EYES ON THE HORIZON

SERVING ON THE FRONT LINES OF NATIONAL SECURITY

GENERAL RICHARD B. MYERS,
USAF (RET.)
WITH MALCOLM McCONNELL

THRESHOLD EDITIONS
NEW YORK LONDON TORONTO SYDNEY

Threshold Editions
A Division of Simon & Schuster, Inc.
1230 Avenue of the Americas
New York, NY 10020

Copyright © 2009 by RMyers and Associates, LLC

First Threshold Editions hardcover edition March 2009

THRESHOLD EDITIONS and colophon are trademarks of Simon & Schuster, Inc.

For information about special discounts for bulk purchases,
please contact Simon & Schuster Special Sales at 1-800-456-6798
or business@simonandschuster.com.

The Simon & Schuster Speakers Bureau can bring authors to your live event.
For more information or to book an event contact the Simon & Schuster Speakers
Bureau at 866-248-3049 or visit our website at www.simonspeakers.com.

Designed by Elliott Beard

Manufactured in the United States of America

10   9   8   7   6   5   4   3   2

Library of Congress Cataloging-in-Publication Data

ISBN-13: 978-1-4165-6012-8
ISBN-10:   1-4165-6012-2

To the men and women who have
served or are serving in the
United States military and their families

Acknowledgments

Writing a book is an adventure. To begin with, it is a toy and an amusement; then it becomes a mistress, and then it becomes a master, and then a tyrant. The last phase is that just as you are about to be reconciled to your servitude, you kill the monster, and fling him out to the public.

—WINSTON CHURCHILL

I am happy to express my thanks to all those who helped sustain and support me through all the aforesaid phases, and especially to those who rescued me from the servitude. I have to express special indebtedness to Brig. Gen. Paula Thornhill, USAF, who was my special assistant when I was Chairman. Her always sage advice and ability to synthesize complex issues were invaluable, then and during the writing of this book, and it is not hyperbole to say this project would not have been finished without her. My National Defense University (NDU) teaching colleague, Dr. Al Pierce, was a terrific alter ego and editor. He provided superb advice on all aspects of the manuscript.

My executive assistant while I was assistant to the Chairman, Vice Chairman, and Chairman, Army Col. Matt Klimow, was an important source of information, especially about the events of 9/11 and the days that followed. His comments and suggestions have contributed greatly to this book. Paul Hanley, my strategic communicator while I was Chairman, provided many insightful comments that helped me with tone and content. Col. Robert Smith, USAF,

Office of the Air Force Judge Advocate General, fully supported the project and added thoughtful comments.

Taylor Wilkinson, my assistant at the NDU Foundation, played a vital role with her note taking and scrupulous research. She was tireless, patient, and always of good cheer. She is a bright young woman with a maturity beyond her years. Jim Shevlin, my previous assistant at NDU, took notes of my early sessions with my collaborator and provided invaluable research help.

Dr. Mark Parillo, of the Kansas State University Military History Institute, was very supportive of the project and provided a researcher to help with the book. Many thanks to Paul Larson, who was very responsive and thorough in answering the many questions. The Joint Staff historian, Dave Armstrong, had the foresight to insist I do history interviews while Chairman. I didn't fully appreciate at the time how helpful these interviews would be in doing the research for this book.

My appreciation goes to Malcolm McConnell, my collaborator and the author of more than twenty-five books. His background in the Foreign Service and his knowledge of national defense issues and organizations gave him a rich background that was very helpful in providing structure and context for my words and stories. Thanks also to his wife, Carol, who, in spite of serious illness, is an essential partner to Malcolm.

Dan Strone and Larry Kramer, my agents, have been my friends and my guides as I entered the unfamiliar world of publishing. They provided great advice and encouragement throughout the process, and I'm deeply indebted to them.

Simon & Schuster editor Kathy Sagan combines the insight, diligence, and perseverance of a skilled publishing professional. She worked hard to help bring this book forth.

It's difficult to find the words to properly acknowledge family members who have been most supportive during this writing process, as well as during a forty-year military career. This book presented one more opportunity for work rather than family to become a dominant force in my life. My deep appreciation and love go to my children, Nicole, Erin, and Rich, and to my sons-in-law, Wade Little and Mike Voto, who understood the commitment. Erin researched a lifetime of photographs to select appropriate ones for this book. My grandchildren, Sophie, Cole, Eloise, and Reed, ages two to six, also played a vital role. A visit to the park or a trip to the ice cream store with them relieved my stress, and served as a reminder of the consequence and import of decisions that were made during my time as Chairman.

This book is a tribute to my wife of forty-three years, Mary Jo. She somehow managed to run twenty-five different homes and raise three children while my duties so often kept us apart. She is an amazing woman who can do absolutely anything she puts her mind to, and she was with me every step of the way through over forty years of military service. I couldn't or wouldn't have served without her. Mary Jo has always been my inspiration, and any success I've had is due to her unyielding love, nourishment of my soul, and common-sense counsel. Above all, she was a great critic who ensured I was never infatuated with power. Without Mary Jo this book would never have been written.

Contents

Introduction

For more than forty years, I had the privilege of wearing my country's uniform—during open war and uneasy peace. In that period, I was fortunate enough to advance from the most junior officer rank of second lieutenant to the Chairman of the Joint Chiefs of Staff, the four-star position held by our country's most senior military officer.

During my four years as Chairman, I served as the principal military adviser to the President, the National Security Council, the Homeland Security Council, and the Secretary of Defense. In addition, I served for almost two years before that as the Vice Chairman, allowing me to understudy the position I'd eventually assume. I was the first Vice Chairman to become Chairman, serving two presidents, Bill Clinton and George W. Bush—the most absorbing, fascinating, humbling, and exhausting period in my life. I hope this book will provide insight into and contribute to understanding of the role of the Chairman and the events of this critical period in our nation's history. "Conventional wisdom" reveals the difficulty in holding up a mirror to reflect a period without the distortion that comes from the perspective of one person's reality.

The events of 9/11/2001 defined my tenure as Chairman. On the eve of taking the oath of office as Chairman of the Joint Chiefs of Staff, following the terrorist attacks on New York, Washington, and United Flight 93, I told Mary Jo, my wife of thirty-six years, "My life won't be my own for the next four years. My focus and priority has to be our military and my job." But I knew we would be in this together, doing our best to represent those in uniform and their families during this demanding time in our nation's history.

In the military, integrity is the cornerstone of everything we do. My parents imbued me with the importance of integrity from an early age. Integrity fosters trust, the foundation for leading a large, complex organization in war or peace. Integrity also underpins ethical leadership. I hoped that the most important attribute I brought to Washington as Chairman was four decades of experiences—forged at all levels—that taught me the priceless nature of ethical leadership.

After the 9/11/2001 terrorist attacks, we certainly needed a foundation of trust linking our armed services and our civilian leadership. This link became more important than ever. Nothing less than the health and future of our democracy were at stake.

Within days of my swearing in, our armed forces were fighting in Afghanistan, engaged in Operation Enduring Freedom to crush the Taliban and al-Qaida. That initial operation was short and decisive. After less than two months, the Taliban were battered into disarray and al-Qaida's fighters had fled across the mountain passes into Pakistan. And twenty-five million Afghans were on a path to freedom and democracy.

At the time, many observers attributed the rout of the enemy to our superior military technology, such as Unmanned Aerial Vehicles (UAVs) and Precision-Guided Munitions, but the true key to our success lay in the "transformation" of our military thinking that provided the mental agility to overcome unexpected and challenging new circumstances. Secretary of Defense Donald Rumsfeld, with whom I worked closely during my term as Chairman, was fond of using Operation Enduring Freedom as an example of transformation at its most effective. He liked to show pictures of our Special Operations Forces troops clinging to the saddles of their charging Tajik ponies—padded cases of laser-targeting equipment and satellite radios banging the riders' knees—as they chased the fleeing Taliban to call down precision air strikes.

After 9/11, transformation of our military became even more urgent, not just another trendy bureaucratic slogan. It marked the creation of an effective twenty-first-century U.S. military through the integration of current and emerging technologies, organizations, and concepts. Transformation at its core is about agile and flexible thinking. It takes place in a complex national security arena and is never finished.

As Chairman, I worked at the strategic level while the combatant commanders, such as Gen. Tommy Franks and Gen. John Abizaid, worked at the operational level of war. My area of responsibility was the globe. I had to understand the nuances and complexities of the myriad security challenges facing our nation so that I could provide the President with the best, most comprehensive military advice possible in the immediate aftermath of 9/11 and on through combat in Afghanistan and Iraq, the Global War on Terror, tsunami relief in the Pacific, and Hurricane Katrina.

My tenure as a general officer was influenced by the Goldwater-Nichols Act of 1986, which reorganized the senior relationships within the Department of Defense. The Goldwater-Nichols Act rightly emphasized the importance of the individual armed services operating together in an integrated, "joint" manner to achieve national strategic objectives. I had learned the nature of these responsibilities in the Far East as the commander of U.S. Forces in Japan in the 1990s, and later as commander of U.S. Space Command and North American Aerospace Defense Command (NORAD). As Chairman, I worked very hard to foster a joint atmosphere in all that I did, down to my personal staff, which came from all branches of the military.

With our nation at war, my fellow Joint Chiefs and I were a very close-knit team, and I have the utmost respect for their professionalism, integrity, and determination to do not only what was best for their service, but what they thought best for their nation. Much of this story is about them, and I wish our citizens could have sat in on our meetings and seen them in action—they would have been proud. Gen. Pete Pace, Vice Chairman, always gave me great advice and was a real support in the toughest times. I could not have survived those six years without the close friendship and collegiality of General Pace and other members of the Joint Chiefs of Staff: Army Chiefs Ric Shinseki and Pete Schoomaker, Chief of Naval Operations Vern Clark, Marine Corps Commandants Jim Jones and Mike Hagee, and Air Force Chief John Jumper.

The combatant commanders are among our military's greatest strengths. They are engaged around the world and are the people responsible for planning and executing our national military strategy. I admire them, and we provided each other great mutual support while I was Chairman: Generals Joe Ralston and Jim Jones, European Command; Admirals Dennis Blair, Tom Fargo, and Bill Fallon, Pacific Command; Generals Tom Franks and John Abizaid, Central Command; Gen. Ed Eberhart and Adm. Tim Keating, Northern Command; Generals James T. Hill and John Craddock, Southern Command; Gen. Buck Kernan and Adm. Ed Giambastiani, Joint Forces Command; Generals Tony Robertson and John Handy, Transportation Command; Adm. Jim Ellis and Gen. Jim Cartwright, Strategic Command; Generals Charlie Holland and Doug Brown, Special Operations Command; and Generals Tom Schwartz and Leon LaPorte, U.S. Forces, Korea.

I had the privilege of serving as Assistant to the Chairman and as Vice Chairman under two outstanding patriots: Generals John Shalikashvili and Hugh Shelton. They always took the time to encourage and mentor me.

Our country owes a great debt to our civilian leadership, too, for the skill and dedication with which they faced grave problems. I learned much working with Secretaries of Defense Donald Rumsfeld, William Cohen, and William Perry, and with Deputy Secretaries of Defense Paul Wolfowitz, Gordon England, Rudy de Leon, and John Hamre.

While Vice Chairman and Chairman, I received enormous support from those on the Joint Staff—dedicated professionals acknowledged by many as the best staff in Washington. Nobody can do it alone, and I had twelve hundred people who were totally dedicated to supporting me and the Joint Chiefs of Staff.

My front-office staff worked under real pressure daily. Mary Turner somehow kept chaos abated and juggled and prioritized an amazing number of calls and requests during my tenure as Vice Chairman and Chairman.

As I served with our soldiers, sailors, airmen, and Marines around the globe in the eventful months and years after 9/11, I was constantly astonished at America's great good fortune to have so many citizens willing to serve, often in harm's way. They confronted every challenge hurled at them—often facing death or terrible wounds—with unparalleled professionalism, dedication, optimism, and effectiveness. They served because they loved their country, their service, and their unit.

They are still out there fighting today, and I remain in awe of them and their families.

PART I

REMEMBRANCE

1

SUNSHINE AND SMOKE

September 11, 2001

Just before 8:45 on the bright Tuesday morning of September 11, 2001, I was waiting in the outer office of Georgia Senator Max Cleland on Capitol Hill. This was one of several scheduled courtesy calls before my Senate confirmation hearings as incoming Chairman of the Joint Chiefs of Staff, America's senior military officer. I had been Vice Chairman since March 2000, serving in both the Clinton and Bush administrations in that capacity.

Max Cleland and I got along well, and he supported my nomination. Like me, Senator Cleland had served in combat during the Vietnam War. He lost both legs and one arm in 1968 when a grenade exploded near Khe Sanh. I had flown 240 "fast" Forward Air Controller, strike, and Wild Weasel missions in modified F-4 Phantoms, many against SAM missile sites in North Vietnam. We had learned a lot about war as young men.

We also worked well as partners in America's enduring yet flexible framework of constitutional government. The military is part of the executive branch. The President requests funding for Department of Defense operations, but Congress controls those funds—and reserves the power to declare war. Therefore the interaction between senior military and congressional leaders is a vital component of our democracy that ideally transcends politics.

Now, with both the Cold War and Operation Desert Storm—our "last" large combat engagement—ended more than a decade earlier, it was possible to hope that there were no imminent major threats to our national security. But I also recognized that hope wasn't part of a senior military officer's job description. Under the oversight of Chairman of the Joint Chiefs of Staff Army General Hugh Shelton, the Joint Staff oversaw the preparation for worst-case war contingencies and the combatant commanders' myriad operational plans (OPLANs). The duties of the Vice Chairman are little known outside the corridors of the Pentagon. Beyond helping coordinate the OPLANs, one of my more exacting assignments as Vice Chairman had been serving as Chairman of the Joint Requirements Oversight Council—which was composed of the four-star vice service chiefs—who approved the requirements of weapons systems being proposed for procurement.

I also served on the National Security Council's Deputies Committee and as a member of the Nuclear Weapons Council. And I represented the Chairman on the Defense Resources Board—which supported the fiscal and personnel structure to the DoD's sprawling bureaucracy. In a large civilian corporation, I would have been the COO, the chief operating officer.

This was very demanding work, but good preparation to serve as the Chairman.

Even if I'd been so inclined, this workload left me no time for politics. But it wasn't just the burden of work: It was against regulations and our military culture for an officer to take part in political activity. This was especially true for a senior officer. And I had always believed that a military career and politics didn't mix. Interaction with the executive and legislative branches, however, was an expected and essential part of being Vice Chairman of the Joint Chiefs of Staff.

Like many of his colleagues, Cleland kept a television set in his outer office tuned to a news network. The first thing I saw on the screen was a live shot of the New York skyline, revealed through a wavering telephoto lens. Black smoke poured from the closer of the two World Trade Center towers, already darkening the bright September sky. At the bottom of the screen, the crawler text announced that a plane had hit the north tower.

Must have been a light aircraft, I thought. *Maybe on a sightseeing flight.*

I entered Cleland's private office, and we chatted a few moments about the aircraft accident in New York.

He had started preparing a pot of tea, but we hadn't taken a sip when a staff person came in from the outer office and informed us that the second tower had been hit. We both knew the interview was over and started out to the TV to see the south tower erupting with smoke and flame.

Cleland looked pale. I suppose I must have, too. This was no light-aircraft accident, but certainly an act of unthinkable terrorist savagery. The only precedent I could imagine for such an attack was December 7, 1941—Pearl Harbor.

My military aide, Army Capt. Chris Donahue, approached us on the way out.

"Sir," Donahue said, "General Eberhart's on my cell phone for you." Ed Eberhart had replaced me as commander of the North American Aerospace Command the year before. Obviously his call was urgent. In this emergency, I had to forgo the luxury of a secure encrypted Red Switch phone and use Donahue's cell.

"Dick," Ed said. "We've got several hijack codes in the system, and I'm working with the FAA to order all aircraft in the national air space to land." Two of NORAD's responsibilities were protecting American air space from enemy aircraft approaching our borders and warning of missile attack.

"That sounds like a good plan, Ed."

NORAD's only role with respect to hijackings was to scramble planes to shadow the hijacked aircraft. The Command was not authorized to order fighters to shoot down civilian airliners. That authority rested with the President alone.

Next, I got a call from Army Col. Matt Klimow, my executive assistant. As we spoke on Donahue's cell phone, the television showed pillars of black smoke erupting from the south tower.

"General," Klimow said in a calm, precise voice, "it looks like there's a major hijacking under way, and I recommend that you return to the Pentagon as soon as possible."

He added that the White House Situation Room had called at 9:16 A.M. to confirm that American Airlines Flight 11 from Boston to Los Angeles had hit the north World Trade Center tower.

"We're on our way back to the Pentagon now," I told Klimow.

As we raced away from Capitol Hill, my security officer took an urgent call.

"Sir," he said, "the Pentagon's just been hit."

I immediately called Matt Klimow back to verify the situation and was relieved when he answered almost at once. "People are running around shouting on the E-Ring corridor," he said. "And all the fire alarms are going off."

"Are you all right?"

"Yes, sir. It must have hit on the west side of the building, near the helo pad."

The Pentagon was such a massive structure that even the crash of an airliner might affect only a portion of the building. In the event of an attack, standing procedures called for the Vice Chairman to move to an alternate command post at a remote location—"Site R"—while the Chairman held the fort at the National Military Command Center in the Pentagon. But Hugh Shelton was airborne on his way to Europe for a NATO meeting and couldn't be back for hours. By law, as Vice Chairman, I was designated acting Chairman of the Joint Chiefs during his absence. And with NORAD and the FAA grounding all flights already airborne in the country and diverting incoming flights from overseas, Hugh might not be able to return—although I knew it wouldn't be easy to stop the combat-hardened former Special Forces paratrooper from heading to the heart of the action.

So my command post had to be in the burning Pentagon.

Looking down the Mall, I saw the cluster of government buildings near the White House. Instinctively, my gaze swept the sky.

"Sir," Matt added, "the White House advised that the combatant commanders will probably want to increase THREATCON as they see fit." In emergencies, the functional and regional commanders in chief had control to adjust the level of protection their forces needed in their geographical areas.

The THREATCON was the alert status that the regional or functional commanders—Central Command, European Command, Space Command, Pacific Command, and so forth—set to defend their forces and installations against terrorist or other threats. If terrorists were executing a complex and massive attack today, our isolated naval, air, and ground bases overseas might be especially vulnerable, so raising the THREATCON was essential. The THREATCON levels increased from Normal, through Alpha, up to Delta. In the next hours, I was sure, over one million American service members around the world would be at their highest level of alert.

Unfortunately, the senior military and civilian leadership in this country was stretched thin that morning. The Chairman was flying to Europe; President George Bush was in Florida, promoting his education initiative; and Secretary of State Colin Powell was in South America, so a significant number of the National Security Council were away from Washington.

At this point, the roles of the military and domestic agencies were being sorted out. Klimow added that the FBI had been designated the lead civilian agency in the crisis, with the military standing by as needed if the terrorist attacks involved weapons of mass destruction (WMD: chemical, biological, or radiological warfare agents).

There was only one current enemy that could have coordinated the suicide hijacking of three airliners, almost simultaneously crashing them into the World Trade Center towers and the Pentagon: Islamic extremists—no doubt commanded by the al-Qaida terrorist movement. This was confirmed later in the day. These terrorists had tried to destroy the Trade Center towers with a massive truck bomb in 1993. Later in the 1990s, their growing organization had attacked American embassies in East Africa. In October 2000, an al-Qaida suicide boat bomb severely damaged the U.S. Navy destroyer *Cole* in the port of Aden, Yemen, killing seventeen of her crew and maiming many more. Al-Qaida's leader was wealthy Saudi radical Usama bin Laden.* Now, as my government sedan sped down I-395 toward the Potomac, it was virtually certain that bin Laden had found the means to export his extreme violence to our shores.

I asked Matt if the National Military Command Center was up and running, knowing I'd need to be where we had the appropriate command and control apparatus. It was. "We're coming in," I told him. "I'll use the River Entrance."

As the sedan merged with traffic onto the Fourteenth Street Bridge, we saw black smoke and orange flame rising from the far side of the dull gray Pentagon. I wondered about my friends and colleagues, about Secretary Donald Rumsfeld and his staff. How many were still alive?

My thoughts were chaotic as the car raced over the Potomac toward the rising smoke. Then, a half-forgotten childhood memory flooded back. I had seen such a greasy black pillar of smoke before.

---

* I have chosen the Department of Defense transliteration of *al-Qaida* and *Usama bin Laden* rather than the civilian, nongovernmental *al-Qaeda* and *Osama bin Laden* spellings often seen in published sources.

2

FAMILY VALUES IN KANSAS

Discipline, Integrity, Hard Work

When I was just two years old in Merriam, Kansas, in the summer of 1944, I witnessed a terrifying incident that scared me so badly my parents were convinced I'd never have anything to do with airplanes.

We lived in this Kansas City suburb in a two-story wood-frame house on a quiet middle-class street bordering a pasture. My dad, Robert Bowman Myers, was a manufacturer's representative for Grayco, which built air-driven and electrically driven industrial pumps and tools, and he also sold other lines of equipment. Pauline Louise, my mother, had taught primary school, but stayed home after I was born.

One sunny afternoon when I was out in the yard playing, a huge four-engine B-24 Liberator bomber roared low overhead, banked steeply, and stalled, crashing nose-first into a vacant lot just a few blocks away. The explosion shook the ground, and I saw the fireball and greasy black smoke boiling above the rooftops.

To a kid of two, this was like the end of the world. I ran into the kitchen, crying uncontrollably, and buried my face in my mother's apron. For several weeks, whenever I saw a plane in the sky, I dashed back into the house, sobbing hysterically. And there were a *lot* of planes over Kansas City in those days. Not only did North American build thousands of twin-engine B-25 Mitchell bombers at the nearby Fairfax plant, Boeing assembled huge B-29 Superfortresses in Wichita, and aircraft like that B-24, en route to Europe from factories in California or training bases in the Southwest, often refueled in Kansas City.

When my mother realized I just wasn't going to wake up one morning, eat my Wheaties, and forget my terror of the big airplanes droning above the house, she took me to see the family doctor. There weren't many child psychologists in Kansas City in 1944, so the doctor approached the problem from a practical point of view.

"What does he *like* to do?" the doctor asked.

"Well," Mom replied, "he certainly likes to eat."

"Fine," he said. "Take him right out to the airport restaurant. Feed him a hamburger and a malted milk and let him watch the planes taxiing, landing, and taking off. If he's still hungry, buy him another hamburger."

Freud probably would not have approved of this approach. But our no-nonsense midwestern family doctor knew a lot about practical child psychology. I quickly came to connect those hulking, noisy machines flying above the house with hamburgers, grilled cheese sandwiches, and chocolate malted milks—not with smoke and flames. But, since this was wartime and food was rationed, it was a good thing the doctor pronounced me cured of my airplane phobia before Mom and Dad ran out of ration stamps.

The test of the cure came a couple of years later when Dad bought us tickets on a TWA DC-3 flight to Wichita. I clomped up the steps and sat on a pillow next to a window so I could see outside. I don't remember anything specific about the short flight, other than a sense of powerful force lifting us up into the sunshine and the flat checkerboard of farm fields stretching below to the horizon. From that day on, I loved airplanes, and that's good, because if I hadn't lost my fear of them, I never would have become a pilot, with flying becoming my passion.

Kansas City was typical of America in those years: Everyone was focused on winning the war. Men of military age not working in defense industries were serving in uniform. Rationing of food, fuel, tires, and clothing was universal. Everyone in my neighborhood had a victory garden. Like most people, we kept ours growing in the backyard well past V-J Day in 1945.

What dim and splintered memories I retain from those very early childhood years are of a general sense of national purpose, of my parents sitting in front of the big varnished cabinet of our radio, listening to President Roosevelt address the country . . . of sad and important events unfolding far beyond the safety of our living room.

My dad was born in Atchison, Kansas, in 1898, so he was too old to serve in the war. He was a risk taker, very skillful at the card table. The story in my family was that Dad supported himself during the lean years of the Great Depression playing poker and gin rummy. His ability to accept risk certainly showed when he became a representative for Grayco Manufacturing, which had its headquarters in Minneapolis.

He wanted a district near our home in Kansas. By then, my brother Chuck had come along, and Dad didn't want to uproot the family during the postwar housing shortage. But the company warned him that the southern Midwest was not very promising. "You don't want that territory," the people in the home office told him.

But Dad took a chance and asked for Kansas and Missouri. He worked hard to become successful. Much of his achievement was due to his ability to read human nature and get along with people. Dad was also a low-pressure guy, equally at ease with a company president or a machinist on the factory floor. And he was honest, never promising more than he could deliver. People liked him and trusted him. I learned the value of genuine friendliness and trust from him when I was just a little kid.

This didn't mean Dad was a pushover at home. He never spoiled my brother or me. But he expected us to be polite and obey adults. I'll never forget my eighth birthday party, a breezy Wednesday afternoon in March 1950. We had relatives and friends of my parents coming over to help me celebrate, but I decided it would be more fun to ride my bike around the neighborhood.

When I finally got back home, my dad pointed up the stairs and said, "Go to your room."

I hoped being exiled from the ice cream and cake was all the punishment I'd get. Not so lucky.

Dad closed my bedroom door and said, "Take down your pants."

He never used his belt, but his bare hand was bad enough. "This hurts me more than you, Dick."

That I found hard to believe. But I knew Dad was disappointed. I was the oldest child, and he expected me to act accordingly. I'd been disrespectful of the family's guests by disappearing before the party even started.

My mother set equally high standards of behavior. She believed in showing respect to others and avoiding selfishness. She emphasized the Golden Rule at every opportunity and that affected my view of how to treat people the rest of my life. These were values that had shaped her life. Her father was a German immigrant named Koerper, a grocer in Kansas City who had gone broke during the Depression by extending too much credit to needy families. Mom graduated from the University of Kansas and taught school, supporting her parents for most of the 1930s. So she and Dad couldn't afford to get married. In that regard, they were like millions of other engaged couples, but they weren't young. In fact, when they finally could marry, Mom thought she was too old to have children. She was thirty-nine when I was born. And Chuck was born two years later.

Mom loved music. She played the accordion, having learned the instrument from her German parents, and the upright piano, which Mom kept in excellent tune—despite the humid Kansas summers and cold, dry winters.

She was determined to make a musician out of me. That meant piano lessons—five *years* of piano lessons. I'll never forget sitting on that thinly padded piano bench with my teacher, Mrs. Wolfe, pointing out the endless stanzas of notes as we practiced key progressions to the beat of her metronome. Through our big picture window, I could see the neighbor kids tossing softballs in the spring or playing touch football in the fall. In the winter, they towed their Radio Flyer sleds to hills in the park, while I sat practicing. A dentist appointment would have been more fun.

But I was learning patience and tenacity, as well as a love of music that endures today, and that prepared me for the high school and college bands I would play in. Once, waiting to play in a recital made me so nervous that I threw up. But my parents expected me to play and persevere—a trait they valued. As my character matured, I, too, came to value that attribute.

It was obvious that they loved Chuck and me and wanted the best for us. Besides his family, cars were Dad's great joy. One summer afternoon he came home driving a canary yellow 1951 Buick Roadmaster convertible. He piled us into the car and drove all around Kansas City with the top down. Next, my dad bought a big Pontiac station wagon with real wood paneling on the doors, a true battleship of a vehicle.

We took that car on a trip east, stopping in Washington, D.C. My parents knew President Harry Truman's private secretary, Rose Conway, and she arranged a private tour of the White House for us.

Waiting beside the long table in the Cabinet Room, we hoped for a peek into the Oval Office that never came, because the President was busy. Chuck and I gazed up at the paintings of sailing ships shooting smoke from their cannons and old guys with whiskers riding horses. Right outside the glass doors were the Rose Garden and the South Lawn, where President Truman greeted visiting kings and queens.

My parents told me, "Take a good look, because you'll never see this place again." Although I certainly did see the White House again, Mom and Dad did not live to share that experience.

I had a very good public school education in the forties and fifties. After my stage fright before that piano recital as a young kid, I became comfortable performing for audiences and drew satisfaction from mastering a new skill. A good part of that was due to my new instrument: the tenor saxophone. At Shawnee Mission North High School, I was the sax and piano player in a small dance band and helped arrange some of the songs.

I was also heavily involved in sports—too heavily—playing on the football, basketball, and track teams. The camaraderie and competition among my teammates were a real pleasure even though team practices, band and glee club rehearsals, and the Latin Club kept me at school until dinnertime almost every afternoon. That didn't bother me because I was slowly learning the value of teamwork and discipline.

So, when I landed one of the two spots on the basketball team reserved for football players at the end of the season, I signed up—but then quit after a day, disappointed that my close friend Sam Keeley had just missed making the team. This was the first time I'd ever quit *anything*. Finally, I thought, I'll have some free time. It didn't happen that way. The football coach, Bryan Sperry, said to me, "Son, if you want to play football again next year I expect you to sign up for winter track in a week." So much for getting a little free time off after school. I still had to walk home each afternoon to a late dinner and homework. Then and there, I decided never to quit anything again.

We had a television set by then, but Mom and Dad were strict about what we watched and when. Homework came first. I understood that my "job" as a teenager was doing as well as I could at school and that *I Love Lucy* and *Dragnet* could wait until I'd finished my math and U.S. history reading. My parents were reinforcing the worth of discipline that I had begun to learn on the football field and the basketball court. This would prove to be far more valuable in my adult life than memorizing who fought the Battle of Tippecanoe.

Mom and Dad also had their own sense of hard-earned discipline, forged in the lean years of the Great Depression, but buffered by my father's innate risk-taking. I'll always remember seeing them sitting at the breakfast room table, counting the money in their bankbooks and insurance policies. Dad, at over sixty years of age, was determined to buy his own equipment distributorship, so that his sons could work with him when he became too old to deal with the exhausting strain of those long road trips.

But he was thinking more about Chuck's and my futures than his own.

Years later, when I was a career military officer, the expression "selfless service" came into the professional lexicon. And when it did, I remembered my mother and father sitting at the table planning to risk everything for their children.

3

SPREADING WINGS

College, ROTC, Pilot Training, Marriage

Although Dad wanted Chuck and me to come work with him one day, mastering another profession seemed more interesting. My math and chemistry courses at Shawnee Mission North High School were fascinating, and veterinary medicine appealed to me.

Kansas State University in Manhattan, about 150 miles northwest of Merriam, had a well-established vet school, having been founded as an agricultural college in 1863 under the pioneering Morrill Land Grant Act. So that's where I headed to enroll in fall 1960. But my dream of becoming a vet, working with livestock and people's pets, did not last long. The assistant dean helping freshmen register explained that while I met most of the requirements for enrolling in the preveterinary course, taking two years of a modern foreign language was a requirement.

"What's your choice? Spanish? German . . . French?"

"How about Latin?" I asked hopefully. "I had three years of Latin in high school. Won't that count?"

I didn't add that I would tear my hair out if I ever had to conjugate another irregular verb. After cramming for a Latin test, I'd wake up in the morning with *augeō, augēre, auxī, auctum* echoing inside my skull.

"I'm afraid not," the assistant dean said. "It has to be a *modern* foreign language."

When I stood to leave, she asked where I was headed. "Let me think about it. Thanks, ma'am." Dick Myers would never hang out his shingle as Dr. R. B. Myers, DVM.

Strolling across the campus, I mulled over my options. When I looked up, I was in front of Seaton Hall, a three-story Kansas limestone building that looked like a fortress. "Engineering" was carved into the lintel above the main entrance. I had originally given some thought to engineering.

I told the assistant dean who greeted me in the large hallway that I wanted to enroll in engineering. He asked what kind of engineering I wanted.

"What kinds of engineering are there?" I asked.

He grinned, probably thinking I was some farm boy who'd just scraped the manure off his boots.

"Well," he said, ticking off specialties with his thumb and fingers, "chemical, electrical . . . mechanical . . ."

"Mechanical," I said without hesitation. Dad had taught Chuck and me a lot about mechanics and I had always had a fascination with motors. I'd built several of my own go-karts out of some pretty basic material. After about half an hour of paperwork, I was signed up.

Because Kansas State was a land grant university, all male students were required to complete a minimum of two years of Reserve Officer Training Corps (ROTC) courses. When the assistant dean asked, "What kind of ROTC do you want, Army or Air Force?" I found that question much easier to answer.

After that brief airplane phobia as a toddler, I'd come to love planes and dreamed of getting my pilot's license. And I was especially drawn to jet fighters. I could trace this fascination to my cousin, Win Koerper, an Air Force lieutenant and aide to the commanding general at Richards-Gebaur Air Force Base on the edge of Kansas City. The Air Force had F-86 Sabre Jets stationed there, and I was thrilled to reach up and run my hands over the smooth and shiny aluminum skin of the fighters, to see the snouts of the .50 caliber machine guns in the nose. The Korean War movie *Sabre Jet* had been one of my favorites, and I was fascinated with the actual footage of combat missions with our guys shooting down enemy MiGs above the frozen Yalu River.

The other relative who influenced me was Sid Newberger, who was married to Dad's sister. Uncle Sid had served in China during World War II and remained interested in the military. Sid asked if I was "considering" any of the service academies when I graduated from high school.

I shook my head sadly. "It would be the Air Force Academy if I could get in," I said. "But you need twenty-twenty vision to apply. And I don't have it."

"Well," he said, "don't give up." I had the idea that Sid regretted not having applied for a Regular Army commission after the war.

With *Sputnik,* in 1957, came the race to deploy intercontinental ballistic missiles. Merriam and a thousand other American cities were now definitely in the Soviet nuclear bull's-eye.

As I started college, the Cold War had entered a new, more dangerous phase. In high school, there had been a vague sense of danger from our protracted confrontation with the Soviet Union. I remember seeing maps in the *Kansas City Star* that showed the combat radius of Russian Ilyushin and Tupolev bombers. Our town was well outside their operational range.

And in October 1962, during the first semester of my junior year, the Cuban Missile Crisis erupted. The Soviets had secretly deployed intermediate-range nuclear missiles to Cuba. The United States had similar weapons based in Turkey. Both sides had longer-range, more powerful missiles on their own territory, aimed at their Cold War opponents. We told the Soviets to get their missiles out of Cuba. They told us, *"Nyet."* For two weeks, America and the Soviet Union teetered on the brink of thermonuclear war. Some nights, trying to study, I lost focus on the differential equations in my textbook and thought about those Russian and American intercontinental missiles poised to fire.

After President John Kennedy ringed Cuba with a naval blockade, Soviet leader Nikita Khrushchev backed down and withdrew the missiles. America and the world could breathe again.

Kansas State was great. That first year, I made some very good friendships that still endure. I also pledged SAE fraternity and moved into the frat house. It didn't cost much more than the dorm, and the food was a lot better. The friendships I made there have lasted a lifetime.

But mechanical engineering was tough. Although I was fairly disciplined, there were lots of demands to support SAE in intramurals and other fraternity events. This all ate into the time for studying calculus, physics, heat transfer, and thermodynamics. And the fraternity house itself was not always conducive to studying. Some of the guys had softer majors that didn't require long lab hours, and they tended to start their weekends early. I hadn't yet fully learned how to prioritize, so midterm and final exams saw me trying to catch up in a quiet rented hotel room where I could study without interruption, hunched over my laboratory workbooks with my slide rule practically grafted to my hand.

The deal with my parents was that they would pay the tuition and house bill, and I would pay for my books, clothes, and all other incidentals. So I found a way to combine business and pleasure. I joined a four-member rock and roll band that we called The Travelers, led by Larry Wellington at Washburn University in Topeka. I played the tenor saxophone and piano. To my great surprise, a local bank was willing to lend me $710 to buy a high-quality Selmer Mark VI sax. I must have looked honest, because all I had to do was sign a loan note and they handed over my check. Playing dances and parties with The Travelers was both fun and satisfying: Our theme song was the classic twelve-bar blues instrumental "Night Train," which has a hard-pounding sax solo. We usually made about ten dollars apiece for a gig, and played about six to eight times a month—good money in the early 1960s.

And one night at a party in Topeka, the audience asked the band to stay late. I walked out of there with thirty-five dollars in my wallet. Dad had bought a '62 Ford convertible that I drove at school. After that late performance, my friend Barry Wilson managed to slide his bass fiddle into the convertible's backseat with the neck jutting forward between our shoulders. That was a fine arrangement, except that the bass completely blocked my rearview mirror. I was heading through the empty streets toward the highway when I heard the police car siren. The officer had clocked me doing forty-five. The fine? He handed me a ticket. I handed the cop the thirty-five dollars I'd just made. It was a solemn and silent ride home.

A few years later, when I was learning to fly Air Force jets, my instructors drummed in a fundamental lesson: "Always watch your six." That was the six-o'clock-position blind spot directly behind your plane from which an enemy attack was most likely to come. A valuable lesson, one I'd already learned on the late-night streets of Topeka.

My ROTC course required attending a short summer camp orientation to the military at Williams Air Force Base southeast of Phoenix: how to wear your uniform—sharply creased with spit-shined shoes—beds made so taut that you could bounce a quarter off them, how to line up your socks and hairbrush in your footlocker. And on it went, a mixture of classroom seminars and lectures, sports, and marching on the drill field in the baking Arizona heat.

We were offered a flight in the T-37 if we wished. I jumped at the chance for my first flight in a jet. I loved absolutely everything about the experience, from getting fitted with the helmet and oxygen mask to the heavy parachute beating rhythmically off your back and buttocks as you walked to the airplane. The flight was surreal in a way, and I remember being fascinated by the pilot executing a zero-G maneuver and putting his pencil in the air right before our eyes. It just stayed there floating magically. Simple stuff now, but then very impressive to a young cadet.

My group of cadets, F Flight, won the trophy for the overall best flight at the summer camp. I thought I made significant contributions to that award. Unfortunately, the training officer running the summer camp didn't feel the same way about me. When I got back to Kansas State in September, the professor of Air Science, Air Force Col. Lee Ruggles, called me to his office and showed me my training report.

The message was short and brutal: "Cadet Myers does not have much of a future as an Air Force officer."

"Sir . . ." I began, but stopped. What could I say? In my view the captain who'd written the report was flat-out wrong.

Colonel Ruggles grinned. He was a World War II veteran who took pride in getting to know each of his cadets. Short, with close-cropped graying hair, he looked every bit the professional officer.

"I wouldn't worry about that too much," he said. He trusted his own judgment and had faith in me.

He convinced me I'd made the right choice in opting to become an Air Force officer. But there were other factors involved in my decision. The Cold War was getting warmer—both in Europe and in Southeast Asia—and the Army was drafting increasing numbers of young men. One way or another, I was going to serve. I preferred to do so as an officer, in the air. I still wished I could be a pilot, but my eyes had me pointed toward navigator training. On the positive side, the B-58 and B-52 bombers and the new F-4 fighter-bombers all had navigators in their crews. So it looked like Lt. Dick Myers would see the world from a navigator's seat.

––––––––––

Once I learned how to study, by my sophomore year, I had more time for a social life. I'd played football in high school and became an end on my fraternity's touch squad. The intramural football game with the Phi Delts was the high point of every fall semester, with the queen of the festivities selected from photos submitted by sororities. A pretty, demure brunette named Mary Jo Rupp was the queen my sophomore year. When she appeared on the parade float in 1961, I decided we had to get to know each other, and managed to drive her home that night.

Mary Jo and I began to date. In those days at Kansas State, dates consisted of slow walks to ice cream parlors and long conversations about suitably serious topics. We started to fall in love.

Meanwhile, I still had to master the mysteries of differential equations, dynamics of machines, and fluid mechanics, to name some of the tougher courses. And in the next two years my ROTC classes also became more demanding. At least ROTC now paid a cadet the princely sum of thirty dollars a month, which in 1962 Manhattan, Kansas, went a long way. I can still remember cashing lots of dollar checks for lunch and getting change back.

After Mary Jo and I met, she'd sometimes come with me to gigs The Travelers played. She got the job of stamping the hands of the paying audience. It's a wonder she stayed with me.

I was still somewhat disappointed that I was destined to be an Air Force navigator, not a pilot. One of our ROTC instructors, a captain named Joel Hetland, had just come back from flying supersonic F-100 fighters in England. He brought a couple of reel-to-reel tape recordings of his squadron mates singing classic flying songs in a Cambridgeshire pub. You could hear the clinking glasses and almost smell the pipe and cigarette smoke. "Bless 'em all . . . bless 'em all . . . Throw a nickel on the grass, save a fighter pilot's . . ."

I thought I would never be part of that elite circle.

My senior year at Kansas State was a grind of rough classes and the encroaching responsibilities of the adult world. I'd be Lt. Dick Myers soon, heading for navigators' training, as well as a married man. In May 1964, I went down to Forbes Air Force Base in Topeka to take my precommissioning physical exam. To my great surprise and even greater pleasure, the doctors now informed me that I had "perfect, twenty-twenty vision." And there was more valuable information from that physical. While being measured for my sitting height, the sergeant said, "Slouch down a little." *I will not,* I thought. *I'll sit up as straight as possible.*

"If you don't slouch down a little," he said quietly, "you'll be over the thirty-eight-inch sitting height limitation for aircrew members."

I must have been nice to that sergeant and he was returning the favor. You never know who's going to hold your fate in their hands, which is a good reason to treat people by the Golden Rule—a lesson my mother had pounded into our heads when I was growing up.

I brought the good news to Colonel Ruggles the next day. "I know it may be too late, sir. But is there *any* way to change from the navigator to the pilot training option?"

Ruggles studied the medical report and sat back for a moment at his desk, probably considering what he could still do. "You've done an excellent job in your course work, Dick," he said. "I'll do my best to get you into pilot training."

He was good to his word and even found me an opening in the ROTC's Air Force Flight Introductory Program, which consisted of thirty-six hours of flight instruction. This was usually just enough to get your private pilot's license. There was a prohibition against participating in this program after your senior year in college, but Colonel Ruggles convinced the Air Force bureaucracy to make an exception in my case.

Mary Jo had graduated cum laude with a BA degree in English in June 1964 and moved to Kansas City to begin teaching. We each felt the deep ache of separation and decided to get engaged at Christmas that year.

———————————

Flying small Cessna two-seat 150s out of Manhattan airport and finishing my degree that fall semester of 1964 gave me a real sense of purpose for the first time. I loved flying, but like most student pilots, I initially had difficulty keeping the plane in level flight with reference only to the horizon. This is one of the first things you have to master when you start flying lessons.

The instructors set me right. "Keep your eyes on the horizon," they said. "If the horizon stays flat, your wings are level."

I learned that lesson early and never forgot it.

Some students had more difficulty than others, but I was lucky and took naturally to flying. I loved the sounds, the smells, and the perspective of looking down on broad areas of the earth that the little aircraft gave me. Between September and December 1964, I racked up the thirty-six flying hours—including the six hours of cross-country flight needed for a private license. In December, I passed my flight exam and could now carry passengers. The first person I took up was my future mother-in-law, Marie Rupp, who was eager to see Manhattan, Kansas, from the air.

In February 1965, I lined up with several hundred graduating Army and Air Force ROTC cadets while an Army brigadier general gave us the commissioning oath. We raised our right hands and swore to "support and defend the Constitution of the United States against all enemies, foreign and domestic; that I will bear true faith and allegiance to the same . . ."

Mary Jo and my mother pinned on my shiny new gold bars.

I was now 2nd Lt. Richard B. Myers, United States Air Force.

While awaiting assignment to an Air Force pilot class, I worked for my dad and rented Piper 180s and slightly larger Piper 235s at Johnson County Airport, a small field near home.

I was now a pilot, a very green, undoubtedly overconfident pilot, but one the Federal Aviation Administration had certified to safely fly himself and passengers.

And, with the utmost audacity—and probably too much confidence—that's what I proceeded to do. Dad had a meeting up at Grayco corporate headquarters in Minneapolis soon after I got my license.

"Say, Dick," he said. "Why don't you rent a plane and fly me up there?"

As I've said, Dad was a risk taker. I rented a four-seat Piper Cherokee 180. Early one crisp spring morning, I did my preflight, checking the engine oil level twice and draining some fuel to be sure there was no water in the line. We stowed our suitcases and climbed on board.

I completed the takeoff checklist slowly, precisely. And then, when the engine had warmed up, I listened to the VHF radio to verify no other plane was in the pattern around the field, set the altimeter, checked all my other instruments again, released the parking brake, and taxied toward the runway.

The takeoff roll for a Cherokee 180 was short. As soon as the nose wheel lifted off the runway, I eased back gently on the control yoke, and we were flying in an easy climbing left turn until we were headed north across the glittering flood plain of the Kansas River.

Dad was grinning like a kid on his first roller-coaster ride. The flight up over the flat expanse of Iowa and Minnesota was smooth. Dad held my folded map for a while and helped me locate landmarks: the water towers with the names of the small towns painted on them, the shiny dome of the Iowa state capitol in Des Moines, and the cluster of lakes surrounding Albert Lea in southern Minnesota. This was the way to travel, no red lights, no traffic backed up in road construction.

Dad finished his Grayco business two days later, and after a short visit to a Wisconsin lake cabin for some cigars, card playing, and drinking, Dad was ready to head home. I filed my flight plan for the return trip to Kansas City. The aviation weather forecast called for "possibly moderate to severe turbulence" along the route we'd be flying. But the Piper Cherokee was a tough little plane, and I didn't think much about turbulence.

To supplement the cabin heater, Dad filled a Thermos with hot coffee. But a couple of hours into the flight, the turbulence hit just as Dad was trying to refill his plastic coffee cup. The weatherman hadn't been kidding. Sometimes the Cherokee rose a hundred feet, only to be smacked down. With the turbulence came a steady headwind that ate up our gas supply. That afternoon, I made an unplanned landing at St. Joseph, Missouri, to gas up the plane. The man I'd rented the Cherokee from had advised me not to waste money by filling the tanks all the way up with expensive hundred-octane aviation gasoline at some other dealer's pumps, so I only put in what I thought we'd need to get home.

But the headwind got even stronger after sunset. I was a very happy young pilot to see the lights of Johnson County Airport around eight that night. And when I was taxiing in after landing I was stunned that one of the gas tanks was empty and the other was low. And I'd landed with the fuel selector on the tank indicating empty.

That was a valuable lesson. Don't try to save a few bucks, because the force of gravity always wins. And never, *ever* neglect the checklist, especially when focusing intently on a challenging phase of flight like a night landing. But that was about the fourth time I'd landed at night, and after that, I was always more alert.

Almost as bad as the fuel scare, when we got home that night, we had to face my mother. She'd been waiting all afternoon for us to pull into the driveway. And neither Dad nor I had thought to call her from the airport in St. Joe. Mother was not amused. Nor was Mary Jo, whom Mom had called earlier to see if we'd checked in. They both expected me much earlier and spent the afternoon and evening worrying. Maybe this was a harbinger of things to come, as Mary Jo would spend many years of our life together waiting for me to return from flying.

On June 5, 1965, I started my Air Force pilot training at Vance Air Force Base near Enid, Oklahoma. Mary Jo and I had set our wedding date at the Kansas State University chapel for that June 12. This gave me enough time to report for the first phase of training, but not time to help prepare for the wedding ceremony.

I planned to drive up to Manhattan as soon as the duty day ended on Friday and, I hoped, make it in time for the rehearsal. My mother had other ideas, as she was worried I'd have so much on my mind I wouldn't watch the road. She hired a man named Sellers from Enid to fly me back to Manhattan—and I bet she checked to see that his fuel tanks were full.

I made it to the rehearsal a little late, to see someone else standing in by Mary Jo's side at the altar. I hurried down to replace him. And our wedding went off without a hitch. Mary Jo was even more beautiful than I remembered, and I felt pretty sharp in the tailored Air Force white jacket mess dress uniform Uncle Sid Newberger had bought me as a commissioning present.

In those days, the bride and groom didn't hang around for the reception. So after greeting people in the receiving line and cutting the cake and toasting with a glass of champagne at the Manhattan Country Club, Mary Jo changed into her going-away dress. After the rice throwing, we climbed into her car and headed down to Oklahoma. Our honeymoon consisted of one night in a supposedly fancy motel in Wichita. But as soon as I carried Mary Jo over the threshold, I could smell mildew, and my shoes squished on soggy carpet. The Arkansas River had recently flooded, and the motel had not quite recovered.

Neither of us complained.

Our lifelong partnership had begun. A recently flooded motel room for our honeymoon suite was just the first of countless adventures we would face together. Mary Jo never complained during the twenty-five moves we were to make and was always ready to face the next adventure cheerfully—from European notions of central heating to insects and the geckos that hunted them in Southeast Asia. She combined optimism with competence. And once the children came along, those attributes gave her the strength to run the family without me, which allowed me to focus on my professional duties.

I owe whatever success I've had to her.

4

EARLY AIR FORCE

Germany, Fighter Training,
First Combat Mission Southeast Asia

Mary Jo and I rented a nicely furnished duplex apartment in Enid, Oklahoma. Vance Air Force Base, where I'd learn to fly jets—"undergraduate pilot training"—was only five miles from town. While I became an Air Force pilot, Mary Jo taught English to six grades and was librarian and sophomore class sponsor at a small school out in the county.

My class of student pilots began training at Vance in June 1965. Our course included ground classes followed by flying with an instructor pilot, first in the Cessna T-37 "Tweety Bird" and then the Northrop T-38 Talon. The T-37 earned its nickname from the piercing shriek of its twin engines embedded in the roots of the straight wings, just below the side-by-side seats in the cockpit. To me, it didn't matter that the T-37 was the smallest, slowest jet in the Air Force inventory. It was still a jet, and they were actually going to *pay* me to fly it.

We trained in teams of four lieutenants, each of whom had already earned his civilian private pilot's license. So at least we knew the plane's nose from its tail—but that was about the only familiar aspect of the Tweet as we dived into mysteries of a more complex aircraft. I now recognized how lucky I'd been to have undergone the academic rigor of mechanical engineering study at Kansas State. After that academic marathon, the T-37 classroom work seemed almost simple.

My team was also fortunate to have 1st Lt. Jerry Gillighan as our instructor. He was demanding, but treated us fairly. Unlike some instructors, who harassed their students—sometimes even yanking the hoses of their oxygen masks in the cockpit to get their attention—Gillighan calmly talked you through every demanding challenge.

Relatively light and low-slung, the T-37 was a very nimble little plane, what pilots call "forgiving." Flying the jet seemed to come naturally to me. And although we could not fly higher than twenty-five thousand feet, I took great pleasure in being able to reach that altitude in one long, slow climb. Our cockpit had twin control sticks like a jet fighter's, rather than the Y-shaped yokes of a civilian aircraft, so I began to feel a solid connection to the plane, as if it were an extension of my limbs. I soon gained an intuitive touch for handling the trainer, taking a bank into a roll or easing back on the stick and watching the flat prairie horizon drop away as I began a loop.

Under Jerry Gillighan's leadership, my team made steady progress, quickly mastering all the traditional flying skills. When we could perform basic maneuvers proficiently, we progressed to aerobatics. We wanted to do well because Gillighan obviously believed in our potential as Air Force pilots. Years later, I realized that Gillighan displayed the ideal attributes of a military leader: the ability to quietly and patiently foster confidence in subordinates without any trace of arrogance or impatience. He worked hard with us, earning our trust and respect in the process. Our other instructors were just as dedicated. They could all teach instrument or formation flying, aerobatics—with an emphasis on tight, steady control—or night flying. I loved that little plane, and after several weeks of dual instruction, I soloed. It's remarkable what you hear when you first solo. Before solo, many of the aircraft's noises were drowned out by the instructor's commentary. I began slowly but happily racking up my flight hours.

But one day, I realized that the Tweet wasn't just a toy. I was alone in the cockpit, practicing aerobatics on the flight range south of the base. The split-S was a basic combat maneuver that allowed a pilot to quickly change heading and drop altitude. It was very useful in evading an enemy approaching from the rear and allowed the pursued pilot to begin reversing positions with his opponent.

I'd flown the maneuver before and was confident that I had it down cold as I slid the throttles back to idle and pushed the stick steadily left until it touched my knee. The plane rolled until I centered the stick and was flying inverted, wings level. Then I pulled the stick back almost against my stomach so that my gloved fist touched the buckle of my parachute harness. The brown wheat fields rose to fill my canopy as the plane dived toward the bottom curve of the maneuver. The dials of the magnetic and gyro compasses turned slowly as we plunged toward the new heading.

But there was something wrong. The chin of my oxygen mask drooped onto my chest. My arms and legs seemed to have thickened into lead weights. And the sunny Oklahoma wheat fields grew dim, drab gray, as the blood rushed away from my brain.

What the hell's happening? I thought.

I was still plummeting, the little Tweet about to become an unguided missile. Using my remaining consciousness, I continued pulling on the stick until I thought I was straight and level again. Under such acceleration stress, my body had literally been heavier than it had on the surface of the earth. The strain of high Gs also forces blood away from the head to pool in the legs, sometimes causing blackout, a sensation particularly familiar to roller-coaster riders starting up after a steep descent. As soon as the G forces dissipated, my vision cleared and I checked my altimeter. I'd managed to pull out several thousand feet above ground level.

Climbing back to my assigned altitude, I realized my mistake. I had entered the maneuver too relaxed and not prepared for the oncoming G forces. The Gs had not been that great, but you needed to be prepared. And, since I belonged to the school of thought that said, if the horse throws you, climb right back on, I proceeded to complete the Split-S perfectly, avoiding any excessive Gs.

My four-man section of student pilots had a solid foundation on which to build when we entered our next, more advanced phase of training. First Lt. Bill Flynn was the instructor in the T-38 Talon. Flynn was an Air Force Academy graduate who had some definite ideas about our training, so he set high goals for us.

Because he knew from experience that the transition from the little Tweet to the T-38 could be a steep hurdle for young pilots, he actively promoted a unique esprit de corps in our group—and in so doing taught us a valuable leadership lesson. One of the first duties he assigned us was coming over to his house and painting the white visors of our flight helmets with a distinctive blue checkerboard. From the start, he made it clear that becoming a U.S. Air Force pilot was a serious and demanding business and reminded us that there were many differences between the two training aircraft.

The T-38 had tandem cockpits, and Bill Flynn usually sat behind me, out of

sight—but never out of mind—making sure I hadn't forgotten the basic classroom and ground simulator lessons.

Unlike the T-37, the Talon was supersonic. The swept-back wings were almost razor sharp; its twin engines had afterburners in which raw fuel was ignited to kick the plane to over eight hundred miles an hour. I was thrilled by its
rate of climb: after a short takeoff roll, I pulled back the stick and the plane
would climb to thirty thousand feet in only one minute. Compared to the tiny
Cessna in which I'd earned my private pilot's license and the T-37, the T-38
seemed like a spaceship. (In fact, all these years later, NASA uses T-38s to help
the space shuttle astronauts keep their flying skills sharp.)

I loved aerobatic maneuvers like rolls, loops, and split S's, in which I had to
closely coordinate stick, rudder, and engine thrust. And now I had a G-suit
to counter the centrifugal force of a tight maneuver. When I was forced down
into the ejection seat, the suit's rubber bladders automatically inflated to clamp
my legs and abdomen, preventing blood from rushing away from my brain—
which might lead from grayout to complete blackout.

We rotated duties—classroom, simulator, flying—and always studied for
the next test in our "spare" time. Once more, I was glad to have spent all those
late nights holed up in one of Manhattan's hotels near the KSU campus, cramming for exams.

The time passed quickly. Several weeks into our T-38 training, we soloed,
and in the coming months mixed solo day and night flights with formation flying and cross-country navigation that took us to bases across the United States.
This phase of pilot training has been compared to drinking from a fire hose—
an appropriate analogy. We were so busy that there was often no time for regular meals, and many of us survived on snack bar hot dogs.

Visual flight gave way to instrument flying, during which we learned to
rely on radio navigation aids. In turn, instrument flying led to mastering instrument landings, a discipline that included descending an electronic glide
slope at precisely the right compass heading, rate of descent, and airspeed to a
runway obscured by a low cloud ceiling or limited visibility. By spring 1966, my
class was combining all these demanding techniques, often alone in the airplane. I certainly found these months invigorating: Some days I'd ride the little
trolley out to the flight line just to watch the aircraft and smell the heady scent
of JP-4 jet fuel. In the classroom, the endless—often frustrating—hours in the
ground simulators were always followed by the all-too-brief exhilaration of actual training missions.

Flynn understood that he was training officers, not just aviators. So one

Friday, he gave us a little weekend homework: writing an essay on the difference between Air Force and civilian pilots. He wanted us to think beyond the exacting demands of our training. The focus of my essay was the need of a "neophyte pilot" about to embark on an Air Force career to examine closely the requisite skills and responsibility of the military pilot. Air Force pilots, I wrote, were part of a military that helped prevent a "large-scale war and protect the United States from any enemy." I stressed the importance of air power in ensuring national survival and world peace. Air Force pilots had to recognize the seriousness of their profession and realize it was much more than just an exciting "adventure." Once an Air Force pilot accepted this challenge, he had to accept the need for "100 percent effort—100 percent of the time, perfecting flying skills down to the smallest detail."

Concluding the essay, I emphasized that the "perfection demanded of Air Force pilots and the responsibilities they shoulder are what sets them apart from the majority of pilots in the air today."

I believed those words then, and I still do.

In August 2001, almost thirty-five years after our T-38 training at Vance, when I had been nominated to become Chairman of the Joint Chiefs of Staff, Bill Flynn sent me a copy of my essay. He closed his thoughtful covering letter, "You have remained true to your words. I am proud to have served with you, even for so short a time."

That June 1966, my folks came down and joined Mary Jo and her family in pinning on my silver wings as a full-fledged United States Air Force pilot. It was indeed a proud moment, but I didn't have much time to relax.

As the year's training was ending, the students stated their preference for the aircraft in which they'd spend the beginning years of their career: multiengine jets like the huge B-52 Stratofortress or four-engine KC135 aerial refueling tanker, the delta-wing F-102 supersonic interceptor, and the McDonald F-4 Phantom, which had become the workhorse fighter-bomber of the Vietnam War. Selection was based on class ranking in academic, flying, and military skills. I scored number two overall out of the fifty-some student pilots who had completed the course at Vance, so I had an open field.

The F-4 looked good for several reasons. First, it was the only fighter-bomber offered to our class, and I had decided long ago that if I had a chance to fly a fighter I'd jump at it. For some reason, big airplanes didn't hold much fascination for me. And by now it was obvious that the originally limited engagement in Indochina had grown into a much larger, long-term war than originally envisioned, and that the Air Force would be deeply involved in Southeast Asia for the indefinite future. Much of the American air campaign involved Air Force and Navy fighter-bombers striking targets in North Vietnam and—secretly—bombing enemy infiltration routes and supply lines hidden beneath the triple-canopy rain forest along the Ho Chi Minh Trail in ostensibly "neutral" Laos and Cambodia.

I was pretty sure I'd be out there flying combat missions and wanted a plane that was in the mainstream action of our Air Force. The F-4 Phantom filled that bill. Although a new F-4 pilot started off as a "GIB" (Guy in Back), I hoped to upgrade to aircraft commander—the pilot flying from the front seat, who made the crucial decisions for the two-man crew. So my training officer and I researched the assignment route that would take me to the front seat as quickly as possible. The word among us was that the fast track to a front-seat upgrade lay in squadrons stationed in Germany. My goal was earning a high proficiency rating as an F-4 backseat pilot in Europe and then transitioning to aircraft commander before heading to Southeast Asia.

Mary Jo agreed with the decision. "Dick, you choose any airplane that will get us to Europe."

She had traveled to Europe as a college student as part of the People to People program, had seen President Kennedy's *"Ich bin ein Berliner"* speech in Berlin in 1963 and had wonderful experiences with the families and people she met. She wanted to share that with me and gain even more experience.

In June 1966, we were assigned to Davis-Monthan Air Force Base just south of Tucson, Arizona, where I underwent intense instruction as an F-4 backseat pilot in a Replacement Training Unit.

The F-4 seemed huge when my class walked around the plane parked on the runway in the baking Arizona sun. With a maximum takeoff weight of over twenty-eight tons, the Phantom equaled the World War II B-24 Liberator heavy bomber that had crashed in my Kansas neighborhood when I was just a toddler. But weight did not degrade the F-4's performance. For years after the Phantom had been introduced in 1960 as the Navy's long-range, all-weather fleet defense fighter, it held the world absolute speed and altitude records: over sixteen hundred miles per hour—Mach 2.2—and more than ninety-eight thousand feet. And it had a distinctly futuristic look, with the tips of the swept-back wings tilted upward ("dihedral") and the horizontal stabilizers of the tail slashing down ("anhedral").

I got my first true impression of the plane's size and power on that initial ground inspection. To examine the two cockpits, I had to climb a vertical yellow ladder ten feet high.

This plane's a real monster, I thought.

The Navy had originally commissioned the Phantom as a fighter that exclusively used air-to-air missiles to defend the ships of aircraft carrier battle groups against Soviet bombers. The Air Force bought the F-4 as a multirole plane that operated as both a fighter and a fighter-bomber. Because the Phantom was designed to withstand the brutal stress of landing on a carrier's flight deck, it had especially robust wings, fuselage, and landing gear and was ideal for carrying tons of bombs and rockets.

And it was in the fighter-bomber role that I was trained on the Phantom. Once more, we combined classroom and ground simulator instruction with flying. The days—and nights—were long. There was so much to learn, and many skills to master to the degree of proficiency that the Air Force demanded. And we were all aware that the air war in Indochina was heating up: American pilots were bombing North Vietnam, as well as the Viet Cong in the South and enemy infiltration routes along the Ho Chi Minh Trail in Laos.

Given the plane's role as both a fighter and a bomber, the cockpit was a complex maze of switches, dials, and caution-and-warning lights. To fly the F-4 well, the pilot had to learn how to focus his attention both "in" the cockpit—on the multiple instruments—and "out" of the cockpit on the other formation members, on navigation tasks, and on watching the surrounding sky for enemy aircraft or missiles. The GIB shared these tasks, but had the principal responsibility for the radar scope. Initially, this seemed one of the most difficult challenges of training for combat in the F-4, but I quickly learned there was much more of interest to look at or look for outside the cockpit—that was where I'd see the enemy (or a craggy mountain looming up).

On a bombing mission, the frontseater had to select and prepare the ordnance he was going to drop by briefly but accurately focusing on the small oval-ended "dog bone" weapons panel beneath the main forward spread of instruments. He had to choose among the munitions slung on pylons beneath the wings, and then (if carrying live ordnance) flip switches to arm the bomb's nose and tail fuses—and set the interval in which they would be dropped. And this demanding task had to be performed while the bombs were still "safe," seconds before the pilot turned on the "master arm," rolled the jet over on a wing, and initiated the optimum bomb run on a predetermined dive angle and at an exact airspeed. During the bomb run, his eyes definitely had to be "outside" the cockpit, especially when flying among mountains. And there was plenty of mountainous terrain in Indochina. But he had to cross-check the gun sight in the air-to-ground mode, trying very hard to arrive at the right aim point, at the right airspeed and altitude, to put the bombs on target.

There was no doubt that we were all headed into combat, and I wanted to be ready for the challenge when the time came for me to go. Because of war-time pressure, the F-4 ground simulators at Davis-Monthan ran on a twenty-four-hour schedule, so I often found myself flying simulator drills late at night after having already spent hours in the classroom and in the aircraft on training flights. One Friday night several months into the course, I finished an exhausting simulator exercise involving air-to-air intercepts, operating the radar in the backseat and directing the pilot where to turn, how hard to turn, and how much power to use in the maneuver. Throw in a couple of emergency procedures and I found myself sweating even though the simulator room was almost cold from the air-conditioning. I was glad when my torment in the "sim" was finally done and the next poor guy could take my place and sweat a little.

I wanted a drink and still had time for one before the officers club closed. My hand was on the club door when I realized I hadn't put on the little dickie neck scarf that then-Col.—later four-star—Chappie James, director of Operations, insisted every officer in his command wear. Chappie James was one of the senior African American officers in the Air Force and had flown over one hundred combat missions during the Korean War. He knew what combat entailed and made sure we took our training seriously. Growing up in the segregated South, he also understood adversity and didn't cut us any slack. That meant we took pride in our uniforms and didn't walk around in a flight suit with a baggy T-shirt showing at the neck. So we wore dickies . . . when we remembered.

But I had almost strolled into the officers club without mine. I tucked it in place and headed for the bar, only to be instantly greeted by hoots of derision. In my haste to correct the deficiency in the dickie department, I had forgotten to remove my hat. An officer did *not* wear his hat in the O'Club bar. By ancient tradition, the cost for that infraction was buying a round of drinks for everyone there. On a Friday night with the place jumping with fighter pilots about to go off to war, that was a pretty expensive lesson for a guy on second lieutenant's pay.

When our weekends became more relaxed after the first exhausting months of training, Mary Jo and I would often join other couples, camping out up in the cool pine glades of Mt. Lemmon in the Santa Catalina Mountains. We'd listen to music on the radio and take hikes, hunting for old Indian arrowheads. It was very relaxing to sit around a campfire, sipping a beer or a glass of wine. We all discussed the future, but nobody talked directly about the war. It was just out there, an invisible, but tangible presence. When one of our small crowd of campers was killed during a training mission on the bombing range, it brought home the hazards of the profession as nothing else could.

We bought a motorcycle for a second "car," and I thought I would be riding the bike to work. But as soon as Mary Jo learned to operate it, I was relegated to our old Chevy. We would ride that Honda motorcycle all over, including our camping trips, and this was a continuation of my lifelong love of two-wheelers, begun in high school when my best friend, Bert Cooper, would let me ride his motorcycle. And then when he went off to Yale, he let me take care of his 250 Ducati motocross bike. I even raced it a bit—with terrible results.

But when the weekends were over, it was back to the grind of training.

My cumulative scores in the F-4 training were high enough for me to get my preferred European assignment: the 417th Tactical Fighter Squadron at Ramstein Air Base, West Germany. Mary Jo was overjoyed, and so was I: I stood a decent chance of earning an upgrade to aircraft commander and going to war in the front seat of an F-4D.

Training wasn't all flying and long hours in the classroom and sims. At the end of our initial F-4 training, we were sent up for the Survival, Evasion, Resistance and Escape School in the Cascade Mountains of Washington State. This was a serious course, which might prove a lifesaver for a pilot forced to eject in Europe or Vietnam—especially in the high mountains. Conditions were meant to be as realistic as possible.

The Cascades were beautiful in November, with the tall pines heaped under heavy loads of snow. But this wasn't a nature hike. Certainly the Prisoner of War phase seemed realistic. The "enemy" instructors would force us individually into a very cramped, freezing wooden box for hours, beating on it with clubs, to see if they could tempt anyone into their warm tents to sit around the kerosene stove with a canteen cup of steaming coffee while divulging military secrets. Nobody succumbed. But some guys came close.

Although the snow in the Cascade wilderness was deep and wet, we were the last class not to be issued snowshoes and had no special clothing or equipment. We had to survive with our leather flying boots and nylon parachute canopies for protection against the bitter cold.

We did learn to survive, however: Layers of nylon from our chutes, sandwiched in insulating pine boughs, became both makeshift parkas and crude sleeping bags. And our campfires were indispensable. The heat dried our boots and warded off frostbite all night. But these fires required a constant supply of wood, and the quest for dry pine or cedar branches never ended. If everyone pitched in and helped find fuel, the chore wasn't too bad. But some guys, exhausted from trekking through the deep drifts, just gave up, and wouldn't lift a finger to help. They were happy to flop down beside the fire and let the rest of us fetch wood for the whole class.

I never would have expected professional Air Force officers to act that way.

They wouldn't last long if this were a real-world situation, I thought.

The course taught me some valuable lessons—both about winter survival and about innate human weakness.

———————

At Ramstein Air Base in Germany, the 417th, fondly known as the "Red Dorks," was unique. We were separated from our parent organization, the 50th Tactical Fighter Wing, which was located farther north at Hahn Air Base, so we operated like the small self-contained unit we were without the normal close wing oversight. Ramstein had pleasant pine and hardwood forests nearby, and the flying weather was generally better than that at the rest of our fighter bases in Central Europe.

The prospect of taking off on a combat mission with a tactical "nuke" slung beneath the jet's centerline belly in bad weather was not appealing. But the grim reality was that the Warsaw Pact and NATO forces confronted each other across the Iron Curtain between the free West and communist East, each side armed with thousands of tactical nuclear weapons. This tripwire stalemate continued day and night for years and decades.

There would be no stand-down, no time-out for bad weather.

So when I sat on nuclear alert in the ready room with Capt. Ralph Van Brunt or another of the frontseaters with whom I regularly flew, we hoped for good takeoff weather, but also hoped the alarm would *never* sound, sending us down that runway toward our target in Czechoslovakia or East Germany.

———————

Our dream of traveling to Europe to fly and tour was definitely realized. Many of our contemporaries had small children who kept them home most of the time. We had decided to put off having children so we could see Europe. My life was basically a cycle of fly, stand alert, take leave. But often it came down to just fly and leave, with my peers standing alert because of their limitations in taking leave—I wasn't too popular toward the end. And with the four-deutsche-marks-to-a-dollar exchange rate in those days and Mary Jo's income from teaching at the base Education Center, we had plenty of money to travel—especially since Mary Jo insisted we use *Europe on $5 a Day* as our guide to where to eat and stay. We chose to live off base in Kaiserslautern when most everyone else lived on base, which enriched our overseas experience. We had a very nice new apartment, but the heat went off at ten every night—going green before it was fashionable.

In August 1968, my squadron transferred out of Germany to Mountain Home Air Force Base in arid southern Idaho. The flying weather was certainly better than in Germany. But in January 1969, my squadron found itself back in Germany, on a temporary assignment to Hahn Air Base. The purpose of this exercise was to demonstrate to our NATO allies—and to the Warsaw Pact—that we could respond quickly to an emergency. After the exhausting transatlantic flight that required seven aerial refuelings, cramped in our cockpits, we arrived at base to be greeted by the local wine queen serving bright green bottles of Mosel. The welcoming ceremony took place in the steam-heated officers club with the aircrew sitting around the edge of the crowded room. As the NATO press officers briefed the media about our high state of readiness, we slumped exhausted, ready for sleep, not combat. Maybe the wine queen was the Warsaw Pact's nefarious secret weapon.

We still faced the dilemma of terrible winter flying weather. The Air Force tried to solve the problem by circling a C-130 cargo plane upwind of the runway and dumping iodine crystals to turn clouds into tiny droplets. But because of the vagaries of the wind, the "clear" air would drift over the runway in uneven patterns. That meant part of the runway was clear while other parts were zero-zero (zero ceiling and visibility). This experiment never became operational.

———————

Back in the States, I would soon be headed overseas again. Preparing for an assignment to Southeast Asia, Mary Jo and I moved to Homestead Air Force Base in southern Florida, where I would complete training as an F-4E aircraft commander.

Here, the intensity increased yet again. One of the skills I had to master was aerial refueling, an essential element of the fighter-bomber's mission. It took a lot of fuel to lift a Phantom carrying a heavy load of ordnance from the runway to cruise altitude. So a typical combat mission profile for an F-4 might call for a rendezvous with a tanker soon after takeoff and then again after returning from the target. All jet fighters at that time were fuel gluttons, and we were always conscious of our fuel status.

Maneuvering an F-4 fast and low on a typical bombing sortie could eat up most of your "gas" in a hurry, and we had to be able to find the tanker flying on its oval track the first time around. Wasting time could lead to empty tanks and flameouts of both engines. And without engine thrust, the Phantom had the aerodynamic lift normally associated with a flatiron—or a brick.

The actual refueling required the ability to keep the F-4 at a steady speed and position just behind and below the tanker's wide horizontal tail stabilizers. The KC135 was the military version of the Boeing 707 airliner and was therefore quite steady in flight. The job of the Phantom pilot was to slide into place beneath the Plexiglas bubble of the tanker's fueling boom operator. Lying on his belly, he would "fly" the forty-foot lance of the boom by delicately manipulating the pair of winglets on the shaft to insert the end nozzle into the F-4's narrow receptacle, located just behind the rear canopy. A satisfying thud and a green positive fuel flow lamp signified a good connection.

———————

At Homestead, day and night aerial refueling, bombing, and gunnery practice at the Avon Park Range in central Florida were interspersed with air-to-air combat maneuvers over water between southern Florida and Cuba. As I trained, I often thought of my overconfident bravado in flying up to Minneapolis and back in that little Piper Cherokee with my Dad. But in combat, I wouldn't have the water towers with the small town names painted on them or the shiny gilded dome of the state capitol in Des Moines to orient me. I was going to war, and by now I recognized that flying fighter-bombers in combat was a very dangerous business.

Like aviators who fought in past wars, I took advantage of the weeks before deployment to enjoy as much of life as I could. More often than not, that included sailing with Mary Jo on Biscayne Bay with a picnic lunch. It was also where we acquired Biffin, our first Old English Sheepdog puppy, who started our lifelong love of the breed.

———————

I was assigned to the 13th Tactical Fighter Squadron at Udorn Royal Thai Air Base and flew my first combat mission on Christmas Eve, 1969.

Although nominally under Thai authority, Udorn was an American base, one of seven in Thailand. We were located on a plateau of rice paddies lying among low hills of scrub jungle near the Mekong River, about three hundred miles northeast of Bangkok. The base was within easy striking distance of targets in both North and South Vietnam, as well as in the Annamite Mountains that ran through southern Laos, forming the spine of Indochina. It was in these steep mountains of triple-canopy rain forest that the North Vietnamese had constructed the hidden network of infiltration routes collectively known as the Ho Chi Minh Trail.

Our primary task was to stop—or at least try to slow—enemy infiltration of men and materiel from feeder routes in North Vietnam, south through the Barrel Roll target zone and down to the Steel Tiger area of operations, which extended to South Vietnam.

The farther north along the Trail, the stiffer the enemy air defenses became. By the time I arrived "in theater," the North Vietnamese Army (NVA) had acquired literally thousands of optically- and radar-controlled antiaircraft artillery (AAA) guns, scores of surface-to-air missile (SAM) sites, and MiG fighter interceptors—many based at sanctuary bases in China. Further, the enemy intensified air defenses along the Trail in the late 1960s, deploying multiple 23mm and 37mm guns. Inside North Vietnam, air defenses along the Trail's feeder routes were steadily upgraded.

By operating so brazenly along the Trail system, North Vietnam had in effect absorbed a big wedge of Laos, even though the kingdom was an officially neutral member of the United Nations. The NVA and their communist Pathet Lao guerrilla allies had fought to overthrow the legitimate royal government from its establishment after the French pulled out of Indochina in the mid-1950s. Our air campaign had two objectives: choking North Vietnamese infiltration to the South and protecting Laos from communist defeat.

But this was not an easy task. It was almost impossible for jet fighter-bombers to stop troop and supply convoys that might consist of tough and well-motivated NVA troops pushing bicycles heavily laden with sacks of rice or crates of ammunition. It was easier to knock out Soviet- or Chinese-built trucks. But the truck convoys rarely moved during daylight, except in the monsoon months when the clouds spilled down to fill the steep valleys between the naked gray limestone ridges and the thick chimneys of the free-standing karsts.

I began my first combat tour in the hot dry season, however, so low overcasts were not a major problem. And we had "fast" Forward Air Controllers (FACs) flying F-4s to guide us to targets. There were also "slow mover" FACs in twin turboprop, twin-tailed OV-10s that could mark targets along busy sections of the Trail.

However, the American air campaign against North Vietnam was fundamentally flawed on the strategic, tactical, and technical levels. The enemy viewed our periodic bombing pauses as showing weakness rather than as inducement to negotiate—which gave them the opportunity to move more troops and war materiel south. If the enemy sent fifty trucks—or five hundred cargo bicycles—and we managed to knock out half, the other half got through. The Annamite Mountains did not provide an open, exposed road network like that in Western Europe on which Allied bombers had attacked German supply lines in World War II. And even where North Vietnamese supply convoys were vulnerable in narrow mountain passes or at bridges, we did not have anywhere near enough precision laser-guided bombs or laser-equipped aircraft and crews to accurately strike these choke points.

Inside North Vietnam, Air Force and Navy planes had to stay in assigned "route packages." It was almost as if the two services were fighting separate wars. Here I gained my first insights into and lessons on "joint" warfare involving separate branches of the armed forces.

The voice channels of our radios were not scrambled, so every time Air Force, Navy, or Marine planes communicated, the enemy could eavesdrop. By the late 1960s, they certainly had had enough time to learn our call signs, because we kept using them. In fact, it often seemed to me that we were fighting World War II battles—over and over again—with far less success.

My early night missions were difficult, not so much due to enemy defenses, but because I was new to combat and there was so much to remember. We basically operated in two- or four-aircraft flights—the Lead, call sign "One," and the wingman, "Two"—flying on opposite sides of an oval holding pattern above the target area. A typical night mission would have a C-130, call sign "Blindbat," dropping "log" marking flares, then one plane at a time would be cleared to bomb at the distances and directions from the dazzling white lights that Blindbat designated.

Early in my tour, I usually waited in the holding pattern for my Lead to roll in and drop his ordnance. And then it was my turn. Most nights were absolutely black except for the magnesium glare of the flares marking the target. Down in the Steel Tiger area closer to the borders of Laos, Cambodia, and South Vietnam, the nights would occasionally light up as fixed-wing AC-119 Stinger or AC-130 Spectre gunships unleashed molten streams of tracers on enemy vehicles caught moving through the darkness.

We began bomb runs by rolling over onto a wing and sliding "down the chute," trying to be as precise as possible with our dive angle and airspeed. The ensuing moments were critical, requiring a rapid sequence of eyes "in" and "out" of the cockpit as I prepared to drop, while keeping the airplane aligned on the target. We tried to release the bombs at seven thousand feet above ground level (AGL) and pull out of the dive at four thousand feet AGL, keeping us out of the heaviest concentrations of antiaircraft fire—a maneuver that always caused our G-suits to inflate.

Bombing at night among the thick towering limestone pillars of the karsts was always risky. The first man lost in our wing after I arrived was Capt. Bill Reed, with whom I'd gone through upgrade training at Homestead. He was a fun-loving guy who drove a beautiful Chevrolet 409 convertible—once right into a fruit stand outside the main gate of the base after a little time at the stag bar in the O'Club. One night he and his backseater rolled into their bomb run and never pulled out.

Climbing out safely from the bomb drop was a crucial maneuver—you never wanted to wait too long and need afterburners to claw for altitude: A Phantom's twin burners glowing an incandescent foundry-furnace orange would attract every antiaircraft gun in the area, allowing the enemy gunners to start tracking you.

But I took my job seriously and always wanted to do it right. If I was going to put myself in harm's way, I intended to hit my target—the first time around. So I was always pleased when the flare plane or FAC radioed with the report of "good bombs."

My next consideration, of course, was making it home alive. Early in my tour I got a taste of what it's like to be shot at. It was another night mission where I could see most everything being shot my way.

We were flying in the Steel Tiger area, and just after I rolled in and was going "down the chute," red tracers surrounded my aircraft. How could they predict so well where a blacked-out F-4 was at night? But they were good. I was almost at the bomb-release point and I didn't want to break off for AAA fire.

So that's what it looks like, I thought. It was difficult to understand how our aircraft was not hit that night.

I now understood the actual possibility of being shot down and forced to eject over the Trail. That was not a pleasant thought to contemplate. During jungle survival school at Clark Field in the Philippines, the instructors had emphasized the grim fate of American airmen captured along the Ho Chi Minh Trail, where the enemy might torture them to death.

So I went into the town of Udorn and had an Indian tailor make me up several custom flight suits out of tough camouflage rip-stop material. The suits had extra pockets where I wanted them for plastic water bottles. Some guys carried a belt of ammunition for their .38 caliber pistols. A handgun was useless against AK-47 assault rifles, so I didn't bother with extra pistol ammo. However, I did take a survival radio and several spare batteries. The radio combined an emergency locator beacon and voice channels that could keep me in contact with U.S. Air Force Search and Rescue (SAR) forces and maybe save my life.

These SAR forces consisted of hard-hitting A-1 Skyraider Sandys, tough prop-driven planes that dated back to the late 1940s. In Indochina, the Sandys escorted HH-3 Jolly Green Giant and HH-53 Super Jolly helicopters deep into enemy territory. If I had to punch out along the Trail, I intended to run, climb, or claw my way up into the forest as fast as possible and call in the SAR forces. And I wanted enough battery power to keep talking them to my position—though I hoped I'd never need to.

In January 1970, Mary Jo wrote to announce she was moving to Bangkok to be near me. We had no children at this point, and if I was going to get shot down or killed she wanted to know what that part of the world looked like and smelled like. She hoped to find some sort of teaching job once she arrived. I tried to convince her that the Department of Defense and the Air Force had a firm policy against dependents coming to Thailand because they could put an undue burden on the limited housing, medical, and commissary services.

Even as I wrote to explain this, I knew better than to try to dictate to this independent woman.

"You mean an American citizen," she wrote back, "with a passport and a visa can't come to Bangkok? I *am* coming."

Midway through my tour, the wing leadership was asked to fill a command post billet in Korea, and the first ones to go would be those whose wives had managed to make it to Thailand. A move to a command post job as opposed to flying combat would not have been career enhancing.

My flight commander, Maj. Robert Smith, strongly advised me to ask Mary Jo to return to the United States or else I was off to Korea. I had what was at the time a very naïve reaction: "Okay, sir," I said. "The squadron's very short of instructor pilots and I don't think the wing will gladly let go a captain with my experience."

Looking back, I know now that having one fewer upstart instructor pilot in

Thailand would not have made much difference to those overseeing personnel moves. I guess I had taken a page from Dad's card-playing bluff habits. It was an audacious comment from a junior officer. But the Air Force backed off, and I wasn't reassigned.

About once every six weeks or so Mary Jo would fly up to the base on a rattling old Thai Airways DC-3 with rice farmers and their chickens as fellow passengers—or sometimes she would take the overnight train. Each time was a unique experience for sure. As much as I liked her being there, it always seemed a little strange to be flying combat missions and have Mary Jo waiting for me at the one decent hotel in town when I got back from dodging ground fire. Mary Jo had to do her own dodging of danger every couple of months. Having a nonimmigrant visa forced her to apply for a new one and leave and re-enter the country every three months. She would come up to Udorn, get a taxi to drive her north to the Mekong River where she would take a little wooden boat across to Laos and then come right back, getting her passport stamped in the process. It was considered too hazardous for the U.S. military to cross into Laos and we weren't allowed to take her route.

By the end of my tour, Mary Jo had three teaching jobs in Bangkok, never used the U.S. medical or commissary services, and probably did more for Thai-American relations than I did turning trees into toothpicks in Laos. She taught adults at a military education center, at a language school run by the U.S. Information Agency and at Chulalongkorn University.

Four months into this first combat tour, I was upgraded again—to fly fast FAC missions. Because enemy air defenses had become so robust along the principal infiltration routes, it was often too dangerous for slow prop-driven Forward Air Controller spotter planes to operate. On Forward Air Control missions, our F-4s carried white phosphorous target-marking rockets on wing pylons and an external 20mm cannon gun pod slung from the belly. The gun pod held 1,250 rounds of ammunition, which allowed us to beat up a truck convoy pretty hard when not guiding in other fighter-bombers—and also to provide support to isolated CIA "Lima Sites" under attack.

On these fast FAC missions, you worked closely with the intelligence folks for details of the threat and the targets you were "fragged" (from fragmentary order) to strike. I learned a lot about the intelligence process one day when another fast FAC from Korat Royal Thai Air Base was badly shot up by an antiaircraft gun in the same area I would be flying in later in the day. His plane suffering hydraulic failure, he landed at our base and I went out to meet the crew. Their F-4E aircraft was easy to spot, having been stitched with 23mm rounds in the nose section. A couple of feet more and they would have impacted in the cockpit area. I asked the crew where the guns were that got them and they pointed out the precise location, as all fast FACs knew the territory we patrolled like the back of our hand.

My mission prep that afternoon included a briefing by the intelligence people, which was thorough—except that they never mentioned the guns that shot up my fellow FACs that morning, yet I knew the crew had debriefed our intel folks.

"Why haven't you mentioned those guns as confirmed antiaircraft positions?" I asked.

Their answer has stuck with me forever. "Well, sir we can't confirm that gun position until Seventh Air Force confirms it."

You've got a plane full of 23mm holes, I thought. *What else do we need to confirm it?* This episode brought home the role intelligence bureaucracy plays even in combat, and it was something I'd fight the rest of my career.

The true dangers of the fast FAC mission became more personal for me when Capt. Ralph Van Brunt, my frontseater from Germany, was shot down at dusk along the Trail. Unfortunately, the Air Force could not launch a Search and Rescue effort because low overcast cloaked the rocky karst pinnacles in the area. In Bangkok, Mary Jo had the painful responsibility of breaking the news to Ralph's wife, Joyce, who also lived in the Thai capital. The next morning, my good friend and veteran fast FAC John Jumper—later Chief of Staff of the U.S. Air Force—used his intimate knowledge of the terrain to guide the prop-driven A-1 Sandy rescue planes down through the thick cloud deck to spot Ralph's flares from his hiding place in the forest. A Jolly Green Giant rescue helicopter winched him up to safety.

Although there was no shortage of skill and courage among our aircrew, we weren't always given logical assignments. One glaring example of weak tactics was our mission of flying fighter escort for the hulking B-52 Stratofortresses bombing the Trail. Our orders were to throttle back to about three hundred knots and take positions off the lumbering bombers' wingtips, in my view acting as bait, tempting the nimble little MiG 17 or MiG 21 fighters to pounce, fire their cannons or heat-seeking rockets, and scoot away. Tactically, it would have been a lot smarter for our fast and maneuverable F-4s to prowl far out ahead to jump the MiGs as they tried to climb up toward the big bombers. But that wasn't the way the 8th Air Force had escorted B-17s and B-24s over Germany twenty-five years before. However, the few times our command-and-control planes did send us on MiG alerts, a flight of F-4s moving out at supersonic speed to intercept them was usually enough to scare the enemy fighters back to their bases. This was a clear case of some officers using the tactics they knew from the past and not adapting to the new realities of warfare—supersonic jets armed with missiles, not just guns.

I left Thailand at the end of 1970 and followed Mary Jo back to Kansas for home leave. Despite the piercing winter chill after a year in the humid heat of Southeast Asia, it was good to be home, back among family and friends. But I had changed and no longer thought of myself as a civilian. At some point in the previous five years, without really realizing it, I had become a career Air Force officer who embraced the unique culture of military life, which was so completely different from my perception of the civilian professional world. There was the camaraderie, of course, but at a deeper level, the military rested on abiding trust: Our lives often depended on that bond of trust. During my first combat tour, I never doubted that the Search and Rescue forces would fly into the most dangerous flak traps the North Vietnamese could devise to pluck me from beneath the triple-canopy forest before the enemy captured me.

But military culture transcended the bravery of combat. Integrity was our watchword. We learned to be honest and forthright with each other in all aspects of our profession. For example, on climbing into the cockpit of an airplane, I implicitly trusted the maintenance crew chief's assurance that the aircraft and its munitions were ready to fly.

Such honesty permeated military life. An officer who was overly ambitious, who tried to manipulate his peers, or who was self-serving didn't last long. Devious attributes were anathema among my friends and colleagues. This is not to say that there were no officers of bad character, but at some point in their career they'd be held accountable. In the military culture I had come to love, you spoke the truth as you saw it and didn't engage in intricate mind games, as the stakes were just too high. A successful military career meant selfless service in a meritocracy where you advanced on the basis of how well you contributed to the mission, not on the basis of your race, sex, or the source of your commission. In fact, the Department of Defense was an American pioneer in actively fostering racial tolerance—which was one of the reasons I stayed in uniform for so many years.

For me another appeal of a military career was the opportunity to serve a cause larger than myself. Certainly I was patriotic, but so were millions of other Americans. What I felt went beyond Fourth-of-July, Pledge-of-Allegiance patriotism. I knew my profession was important for our country, more valuable in fact than the relatively modest salary I earned at that time. When I raised my hand and swore to protect the Constitution I felt a pride that has never diminished. Later in my career, I studied the lives of Generals Hap Arnold and Dwight Eisenhower. Both these World War II leaders epitomized my concept of service to one's country. Between the two world wars, Arnold turned down a lucrative and prestigious offer to head Pan American Airways and stayed in the Army Air Corps—even though his own military career was stalled. In the late 1930s, Eisenhower accepted noncommand staff assignments because that was where he was needed as America prepared for war. It wasn't until after Pearl Harbor that Eisenhower was awarded command as a flag officer and Arnold took command of the Army Air Force.

After I retired, I spoke to a group of investment bankers and their dinner guests. One banker, a self-confident man in his forties, approached me over cocktails. "General," he said, "it must have really bothered you to make so little money during your long career."

"You know," I answered, "I never really thought about it."

"No," he insisted. "You *must* have thought about it. And it must have been something you and your peers talked about it."

Arguing all night about this point would not have convinced the guy, so I backed off and found a new conversation.

The exhilarating nature of flying fighters and the attributes of the military culture were the main reasons I was hesitant to return to civilian life as the end of my initial five-year commitment approached.

But back in Kansas City, my dad and brother Chuck were hoping I would join them in the family business in 1971.

"I can't do it this time, Chuck," I explained. "I've got an assignment coming up that's going to extend my active-duty obligation."

"An important job?" Chuck asked.

"It will probably save a lot of American lives and maybe even help end this damn war."

That assignment was flying Wild Weasel Suppression of Enemy Air Defense (SEAD) missions. By 1972, when I returned to Indochina for my second combat tour, the sky above North Vietnam and Laos had become a sophisticated and deadly electronic battlefield. The approaches to the Ho Chi Minh Trail bristled with radar-guided SA-2 Guideline missile sites. So the Navy and Air Force finally joined the twentieth century by deploying relatively effective electronic countermeasures.

Our Wild Weasel aircraft was a heavily modified F-4. The nickname derived from the four-legged weasel's instinctive ability to penetrate prey's dens—often in the dead of night. The planes were laden with electronic detection and jamming equipment as well as AGM-45 Shrike missiles that could seek out and destroy enemy radar antennas. That was the theory at least. In addition we would also carry cluster bomb units (CBUs) to drop on any SAM sites we could visually identify.

In reality, a Shrike had a range of only about twelve miles—half that of an SA-2—and was much slower. This meant you had to get close to the SAM site after your plane was detected by the enemy radar and remain within range long enough for your Shrike to detect the radar antenna and do a crude estimate of the range to the SAM site—called the "dip check."

I was stationed at Korat, Thailand, and the guys in the officers club who flew normal missions would sometimes look at me quizzically when they recognized the Wild Weasel patch Velcroed to the shoulder of my flight suit. The patch *was* intriguing: a little orange cartoon weasel, its fur and tail frazzled perhaps from electronic static and the acronym YGBSM at the bottom. This stood for "You Gotta Be Shittin' Me," the reputed reaction of the electronic warfare backseater on seeing his first SA-2 coming at him.

The idea of flying close enough to enemy missile sites to strike them with radar-homing weapons—or dodging and outflying the SA-2 once it was launched—initially did seem near suicidal. As one Wild Weasel pilot told us being trained in Japan, "Flying these missions is a manly sport."

That was an understatement. On one of my first duels with a SAM site up in Route Pack 3 in North Vietnam, my electronics warfare officer got the launch indications on his scope as the missile rose from the site. We were too far away to fire one of our Shrikes, so my backseater turned up the power on all our radar-jamming equipment, and I started my evasive maneuver. On a night mission like this, you had the advantage of quickly telling whether the SAM was homing on you. This SAM kept on coming, straight at us. I swallowed hard and used the tactics I'd been taught.

After turning to keep the SA-2 steady on my right wingtip, I paused and then nosed over into a shallow dive, slowly increasing my speed as the missile approached, the glare of its rocket plume growing brighter. The Soviet-made

SA-2 was designed to defend against high-flying bombers, which lacked good maneuverability. So the idea was to get the missile heading down, and then pull up at the right moment. The telephone-pole-like SA-2 Guideline missile was not strong enough to stay with our Phantom. As I pulled up, the incoming SAM undershot us, broke apart, and exploded about three miles away.

Despite the cockpit air-conditioning set on Max, I was dripping sweat as we turned back to our patrol sector. Even though the Air Force had trained Wild Weasel crews well, this was very hazardous duty. But all our crews were volunteers who flew these missions with full knowledge of the risks. So we mastered the fear we all felt. We flew missions. We dodged SAMs. Some crews did not come home.

The more we improved our tactics, the more the enemy kept pace. Somebody commented that flying Weasel missions was like kids playing flashlight tag. Actually, our missions seemed more like heavily armed thugs stalking each other in a pitch-dark alley. But we didn't use the visible bands of the electromagnetic spectrum: We "saw" and were seen with radar and radar receivers. Once the North Vietnamese understood our tactics, they kept their radars on standby and tracked the telltale signature of their prey's electronic countermeasures. This wasn't a game of cat-and-mouse; it was a contest between two fierce predators.

In October 1972, the Nixon White House began Operation Linebacker I, sending giant B-52 bombers to strike targets in the southern provinces of North Vietnam. These missions were intended as retaliation for a renewed NVA ground offensive in South Vietnam, despite the protracted peace negotiations under way in Paris. The North Vietnamese diplomats walked out of the talks. We kept bombing.

On the night of November 22, I was flying SAM suppression for B-52s in Route Package 3. Having fired my Shrikes, I rolled over and headed west toward Thailand. I hadn't proceeded very far when I heard an urgent radio message for any aircraft with "sufficient remaining fuel" to return to base, and for those needing midair refueling to stand by on the tanker for a possible Search and Rescue (SAR). One of the B-52s we had been escorting, *Olive 2*, had not checked in posttarget. We didn't know it at the time but that B-52 had sustained heavy battle damage from a SAM hit. As I quickly calculated how much flying time I had with the fuel on board, Capt. Don Triplett, my electronics warfare officer in the backseat, recommended we head home as there were enough folks going to the tanker for any possible SAR.

We were climbing to thirty thousand feet, enjoying the cooler air being put out by an air conditioner that always worked better at altitude. It was a beautiful night with the moonlight turning the Mekong River into a shimmering ribbon as we passed into Thailand.

Don and I were discussing the fate of *Olive 2*, wondering where she was, when suddenly straight ahead at twelve o'clock it looked as if the sun just appeared. There was a rolling orange fireball. We were near a tanker refueling track and I initially thought there'd been a midair collision. A massive wing cartwheeled past us, and the rest of the flaming debris cascaded into the Thai rice paddies below. My earphones sounded with the multiple "whoop-whoop-whoop" of the emergency beacons packed in the bomber crews' survival gear. Hearing the numerous beacons, I knew we had found *Olive 2*.

I reported the bailout location to the tower at Nakhon Phanom Air Base and orbited the area until the Jolly Greens arrived on the scene. All of the *Olive 2* crew were picked up successfully. When we landed back at base, we probably had enough fuel left to stay airborne another ten minutes.

In December 1972, the United States initiated Operation Linebacker II, the so-called "Christmas bombing" during which waves of B-52s and fighter-bombers struck previously prohibited targets in the Hanoi-Haiphong area. The strategic objective of the operation was to force the North Vietnamese back to the Paris peace negotiation table.

Unfortunately, it was a costly operation, during which a number of B-52s were needlessly shot down due to the unimaginative, rigid tactics that the Strategic Air Command (SAC) employed. The first night, three went down over Hanoi, and during the next week, the North Vietnamese SAMs destroyed twelve more. This tactical disaster—with strategic implications—drove home some key points to me: Courage and integrity are not enough on the battlefield; imagination and flexibility are qualities every military leader must possess.

One of the operation's most serious tactical flaws concerned the pattern of three-bomber "cells" repeatedly flying nearly identical routes at predictable altitudes to and from their targets and then banking away over the heavily defended target area after dropping their bombs. On the outbound turns, the bombers' powerful radar jammers were deflected upward and sideways, away from the SAM sites, which allowed the SA-2s to penetrate the Americans' protective electronic cloak. Worse, SAC mission planners initially had not integrated Wild Weasels into the mission profiles. It was only after the first night, when those three big bombers were shot down and fifteen American airmen were killed or captured, that the Weasels were allowed to know the details of the bombers' tactics and provide the best protection we could all the way to "downtown" Hanoi.

But once we were coordinating our tactics, mission profiles changed dramatically. Cells of B-52s now approached their targets simultaneously from different directions and at staggered altitudes, and most important did not turn while over SAM territory. The Wild Weasels ran interference and always tried to put a Shrike on a SAM site before the missile could intercept the bomber. These new tactics overwhelmed enemy air defenses, and the North Vietnamese expended their reserves of SA-2s without blunting the American bombing offensive.

Complacency lay at the root of the initially inflexible mission planning. For years, B-52s had droned along at high altitude, dropping thousands of tons of bombs into vast areas of jungle in the South and Laos that were virtually devoid of antiaircraft defenses that could reach them. But when SAC employed this same approach in the most heavily defended air space in the world, the Air Force flirted with disaster. Not only were we losing unacceptable numbers of B-52s and airmen, the enemy was exploiting the notoriety of purported "carpet bombing." Until we changed tactics, we risked losing both the tactical struggle and the propaganda battle: It was possible that the enemy might beat us in the sky above Hanoi and on the global media stage.

Among the root causes of the ineffective air campaign in Indochina were our eight separate and often poorly coordinated air forces: The 7th Air Force was based in Saigon and ran missions in South Vietnam, sharing responsibilities with 13th Air Force, which had its headquarters in Udorn, Thailand. The U.S. Navy and Marine Corps had their own air commands. The headquarters of 8th Air Force on Guam controlled all B-52 and tanker missions. Within South Vietnam, the U.S. Army had a big transport and attack helicopter operation. Military Airlift Command was responsible for hundreds of transports and civilian charter planes flying in and out of Indochina. And in Laos the CIA operated its own secret "air force" of transports and prop-driven T-28 attack planes. Writing coherent orders to control this huge, unwieldy effort was often impossible.

The lesson of Linebacker II was that a nation at war can't afford to have several air forces, but must coordinate *all* its technological, tactical, and diplomatic assets toward a common strategic goal. The Air Force and Navy each had its own dedicated electronic warfare aircraft, but neither service synchronized its employment to the optimum possible degree when the campaign began. It was almost as if Air Force and Navy airmen were fighting separate wars, while the slow, vulnerable B-52s were left relatively unprotected for more than ten nights over North Vietnam.

(And it would not be until the Goldwater-Nichols Department of Defense Reorganization Act was passed in 1986, mandating that the services integrate their capabilities, that real progress was made.)

By January 1973 we had shifted tactics, which allowed the United States to achieve its strategic objective: Our big bombers were no longer clumsy bludgeons, but had instead become a devastating force that the enemy could no longer resist.

My dad had been hospitalized, and was reportedly not going to make it, just before Linebacker II began. I returned home on compassionate leave. In Kansas, I didn't believe Walter Cronkite's initial account of B-52s striking Hanoi: Those big planes *never* bombed that far north. When I found that the story was true I was very frustrated trying to get back to Korat with no special travel priority. The bombing eventually had the intended effect: The North Vietnamese returned to the Paris peace talks, and they negotiated seriously this time.

When in Kansas City while Dad was recuperating, my brother Chuck asked me the inevitable question.

"Dick, you *will* be coming home to join the business pretty soon, won't you?"

"You bet, Chuck . . . but I just have to check on what the Air Force might have in mind for me to do."

As events played out, the Air Force did have some very interesting jobs waiting for me.

PART II
LEADERSHIP

5

HONING SKILLS

*From Fighter Weapons School Instructor
to Major General*

Mary Jo and I left the Far East in the summer of 1973 just after the last American combat forces were withdrawn from Vietnam following the Paris Peace Accords. We and our two little children, Nicole and Erin—who had both been born on Okinawa—boarded a military charter jet on a sweltering afternoon at Kadena Air Base on the Japanese island of Okinawa and began a thirty-odd-hour marathon series of flights back to Kansas. The children had confusing birth certificates: Nicole was born when the island was U.S.-occupied territory; Erin was born in 1973, one year after Okinawa reverted to Japan, a process the Johnson White House began and the Nixon administration completed.

Thank goodness the scrambled paperwork did not make traveling with the children even harder: Flying with a toddler and a newborn baby was a challenge. Crossing the Pacific in a jammed DC-8 with the cabin atmosphere a blue haze of cigarette smoke was the proverbial trip from hell, which included stops at six airports and one bus ride before arriving in Kansas City.

"The children seem a little fussy, Dick," my mother commented when we finally reached Merriam after more than a day in airplanes and terminals.

"Believe me, Mom," I said, handing her squalling Erin, "they've good reason."

At least I wouldn't be going back to combat, I thought. And maybe . . . just maybe, the peace would prove permanent.

But tragically, that fragile peace did not last. Probably one of the war's most humiliating and haunting images appeared on front pages and television screens around the world on April 30, 1975: the line of desperate Vietnamese refugees clawing their way up a ladder toward a Huey evacuation helicopter perched on the narrow roof of an American housing compound in Saigon. But the enemy tanks were already rolling into the city, and most of these frantic people never escaped.

South Vietnam collapsed, followed in turn by Cambodia and Laos. The debacle seemed complete.

But the worst had not yet begun. In Cambodia, the Khmer Rouge, a communist-led, largely peasant guerrilla army, swept into the cities and drove several million people into rural killing fields. When the carnage had ended, almost one-third of the country's population, between 1.5 million and 2 million innocent men, women, and children, had been slaughtered. In the eyes of fanatical Khmer Rouge leaders, these people's crimes ranged from Western "intellectualism" (teaching or attending school, even wearing glasses or a wristwatch), to belonging to ethnic or religious minorities, to running shops and small businesses.

Before the victims were butchered—many with shovels, clubs, or simply buried alive—most were tortured into confessing their crimes. The Khmer Rouge watchword at the time was, "To keep you is no benefit. To destroy you is no loss."

In Vietnam, less brutal repression was under way, with hundreds of thousands of former Saigon military officers, soldiers, and civil servants herded into isolated rural re-education camps—which they were forced to build themselves while subsisting on starvation rations. Later, academic researchers in America and Europe estimated that at least 165,000 people died in these camps.

For those of us who had fought to protect our South Vietnamese ally, this tragedy was embittering. Even though I had not personally been called a "baby killer" on returning home (as had several friends), it was obvious that America's general public opinion of the military had reached a historic low. I'll never forget being advised to "get out of uniform and into civies" as soon as possible after my World Airways charter landed in California in 1972 as I was returning to be with my hospitalized dad.

After the fall of Saigon, many young officers like me re-examined the strategic foundation of the Vietnam War. In 1975, it had become accepted in the military that America had won all the battles but had lost the war. There was certainly some truth to that argument. However, the heart of the issue was that U.S. forces had developed effective tactics in Indochina, but our civilian leadership had ignored the principle that these tactics must advance from a solid strategic foundation.

But the United States had grown so war-weary by 1973 that two years later the national leadership refused even to consider exploiting our military superiority to compel North Vietnam to adhere to the terms of the peace agreement and instead simply accepted communist victory following our withdrawal. A significant force of B-52s remained based in the Far East, but we chose not to use them to destroy the massed enemy forces moving on Saigon. As it had from the beginning of the conflict, fear of overt Chinese or Russian intervention—or at the least, expanding the war to a much wider international conflict—seemed to paralyze our political leadership. Victory, it appeared, was not an option. That was a strategic decision. Tactically, we had dominated the battlefield; strategically, we had lost the conflict.

Most of the nation was happy to see us out of Vietnam, no matter the cost to our former Indochinese allies. Our leaders had never successfully articulated to the American people what our country had at stake in Southeast Asia. As a student at the Army War College in 1981, I heard Secretary of State Dean Rusk respond to a question from a student about whether there had been "a deliberate decision not to try to get the American public behind the war." Even though our military engagement in Indochina lasted twice as long as America's involvement in World War II, we never created a domestic agency analogous to the Office of War Information of the 1940s to encourage patriotic support for the conflict. Also, in the 1960s and 1970s, America did not have a single unifying strategic goal like the "unconditional surrender" of the Axis powers, which emerged from the Allies' Casablanca Conference of January 1943.

World War II was the last total war America fought. The Korean "Conflict" of 1950–53 was constrained by geographical scope and strategic objectives—and was the struggle that came to define limited war, which can be so difficult to explain to the public in terms of what is at stake, what victory means, and how to describe progress toward it. These same constraints dominated the Vietnam War.

Most of us in the military, however, understood the central truth that our failed effort in Indochina was a defeat on only one front in the wider and longer Cold War. Rather than foreshadowing a general disengagement from that larger conflict, the collapse of South Vietnam served as a warning that the American national security establishment had to reinvent itself based on an all-volunteer force, innovative technology, and a more realistic blend of practical strategy and flexible tactics.

For those of us who had served multiple tours of duty during the long Indochina war and who later became senior military leaders, the lessons learned from our service were obvious. Personally, it was often disheartening to fly combat missions as America's "Fight-Talk, Talk-Fight" strategy unfolded. Our bombing pauses allowed the enemy breathing room to rest and rearm, only to resume offensive operations when they chose to do so.

In any conflict, our forces should be committed in appropriate strength, with clear objectives, which keep relentless pressure on the enemy to capitulate—as was eventually the case after the Linebacker II bombing campaign drove North Vietnam back to the negotiation table in Paris. Further, American armed forces should not be committed to war without a "reasonable assurance" of the continued support of U.S. public opinion and Congress. (In retrospect, virtually none of these elements existed when we began throwing combat forces piecemeal into Southeast Asia in 1964.)

If you survive combat, the experience is a great teacher. You learn to trust other flight members, to control fear, to avoid panic, and to stay focused on the mission.

But there were times during my two combat tours when I found myself flying with pilots who clearly lacked the skill and decisiveness to complete the mission without endangering other planes in the flight. So, during the post-mission debrief, if they tried to make excuses for their sloppy flying or in-flight decision-making, either I or another experienced pilot would take them to task.

"I'm going to have to throw the bullshit flag on that," we'd say.

Like a football official's bright yellow penalty marker, the virtual bullshit flag kept us honest. It was one thing to exaggerate when describing a fishing trip or a friendly softball game. But trying to duck responsibility for poor performance in the air or not knowing what you were talking about in a mission or debriefing could get people killed or jeopardize mission success. So it was the duty of everyone in a flight to throw the bullshit flag when necessary. No one was immune, from the wing commander, to instructor pilots, to the least experienced aviator. We needed men who were willing to swallow their normal fighter pilot's ego, learn from their mistakes, and apply those often painful lessons to improving their skills.

Our experiences in Vietnam, both good and bad, gave us the courage and determination to change the way we trained in the tactical aviation business. Flexibility and innovation were now our watchwords. They thrust many of us into efforts to change our Air Force after Vietnam and became an important part of who I was and still am.

This principle was embedded in the ethos of the combat airman and was central to the culture of the Air Force Fighter Weapons School at Nellis Air Force Base, outside Las Vegas, Nevada. When Saigon fell, I was an instructor pilot in the 414th Fighter Weapons Squadron at Nellis. The Air Force's Fighter Weapons School was the rough equivalent of the Navy's Top Gun course. Only the most highly skilled and promising Air Force pilots were selected for the weapons school. Our goal was to forge skilled instructors who could take what they had learned in the Nevada desert back to their squadrons around the world, and in turn, raise the proficiency of every member of their squadrons through in-flight and classroom instruction. On completion of the four-month course, each pilot or backseater earned the right to wear the coveted graduate's patch on his flight suit, an arrowhead shape with a bomb or rocket striking the bull's-eye of a target ring. Becoming a "patch wearer" was a great honor and those who wore it were highly respected throughout the chain of command.

The Air Force had to retain all its best, combat-tested pilots following the debacle in the Far East. A lot of experienced military aviators had become disillusioned and left the Air Force to take airline jobs. It was hard to blame them: Flying as a civilian offered a regular schedule, a chance to put down roots in a community, and far better pay.

For me the excitement of flying fighters and teaching at the Air Force's premier school overcame any thought of leaving the service. Two of my fellow instructors at the weapons school—and two of my closest friends with whom I'd shared combat and a tour in Okinawa—went on to be leaders in the Air Force. John Jumper became the Chief of Staff of the Air Force while I was Chairman, and Ron Keys rose to lead the largest major command, Air Combat Command. Both retired as four-stars. I'm sure our military sacrifices together helped build the tremendous love and closeness that endures between our families today.

For those of us who did choose to stay in uniform, it was obvious that the armed services had to shake off the ashes of defeat and work to improve both national strategy and tactics. The Cold War was still a fact of life, and the Soviet Union and its allies were investing heavily in their military, introducing new lines of aircraft and weapons systems at an alarming rate. Although their new fighters, such as the MiG 23, did not match all the capabilities of our F-4, the Soviets were deploying these aircraft in frightening numbers. And the newest Soviet planes emerging from Mikoyan and Sukhoi designs bureaus also had advanced offensive avionics such as look-down/shoot-down radar—systems similar to those we had developed for our newest combat plane, the F-15 Eagle. The combined threat of potentially overwhelming aircraft numbers and innovative avionics made the Soviet Air Force increasingly dangerous. The East-West arms race in the air was accelerating.

But the relentless Soviet drive for military superiority was not limited to airpower: Our Cold War enemy was developing new land- and sea-launched intercontinental ballistic missiles, surface-to-air missile systems designed specifically to shoot down aircraft that could maneuver well, surface ships, and submarines, as well as powerful main battle tanks like the T-72 and infantry fighting vehicles.

Learning how to counter the emerging Soviet threat was one of the tasks we faced at the Fighters Weapons School. A major element in our tactics of the 1970s was the penetrating of enemy air space, employing electronic countermeasures and destroying his offensive air capabilities, as well as the command-and-control system he would rely on to mount offensive war.

As an instructor pilot at Nellis, I felt a personal sense of responsibility in helping train my peers to meet their increasingly complex Cold War duties. But my own responsibility increased when my squadron leader, Lt. Col. Paul Chase, called me to his office one morning.

"Would you like to be an instructor in the air-to-air flight or become the new air-to-ground flight commander?" he asked.

My mind raced as I wondered what was happening. "We have an air-to-ground flight commander," I blurted out to Colonel Chase.

"The current commander will be relieved when he lands from this morning's flight and will be asked to clean out his things by noon," he said.

I learned that this officer participated in all decision-making in the squadron, but when the leaders made a decision he didn't like, he became a very vocal public critic of leadership. This had been going on for months.

My mind jumped to others who might outrank me, particularly a peer who had just had an early promotion to major.

"The fellow promoted to major doesn't have the competencies we're looking for in our leadership," Colonel Chase said.

So it was up to me to decide whether to choose the more prestigious air-to-air flight, where the focus was on aerial combat which required instructors who could best maneuver in that three-dimensional arena, or take command of the air-to-ground flight. My experience as a fast FAC and Wild Weasel formed my strongest suits. "I'd be honored to be the air-to-ground flight commander," I told my boss. As anyone in the military knows, command opportunities are rare, and when you're offered the privilege to command others, you have to take it before someone changes his mind.

By the time I became an instructor pilot at the school, I had acquired some definite ideas about leadership. First, a leader had to actually lead, not rule by arbitrary edict. During my ten years as an Air Force officer, I'd encountered both good and bad leaders. One of my first squadron commanders was so rigidly authoritarian that his flight commanders and other key subordinates were not open or honest with him. In his arrogance, he didn't feel the need to treat his pilots with respect. This drove many of them into the open arms of the airlines, which were more than happy to welcome experienced jet pilots. Ideally, the members of a military unit had to know what their leader expected of them and that their commanding officer understood the full nature of their responsibilities and was also capable of performing them.

Every squadron I ever served in or commanded had a traditional varnished "scoreboard" near the entrance of the headquarters that ranked the individual pilots and weapons systems operators in order of their proficiency in air-to-air or air-to-ground skills. A veteran lieutenant colonel commander of the unit might have earned the coveted position at the top of the board—or a new second lieutenant could be the best. This was not a question of a man's military rank, but rather of his hard-earned ability as an aviator.

Early in my flying career, I learned that a leader *earned* respect; respect did not magically accompany rank. In fact, no matter how many assignments or how much success, when you reported to a new flying unit, one of the organization's best instructors took you out to see just how good you really were. You had to establish your credibility each time you moved to a new base. The military offered opportunities to succeed irrespective of rank, as well as race and gender.

President Harry S. Truman racially integrated the services, and two decades later we began to aggressively open up traditionally male career fields to women. This achievement meant a lot to me personally. Successfully achieving diversity was an important reason I stayed in the military: Everyone is treated the same and the armed services comes as close to a meritocracy as any organization I know.

During the mid-1970s, the Air Force began the experiment of introducing women mechanics on the flight line, including service ramps at the Nellis Fighter Weapons School. This duty had traditionally been the exclusive purview of men, and a lot of the more macho mechanics and airmen didn't like the change. But when some of them came grumbling to me that "girls" just weren't strong enough to lift mechanics' heavy, multidrawer tool chests, they didn't find a sympathetic audience. For openers, I was the father of two daughters, and I wanted them to grow up in a world in which their opportunities would not be limited by their sex. Also, the men's argument that women weren't strong enough to do the job was patently ridiculous: All the male mechanics pulled their toolboxes on wheeled dollies.

The women arrived. They did their jobs. None of them made serious mistakes. Clearly, the experiment was a success. Soon there were women mechanics at every Air Force base. The range of Air Force assignments open to women continued to expand, to include female transport, tanker, and helicopter pilots—and later, pilots of every combat aircraft in the Air Force inventory. During the post-9/11 combat in Afghanistan and Iraq, a large number of women pilots were flying dangerous and complex missions, and a proportional number of female mechanics and armorers kept their aircraft flying.

As a three-star general commanding U.S. Forces in Japan in 1996, I flew a training sortie with one of the first female F-15 Eagle pilots. She was fully integrated into that combat wing because she had *earned* the respect of her fellow pilots. Flying with her and other F-15s on an over-water training range near Kadena Air Base, I heard something I had never heard before, a female voice announcing in my earphones:

"Kill the F-15 in a left turn, ten thousand feet."

Hey, that's me! As an adversary pilot that day, she had maneuvered undetected to arrive in simulated kill parameters behind me.

Women have demonstrated their invaluable contribution to the armed services and America's national security, and they have come to constitute fully 15 percent of service members.

In 1975, my dad's heart finally gave out. When I was back home in Kansas for the funeral, my brother, Chuck, posed the inevitable question: "Any chance you'll be coming home to go to work in the business now, Dick?"

But I had just signed on as the Nellis air-to-ground flight commander and wasn't free to resign my commission. "Not right away, Chuck. It'll be at least a year or two longer."

That period certainly stretched on.

While still at the Fighter Weapons School and on the promotion list for major in 1976, I began a sequence of challenging and diverse assignments. Among the first was being sent on temporary duty to Iran to help set up an electronic warfare training range for the Iranian Air Force. After several successful weeks of working with the Iranians, I was eager to return to the family and Nellis. But when I arrived at the terminal in Tehran for departure, there was a message from Chuck waiting for me. "Dick, Mom is very ill in the hospital and not doing well. Better come through Kansas City on your way home."

During my eleven years in the Air Force, Chuck had to shoulder the responsibility of caring for our aging parents without me to help. Much of that time I was overseas, a very long way from the Midwest. Chuck took over managing the daily details of helping with their lives, driving Dad to work and checking up on both of them regularly. I would have gladly assumed those tasks, but was prevented by duty and distance. Chuck never complained or made me feel guilty about not being there.

I reached Kansas City about twenty hours later and met my mom's sister, Margaret Lembke, and my brother at the hospital. Before I entered Mom's room, they both warned me that she was essentially comatose and wouldn't recognize me or be able to gesture in any way. But when I leaned over the bed and said, "Mom, Dick's home." She opened her eyes, rose from the pillows, and gave me a big hug. She then lay back down, and later that night she died. Clearly, she had been keeping death at bay until both her boys were home.

One of the strengths of the military services is interweaving formal education requirements into the course of a normal career. In June 1977, after spending ten months at the Air Command and Staff College, at Maxwell Air Force Base, Alabama, I was a Distinguished Graduate and simultaneously received my

MBA from Auburn University. Four years later, after early promotion to lieutenant colonel, I would continue my formal professional military education at
the U.S. Army War College.

My true military education continued beyond the classroom. In the late 1970s,
serving as a major on the test and evaluations staff of the Air Force Directorate of Operations in Washington, I gained unique insights on how the real
world of national security decision-making worked inside the Capital Beltway.
My responsibilities included trying to augment the capabilities of the electronic
warfare ranges out at Nellis, beefing up the computerized instrumentation,
and threat simulation to increase the realism of the war-fighting instruction.

Nellis had become the Air Force's location of choice for our most demanding aircrew training. The huge desert base was the site of the expanding annual
cycle of demanding Red Flag exercises in which Tactical Air Command fighter
(and later bomber, tanker, transport, and most of the other Air Force specialties) crews faced "aggressor" aircraft and a very realistic integrated air-defense
system, which included multiple Soviet SAMs and AAA. Analysis of aircrew
survivability in the Vietnam conflict showed that most pilots were shot down
in their first ten missions. If they made it past the first ten sorties they had a
good chance of completing their combat tour. Red Flag attempted to replicate
those early combat missions. Soon, aircrew from NATO and our other close
allies, such as Australia, would sharpen their skills in the most demanding
training regimen we could provide.

In the late 1970s as the Red Flag program grew, Nellis competed for funding
with Eglin Air Force Base in the Florida Panhandle, which had a large test and
evaluation program for air-delivered munitions. And that base was right in the
middle of the district of one of the most senior Democrats in the Democrati-
cally controlled Congress, Representative Bob Sikes. Needless to say, for years
the Eglin program was consistently better funded than Nellis, which was in a
Republican district.

I was given the unenviable task of going up to Capitol Hill to explain the
situation to Congressman Sikes. I'd brought along several charts and graphs
with bulleted talking points, which I hoped would convince Sikes to open the
budget purse enough for the Nellis test and training instrumentation upgrades
to move forward. But before I got very far in my sales pitch, the congressman
pushed the papers aside.

"Tell me, Major," he said. "Just what will all this do for *my* district?"

The Air Force budget people had prepared me for this, and I laid out some charts that spoke directly to the subject. So I proceeded to explain that the Eglin complex would always be important and not replaced by Nellis. In addition, all the equipment in the budget was to be procured through a large office on Eglin and some of the equipment would even be made by Florida contractors. I must have been convincing, because the next budget was the first in which the requested Nellis funding was granted.

The lesson I learned from this episode reinforced House Speaker Tip O'Neill's sage maxim, "All politics are local." In some minds national security often had less to do with the merits of a particular base or weapon system than with the jobs and budget dollars they would bring to a congressional district.

Years later as a senior Pentagon general officer, my colleagues and I lived this adage every day.

The best part of my first Pentagon tour was a late dividend—the birth of our third child, Richard Bowman, Jr., in 1979. Our family was now complete.

A senior service college assignment was meant to broaden an officer's horizons, allow him to move beyond the formal structure of professional education specific to the Army, Navy, or Air Force, and afford the opportunity to develop relationships with peers from those branches. In 1980–81 at the Army War College in Carlisle, Pennsylvania, I could pursue my interest in military history and leadership, and I met Professor Dick Kohn for the first time. In his course, he brought in biographies of great military leaders, and we had the chance to discuss their leadership style and how they made their crucial decisions. We also spent considerable time studying leadership from an academic perspective and finally wrote a paper on our personal leadership style. Mine was one of only a few that were published by the college. For me, this effort and these courses provided excellent insights into leadership development and allowed my philosophy to grow and mature.

Following that year at the Army War College, I was assigned as operations officer and then appointed commander of the 335th Tactical Fighter Squadron, an F-4E unit at Seymour Johnson Air Force Base, North Carolina.

Up to that point, commanding a squadron had been my ultimate career goal, and I never thought I'd advance beyond it. This assignment was analogous to an Army officer commanding a battalion or a Navy officer becoming the captain of a ship.

But for a while, it looked as if I'd *never* get my chance at squadron command. I went to the 4th Tactical Fighter Wing as the chief of Weapons and Tactics, and had been told a squadron command assignment would be forthcoming. But those jobs were all filled, and I was one of seven officers vying for three command positions. One of those officers was a very close friend, Tad Oelstrom. Tad was an Air Force Academy graduate and excelled in all he did. We had been friendly competitors for years. He won most of the awards when we were at the Fighter Weapons School together over ten years earlier, and we had shared many assignments. He and his wife, Sandy, were—and remain— among our closest friends. I dreaded competing against Tad.

Meanwhile, I headed the wing's Gunsmoke team. The Gunsmoke competition for bombing and air-to-ground usually took place every two years, and winning was considered very prestigious.

———————

My chance for command improved dramatically when the commander of the 335th Tactical Fighter Squadron accidentally hit a target-towing jet out on the aerial gunnery range. The safety rules about such live-fire training were ironclad: *Never* shoot at a target dart rolling in the slipstream, because there was a risk of striking the tow plane. But he had fired his 20mm cannon, and he had hit the tow plane. He was relieved of command, both for breaking the rules and for an obvious display of poor judgment. As you might expect, the tow crew was not too pleased.

I was appointed operations officer in 1981. In about a year I took command of the 335th Tactical Fighter Squadron, nicknamed the "Chiefs" after the squadron patch, which had an Indian chief in the center. (Incidentally, Oelstrom took command of a squadron at much the same time.) As a squadron commander in my first "big" assignment, I was also put to the test. A situation developed in which the A Flight commander failed his tactical evaluation check. It wasn't even close—he flat-out failed—and this created a dilemma: I couldn't expect one of my squadron leaders to retain the credibility and confidence to lead with a failed check ride on his record. In order to be as fair as possible, I removed him but ensured he got a position on the wing staff where I thought he would perform well.

When I became squadron commander, Mary Jo became the leader of the squadron wives, a volunteer organization that helped with information flow and morale. It was a demanding, but unofficial, full-time job, with so many officers and enlisted airmen and their families constantly on the move. But she has a gentle, guileless persona, and she is strong and tireless. I couldn't have been as effective a commander without her support and leadership among the squadron wives and families.

———————

After coming out on the colonels list in 1984, I left squadron command and was assigned to Headquarters Tactical Air Command as the deputy in the office of Personnel Plans and Readiness. I was sure this was the end of my career, as my contemporaries were getting flying assignments in the newer F-15 or F-16 aircraft. I knew nothing about the job. As it turned out, I learned more about how the Air Force personnel system worked and how to take care of your people from this assignment and my new boss, Col. Norm Lezy, and his boss Col. Billy Boles, than I had in my previous almost twenty years of service. I moved from the personnel position to the Inspector General Team as a Team Chief working for Brig. Gen. John "Jake" Jaquish. He was instrumental in my becoming commandant of the Fighter Weapons School at Nellis. (I would work again for Gen. Jaquish at the Pentagon and always appreciated his guidance and the confidence he showed in me.)

The Nellis commandant position was considered a plum job given only to those with the credibility to lead the best young officers, all at the top of their game. By now, my brother, Chuck, asked much less frequently when I planned to return to Kansas to work in the family business. But I knew he still hoped I'd retire from the Air Force and come back because he'd renamed the company "Myers Brothers."

This made good business sense, because he could always gain a strong negotiating position by saying, "I'll have to check with my brother before deciding and get back to you." Of course I never heard a thing from him on business matters. My bonds with my brother and Kansas remained strong.

In 1985, the Nellis Fighter Weapons School was a much different place than it had been twelve years earlier. We now worked with the airborne warning and control (AWACS) system and flew intricate, demanding missions during the last phase of our courses. These were large "gaggles" of planes on long, complex operations, always pitting allied aircraft against aggressors flying supersonic F-5Es as well as the latest generation of simulated Soviet surface-to-air missile systems employing the most recent tactics.

The Soviet SA-2 missile I first encountered in Vietnam had evolved from a German World War II design for use against slower and less maneuverable bombers such as the B-17. The next-generation Soviet SA-3 missile systems were designed to counter our fighter-bomber threat.

At Nellis, the Air Force worked hard to sharpen the skills needed to support rapidly evolving battle tactics. And we had new aircraft to accomplish our expanded mission. The futuristic-looking F-16 Fighting Falcon became an operational Air Force multirole fighter in the late 1970s. It was designed to be lightweight, fast, and highly maneuverable both as a high-altitude air-to-air fighter and as a nap-of-the-earth fighter-bomber. On a ground-strike mission, the Falcon could fly hundreds of miles and accurately deliver a variety of weapons in poor visibility while defending itself against enemy aircraft with advanced air-to-air missiles and using electronic countermeasures against enemy SAM batteries.

The F-16 was the first operational "fly-by-wire" jet. Hand pressure on the computerized side stick sent electronic signals over multiple redundant circuits through the central processing unit and on to the flight controls. The side-stick controller moved only a maximum of three-eighths of an inch. Unlike conventional planes, the Falcon was inherently unstable in flight, and the central computer had to send hundreds of corrections a second to the controls, even when the pilot did not make any conscious moves.

The joke among Falcon pilots in some phases of air combat, especially when you flew just above stall speed, was that you weren't flying the plane, the fighter's designer, General Dynamics, was. Still, it was an absolute joy to fly. I'll always remember, on one low-level training mission, rushing along at a couple of hundred feet at five hundred miles per hour, the edge of the Grand Canyon coming up in front of me. As I passed the rim of the chasm, the earth fell away and I felt like Luke Skywalker in the *Star Wars* movies. Sitting out very far in front of the aircraft with such tremendous visibility that day, it was easy to believe that whatever I commanded the jet to do, it *could* do. If I'd wished (and if I had the permission of air traffic control), I could have pushed the throttle forward to the afterburner position and climbed into the dark blue daylight close to fifty thousand feet in just a couple of minutes. *And they pay me to do this!*

As the multirole Falcon was deployed through the Air Force and allied nations, innovative training programs honed our pilots' skills, and we developed effective tactics to overcome the Soviets' advancing technology.

This expansion stemmed in part from the new AirLand Battle doctrine, which the Pentagon had adopted in the early 1980s. It was a major shift in strategic thinking from the "Active Defense" approach to dealing with the numerically superior Soviet and Warsaw Pact forces in Central Europe. Under the new doctrine, our ground forces would engage and destroy the enemy's advancing front-line units while our Air Force would strike deep, attacking rein-forcing elements at choke points, such as bridges, tunnels, and road junctions as far as 150 miles behind the front. This was an innovative approach, but it was still fairly rigid: The AirLand Battle doctrine assigned the Army and the Air Force responsibilities for their own sectors, "deconflicting" rather than inte-grating their efforts. It always seemed to me we could do better than just de-conflict our actions.

———————

Among the most positive aspects of being commandant of the Nellis Fighter Weapons School was working with the outstanding instructors and young captains who had competed for and won admission to this prestigious course. Their skill, energy, and dedication bolstered my faith in the future of the Air Force. One of my primary responsibilities was to keep these leading-edge thinkers and doers from going over the edge from realistic to dangerous training—a challenge that kept me on my toes.

I got a lot of support from my wing commander, Brig. Gen. Joe Ashy, a fair but demanding taskmaster. He proved a great role model for how to lead and how to command. I would work for Ashy again back at Langley, and we remain good friends today.

Helping select each year's students from the large pool of qualified appli-cants for the four-month courses was one of my most important responsibili-ties. Given the limited number of available student slots, selection was a very competitive process, and it was essential that these slots went to the most qual-ified candidates. Conversely, the process had to be protected from inappropri-ate pressure by senior officers trying to influence selection and get their favorite person in the course.

This was precisely the situation I faced when I arrived at Randolph Air Force Base in San Antonio, Texas, to be the president of one of the selection boards. My host at Randolph, Col. Don Peterson, handed me a note from the three-star general commander of one of the numbered air forces, the unit re-sponsible for about half the fighters in the United States. On the note was the name of a young F-15 pilot. "He's my number-one choice for Fighter Weapons School," the general wrote. The curt message was clear: Accept this guy be-cause I say so.

That was way out of line. This board was supposed to conduct a selection process free of command influence. I called my wing commander at Nellis to get his guidance. "What should I do?" I asked.

"Well," the wing commander said, "I guess we'll have to accommodate the general, as he's a senior leader in our tactical air forces."

But that was hard to swallow. After Vietnam, we had been rebuilding the Air Force based on a solid foundation of integrity. What the general had requested clearly smacked of favoritism and was outside the board process we were sworn to uphold. Without telling anyone, I decided not to inform the other board members about the general's message and to let the chips fall where they might.

When I called him after the panel did not select his candidate, I did a lot more listening than explaining.

"Well, Colonel," he huffed at the end of the call, "I guess being a three-star general in the U.S. Air Force doesn't mean much anymore."

Before I could answer, he slammed down the phone. *There goes my career,* I thought. Maybe it *was* time to speak to Chuck about that job at Myers Brothers. But before I did, I called my wing commander at Nellis again to report on the situation. In the end, my two-star boss supported my decision, and the argument went up the chain of command way above me.

I survived the confrontation, having learned the lesson that acting with integrity was not always easy. But it *was* the only course open if you wanted to sleep well at night and if you wanted to protect the larger integrity and culture of our great Air Force.

I left Nellis in September 1986 to take command of the 325th Tactical Training Wing at Tyndall Air Force Base, one of several former World War II bases in the Florida Panhandle. Commanding a training wing normally would not have seemed especially challenging or stressful after my intense experience as commandant of the Fighter Weapons School, but the wing was training pilots to fly the state-of-the-art F-15 Eagles, the best air-superiority airplane in the world, which had entered the Air Force inventory in significant numbers. Maj. Gen. Pete Kempf, commander of the Tactical Fighter Weapons Center at Nellis and the fellow who stood up for me after the selection board process at Randolph, and also my wing commander at Seymour Johnson, asked me to come into his office just before I left for my new assignment. It was a Friday evening and General Kempf was about to fly to the East Coast. I appreciated his taking the time when his schedule was so hectic to offer me advice on my first wing command.

After lots of detailed suggestions on a wide variety of topics, he ended by saying, "Just be yourself and do it your way . . . if you do well, we'll all applaud. But if you *fail*, at least we can use you as a bad example." He was not smiling; he was very serious.

My first task at Tyndall was qualifying as an F-15 pilot. In the right hands, there was no plane in the world that could compete with the Eagle. But I had only ten check rides to qualify and had to jam a lot of work into them. The cockpit of the F-15 was crammed with all the most innovative features available in the mid-1980s, including radar that could lock onto both high-flying targets and low-flying enemy jets. And the plane's designers had ingeniously solved the "head-in, head-out" of the cockpit problem that had plagued fighter pilots for decades. The HOTAS (hands-on-throttles-and-stick) system allowed the pilot to keep his eyes outside the cockpit while activating key controls. Further, a transparent head-up display beneath the forward canopy presented important flight, target, and weapons data.

The plane's amazing power also permitted tight turns without loss of speed—providing the pilot was experienced and fit enough to withstand the G forces generated in these maneuvers. Both physical fitness and mental acuity were on my mind when I began flying Eagles as a colonel at age forty-four, along with hotshot captains or first lieutenants around half my age.

One of our tasks in the wing was to check out pilots from the Air National Guard converting from F-4s to the F-15. You got a real variety of capabilities in these units compared to active duty squadrons. One afternoon a squadron commander came to me and announced that some of the more senior pilots with a particular Guard unit weren't passing the course. The Guard squadron leadership was pressing to have us graduate them anyway, saying they would "fix the problem" back at their home base. After all, washing out would be embarrassing to these more senior individuals.

After thinking about this for a few moments, I threw a bullshit flag. "They either meet standards for graduation or we don't send them home qualified in the F-15." This started a little bit of lobbying for me to relent, but once I had carved out the high ground, it was easy for me to hold my position. These pilots returned unqualified in the F-15, and I'm sure that was somewhat embarrassing. But just think how much worse than embarrassment it would have been for their unit and for the Air Force if we had passed them and they had injured themselves or someone else and lost airplanes in the process. I must have done okay for an old guy because when I completed this assignment less than a year later, I went on to command the 1st Tactical Fighter Wing at Langley Air Force Base in the Virginia Tidewater area, one of the oldest, most prestigious wing commands in the service. There was a downside to this great opportunity. Mary Jo and I spent only nine months at Tyndall; we totally missed the scallop season, which would have allowed us to gather them in the bay right behind our home.

The challenging series of assignments during these years had frequently uprooted my family, sometimes within a matter of months after settling into a new town or base. Air Force kids, like children in other service families, had to learn self-reliance and not to let the next impending move disrupt their academic work. This could prove very difficult, so I was especially proud of our oldest daughter, Nicole, who was starting her fourth high school in three years when we arrived at Langley.

In 1976, the 1st Tactical Fighter Wing had been the first to begin flying the F-15. After the unit was equipped with its full complement of seventy-two Eagles, its three squadrons began the hard process of getting "trained-up" and combat qualified. When I arrived in June 1987, the 1st Tactical Fighter Wing had dual operational missions: continental air defense and defending Saudi Arabia and other Persian Gulf allies.

I wasn't at Langley very long before it became clear the wing was not ready to go to war in the Gulf. The unit was long overdue for an operational readiness inspection, and there were deficiencies, particularly in the Gulf deployment scenario, that had to be corrected before the inspectors paid their next visit. In this deployment, we faced the complex task of moving all our people, ground equipment, and aircraft to the modern facility of King Abdul Aziz Air Base in Dhahran, Saudi Arabia, virtually within hours of receiving orders.

But the wing and its commander had other responsibilities that could interfere with our principal mission, if I allowed them to do so. The 1st Tactical Fighter Wing was the host organization for all the other units based at Langley, including the headquarters of the Tactical Air Command (TAC), led by a four-star, Gen. Bob Russ. This meant that the commanding general's lawn—and those of his subordinate generals—and the base itself, had to be kept manicured, the streets free of potholes, and the base's overall appearance flawless. (So, besides commanding a combat fighter wing, I was Langley's Commander in Chief for "weeds, seeds, roads, and commodes.") This disciplined attention to detail was supposed to show the other TAC bases how it was done. To say the least, these responsibilities could be a distraction from preparing for combat for the wing commander and his staff.

Once, I was even called into the office of a two-star on the TAC staff and asked why the Base Exchange cleaners, a contractor-run operation, had overpressed and ruined his suit. Such distractions could monopolize my and the wing's time just trying to please the many senior personnel on the base. When I took over the unit, I initially found myself a little conflicted about where to put my priorities, and I was spending far too much of my time trying to extinguish such annoying but minor fires. (I even carried extra light bulbs in the trunk of my staff car to replace the many lights we had around our well-used Distinguished Visitor Quarters.)

Bob Russ was a veteran fighter pilot known as a fair but demanding leader. My predecessor had done a great job of "working" General Russ's Langley priorities, but the readiness of the wing to go to war had suffered. I faced the choice of either focusing on him and his subordinate generals on the staff or shaping the wing into an effective fighting organization. If I made pleasing General Russ a priority, I'd probably be promoted to general officer and land a series of increasingly important assignments, but if I neglected the wing's readiness, I'd be evading my principal responsibility. I'd learned enough about leadership to recognize my only choice.

I explained the situation to Mary Jo. "One day I might have to take the wing to war in the Middle East," I said. "And they're just not ready to go." With General Kempf's words in my mind, about using me for a bad example if I failed, I told her, "I'm going to let the chips fall where they will and do the job I'm getting paid for."

"Do what you have to, Dick," she said. "You know I'll support you for doing the right thing."

After all, retiring as a colonel and going back to Kansas to work with Chuck in the family business was not the end of the world.

Each day, we still were aggressively trimming trees and hedges, filling potholes, and painting lines in the officers club parking lot, but I now concentrated on getting the wing ready for the operational readiness inspection (ORI)—even when I heard the occasional grumbling from some of the lower-level brass in TAC headquarters.

Training for deployment to Dhahran became our most important mission. The runways and parking ramps at Langley were ancient, dating back to World War I. But we worked hard to duplicate the layout of the Dhahran ramps and hangars, so that our fuel trucks and maintenance crews faced a realistic atmosphere in our training exercises. And we enhanced that realism by simulating attacks from chemical and biological weapons, which meant that our ground crews and pilots had to work in sealed protective suits. I even told the ground crews to forgo their practice of ordering from the local Pizza Hut when we were in exercise conditions.

"You won't be eating commercial pizza on the ramp at Dhahran," I told them confidently.

During the long training exercises, wing personnel subsisted on sandwiches from the mess hall or cold MRE rations, which they ate at our designated "clean area" away from the flight line. One evening just before the ORI, Mary Jo and I came home from a dinner to find that one of the fighter squadrons had "decorated" our two-story home with camouflage, complete with sandbags for pillows in our bed. This was meant to get the warrior spirit going in the wing. This rigorous degree of realism had the desired effect, because the wing passed the operational readiness inspection exercises that replicated both the complex deployment and employment phases.

But I might have been a little overzealous about canceling the troops' Pizza Hut carry-out orders. In August 1990, the 1st Tactical Fighter Wing was the first Air Force combat unit to deploy to Saudi Arabia during Operation Desert Shield in the first Gulf War. A few weeks later, I received a large, odd-shaped package at my new office in TAC headquarters. In it was the top of what looked to be a pizza container, grease and all. There was Arabic writing on the front and a message printed in a neat pilot's hand.

"Sir," Lt. Col. Fred Pease, my former inspection officer at the 1st Wing, had written, "just thought you should know, we're enjoying our *delivered* pizza on the ramp here. Guess we were wrong."

Gen. Bob Russ apparently liked the way I led the 1st Tactical Fighter Wing—even if some of his subordinates moaned about a few untrimmed trees on their streets—because he took me on as one of his "projects" when I completed my command. For the next three years I advanced through a variety of staff assignments at TAC headquarters, finishing as Deputy Chief of Staff for Requirements, which meant I had to be intimately familiar with every element of the operational necessities for this huge global command. This also meant knowing all the new equipment programs that would take our tactical air force into the twenty-first century. Bob Russ was particularly adept at developing officers for more responsibility, and this was certainly true with me. His impact on future Air Force leadership was unmatched, before or after his command of TAC.

For me, one of the most interesting aspects of this job was gaining an appreciation of the vital role the reserve component played in overall Air Force readiness. The fighter, tanker, and transport wings of the Air National Guard and Air Force Reserve contained some of the best pilots and ground support personnel in the Air Force. As they would repeatedly demonstrate over the coming years, serving in a "part-time" capacity did not diminish the effectiveness of these airmen.

I was in that staff position at TAC headquarters when my promotion to brigadier general was announced. Since my mother and father were no longer living, Mary Jo's parents substituted and accompanied my brother, Chuck, to the ceremony at which my first star was pinned onto the shoulders of my uniform.

(After Mom and Dad died in the 1970s, my mother- and father-in-law, Clarence and Marie Rupp, became my surrogate parents. They were great citizens, for many years never missing important family occasions. Always enthusiastic about my career, they attended promotion ceremonies and service school graduations and visited us wherever we were stationed.)

"Well," Chuck said as he shook my hand, "I *finally* get the picture. You're not coming back to Kansas City."

"Not for a while," I replied.

I was serving as the TAC Deputy Chief of Staff for Requirements when Iraq invaded Kuwait and Operation Desert Shield evolved into Desert Storm. Proud that the F-15 Eagles of my old 1st Tactical Fighter Wing arrived in the war theater after a seventeen-hour flight with seven midair refuelings, I was especially interested to see how the unit would perform against Saddam Hussein's large and modern air force.

The Eagle's suite of weapons included long-range AIM-120 AMRAAM radar-guided missiles that could engage targets far beyond visual range. The missile was a "launch-and-leave" system that at a certain range to the adversary sought out enemy planes without input from the F-15 pilot or the fighter's weapons system.

With Desert Storm about to begin that winter, we had to make a decision on whether to install newly available radar software on the plane to accommodate an upgraded missile. I strongly recommended against this change, because there might not be enough training time on the new cockpit displays before the F-15s faced combat. As events unfolded, the Eagle pilots did not need this new software: They racked up a 33–0 aerial combat score against Iraqi fighters, a tally so lopsided that 115 Iraqi aircraft fled to seek sanctuary in neighboring Iran, where they were impounded.

There was a story around the Air Force at the time that the most dreaded message an Iraqi pilot could hear over his radio was the tower telling an Iraqi pilot, "You are cleared for takeoff."

Another fascinating task I had during the hectic weeks leading up to Desert Storm was working with Northrop Grumman to prepare the new Joint Surveillance and Target Attack Radar System (JSTARS) for deployment to Saudi Arabia. This was a joint Air Force–Army project involving a powerful and sensitive radar array shaped like a canoe slung under the belly of an E-8, the military version of a Boeing 707-300 aircraft. In theory, the JSTARS could pierce darkness, clouds, and *shamal* sandstorms and essentially detect and track anything that moved, including enemy tanks, trucks, and low-flying helicopters normally lost in the ground clutter by other radars. This would give our commanders in the war zone an enormous advantage as Iraqi forces maneuvered across the vast, featureless desert.

But there was one major problem with the system as the deadline we'd given Saddam Hussein to remove his forces from Kuwait approached, and the Iraqis showed no sign of budging: There were only two JSTAR prototypes in the research and development phase, and we didn't have trained Air Force operators to use them.

When General Russ asked me who should lead the Joint Stars deployment to Desert Storm, I immediately volunteered my deputy, Col. George Muellner. He and I worked hard to get the two JSTARS up and running for deployment if the United States and its Coalition allies were forced to launch an offensive ground operation to liberate Kuwait. One of our problems was that we couldn't just order Northrop Grumman's civilian employees and subcontractors into a war zone—where Iraqi Scud missiles were already striking our bases. Some of the civilian engineers became nervous when we put them through modified training to cope with possible chemical or biological attacks.

To their credit, the JSTARS civilians did deploy. The crews of the two prototypes flying racetrack oval courses high above the Iraqi border overcame all the expected technical glitches—including some that forced engineers to change radar waveforms from the belly of these circling giants—and performed brilliantly. The two prototypes flew forty-nine combat missions, denying Iraqi mechanized forces freedom of movement both day and night. This system was, as we used to say, very much a "force multiplier," and would go on to make a big difference in the 2003 major combat in Iraq during severe sandstorms.

I was promoted to major general in 1992 while serving in the Office of the Assistant Secretary of the Air Force for Acquisition at the Pentagon. Any tendency toward hubris that the two stars on my shoulders might have triggered was quickly extinguished: Major generals were far from rare in the building's vast corridors. So I remembered what I'd learned in my life up to that point: Hard work and integrity were what was essential if your boss thought you had more potential.

At this assignment in acquisition, I found that the Air Force had a wide slate of potentially fascinating weapons, intelligence, and command-and-control systems. But, with the Cold War over and following our victory in Desert Storm, Congress was disinclined to fund all the weapons we might want. The phrase "peace dividend" echoed across Capitol Hill and the executive branch, and many believed the long post–World War II era of armed confrontation with the East Bloc was the last major conflict America would ever face. In their opinion, the United States was the sole remaining superpower, so there was no need to develop so much expensive new military technology.

This viewpoint, however, seemed to me dangerously shortsighted. China had thermonuclear weapons and missiles for delivery and was rapidly expanding and modernizing its military, with a stated long-term goal of overwhelming Taiwan. India had tested an atomic bomb in the 1970s, and the international intelligence community estimated that it was planning to enlarge its nuclear arsenal. Its bitter rival on the Subcontinent, Pakistan, was working hard and fast on its own nuclear weapons program. Following his country's defeat in the 1991 Gulf War, Saddam Hussein's Baathist government had formally agreed to dismantle Iraq's weapons of mass destruction program, but a year after the ceasefire, his regime was still placing obstacles in the path of United Nations weapons inspectors. North Korea remained the world's sole surviving Stalinist dictatorship under "Great Leader" President Kim Il-Sung. He was in failing health and had turned over command of the bloated and well-armed military to his emotionally erratic son, Kim Jong-Il, who at one point proclaimed he would turn Tokyo into a sea of fire. In the Middle East, tensions remained high between nuclear-armed Israel and radical Palestinians, who were supported by Syria, Iraq, and sympathetic Gulf Arabs. Further, Iran backed terrorist groups like Hezbollah and had embarked on a quest to develop longer-range missiles.

From my perspective, the world hardly looked peaceful—and definitely not stable. So deep cuts to America's armed forces did not seem like a wise policy option, but because budget cuts were inevitable, we were going to have to learn to do more with less—or at least with a radically different mix of weapons, doctrine, and strategy. The services were already reduced by about one-third in terms of their personnel strength. The Department of Defense budget had fallen below 3 percent as a percentage of the Gross Domestic Product for the first time since Pearl Harbor had thrown America into World War II, but our military was deploying to hot spots more in the decade of the nineties than ever before. To support this activity with a decreasing budget, our nation's senior leaders robbed the new equipment procurement accounts. (And the so-called "procurement holiday" of the 1990s still haunts us today.)

———————————

In September 1992, I was invited to represent the U.S. Air Force at the Moscow Air Show, held at Ramenskoye Air Field near Moscow. With the Cold War officially over, the Russians were eager to practice capitalism by showcasing their military aircraft and other hardware on the international arms market. This was understandable: Design bureaus like MiG and Sukhoi had lost most of their generous state subsidies, and they needed foreign sales to stay in business.

It felt strange to be walking along the rows of mottled gray combat planes in the company of our embassy air attaché, Russian Air Force officers, and Russian civilians. Eighteen months earlier, this base would have still been a top secret site, from which foreigners and most Russians were barred. Before leaving the air show, I met a group of World War II veterans, the chests of their rather threadbare suit coats lined with medals and ribbons. Many of them came up and made a point of reminding me that Russia and the United States had been allies once.

One old gentleman with a tobacco-stained mustache addressed me through an interpreter. He pointed his cane at the parked ranks of MiGs, Sukhois, and military helicopters.

"Is this equipment any good?" he asked.

"Some of it is *very* good, sir."

He frowned. "Well, it better be, because we have a lot of tanks and planes—but we don't have washing machines."

That stark complaint epitomized the Cold War from the Russian perspective. And I was going to learn in short order just how good that equipment was.

The next day, I was briefed for a demonstration ride in the Mikoyan-Gurevich Design Bureau's MiG 29 Fulcrum, one of the world's most maneuverable fighters. I'd be flying with the chief MiG test pilot, Valery Menitsky, a fireplug of a guy with a strong handshake and pale blue eyes, a Hero of the Soviet Union.

"Call me Dick," I said as he coolly eyed my general's stars and service ribbons. But he apparently had never heard the name "Dick."

"Okay, Duck," he replied, almost exhausting his English.

While our hosts tried to find a G-suit long enough to fit me, Valery briefed me on the flight. He had a list of the ten planned aerobatic maneuvers, beginning with simple aileron rolls and proceeding to high-G loops, a split-S, an afterburner climb, tail slide, and a variety of other maneuvers to highlight the aircraft's performance.

My new Russian friends had one request before we departed for the flight line. They said that either crewmember could initiate ejection from the aircraft and asked if I would permit them to disable my ability to start the ejection sequence. I think they were worried that this unknown American general might just lose his bearings and eject a Hero of the Soviet Union. To my Russian friends I answered, "I'd be happy with you disabling my ability to eject." To myself I said, "What we do for our country."

The design bureau found a G-suit belonging to a lanky Kazakh cosmonaut, and I strapped into the backseat of the Fulcrum. When Valery had started the engines and completed his ground checks, he announced, "Takeoff. Okay, Duck?"

We were airborne after a takeoff roll of only fifteen hundred feet and shot up to a hard right turn at six thousand feet. "Duck okay?" Valery asked.

"Duck okay," I answered.

"Number one," Valery said.

This was a six-G loop, and I was prepared for it. "Okay, Valery," I grunted.

The G-suit worked perfectly—but I think Valery expected me to get sick, especially if their intelligence about us was as bad as ours about them. I'd never been sick in an airplane in my life, and I wasn't about to start now.

"Duck okay?" Valery said.

"Duck okay," I answered.

Valery said, "Number two."

And so it went, right through the tail slide, in which he put the nose straight up and throttled back to zero airspeed before sliding back to controlled flight—a very effective maneuver for showing the inherent stability of the MiG 29. The Fulcrum was an impressive plane. Valery was a great pilot, although I think he was a little disappointed at not having made this American general airsick.

The larger purpose of the visit was to continue "military-to-military" relations with the former Soviet Union, as America and Russia began the complex business of standing down from what had been a quasipermanent state of war since the late 1940s. This assignment included working with Russians to identify areas of technical cooperation to help ease their transition from communism to a market economy that would tap their vast pool of scientists and engineers.

In summer 1993, I was nominated for promotion to lieutenant general and appointment as Commander U.S. Forces Japan and Commander Fifth Air Force at Yokota Air Base near Tokyo. While my candidacy was still pending approval at the Senate Armed Services Committee, and before I left for Japan, however, I encountered another of those ethical dilemmas that tested my integrity *and* my future career.

One morning in late August I got a call from a senior officer known to be close to Gen. Merrill "Tony" McPeak, Air Force Chief of Staff, and to Defense Secretary Les Aspin. This officer had helped plan the successful air campaign against Iraq during Operation Desert Storm, and many considered him a shoe-in to receive his fourth star.

I was slated to be on the promotion board evaluating one-star candidates for major general. In order to eliminate outside influence, regulations did not allow board members to discuss any aspect of the process with outsiders.

But obviously the officer who called me had his own agenda. He met me in his office and named a brigadier general the board was about to consider. "The Chief doesn't want him promoted," he said with characteristic bluntness. In other words, if Dick Myers knew which side his bread was buttered on, he'd blackball that guy, always keeping in mind that the Senate Armed Services Committee had not yet confirmed my own recent nomination for another star and assignment to Japan.

I double-checked the regulations to be sure where I stood. Before the board convened, we would all have to sign a statement attesting that no one had tried to influence our decision. Here was one of those rare but glaring examples of senior officers interfering with formal procedure, a case made especially serious because it could distort the meritocracy of the promotion process. I was profoundly disappointed that a senior officer had tried to influence the promotion board process. This was reminiscent of the attempts earlier in my career to influence the selection of the Weapons School candidates and the certification of Air National Guard pilots.

That Labor Day weekend, Mary Jo and I played tennis with Lt. Gen. Mike Ryan, assistant to the Chairman of the Joint Chiefs of Staff, and his wife, Jane. The Ryans were among our closest friends, and he would go on to become the Chief of Staff of the Air Force, as his father had decades before. Mike was also on the promotion board.

As we were talking I said, "Mike, I have a dilemma. I'm on the upcoming two-star promotion board and somebody tried to influence me. How do I handle this?"

"That's interesting, Dick," he said. "I'm also on that board and *somebody* tried to influence me, too."

When the promotion panel met at Andrews Air Force Base the next Tuesday, three of us reported the attempt at unwarranted influence to the board. Board chairman Gen. Lee Butler, commander of the United States Strategic Command, ordered us to recuse ourselves from the board, and later we were asked to brief Air Force Secretary Sheila E. Widnall. She listened to what we had to say and immediately called on the Air Force and the Defense Department's Inspector General to launch a formal investigation.

I sure didn't need a messy scandal with my own promotion still pending confirmation in the Senate.

The officer who'd tried to interfere was known as an effective player in the Pentagon under President Clinton's first Secretary of Defense, Les Aspin, and on Capitol Hill. If he survived the investigation, he and his allies in Congress could have sharp knives ready for the three-stars who had had the audacity to defy him. But I could not give in to that improper pressure, either. So I'd done what I had to do.

I called Mary Jo. "I hope you haven't finished packing," I said. "And I hope you've still got your teaching certificate up to date."

The joint IG investigation was less than rigorous. It was based mainly on "he-said, I-said" evidence: sworn affidavits from the three lieutenant generals on the board the officer had tried to sway, plus my office telephone log in which I noted the time and date, but not the details, of his call. However, this was sufficient to convince the inspectors that he had breached regulations—despite his own sworn statement that he had not even known the three of us were on the promotion board, so certainly could not have tried to influence us.

Secretary Widnall issued a letter of admonishment against him, a step that effectively ended his career. His friends on the Senate Armed Services Committee did their own investigation in determining what grade to retire him in. This mostly friendly group approved his retirement as a three-star.

———————

Once more, I had acted in what I thought was the best interest of the Air Force. Many had done so before, and I hoped many would do so in the future, no matter what the potential consequences.

I had also gained firsthand experience with the invisible but sometimes dangerous vortices of power swirling within the Capital Beltway like hidden currents beneath the surface of a river.

In almost thirty years in the Air Force, I had learned a lot about the values my parents had inculcated in me at home: Work hard, tell the truth, and earn the trust of your colleagues. In 1973, I was a captain coming out of Southeast Asia, thirty-one, experienced in combat, but with a limited perspective on the military and geopolitics. Now I had learned much more about the texture and complexity of national security issues and also experienced some of the personal demands that service at senior levels placed on its officers.

Early instruction from Dad (November 1944). My parents married late in life because of the Great Depression and never thought they could have children, so were delighted to find out otherwise.

My parents, Bob and Pauline Myers, Merriam, Kansas (circa 1950). In the years before air-conditioning, summer evenings after dinner were spent outside. We usually listened to the ballgame while my parents drank iced coffee, and Mom always spoiled us with an ice cream.

Mary Jo with her parents, Clarence and Marie Rupp, at graduation from Kansas State University in June 1965. When my parents passed away in the mid-1970s, Clarence and Marie became my surrogates and were the best in-laws one could ask for. They were very supportive of us and my career, even taking Biffin, our six-month-old, ninety-pound Old English Sheepdog puppy, for a year while we went to Thailand during the war. This experience required replacement of the living room carpet after Biffin moved out.

The getaway: I captured my lovely bride and we were off, albeit only for a brief getaway, as I was due back at pilot training the next day (June 12, 1965).

Receiving my pilot wings with Mary Jo by my side—an exciting day for me and my whole family (June 1966). The Vietnam War was on everyone's mind.

Reunion of the Pogo Club, my be friends in high school (Decembe 1966): I'm on the left, next t Bert Cooper, who became a lawye Stuart Burns, who became a doctor veterinary medicine, and Sam Keele who has a Ph.D. in economi

Posing with my responsive, supersonic T-38 Talon II trainer at Vance Air Force Base, Oklahoma (March 1966). This experience fueled my desire to get an assignment to a fighter after graduation. Note the blue checkerboard helmet visor that Lt. Bill Flynn had all of his students paint.

The 417th Fighter Squadron at Ramstein, Germany, in 1967: Tad Oelstrom, bottom row, left, remains a steadfast friend and retired as superintendent of the Air Force Academy. Steve Melnick, third from the left, was killed in Vietnam. Maj. Fred Phillips, back row, left, was a great flight commander for a young pilot, and Ralph Van Brunt, back row, far right, taught me a lot as my aircraft commander (the F-4 had two pilots in the cockpit at this time).

With David Haas, my backseater in Vietnam, sitting on five-hundred-pound bombs loaded on our F-4 Phantom at Udorn Air Force Base, Thailand (June 1970).

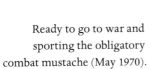

CAPT. RICHARD MYERS
KANSAS CITY, KANSAS

Ready to go to war and sporting the obligatory combat mustache (May 1970).

Receiving the Distinguished Flying Cross from Col. Bob Titus, the wing commander of the 18th Fighter Wing, after my first combat tour in Southeast Asia (March 1971). Kadena Air Base, Japan.

Our family was complete when Richard Bowman Myers, Jr., joined his two sisters, Nicole Marie (left), age eight, and Erin Louise (right), age six (Christmas 1979).

The move from Nellis Air Force Base in Las Vegas to Tyndall Air Force Base in Panama City, Florida (August 1986), was the fifteenth of twenty-five moves we made during my Air Force career. The truck broke down only three times, and the boat came unhitched only once.

Gen. Robert Russ, commander of Tactical Air Command, Langley Air Force Base (September 1989), was a great leader and an important mentor. He assigned me to two wing commands and four subsequent positions on the TAC staff.

Prime Minister Hashimoto of Japan welcomes Ambassador Walter Mondale and me to his residence for dinner and a discussion of Japanese-U.S. national security issues (1995).

My outgoing change of command at Yokota Air Force Base (June 1996). Gen. John Lorber, Commander of Pacific Air Forces (center), officiated and Ralph "Ed" Eberhart (left) assumed command of U.S. Forces Japan.

As Assistant to the Chairman of the Joint Chiefs of Staff, I had the pleasure of accompanying Secretaries Warren Christopher and Madeleine Albright on many visits around the world. Here an Army officer points to something of interest to me, the Secretary, and the U.S. Army Commander, Korea, across the DMZ looking into North Korea (February 1997).

At the four-star promotion ceremony preceding my assignment to Pacific Air Forces are, from left, my niece Julie Myers; my brother, Chuck; our son, Rich; Mary Jo; me; our daughter Nicole, and my other niece, Jennifer Myers (June 1997).

With good friend and golfing buddy Gen. Shigeru Sugiyama, Chief of the Japanese Air Defense Force, and later, their Chairman of the Joint Staff Office. Maggie Surls (middle) was my interpreter and advisor on all things Japanese. She made me sound eloquent, witty, or whatever the situation called for, and did much to facilitate relationships between the U.S. military and the Japanese. Many USFJ commanders would have been lost without her (May 1997).

My first command as a four-star general was Commander of U.S. Pacific Air Forces, Hickam Air Force Base, Hawaii (December 1998). As I stood near the memorial to Pearl Harbor, site of our country's last surprise attack, I could not have imagined we would witness another just three years later.

6

DIPLOMACY AND MIGHT

Japan Joint Command,
Assistant to the Chairman, Space Command

Flying out to Japan with Mary Jo and our third child, Rich, now a teenager, on a 747 jumbo jet in November 1993 felt much different from our trip back from the Far East in 1973. Then I had been a captain returning from a war that would be lost. Now I was a three-star general who had added what I hoped was a long-distance contribution to the lopsided victory that liberated Kuwait from Saddam Hussein. But the tearful good-bye with our daughters at the airport was painful. Nicole would be graduating in a couple of months and had to find a job because she had no home to go home to, and Erin was off for a semester abroad in Italy.

In addition to family separation, other challenges awaited me in my first joint assignment as Commander of U.S. Forces Japan. I would be in command of forces from all four services in the defense of Japan and subordinate to the U.S. Pacific Command (PACOM) in Hawaii. Under the post–World War II treaties that had evolved between our two countries, I was also responsible for developing plans for the defense of Japan. In peacetime, I represented PACOM in relations among all Defense Department elements, military and civilian, the Ambassador, and the Japan Defense Agency.

My headquarters was at Yokota Air Base about thirty miles northwest of the Tokyo megalopolis near the foothills of the Okutama Mountains. The base itself was a small military city with over fourteen thousand uniformed American personnel and civilians. Most of the 5th Air Force units at Yokota were occupied with airlift, logistics, or medical evacuation.

The combat muscle in Japan was in the 7th Fleet at Sasebo on the southern island of Kyushu, the Third Marine Expeditionary Force on Okinawa, the Air Force's wings at Misawa and Yokota, and the huge 18th Wing at Okinawa's Kadena Air Base. The total U.S. strength on Okinawa was just over twenty-five thousand, a very heavy presence on a relatively small island, which had reverted to full Japanese sovereignty in 1972 after seventeen years of post–World War II American occupation. All told, U.S. forces in Japan included over forty thousand uniformed service members and several thousand dependents.

My duties combined diplomacy and traditional military command. Following the disaster of World War II, the Japanese people had rejected the militarism that had left the country in ruins and had opted instead for a small "self-defense" force under the protective umbrella of the United States. But by the 1990s Japan's military had grown, and it had become increasingly clear that Tokyo would have to shoulder more of the country's expensive defense burden. I was there at a time when America was moving beyond the goal of protecting Japan from the Soviet Union to a new, less-defined mission of ensuring Japanese security in the post-Soviet era. Providing support to Japan in the case of conflict in Korea and underpinning regional security and stability remained an important, enduring mission.

During my tenure, the delicate issue of sovereignty lay just below the surface of Japanese-American relations. Although Tokyo sought the shield of America's military, few Japanese politicians wanted to be reminded of this dependence, and the American bases on Japan's soil were a constant reminder.

No knowledgeable observer of the strategic situation in the region disputed the need for the American military presence. The nearby Korean peninsula was a virtual powder keg, with communist forces that included an army of over one million men in the North periodically threatening the American and South Korean units stationed along the Demilitarized Zone (DMZ)—both sides of which, ironically, were among the most heavily *militarized* zones in the world. Seoul and much of South Korea's industry lay just to the south, within communist artillery range. A few hundred miles west, the People's Republic of China regularly flexed its growing military muscles against the noncommunist Republic of China on Taiwan.

Our bases on Okinawa lay almost equidistant between Korea and Taiwan. Given Japan's focus on defense of its Home Islands, it was obvious that America's robust military presence in Northeast Asia discouraged aggression and promoted regional stability.

But not every senior American official in Japan agreed that our very visible bases were worth the discontent among Japanese civilians they often provoked, especially during artillery or tactical air training exercises. Ambassador Walter Mondale, Jimmy Carter's Vice President, had arrived at the American Embassy in Tokyo just before I took over at my headquarters at Yokota Air Base. His stated goal was to improve bilateral relations between our two countries, and he asked me early in his tenure why America had so many military forces in Japan.

I convinced the Ambassador to join me on a tour of the Korean DMZ. Although United States Forces Korea was a separate and independent command, my headquarters maintained close relations with the Army, Navy, and Air Force units stationed on the peninsula and often observed their military exercises via electronic datalink from our own command post in Japan. If conflict ever spilled over the DMZ, we all would have to depend on each other: That was the point I wanted to make.

"Mr. Ambassador," I told him, "it would be good if the two of us could visit Korea, talk to our diplomatic and military leadership in that country, and tour the DMZ."

The Korean DMZ is a pretty dramatic piece of ground. Two and one-half miles wide, the zone snakes across the peninsula from the Yellow Sea coast in the southwest to the Sea of Japan in the northeast, crossing the thirty-eighth parallel, which had been the border between the north and the south before the massed communist armies invaded in June 1950. Three years later, in June 1953, the bloody conflict ended in stalemate and an armistice—but no peace treaty. The two Koreas were still officially at war with a ceasefire, not a peace treaty, in place. The DMZ followed the ridges and valleys of the ceasefire line, incorporating minefields, barbed-wire fences, and watchtowers on the southern and northern sides.

This was the world's tensest frontier, with almost two million North and South Korean and American forces confronting each other across the line. The U.S. 2nd Infantry Division, with integral armor, artillery, and assault helicopters, constituted the principal American ground combat strength. The division was garrisoned in bases south of the DMZ. In many ways, their mission was to serve as a "tripwire" to discourage North Korean aggression. Republic of Korea (ROK) combat units were spread among the American forces all the way to the eastern end of the DMZ.

Beginning just across the DMZ and spreading north, the North Koreans had positioned over a million troops, mostly in infantry, artillery, and Special Operations commando units. There could be no doubt about North Korea's aggressive intentions. In the mid-1970s, ROK units began discovering deep tunnels under the DMZ that the North Koreans had hewn from solid granite. These invasion tunnels were wide enough to accommodate the quick passage of division-size assault forces, including armored vehicles. The North claimed the tunnels were abandoned "coal mines" and even painted the granite black to support this ludicrous assertion. Perhaps you could question the North Koreans' intentions, but not their capability. We had to be ready to "fight tonight," as the U.S. forces in Korea often said.

Ambassador Mondale and I flew up from Seoul by Black Hawk helicopter and continued north by road in an Army Humvee to stop below Panmunjom, site of the Joint Security Area. This was where American and South Korean officers of the United Nations Command met periodically with their North Korean counterparts—often with the Americans and their allies being forced to endure threats and insults. The Joint Security Area was even more bizarre than the rest of the DMZ.

A girded structure half as tall as the Eiffel Tower, from which flew the huge flag of the Democratic People's Republic of Korea, stood near the "Peace Village" of Kijong-dong. This was a cluster of shoddy concrete apartment buildings that the communists claimed were home to two hundred families. But observers on the south side of the DMZ never saw families, only soldiers in civilian clothes trucked in each morning to sweep the streets and hack weeds with sickles. Each night after the "villagers" left, lights in the same windows of the same apartments snapped on in unison. Close examination of this Potemkin village with binoculars revealed that many of the windows were missing glass.

When Ambassador Mondale and I arrived at the observation post near the Joint Security Area, the North Korean loudspeakers were playing loud patriotic music. There was a ridiculous side to this transparent propaganda, of course, but there was nothing farcical about the nearby invasion tunnels, or about the massed, yet hidden, North Korean firepower that faced us from across the DMZ.

The North Koreans had deployed thousands of truck-mounted heavy rocket launchers and self-propelled artillery pieces in hardened cave shelters dug into the north slopes of the ridges, shielded from direct fire from the south. If they chose to attack, the communists could unleash a holocaust on the sprawling Seoul-Inchon National Capital Area—home to 23 million South Koreans. Intelligence estimated the North Korean Army could fire between four thousand and ten thousand rockets and artillery shells a *minute* in the initial salvo on greater Seoul. Before ROK and American forces could react, these mobile, long-range weapons could dart back into their cave shelters, and then roll out to fire more devastating salvos. (North Korea also had over six hundred surface-to-surface missiles, potentially with chemical, biological, and perhaps even nuclear warheads, that could threaten targets ranging from South Korea to Japan.)

As we drove east from the Joint Security Area along the well-paved military road that skirted the DMZ, I summarized for the Ambassador the U.S.-ROK Operations Plan to defend the South. The U.S. 2nd Infantry Division had devastating Multiple Launch Rocket Systems and long-range Army tactical missile units poised for retaliatory strikes on North Korean rocket and tube artillery literally within minutes of the first enemy salvo. Our forces had counter-battery radar and sensor systems that used powerful computers to precisely target rocket launchers and guns firing from the north. And our tactical air forces and bomber forces had key artillery and other important targets already planned.

But unfortunately, our ground forces, Air Force, and Navy units did not possess sufficient precision-guided "smart" weapons to quickly neutralize the long-range artillery threat to South Korea's densest population center. Although the world had grown accustomed to video footage of laser-guided bombs striking Iraqi targets with surgical precision during Operation Desert Storm, our forces defending South Korea needed such weapons, and the satellite-guided weapons still in development, in much larger numbers to fully counter the communists' overwhelming conventional firepower. It would be several years before they reached our forces in the region in sufficient numbers.

Meanwhile, we had to hope that our lead in counter-artillery weapons would continue to serve as a strong deterrent to North Korean attack—as the best intelligence estimated it would.

Intelligence, however, is always a prediction based on judgment, probability, not on certainty, although there was a consensus in our intelligence community that the Korean communists did not want to see their huge military—on which their state depended—mauled by more technically advanced American and ROK forces. In other words, the American presence in Korea served as an invaluable deterrent, at least for the time being, but no one could predict the future actions of North Korean President Kim Jong-Il. Not only was he a ruthless dictator, he was dangerously unstable, which made planning for military options very difficult.

But one thing was certain: South Korea had to depend on its American ally to provide a credible restraint to aggression from the north. I explained to Ambassador Mondale that it wasn't just U.S. forces based in South Korea that provided this deterrent; Japan was a critical link in our defense of the peninsula. Within hours of an initial North Korean attack, all American military facilities in Japan would be operating on wartime footing. Our naval base at Sasebo would supply fuel and munitions to 7th Fleet aircraft carrier battle groups responding to a shooting war in Korea. Kadena Air Base on Okinawa would about double in the number of aircraft and dispatch multiple squadrons of F-15 Eagles to engage enemy aircraft, while F-15E Strike Eagle fighter-bombers would stage out of the base en route to the combat zone. Kadena also had tankers and AWACS, as well as some intelligence-gathering aircraft. Our F-16s at Misawa had the Wild Weasel mission and the C-130s at Yokota would conduct the tactical airlift mission. Of course, as soon as the balloon went up there would be a huge flow of aircraft into Korea and Japan. It was air power that would initially blunt the North Korean attack while we waited for ground forces to arrive from the United States for the follow-on fight.

The Ambassador stared across tangled brush masking the minefields of the DMZ, somberly weighing what we had seen and what I had explained about the North Korean threat. But there was one dismal fact I had not yet stated. I did so now: "Mr. Ambassador, if the North Koreans attack, there would never be any doubt about the outcome . . . but the casualties on both sides would be too horrible to contemplate." After our visit to the DMZ, Ambassador Walter Mondale fully appreciated the importance of U.S. forces and bases in Japan.

I had learned some lessons, too: specifically, how to best work with my senior civilian counterparts toward solving common problems. It was easy for people in our government's civilian agencies, such as the Departments of State, Treasury, or Commerce, to view the world through the perspective of their own special interests, and the military also often wore blinders. The fact was, however, we were all pulling the same cart and had to work together. I was new at this and had a lot more to learn about integrating the military and civilian sides of government. Mondale was a great teacher in this regard, and in my view a superb leader of the U.S. Embassy's Country Team, of which the senior members of U.S. Forces Japan headquarters were an integral part. The Ambassador always made sure the military voice was heard on security issues.

Before dawn on January 17, 1995, the industrial port of Kobe was struck by a powerful earthquake that devastated the city, decimating the city's disaster relief personnel and cutting off the surrounding region from the rest of Japan. I was at the embassy in Tokyo, attending a meeting with the Chairman of the Joint Chiefs of Staff, Army Gen. John Shalikashvili. When word came of the Kobe earthquake, Ambassador Mondale left the conference room to gather more information. General Shalikashvili said it was imperative for the United States military to begin organizing a disaster response to provide whatever the Japanese needed. But when the Ambassador returned, he announced in a relieved tone that the quake wasn't nearly as bad as first feared, and that fewer then three hundred people were thought to have died. We checked with our Japanese Self-Defense Forces contacts, who told us that the Kobe city government had not requested their assistance.

As the coming hours and days unfolded, the true enormity of the Kobe disaster was revealed. The final casualty count would be over sixty-four hundred dead, with thousands more injured.

Why hadn't the Kobe municipal government called for immediate assistance from the Japanese Self-Defense Forces and the American military? Both could have provided medevac helicopters and field hospitals. The reluctance to seek outside help was partly due to the sheer magnitude of the disaster and to the fact that the mayor's reporting stations had been wiped out. But there was also a tradition of ingrained antimilitarism in the people of Kobe and their elected officials. This was just one example of Japan's ambivalence about the military, either those wearing their country's uniform or that of the United States.

The interface between the military and natural disaster relief is often difficult. As with so many other formative experiences in my career, I recognized similarities to the Kobe quake ten years later during the 2005 Hurricane Katrina recovery. The President's office tried to establish unity of command among all military forces participating in relief operations. There were National Guard, Reserve, and active duty units involved with command splintered among the state governors and the Department of Defense. But the governors of the two hardest-hit states, Louisiana and Mississippi, rejected unity of command. Fortunately, the active duty commander, Army Lt. Gen. Russ Honoré, a New Orleans native, had the contacts and personality to informally establish effective command.

In central Tokyo during the morning rush hour on March 20, 1995, members of the violently apocalyptic Aum Shinrikyo cult released deadly sarin gas on several subway lines. The cult members hid the nerve agent in liquid form in plastic bags rolled in newspaper, which they pierced with sharp-tipped umbrellas before leaving the subway cars at crowded stations. As the invisible, odorless gas spread through the jammed subways, twelve passengers were killed, fifty others were severely injured, and five thousand more were either transported or made their own way to hospitals. Panic gripped Tokyo's dynamic heart for hours.

The next day, my driver, Kobiyashi-San, a stern man in his sixties, drove me, my military aide, and my interpreter, Japanese-American Maggie Surls, slowly past the Kasumigaseki station. Kobi-San had come to Tokyo at a young age right after World War II. He applied and got a job as a driver with General MacArthur's headquarters. He had been driving for U.S. Forces Japan ever since. He knew every road in the Kanto Plain and we became good friends. Fishing was his passion and he took me trout fishing in the mountains just west of Yokota.

"This is one of the worst-hit places, sir," Maggie said, translating Kobi-San's comments.

"Kobi-San," I said, "you really think it's a good idea for us to drive by here?"

"Oh, it's okay, General," he answered. "We've got protective masks in the trunk."

In the trunk, I thought. Had there been a cloud of sarin lingering nearby, we'd all have been dead before he could pop the trunk of the sedan to grab the protective gear.

Driving toward the embassy through the morning traffic—which was much thinner than normal—I reflected on the deadly mix of violent fanaticism and weapons of mass destruction (WMD). Aum Shinrikyo was an isolated suicidal doomsday cult composed of mentally unstable people. But there were too many leaders of rogue states—Iraq, North Korea, and Syria came to mind—

making reckless comments to allow one to ignore the existence of WMD in the contemporary strategic arena.

Sarin was not hard to make. What would the impact of such an attack have been in New York, Washington, or London?

———————

In summer 1995, Mary Jo and I joined Ambassador Mondale on the volcanic island of Iwo Jima for a ceremony marking the fiftieth anniversary of the end of World War II in the Pacific. Three planeloads of Marine veterans of the terrible battle sat in rows of chairs on the hot black volcanic sand, listening to the officials' speeches, undoubtedly absorbed in memories of the friends who had died there. The most poignant remarks came from the widow of Lt. Gen. Tadamichi Kuribayashi, the commander of the Japanese troops in 1945, who had died with his troops. Through an interpreter, the frail old lady spoke of the hatred of the past giving way to the cordial and fruitful relationship Japan and the United States enjoyed today. At the end of her comments, the Marine vets rushed forward. This was an amazing moment, not knowing what memories or bitterness these American veterans held. But all they wanted was to pose for snapshots of them shaking her hand. This warm image said a lot about the reconciliation the two countries had achieved.

———————

The next spring, during the run-up to the Republic of China elections in Taiwan, Beijing tried to intimidate Taiwan by firing missiles dangerously close to its territory. The United States responded by ordering two aircraft carrier battle groups to the waters near Taiwan. With this demonstration of American resolve to support its Taiwan ally, Beijing stepped down to defuse the tense confrontation.

In a conversation with Ambassador Mondale, I asked if the United States had been keeping the Japanese government informed of American objectives and all the logistical support flowing from its territory to our naval forces involved in the crisis. We had not. So Mondale and I received permission from Washington to brief Foreign Minister Yohei Kono on the crisis. We could see the immense relief in Kono's eyes as we spoke. Until we called on him, the Japanese government had no idea of what our exact intentions were. It wasn't the first time—nor, unfortunately, would it be the last—that we neglected to keep our friends and allies informed of our military planning and activities.

Two years into my assignment in Japan, a shocking incident occurred on Okinawa that seriously strained relations between our two countries and their armed services. Over the long Labor Day weekend in 1995, two Marines and a Navy hospital corpsman abducted, beat, and raped a twelve-year-old Japanese schoolgirl. Based on information from another Marine who backed out of the crime, American military police quickly arrested the three. They admitted buying duct tape to bind the girl and renting a minivan to transport her. The three found the slight child alone after dark outside a stationery shop and drove her to a remote sugarcane field, where they beat her and one raped her. The other two claimed they could not complete the sexual act once they realized how small the girl was.

Nevertheless, all three were charged with kidnapping and aggravated sexual assault—offenses that could have brought them life without the possibility of parole or even the death sentence under the American Uniform Code of Military Justice (UCMJ). The Status of Forces Agreement between America and Japan gave primary jurisdiction to the U.S. military in such cases. After consulting my command's Judge Advocate General, Col. A. J. Cunningham, we began looking at the charges against the three confessed criminals that might be appropriate under the UCMJ, including capital charges.

The Japanese government vigorously objected and demanded that the Americans be turned over to the local prosecutor in Okinawa for trial. Under our chain of command, I could have let the Marine general in charge of the III Marine Expeditionary Force handle the matter. But I decided this was such an important matter that the American "face" to the Japanese public and media should be at Headquarters, U.S. Forces, Japan, and I would be that face. This was not a pleasant task but very important to U.S./Japan relations and I wanted it done right.

Public outrage and anti-American fury on the island had reached an explosive level, with demonstrations surging outside our bases. So I conferred with Ambassador Mondale and PACOM commander Adm. Richard C. Macke, recommending that we defuse tensions on Okinawa by transferring the three American servicemen to Japanese authority, which in any event would be the ultimate outcome of the legal proceedings under the Status of Forces Agreement once they were indicted for such serious felonies. Mondale flew to Okinawa and apologized to the island's governor, Masahide Ota, for the "suffering" the rape had caused the girl, her family, and all the people of Okinawa. Speaking for the U.S. forces in the country, I told my counterparts in the Japanese military, "This criminal act does not stand for America and will not be tolerated by us." Public expressions of remorse—followed by concrete actions—are deeply rooted in Japanese culture. Our apologies and the transfer of the prisoners went a long way toward cooling the flaring indignation on the island.

But in November, Japanese fury blazed again when Admiral Macke made insensitive and ill-advised remarks. In an impromptu PACOM news conference, Macke commented on the vicious crime, "I think it was absolutely stupid. I have said several times: For the price they paid to rent the car used in the abduction, they could have had a girl [prostitute]."

The stunned journalists in Washington hardly had time to file their stories before President Bill Clinton ordered Defense Secretary William Perry to relieve Macke of command. I had always considered Admiral Macke a good boss and I was sorry to see him end his career in this way.

Meanwhile the trial proceeded on Okinawa. After pleading guilty, the three Americans sought mercy from the three-judge panel that tried the case and were sentenced to between six and a half and seven years. Ironically, this was a much milder prison term than they would have received at a U.S. court-martial.

The fundamental issue of American bases on Okinawa remained unresolved. So the U.S. government used the rape incident to work with the Japanese toward moving our relations with Japan forward. It was important to try to lessen the burden of the people of Okinawa, especially, as such a large percentage of our forces in Japanese territory were stationed there. The State Department and the White House negotiated a summit meeting between President Bill Clinton and incoming Japanese Prime Minister Ryutaro Hashimoto. The question of the American military presence in Japan was only one of several points of contention between our two countries, but the public clamor over the Okinawa rape was an ideal catalyst to bring the two leaders together.

In April 1996, Clinton and Hashimoto met in Tokyo and worked out an agreement that planned a significantly reduced U.S. military footprint on Okinawa, which helped smooth Japanese feelings, but did *not* weaken America's position. It was during this period that I fully began to appreciate the intelligence and energy of my deputy, Marine Maj. Gen. Pete Pace. He would go on to become my Vice Chairman of the Joint Chiefs of Staff and would replace me as Chairman when I retired in 2005.

Among the summit's notable achievements was a joint declaration that reaffirmed American military presence in Asia was "essential for preserving peace and stability." This was virtually a truism, but the Japanese placed great stock in formal statements. The two leaders agreed on the necessity to promote policy coordination, including studies on bilateral cooperation in dealing with situations that might emerge and have an important influence on the peace and security of Japan.

Expanding on the theme of the U.S.-Japanese relationship, the two leaders called it "the cornerstone for achieving common security objectives" and stability in the region. In more concrete matters, the Americans agreed to return an air base, a port, and related military facilities to the government of Okinawa. One important outcome of this summit was that we had begun to break through the old inhibitions in bilateral military planning. All told, Japanese-American security relations had not been so vigorous in years.

"Back in Kansas," I told Mary Jo, "they'd call that making lemonade out of lemons."

———————————

One of our major accomplishments after the summit was to convince the Japanese to participate in after-action reviews of our joint and combined exercises. It was part of our U.S. military culture to have brutally frank, no-holds-barred after-action reviews, with the people doing the critique perfectly comfortable telling a private or a general he had screwed up. This kind of candor didn't happen in the Japanese military. Lower-ranking officers criticized their superiors only if they wanted to find a new profession. During one of our exercises, I asked my Japanese counterpart and his staff to sit in on our after-action review. General Nishimoto, Chief of the Joint Staff Office, eagerly joined us and quickly embraced the notion that honest after-action reviews made you stronger. He said he wanted to participate in next year's exercise. You could hear the twelve-molar sucks from his staff in the back of the room.

———————————

The last year of my command in Japan had sometimes been tense and demanding, but overall, we thoroughly enjoyed our tour of duty. We came to genuinely love the country and grew close to our Japanese civilian friends and military counterparts and still are in contact with many. Visiting our home today, it's easy to see the influence of Japanese arts and crafts. Mary Jo was so taken by the fine embroidery of the traditional obi, the wide silk waistband of a kimono, that she spearheaded the publishing of a book through the officers' spouses club called *Obi Ties East and West*.

Our Japanese friends were hospitable and genuinely pleased that we appreciated their country. Whenever Mary Jo and I traveled with them to Kyushu, Hokkaido, or Shikoku, we always stayed at tastefully decorated traditional hotels and inns, many with rock gardens and elaborately pruned bonsai trees. Our Japanese hosts also knew where to find the most authentic local cuisine, which was usually based on raw, pickled, or smoked fish, washed down with copious amounts of sake or beer.

Eating fugu, blowfish, was one rite of passage that required ramping up our nerve to attempt. Unless the dish was properly prepared, eating raw morsels of blowfish could be a deadly cross-cultural experience, because parts of the fish were extremely poisonous. My Air Self-Defense counterpart, General Sugiyama, invited us to his home for the traditional initiation. Figuring that he would have hired one of Japan's premier fugu chefs who knew how to avoid the most toxic internal organs to ensure our meal was as safe as possible, I seized my chopsticks and got to work. Dipped in the pungent sauces, the fish was delicious. Mary Jo ate right alongside me, probably figuring it might be best to go out together. (Only later did we learn that Sugiyama's "experienced chef" was actually an officer on his staff who prepared fugu as a hobby.)

"Do you have such a thing in your country?" General Sugiyama asked politely.

"Oh, yes," Mary Jo said with a straight face. "It's called Jack in the Box."

That fast food chain had recently suffered a serious *e. coli* contamination incident in which a number of customers died after eating undercooked burger patties. But I wasn't deterred: As much as I loved Japanese cuisine, after returning from a trip, I always felt starved for warm, solid American food, and the first stop I'd make back inside the base was the Burger King for a Whopper and fries.

Traveling and living outside the protective gates of American bases overseas, however, came to form an important part of who we were. We were exposed to German, Thai, and Japanese cultures in ways American tourists rarely experience, which strengthened the bonds among our friends and colleagues. Years later, this appreciation of foreign cultures helped me in my dealings with senior military officers and dignitaries around the world.

In June 1996, we left Japan and I took up my new assignment as Assistant to the Chairman of the Joint Chiefs of Staff, Army Gen. John Shalikashvili.

The Chairman was a robust and sophisticated soldier who'd been born in

Poland in 1936 to Georgian refugee parents. Shalikashvili was sworn in as an American citizen in 1958 and drafted into the Army. He later served as a senior adviser to the South Vietnamese Army. Known informally as "Shali" because his Georgian name was difficult, he advanced steadily, further proof of meritocracy in a military career.

President Bill Clinton nominated Shalikashvili to replace Colin Powell as Chairman. As General Shali's assistant, I found him to be a forthright leader who gave his subordinates considerable independence while also expecting initiative and responsibility.

I assumed my duties among the offices and conference rooms on the second floor of the Pentagon's outer layer, the E-Ring. This was the Chairman's territory, a favored site with windows facing the Potomac and Washington. On my first day at work it was clear that the job would not be just another senior military assignment. Even though I had served in joint commands, I had never worked so close to so many members of all the armed forces. The commissioned and noncommissioned officers I met wore a variety of different uniforms: deep Army green, different shades of blue among the Navy and Air Force, and the olive green of the Marine Corps. They were often referred to as "purple suiters" because if you blended all the uniforms' colors the result would be purple.

At this level of the joint world, I was operating in an environment that had been radically altered by the restructuring of the armed services, which began with the Goldwater-Nichols Department of Defense Reorganization Act of 1986 (GNA). Named for its sponsors, Arizona Republican Senator Barry Goldwater and Alabama Democratic Congressman Bill Nichols, the act made the JCS Chairman the principal military adviser to the President and the National Security Council. Previously there was no principal military adviser, as the responsibility was shared by all the Joint Chiefs of Staff. Goldwater-Nichols also empowered the combatant commanders and gave them responsibilities that encroached on territory that had been the service chiefs' domain. For instance, combatant commanders now had a greater say in priorities for acquisition and procurement of systems and allocation of resources, an area previously the purview of the chiefs. The act also gave the Secretary of Defense more authority and streamlined the chain of command that now ran from the President through the Secretary of Defense and directly to unified combatant commanders—four-star generals or admirals with joint responsibility in a regional or functional area: U.S. Central Command, U.S. Pacific Command, U.S. Strategic Command, U.S. Transportation Command, and so forth.

Although the Chairman was the senior ranking officer in the armed services, he did not exercise military command over the Joint Chiefs, any of the armed services, or the combatant commands. The responsibility of the services was to organize, train, and equip soldiers, sailors, airmen, and Marines, while the combatant commanders deployed and led them in military operations. The combatant commanders also continued to be deeply involved in operational planning.

Under the act, while the Chairman was the principal military adviser to the President and the National Security Council, he had to reflect the services chiefs' advice if it differed from his own. And by law they retained the right to consult the Secretary of Defense or the President if they so desired.

But I must note that during my tenure as Chairman, I was never in a position where one of the service chiefs and I had different advice to offer our civilian superiors. I worked hard to keep the chiefs informed and always tried to ensure that we were in agreement on the advice we would give the President, the Secretary of Defense, and the NSC.

The Goldwater-Nichols Act was implemented to overcome interservice problems that had become serious during the Vietnam War and had reached crisis level by the 1980s. The services had competed for resources and strategic authority for decades during and after World War II, and interservice redundancy and inefficiency had become a problem that had to be addressed and corrected.

The branches of the armed forces often sought to "get their share of the action," which undercut smooth coordination during joint operations—especially those demanding a synchronized and flexible interservice partnership. Sometimes the services seemed intent on maintaining the upper hand with their rivals on the E-Ring. Inevitably, this resulted in flawed planning for joint operations and in even worse execution.

Two of the most glaring—and disastrous—examples of muddled operations were the failure of the Iranian hostage rescue mission in April 1980 and the badly executed U.S. invasion of Grenada in October 1983. In the Iranian operation, eight Navy RH-53D Sea Stallion helicopters—flown by Marine aviators—off an aircraft carrier in the Indian Ocean were to rendezvous at a remote Iranian site code-named Desert One with Air Force C-130 transports carrying fuel, equipment, and members of the Army's elite Delta Force. A minimum of six helicopters was needed to fly the Delta Force team north to Tehran, link up with CIA operatives, enter the U.S. Embassy compound where the hostage diplomats were held, and lift them out by helicopter to a nearby Iranian air base that Army Rangers had secured. The operation involved the Navy helicopters, Marine Corps aviators, Air Force, Army Rangers, and the Delta Force—as well as the CIA. One problem with preparing for the ultrasecret mission was that operational security often prevented the rigorous complete training exercises required for complex clandestine endeavors. The elaborate plan failed, ambushed by a desert sandstorm, equipment breakdowns, and inadequate planning.

After the commander, Army Special Forces Col. Charles Beckwith, aborted the mission, exhausted aircraft crews tried to maneuver for takeoff in the blinding dust. A Sea Stallion and a C-130 collided in a blazing explosion that killed eight and badly injured four. In the ensuing shock and confusion, the force abandoned relatively undamaged helicopters. Iran's revolutionary government derived maximum propaganda value from the debacle and held the hostage American diplomats captive until the very end of President Jimmy Carter's term.

The after-action report cited rushed mission planning, the inability of the service branches to coordinate their actions, and inefficient command and control. Everyone involved seemed to have forgotten the adage that an operations plan is excellent until the first shot is fired—or the sandstorm blows. The failure at Desert One did lead directly to the creation of the joint U.S. Special Operations Command that unified all our land, sea, and aviation Special Ops forces.

Although the 1983 U.S. invasion of the Caribbean island of Grenada accomplished its objectives—unseating the local left-wing strongman and his Cuban allies and rescuing American medical students—the hastily planned and executed operation also exposed a glaring lack of coordination among the Navy, Army, Marine Corps, and Air Force units involved. Army Rangers in the south could not communicate with Marines operating in the north of the island because their radio sets did not share common frequencies. Some units were forced to rely on outdated tourist maps to call in artillery support or air strikes. More unsettling was the case of Navy SEALs pinned down by heavy fire near the island capital of St. Georges who saw AC-130 Spectre gunships circling overhead but could not communicate because the Air Force and the Navy had incompatible radios.

Such shortcomings had all but disappeared during the much larger and complex Operation Just Cause, the U.S. invasion of Panama in late December 1989. Over fifty thousand personnel from all four services worked in well-coordinated unison under the leadership of Southern Command commander-in-chief, Army Gen. Max Thurman, to overthrow dictator Manuel Noriega and secure the Panama Canal for international shipping.

A year later, Commander of U.S. Central Command, Army Gen. Norman Schwarzkopf, led an international coalition ten times larger in Operations Desert Shield/Desert Storm, which severely mauled Saddam Hussein's Iraqi forces forcing their withdrawal from Kuwait.

Due in large measure to the Goldwater-Nichols Act four years earlier, Desert Storm was a much better example of multiservice operations than previous efforts. But despite the overwhelming victory, significant multiservice operational problems were evident: Instead of a single, focused ground-air offensive that would have concentrated our firepower on the enemy, the air and ground campaigns were separate and sequential. The efforts were "deconflicted"— with air or ground units separated by time or distance—as in the AirLand 2000 doctrine, not integrated. When our fighter-bombers and attack helicopters did provide close air support, there were too many fatal friendly fire incidents. Our aircraft had no way to positively identify the armored vehicles moving through the swirling dust. We had to rely on traditional orange recognition panels that were hard to see in darkness, or, as a last resort, put light bulbs inside tin cans, which flickered dimly in aircraft infrared targeting systems.

In addition, the public did not understand the importance that laser-guided bombs played in the victory: Only about 10 percent of the aerial ordnance used in Desert Storm was precision-guided—even though CENTCOM public affairs efforts tried to leave the impression that our arsenal of smart weapons was virtually limitless by repeatedly showing footage of laser-guided weapons striking their targets. Part of this effort was sound psychological operations against the enemy, part was to reassure the home front.

But the fact was that about 90 percent of the ordnance dropped during Desert Storm was the type of "iron bombs" that the B-24 Liberator that crashed in my neighborhood during World War II could have dropped.

Yet the post–Cold War "peace dividend" policy that appeared so quickly after Desert Storm dictated that the American military was going to have to get by with fewer people and less equipment. The Defense Department would have to find better ways to do its job.

By the time I became Assistant to the Chairman in July 1996, the services and the Pentagon's civilian leadership had resolved many of the problems inherent to the Goldwater-Nichols legislation, but there was still lingering strain among the service chiefs of staff and the combatant commanders. This often became evident during the conferences among combatant commanders and service chiefs that I attended. Sometimes, the tension around the table was palpable. It was as if everyone was walking on eggshells, so wary of their counterparts' prerogatives that it was difficult to accomplish much.

The chiefs now trained and equipped forces but did not lead them. This was the responsibility of the combatant commanders, who also developed the operations plans for the use of those forces. The service chiefs in their Joint Chiefs of Staff roles, however, would review and make recommendations to the war plans, as we did for the plans for Afghanistan and Iraq.

This arrangement was bound to create tensions, because each service chief wanted his branch to have a piece of the action—literally—when an operation unfolded; for example, during the Panama operation, the Navy obtained the seizure of waterfront Patilla Airport for the SEALs, normally an assignment for Army Rangers.

Initially I found representing the Chairman in the Washington interagency world challenging because I had limited experience working closely with senior civilian peers outside the Department of Defense. I was the official liaison between General Shalikashvili's office and the State Department. To function well, I had to learn to evaluate many interrelated aspects of national security policy—civilian as well as military—that I had never considered before, other than at the Army War College. And I also got to travel with the Secretary of State as part of my duties. Both Secretary Warren Christopher and Secretary Madeleine Albright treated me as one of their closest advisers and I was in essentially every meeting they had with their counterparts or heads of state around the world. You couldn't pay for this type of education, and it would come to be a great benefit in my later career.

This assignment gave me my first direct access to high-level strategic intelligence, based on ultrasensitive agent (human) reports, electronic collection and analysis, and remote imagery sensing (observation from aircraft or satellites). My initial impression was that this intelligence was probing and exhaustive.

But it wasn't long before I saw that the raw information from which the intelligence was assembled arrived through narrow vertical "stovepipes" of secret data that each intelligence collection agency often jealously guarded. Ostensibly, the intelligence agencies needed such restrictions to protect their sources, methods, and procedures from leaks that would expose valuable agents or technical processes. Although the intelligence community acted in good faith, the stovepipes prevented its members from fully coordinating and sharing as they should have, making any products less useful.

At a 1996 NATO conference in Brussels, France stunned the world by announcing its interest in re-entering the integrated command structure from which President Charles de Gaulle had precipitously withdrawn thirty years earlier. The U.S. government response was to welcome the positive French "demarche."

France had never left the alliance itself and had fought with the Allied Coalition in Operation Desert Storm. The French were now patrolling the southern and northern no-fly zones in Iraq alongside American and British aircraft. And in 1995 the French had joined NATO air and ground forces applying military pressure on the Serbs to lift their brutal siege of Sarajevo, the Bosnian capital. Now it looked as if Paris might be ready to rejoin NATO's military command formally, but everyone knew dealing with the French on such a delicate political issue could be difficult.

True to form, it wasn't long before Paris announced its terms for re-entering the NATO military structure: They insisted that a French four-star command one of the senior billets, possibly in the Southern Region. This was unacceptable. France had sizable armed forces compared to other NATO countries and did possess a nuclear *Force de Frappe,* but it would first have to rejoin NATO militarily and then the allies would go through the standard process of determining which countries got which flag-officer billets—always a sensitive and hard-fought business.

General Shalikashvili asked me to fly to Paris to determine France's expectations, which were no doubt based largely on a sense of bygone *gloire.* I had lunch with Air Force Gen. Jean-Philippe Douin, Chief of Staff of the French armed forces, at his resplendent office suite in the *Etat Major des Armees* with the Eiffel Tower dominating the view through the tall, polished windows. He was a very charming man, and I felt a great deal of pressure as he laid out France's position, but I remained reticent. I was in Paris to learn their position, not to negotiate.

Later, I returned to Paris with Clinton's National Security Adviser, Anthony Lake, who met with his French counterpart to conduct the actual negotiation. Several of us were sitting around the table with the French team when Tony's counterpart told us all, "Well, of course you know we consider the Mediterranean a French lake."

I could see that Tony, normally an unflappable former Foreign Service officer and academic historian, came close to losing his cool at that brash assertion. As a young diplomat in South Vietnam he had served amid the crumbling ruins of France's empire. He mentioned his history credentials and pushed back hard on this concept of French dominance in the Mediterranean, but then returned to the matter at hand. There would be flag officer positions available to the French, should they choose to re-enter NATO militarily—but for the moment, all the four-star berths had been allotted to the countries already militarily integrated into the alliance. Despite the comfortable temperature in the old high-ceilinged office, a decided chill seemed to have settled on the Empire tapestries and furniture.

I recalled Winston Churchill's adage after the tense Tehran Conference he attended with Roosevelt and Stalin in 1943: "The only thing harder than working with allies is working without them." Churchill's ironic conclusion resonated in Paris during our negotiation.

We ended the meeting where it began: General Douin would continue to attend sessions of the alliance's military committee, but France's future military integration in NATO remained unresolved.

My first exposure to high-level diplomacy was instructive. Working with NATO in the future would not be easy. And it turned out that working with the American bureaucracy was also difficult.

As we were preparing to leave the American Embassy for the airport, my executive assistant, Army Col. Matt Klimow, nervously explained that, while I had a reserved seat in Air France business class (per Pentagon policy for three-star officers), Tony Lake and his small party were flying coach.

"That won't do, Matt," I said. "We can't have the President's National Security Adviser flying coach while I'm up front drinking free champagne."

The embassy travel people thought they'd solved the problem by getting us all business-class seats, but the arrangement fell through when we reached the airport.

"Tony," I told Lake, "we've got a big problem. I'm in business class but you're not. I want to swap seats with you."

Lake shrugged. "Dick, sit down and stop worrying about it. That's just the way Washington is these days."

The Clinton White House was still under investigation for the 1993 firing of the West Wing travel office staff. So to avoid appearances of impropriety at that point, cabinet secretaries were the only civilian officials authorized business-class air travel.

I hated the thought of the President's National Security Adviser scrunched up in a narrow seat back there in the coach cabin while I had room to stretch my long legs, but that was Tony's way: He was a gentleman, never an officious stickler for protocol. We always got on well.

The episode reminded me of the prevailing misconceptions about relations between the military and the Clinton administration. According to conventional wisdom, the White House did not understand the military and didn't care to learn. This conclusion was based in part on separate incidents that, combined, made ample grist for the mills of columnists and radio talk show hosts. In 1993, Army Lt. Gen. Barry McCaffrey met a female White House staffer leaving the Southwest Gate. When he said, "Good morning," she replied, "I don't talk to the military." McCaffrey complained, the White House tried unsuccessfully to identify her and punish her impolite behavior—and the news media had a field day, alleging the incident reflected Clinton's own view of the military. Later that year, Army Rangers and Special Operations troops suffered heavy casualties in Somalia's strife-torn capital, Mogadishu. The press tried to lay the blame for tactical mistakes on Bill Clinton's desk, a groundless accusation.

While the Clinton administration's alleged disdain for the armed services did make for lively reading and talk shows, I had learned from personal experience that the impression was based on a false assumption. The President and his national security team respected the military, and Clinton himself appreciated that the military would accomplish what he wanted done. I met President Clinton and the First Lady in 1995 at a PACOM commanders' conference in Hawaii when they were returning from a summit of the Association of Southeast Asian Nations. He could discuss the fine points of strategic issues as well as any flag officer, and Hillary Rodham Clinton was passionately interested in the programs that affected military families and elected the next day to tour facilities on Marine Corps Air Station Kaneohe instead of spending time with her daughter.

I had the chance to observe firsthand the subtle diplomatic skills of the Clinton administration when I accompanied the President's party, including Secretary of State Madeleine Albright and her deputy secretary, Strobe Talbott, to Helsinki in March 1997 for a summit meeting with Russian President Boris Yeltsin.

I had been the military representative on Strobe's Russia group that was grappling with U.S.-Russia and NATO-Russia policy. The seemingly most contentious issue, NATO expansion east, was one of the main items on the agenda. We wanted to extend membership to the former Warsaw Pact nations of Hungary, the Czech Republic, and Poland. Before the meeting, Boris Yeltsin restated Russia's opposition to NATO's eastward spread, but then announced in Helsinki that his government was eager to put the Cold War behind them. Surprisingly, that potentially intractable question was relatively quickly resolved, with the Russians accepting a new NATO-Russia charter "in order to minimize the negative consequences" to their country, such as isolation from Europe. In turn, Clinton's team agreed to back a larger Russian role in international economic institutions and support Moscow's membership in the Group of Seven leading industrialized nations.

As the representative of the Chairman of the Joint Chiefs, I provided expert advice to the civilian negotiators establishing a framework for a new Strategic Arms Reduction Treaty to replace the 1992 START II agreement. In this area, Clinton and his senior foreign policy advisers also achieved unexpected triumphs in nuclear arms reductions, breaking a stubborn deadlock.

But the Russians entered the talks worried that superior American missile defense technology would drastically weaken the massive long-range and theater ballistic missile arsenal the Kremlin had inherited from the former Soviet Union and on which Moscow depended for its sense of security in a hostile world. The initial Russian negotiating position was to demand a "speed limit" be placed on American interceptor systems under development for protection against short-range missiles such as the Scud. During Operation Desert Storm, a Scud had scored a direct hit on an American barracks in Dhahran, killing twenty-seven service members. So we had development of theater missile defense systems high on our priority list, and we all worked long into the night to convince the Russian team that their speed limit requirement was impractical and hammered out wording that was acceptable to both sides.

For me, participation at the summit—albeit as a rather small player—was a fascinating experience, which made tangible the connection between strategy and high-level diplomacy. When Yeltsin arrived in the meeting house, fresh from his hospital bed where he had nearly died from heart disease, I heard his deep booming voice reverberate off the ancient walls. He sounded fine to me and I saw the perspiration on President Clinton's face as he sat in his wheelchair, one leg immobilized, still in pain from a knee injury incurred only days before. Afterward, Madeleine Albright announced that the Helsinki summit had produced "historic progress in European security, nuclear arms reduction, and economic cooperation with Russia."

Well, I thought, flying back to Washington in the comfort of *Air Force Two,* the President's backup plane, *I've done a lot of interesting things in my career, but this is the first time I've been an eyewitness to history being made.* With the Cold War declared over, I figured that I probably would not have enough time left to witness more while wearing my country's uniform.

———————

In spring 1997, Air Force Chief of Staff Ron Fogelman called me to his Pentagon office.

"Dick, we want to send you out to Hawaii to take over PACAF for two or three years. You can retire after two if you think you've accomplished what you want or go until three years and retire at the thirty-five-year point."

This was good news: The assignment brought a fourth star and the prospect of living in the comfortable Pacific Air Forces commander's quarters on Hickam Air Force Base near Pearl Harbor. The kids wouldn't have to worry about expensive hotels when they came to visit.

PACAF was one of the largest, most diverse commands in the U.S. armed forces. Our area of responsibility stretched from California to the Far East and on to India, from the North Pole to Antarctica, covering an area of forty-four countries with a population of almost three billion. The large components in my command were the Fifth Air Force in Japan, the Seventh Air Force in South Korea, the Thirteenth Air Force on Guam, and the Eleventh Air Force in Alaska.

One of the challenges I faced leading PACAF was adjusting to the accelerating speed at which military innovation was pushing change in strategic doctrine. Dramatic innovations were taking place in the area of Precision-Guided Munitions, which I had helped shepherd through the requirements and acquisition process in the early 1990s when I was in the Air Force acquisition business in the Pentagon. They were now completing their research and development phases and beginning to appear in operational units deployed around the world.

The Joint Direct Attack Munition (JDAM) was a true quantum leap in combat effectiveness, a relatively inexpensive "bolt-on" conversion kit that transformed standard unguided bombs into precision-guided weapons. After the first Gulf War, the Pentagon placed high priority on developing drop-and-forget guidance for aerial munitions that would operate effectively day or night, impervious to overcast, smoke, or sandstorms. The weapon would follow an unerring glide path to a target's exact geographical coordinates as transmitted in data from a constellation of orbiting Global Positioning System (GPS) satellites.

The JDAM cost only $18,000, compared to $730,000 for a Tomahawk cruise missile. And, when dropped from high altitude, the JDAM had the ability to guide itself autonomously to its target more than ten miles away. The weapon system gave new life to the older aircraft and had great potential against the North Korean long-range artillery in the mountain caves above the DMZ. Working the kinks out of the weapon took time, as it required aircraft modifications, but the doomsday specter of attack from massed North Korean artillery began losing much of its menace.

It is important, however, to remember that innovative weapons seldom provide a panacea to strategic problems. In spring 1999, NATO unleashed a bombing campaign against Serbia, Operation Allied Force, in response to the Serbs' ruthless oppression of ethnic Albanians in the southern Yugoslav province of Albania. The campaign was large, involving bases in most NATO allies and over one thousand aircraft, which struck Serb military installations and civilian infrastructure. JDAMs were used in combat for the first time, on the whole with spectacular success.

When a mishap did occur it could be big and politically costly. On the night of May 7, 1999, a B-2 Spirit stealth bomber flying a thirty-hour round trip mission from Whiteman Air Force Base, Missouri, dropped JDAMs on the target coordinates shown on the map to be the Yugoslav Federal Directorate for Supply and Procurement in Belgrade, a vital link in the Serb war effort.

The JDAMs struck their aim-points precisely. Unfortunately, the building they hit was the Chinese Embassy. Three Chinese diplomats were killed, and Beijing accused America of deliberately targeting their embassy, but there was a more mundane explanation. The CIA had provided the coordinates from an out-of-date map; the Air Force loaded those coordinates into the JDAMs, and the bombs worked perfectly.

The lesson learned was brutally clear: Precision weapons strike their aim points. It is the responsibility of those who employ them to be certain target coordinates are correct.

In summer 1998, seven months before the Belgrade incident, I got a call from the Air Force Chief of Staff's office. My good friend Mike Ryan said, "The SecDef would like to send you to Colorado Springs to take over Space Command."

So much for two or three years in the Hawaiian sun.

I would wear four joint or Air Force hats in the new assignment: Commander in Chief, North American Aerospace Defense Command (NORAD); Commander, U.S. Space Command (both joint jobs); Commander, Air Force Space Command; and Defense Department manager for contingency support of the Space Transportation System (the Space Shuttle). As with PACAF, running this command demanded a diversity of skills. For example, U.S. Space Command had the demanding responsibility of keeping precise track of the thousands of satellites large and small—some active, most not—as well as the virtual swarm of orbiting space "junk." This was not a hobby: We had to be able to instantly determine if an object on the radar was a fuel tank from an American or Russian booster launched in the 1960s or an incoming missile warhead.

I was not a specialist in space operations, but I was an engineer and had several years' experience commanding large units, so I knew how to recognize problems and set about solving them.

The Titan IV launch rocket presented one of the first major problems that I had to deal with when I took command at Peterson Air Force Base in Colorado Springs. I'd hardly had time to set up my desk when my executive assistant, Col. Roger Burg, entered my office on August 12, 1998.

"General," he said, "a Titan IV launching a big recon satellite exploded twenty seconds after liftoff at the Cape."

"How often does this happen?" I asked.

"Sir," he said, "this is very unusual and it doesn't happen very often."

That was terrible news: Before the *Challenger* disaster in 1986, the United States planned to shift all large payloads—civilian and national security—from expendable boosters to the space shuttle. But when the shuttle proved prone to accidents and flight delays, the Air Force sought reliable boosters to lift large, expensive intelligence and military communications satellites into orbit. So the Defense Department reverted to the huge Titan IV expendable booster to launch these critical payloads while awaiting development of the new heavy-lift Evolved Expendable Launch Vehicle. In 1998, the Lockheed-Martin factory near Denver was building the last Titans under contract, and the assembly line would then shut down.

The Titan IV had flown flawlessly for several years, but a panel from Space Command investigating the August 12 accident determined that faulty wiring in the Titan IV had triggered the destruction of the booster rocket and the unique-design, highly sophisticated spy satellite belonging to the National Reconnaissance Office—a combined loss of almost one billion dollars.

But there was worse to come: In April 1999, the next two Titan IV launches, less than three weeks apart, ended in catastrophic failures of either the booster rocket or its Centaur upper stage. More expensive national security satellites became so much junk on the ocean floor or were marooned in a useless orbit.

This string of disasters could not continue unchecked. Space was essential to our national security. I was the commander, and it was up to me to stanch the hemorrhage of irreplaceable equipment and money and restore a sense of pragmatic optimism among the thousands of civilian contractors and Air Force launch support crews.

I worked with the Air Force leadership to order an immediate moratorium on Titan IV launches and asked the Pentagon to stand up an independent assessment group headed by Gen. Larry Welch, former Air Force Chief of Staff.

My command got terrific support from General Welch's group. Their main findings focused our attention on existing problems in space operations and offered solid guidance on resolving the situation. This guidance involved achieving a dramatic improvement in mission success using existing launch boosters such as the Atlas, Delta, and Titan IV already in production or in inventory while the government worked with contractors to develop the Evolved Expendable Launch Vehicle.

The Welch panel determined that equipment design and engineering, when combined with program management problems in both industry and the Defense Department, "played a prominent role in failures and near misses." We had to bring operational discipline to a business in which every launch was treated somewhat as a science project. Henceforth, everyone involved in building and launching space hardware had to follow strict checklists and know the limits of their authority. People had to be held accountable if mission success was to be achieved. And once the booster and payload were mated and ready for launch, there could be only one boss from the many different organizations involved, and that was the space wing commander.

There were ten more Titan IV missions launching national security payloads valued at $4 billion scheduled to be flown. Each payload was unique, which left no margin for error. (It was interesting that in a business in which we knew we'd have failures, historically around 10 percent, we didn't build spares—too expensive, as the rationale went.) But the existing pattern of building and launching "satellite constellations" based on an assumption of a 100 percent success rate was "unrealistic." Space operations were a complex, inherently risky business. So everyone involved was going to have to bear down and pay much more attention to detail. Nobody wanted another launch failure. Each of the remaining Titan IVs had to operate perfectly.

As we were implementing the many recommendations from the Welch group, I was asked by the contractor to talk to the folks who made the big booster at the plant just outside Denver. I enthusiastically accepted. I stood on a platform in the middle of the factory and addressed the hundreds of people who were responsible for assembling the Titan IV. I simply told them that we had a lot at stake, "our national security," and that all of us had to be as close to flawless as humanly possible from then on out with our Titan launches, and that this process started "right here at the factory." I challenged them to be perfect, noting that the odds were against them. They responded as motivated Americans have always responded and produced ten perfect Titan IVs, even though their assembly line was about to become extinct. The launch crews also performed perfectly. Defying all odds, the last ten Titan IV missions were absolutely faultless.

This had been a vital task. It was the policy of the United States that we would not be the first country to introduce weapons in space, but much of America's national security depended on military space operations. All our armed services relied on satellites for navigation, secure communications, meteorological support, and intelligence. The most sophisticated orbiting platforms under the control of the National Security Agency and the National Reconnaissance Office could eavesdrop on communications or scan the earth's surface across the electromagnetic spectrum, sending back detailed digital imagery day or night in any weather. And many of these large, heavy payloads needed the muscle of the Titan IV to reach space.

At my first combatant commanders' meeting in fall 1998, I got a real surprise. I had attended these Pentagon conferences before as the assistant to the Chairman. Following tradition, the combatant commanders at this meeting were seated around the big mahogany table in order of their time in command, so I sat next to Army Gen. Peter Schoomaker, commander of the U.S. Special Operations Command. (In 2003, he returned to active duty as the Army's Chief of Staff and worked closely with me on the Joint Chiefs of Staff.) Usually, not much that was controversial was discussed at these sessions, nor were major decisions made. This one was different.

Dr. John Hamre, the Deputy Secretary of Defense, had been worried about the department's ability to defend our networks—our "cyberspace." Once he'd asked a group in the Pentagon, "Who is in charge of cyber security?" Everyone raised his or her hand, meaning in effect that no one was in charge.

At this commanders' conference Dr. Hamre stated that he thought the mission of Computer Network Defense (as we called it then) should go to one of the unified commands. But which one? He explained that the geographical commands weren't suited because they were focused only on one region of the world, and this issue would have to be addressed globally.

His conclusion was that this new mission fit pretty neatly into Space Command's portfolio. It was a command that looked globally, was used to working in the virtual world, and had the talent to get this new responsibility moving. At the end of his discussion he asked the other commanders what they thought. They turned to face me: It seemed that they were all too eager to give this hot potato of a mission to SpaceCom.

"Dick," Dr. Hamre said, "are you willing to accept this new mission?"

"Of course," I said, not knowing exactly what I was signing up for. My staff hadn't been warned that this discussion was pending, so I had to go on my gut instinct.

That set in motion a flurry of activity as we tried to learn about this new mission of cyber defense. I asked Mitre Corporation, a federally funded, not-for-profit research center, to come to Colorado Springs and conduct a series of classes to educate us on the threat. Mitre often worked with the Pentagon and other government agencies on complex high-technology problems. I traveled with my staff all over the country to learn about the challenges of defending our networks. We visited major companies, such as Microsoft, and several of the important carriers handling internet traffic. We also started working closely with the intelligence agencies, particularly the CIA and NSA.

We weren't lacking for work at Space Command, but there is nothing more challenging than beginning a new mission, especially one as important as this one. And I believe we were very successful, as the structure, relationships, and procedures we put in place essentially continue today.

My command learned that the cyber threat had many dangerous facets and tentacles. Our country was vulnerable on multiple levels: Cyber warfare could be unleashed by individuals or by nation-states against national security or commercial systems worldwide, which might never realize they were under attack. The more sophisticated a country's information technology became, the more vulnerable it was. One of Space Command's first responsibilities was to work with the U.S. military to bring coherence and focus to the doctrine, organization, and training needed to counter the threat.

One of the unintended consequences of this new mission was that Space Command would become the "supported commander" for Computer Network Defense operations, rather than taking its usual "supporting commander" role for all other operations. This would ruffle some feathers in other commands, and just before I left, we received a message from the Chairman of the Joint Chiefs officially naming us the supported commander for a highly classified Computer Network Defense mission.

It seemed that Space Command was coming of age.

Meanwhile, I was faced with another complex challenge, also related to computer technology. In the late 1990s, the world began to address what became known as the "Y2K Problem": the advent of the year 2000. Since calendars had been adjusted so often since classical times, entering the third millennium was more of a cultural artifact than an event that affected our daily reality—except for one thing: A large percentage of the computer systems that controlled everything from traffic lights to the launch of nuclear missiles depended on internal clocks that could malfunction at the stroke of midnight on January 1, 2000.

Most of the world's software experts were confident the problem could be solved with digital "patches" inserted into the computer code. They were confident but *not* always certain. It was also no secret that some of Russia's older missile systems depended on obsolescent computer hardware and software, so we could not ignore the specter of their warning system's malfunctioning, potentially resulting in an accidental New Year Russian missile launch. The U.S. and Russian governments agreed to establish the Center for Year 2000 Strategic Stability at Peterson Air Force Base, with Russian military officers working side by side with Americans monitoring missile launches and any anomalies in space. This was obviously reassuring, as the media had many stories about the potential for Armageddon.

The international team was assembled by December 1, 1999, standing three shifts around the clock and adjusting to working through interpreters.

Well, I thought, *at least they won't have to hear, "Okay, Duck?"*

But New Year's Eve did not pass without an alarming incident. Around 9:00 P.M., just as I was about to begin a CNN live interview on the Y2K issue in the NORAD Command Warning Center in Cheyenne Mountain, infrared sensors on American satellites detected the unmistakable heat signatures of three missiles launched in southern Russia. We had to close the curtain to hide the center activity from the CNN cameras while we analyzed the situation. For several anxious minutes, as the rocket plumes climbed to the edge of space, we could not determine the nature of the events.

Were these accidentally fired intermediate- or even intercontinental-range ballistic missiles targeting Western Europe or the United States? If the missiles were aimed at America, we would have about thirty minutes to retaliate. But what response would President Clinton order—a nuclear counterstrike for what was almost certainly an accidental launch?

The joint NORAD-Russian team immediately sprang into action to determine what was happening. The Russians spoke anxiously by secure satellite phone to Moscow; NORAD refined its data. Within minutes we saw that the three launches were short-range Scuds the Russians had fired against rebels in Chechnya and had nothing to do with Y2K. We relayed this to our Russian counterparts, and I think they were impressed with our capability to quickly resolve any ambiguity in the analysis of the Scud launches.

While I was confident that all our extensive Y2K work in the previous two years would ensure reliable systems, I did sleep in my office in Cheyenne Mountain that New Year's Eve, forgoing the party scene to be near the command center just in case.

In late summer 1999, Army Gen. Hugh Shelton, Chairman of the Joint Chiefs of Staff, came to Colorado Springs to meet with me and my staff and for the usual briefings on the command. I'd met Hugh when he'd been commander of the U.S. Special Operations Command and thought highly of him. He was a decorated former Green Beret who had fought two combat tours in Vietnam. We were of the same generation: While I was dodging SAMs over North Vietnam, Hugh was fighting down in the jungle.

I knew he would be needing a new Vice Chairman of the Joint Chiefs of Staff and wondered if he'd come to size me up for the job. If so, I must have passed that test, because Hugh called me in early October. He wanted me as his Vice Chairman to replace Air Force Gen. Joe Ralston, who was headed to Europe to become Supreme Allied Commander at NATO.

I called Mary Jo. "Get the suitcases out of the closet. We're going to Washington again." This would be the third position from which I thought I would retire.

7

PRESIDENTIAL ADVISER

Vice Chairman, Then Chairman
of the Joint Chiefs of Staff, the Rise of al-Qaida

In September 1999, before testifying to the Senate Armed Services Committee on my nomination as Vice Chairman of the Joint Chiefs of Staff, I answered a detailed questionnaire. Many of the questions were routine; others probing. I was leaving the relatively predictable milieu of joint command and entering a world that some of my peers had ironically dubbed the "Washington Area of Operations." Here, to be successful, I would have to deal with members of Congress and senior bureaucrats, and they could have a much different agenda from the military's. But I had to work with them in a straightforward manner, as I had been taught in the military culture, a culture which often could be very different from the civilian government world. I hadn't served full-time in Washington since I was a three-star assistant to General Shali in 1997, so my understanding of this new challenge was still evolving.

The Armed Services Committee questionnaire provided the chance to express my views on the complex relationship among the Vice Chairman, the Chairman, the Joint Chiefs of Staff, the civilian leadership of the Pentagon, and the President. One of the most important questions—asked of all senior officers—was whether I would give my personal views in congressional testimony even if they differed from those of the "administration in power." My answer was a straightforward "yes." Civilian political appointees are not asked this question.

Following tradition, I formally pledged my full support to the Constitution, the President, the Congress, the Secretary of Defense, the Chairman of the Joint Chiefs of Staff, and the men and women of the armed forces. But I did not name any of these officials. If confirmed, my term would begin in March 2000—an election year—and extend into a new administration. On January 20, 2001, when the incoming President took his oath of office on the Capitol steps, I would have a new Commander in Chief, even though it was President Clinton who had nominated me and under whom I'd serve my first year as Vice Chairman. The political party of the new President would not enhance or diminish his constitutional authority, and like my peers, I would salute the outgoing and the incoming Presidents with equal sincerity.

Although I didn't expect my confirmation to be politically contentious, controversy was possible on specific issues, because Congress was controlled by Republicans and the White House by the Democratic Clinton administration. I knew full well that there would be times when attempts would be made to pull me into partisan debates. But my challenge was to remain politically neutral, avoid partisan traps, and respond to congressional questions in a forthright and honest manner. I felt very strongly then, as I do now, that the professional military must be completely apolitical, so I had even stopped voting upon reaching senior flag rank, as General Marshall had done while he was in office.

The Senate Armed Services Committee sought my opinion on the Goldwater-Nichols Act's (GNA) impact on the military "reforms" the law initiated. I stressed that the act had dramatically strengthened "the war-fighting capabilities of our combatant commands and facilitated the evolution of a truly joint force."

But this was still very much a work in progress: Not all the goals of a joint force had yet been achieved.

The committee asked for specific comments on the "areas of responsibility" I anticipated Chairman of the Joint Chiefs of Staff Hugh Shelton would assign me. This was the type of question all candidates for Vice Chairman answered. To the best of my understanding, my responsibilities were clearly specified under Title 10, United States Code. Beyond the standard duties, I would have the responsibility of serving as Chairman of the Joint Requirements Oversight Council (JROC).

Most Americans, including the majority of Congress, had never heard of the JROC, and only a handful understood the importance of the body. Despite its obscure status outside the Pentagon, however, serving as chairman of the JROC would be among my most critical duties. Under the Goldwater-Nichols Act, the council was composed of the vice chiefs of staff of each service and the J8 of the Joint Staff, who was responsible for analysis of force structure and overseeing the resources of the armed forces.

In the JROC, the traditional pattern of the service branches rubber-stamping an aircraft, ship, or armored vehicle that was favored by one—with the expectation that their counterparts would do the same for *their* favorite plane, tank, or artillery system—would have to change. And I would be responsible for continuing to implement that change.

I remembered a JROC meeting I had attended as a two-star on the Air Force Staff. The issue under discussion that day was a new Army anti-armor weapon system. All the members seemed inclined to back it. But then the JROC chairman, Adm. David Jeremiah, asked a simple question: "How many similar anti-armor systems do we already have in the Department of Defense inventory and how many do we *need*?" Nobody sitting around the table knew for sure, but the members estimated about twenty-five.

Unfortunately, we hadn't had the processes or the analytical tools in place during the early 1990s to properly answer Admiral Jeremiah's question. Now, however, we were much closer to being able to do so, and I would spend a great deal of time as Vice Chairman with the service chiefs, trying to develop a process that would answer such important questions. This exacting process took up a significant part of my time as Vice Chairman. The task occurred outside public scrutiny, but my evolution as a senior military leader matured as I worked side by side with my flag-rank colleagues, shaping our future military.

When I became Vice Chairman, the Defense Department was continuing the process of "transformation," moving into the twenty-first century toward a leaner, more flexible structure and away from the vestiges of the Cold War. Under the concept of transformation I believed in, we needed new organizations, doctrine, and training as well as material solutions that took advantage of rapidly changing technology, which would allow us to function as effectively as possible in the multidimensional "battlespace" (land, sea, undersea, air, space, and cyberspace). Most important, our military leadership would have to be agile and flexible, as would the capabilities of our services. In my view, real transformation happened first "between the ears," not in a new technology or system. Abandoning stale approaches and embracing new ways to defend the nation and support its armed forces were the keys to transforming the military.

Transformation would apply to the new security arena, in which the risk was less defined than the Soviet threat and more uncertainty entered in the security equation. Since technology was changing rapidly and was almost always expensive, we had to maintain control of our limited budget: Any acquisition of costly new weapon systems had to be carefully weighed. Because uncertainty characterized this period, the members of the JROC sensed that major transformation was looming on the horizon, making our task all the more urgent.

Whatever the nature of the new administration that would take over on January 20, 2001, the American military would have to accelerate the process of transformation. The Clinton administration had made some significant advances in military transformation, particularly in overseeing development of GPS-guided JDAM bombs, new sealift ships, and Unmanned Aerial Vehicles (UAVs). But transformation is an unending task and much remained to be done.

At the Citadel in Charleston, South Carolina, in September 1999, Republican presidential candidate George W. Bush had made a major speech on the challenges the armed services faced and the need for transformation. Beyond the strength and patriotism of our young men and women in uniform, Bush said, our national defense needed thorough modernization. This ranged from a practical shield against intercontinental and theater ballistic missiles launched by rogue nations, to strengthening the intelligence community to penetrate international terrorist networks both here and abroad. We must also develop long-range strike capability and Special Operations Forces (SOF) to launch a "strong and swift offense" against terrorists. Bush emphasized that power "is increasingly defined, not by mass or size, but rather by mobility and swiftness. Influence is measured in information, safety is gained in stealth, and force is projected on the long arc of precision-guided weapons. This revolution perfectly matches the strengths of our country—the skill of our people and superiority of our technology."

Reading a newspaper account of the Citadel speech, I saw that Bush had done his homework and was passionate about making our military more relevant in the twenty-first century. I thought it was good to see a presidential candidate speak seriously about military matters. I hoped that other candidates would give similar thought to the need to continue our transformation efforts.

————————

As Vice Chairman, I was a member of the National Security Council Deputies Committee and charged to stay abreast of operations and policy debates. The committee was made up of the "number twos" of the principal NSC members. The deputies usually analyzed the issues first and then presented options to the principals, the leaders of the departments and agencies represented on the National Security Council. In some cases the Vice Chairman would represent the Chairman at Principal Committee or National Security Council meetings in the Chairman's absence.

Senator John Warner wrote me to say he wanted to be sure I clearly understood the national chain of command that GNA had established. He formally reminded me that it ran from the President to the Secretary of Defense and on to the combatant commanders. "Other sections and law and traditional practice, however," he added in his letter, established "important relationships" in the national security structure. Senator Warner asked me to describe my understanding of the relationship of the Vice Chairman to the senior positions in the Defense Department. These included the Deputy Secretary; the under and assistant secretaries; the Chairman of the Joint Chiefs of Staff and his assistant; the Director of the Joint Staff; the secretaries of the military departments; the Chiefs of Staff of the services; and the combatant commanders.

I outlined my understanding of the functions of the Office of the Secretary of Defense (OSD), the Chairman of the Joint Chiefs of Staff, the Joint Staff, and the combatant commanders. I saw the Chairman's office and the Joint Staff working as collaboratively as possible with the under and assistant secretaries of defense. In addition, the Chairman would be the spokesman for the combatant commanders, linking them to elements of the entire Department of Defense. The Joint Staff was a large, complex organization, assembled to support the Chairman, the Vice Chairman, and other members of the Joint Chiefs of Staff in their responsibility to provide military advice to our national leadership. It was composed of over a thousand men and women of the uniformed services and civilians, divided into eight major directorates led by flag officers and focused on traditional areas of responsibility, from J1 (Manpower and Personnel), to J2 (Intelligence), to J3 (Operations) . . . to J8 (Force Structure Resources and Assessment).

One of my most important missions was to advise the Secretary of Defense. A critical element was to maintain close contact with Deputy Secretary of Defense John Hamre, the second-highest-ranking Pentagon official, and other senior OSD officials. The one with whom I worked closest was the Undersecretary of Defense for Policy, Walt Slocombe. We'd first met in Japan and got along well. My most important relationship was with the Chairman of the Joint Chiefs of Staff. Although Gen. Hugh Shelton was the principal military adviser to the National Command Authority (NCA), the Chairman was not in the chain of command. But by custom, the Secretary of Defense had always directed that all communications addressed to him pass though the Chairman. Because of my close partnership with Hugh I would see all the important messages. This flow was instrumental in enabling the Chairman to oversee the combatant commanders' activities, be their advocate, and stay informed so he could provide military advice to the President, the Secretary of Defense, and the NSC. I would be at the nexus of this relationship, which acted largely out of public view.

The fact was that the majority of Americans did not understand the statutory powers of the OSD, the Chairman of the Joint Chiefs of Staff, his Vice Chairman, and the combatant commands, which were delineated in great detail in Title 10 of the U.S. Code. After all, the Cold War was over; the United States had emerged from the long struggle as the sole remaining superpower.

———————

The Senate confirmed my nomination that fall, and I was sworn in as the Vice Chairman of the Joint Chiefs of Staff on March 1, 2000. I entered the position with complex emotions. I felt well prepared for the duties I would be asked to undertake, and I hoped I was worthy of the tremendous responsibility I'd just been given.

Within a few months, after visiting the combatant commanders' headquarters and working almost daily on difficult JROC issues, I felt that I'd gotten a fair understanding of the Vice Chairman's complex job. Above all, I came to view my responsibilities from a global perspective, weighing the strategic challenges and potential contributions that all the armed services brought to the table. I had begun my military career as a second lieutenant Air Force pilot thirty-five years earlier, but my horizons had widened to almost unrecognizable dimensions since then. Even so, as a four-star general and Vice Chairman of the Joint Chiefs of Staff, I had to keep my eyes on the horizon just as carefully as I had flying those little Cessna 150s out of the Manhattan, Kansas, airport.

Being chairman of the JROC was every bit as interesting, and as challenging, as I'd anticipated, especially because Hugh Shelton expected decisiveness and a service-neutral perspective on my part, although some of my fellow council members were occasionally torn between advocating what their particular service sought and advocating what the DoD really needed.

Shelton was a tough soldier who had fought two tours in Vietnam as a young Green Beret and an Airborne officer. He'd commanded infantry forces at division level and been the J3 Operations Officer of the Joint Staff before serving as commander, U.S. Special Operations Command. His resolve and integrity were well known to all who worked with him, and so was his reputation as a thoughtful, no-nonsense officer.

The Chairman wanted the JROC to do its job in a truly "joint" manner, to think beyond parochial service loyalty, and to help modernize the entire armed services establishment. I certainly agreed: My having a joint perspective was important to maintain credibility among my colleagues. There would always be a few who saw the world through the prism of their individual service's interests, although the council members were usually able to overcome service bias for the greater good.

Early in my JROC tenure, we grappled with a typical procurement issue: the design and budgeting of advanced secure satellite communications systems. The proposed new "constellations" of communications satellites operated on the extreme high frequency upper end of the radio band. Their encrypted up- and down-links were virtually immune from jamming and eavesdropping. Capable of linking surface units via satellite to each other to overhead reconnaissance platforms, to regional command centers, and to combatant command headquarters, in voice, visual image, and data stream, the new generation of communications systems was highly valued—especially by surface combatants—and promised to cut through the blinding "fog of war" that had gripped battlefields for millennia. I learned in my time at U.S. Space Command that these systems were critical to a transformed military capability.

But the architecture of the system—including the satellites, launch services, and ground stations—could be a budget-buster for the service shouldering the lion's share of the burden, in this case, the Air Force. The Army, Navy, and

Marine Corps wanted the new satellites, and they wanted the Air Force to pay for them out of its budget. Even inside the Air Force there were those who wanted the capability and who weren't sensitive to the cost and budget implications for their parent service.

The arm wrestling began. But we eventually ended up with an equitable distribution of costs and benefits. Although the JROC tended to favor the warfighters, we also had to be sensitive to costs: A new system that a service might covet could also prove so expensive that it would take away resources needed elsewhere.

Beyond this particular system, I made sure we tried to develop new ways to think about military requirements. Was a proposed weapon or system redundant or did it fill a definite joint need? Did it fit in with the way we thought we'd fight? The JROC began working on operational concepts, not just hardware. Operational concepts were formal documents that we developed on how we would fight. The service chiefs and combatant commanders became personally involved in writing these documents. This was good: Over the years I'd learned that engaging the senior people early in the decision-making process bettered the chances of reaching a sensible solution and compromise where required.

The JROC helped accomplish some of the transformation goals that I thought were so important for our Armed Forces.

———————

In summer 2000, European Command (EUCOM) and the Joint Chiefs became involved with the secret effort to capture two of the worst war criminals to emerge from the years of bloodshed in the former Yugoslavia: Ratko Mladić, commander of the Bosnian Serb Army in the mid-1990s, and Radovan Karadžic, political leader of the separatist Serb Republic of Bosnia. Together, they had directed a campaign of brutal ethnic cleansing, widespread torture and assassination, and outright massacre of Bosnian, Croat, and Muslim civilians.

Although we tried hard to capture them with Special Operations Forces raids, the two war criminals slipped through our net. We gathered a lot of fascinating intelligence, almost all of it concerning where they had just *been,* not where they were going to be.

Any time our military needed authority to use forces outside the European theater of operations, Supreme Allied Commander, Europe (SALEUR) Gen. Joe Ralston would call me to get the Secretary's verbal approval to deploy troops. One reason Joe had no qualms about waking me in the middle of the night was that he had been in my shoes for four years—and, he'd always say with a chuckle, "It's a lot easier to wake up the Vice Chairman than the Chairman."

On several occasions we sent in Special Ops teams to lie in roadside ambushes or search fugitive safe houses. Although we were successful in capturing lower-level indicted war criminals, and even though we had hundreds of people dedicated full-time to capturing Mladić and Karadžic, they evaded us.

We remained hopeful of unraveling their patterns of behavior—telecommunications, the movement of known associates or family—that might deliver the "actionable intelligence" we sought. But we never received intelligence precise enough to allow us to launch a successful special operation. And we couldn't just launch cruise missiles against fugitives' boltholes, especially in cities where a significant number of civilians might be at risk.

The lesson learned from the unsuccessful manhunt for Karadžic and Mladić was that capturing individuals, as opposed to groups of enemy combatants, was extremely difficult. Further, the two had achieved hero status in the eyes of nationalist Serbs and could expect that the shield their followers held over them would remain in place indefinitely.

It was not until late July 2008, over twelve years after the Bosnian War, that Serbian authorities finally captured Radovan Karadžic and started the process of extradition to the international tribunal in the Hague. Mladić remains at large.

Their long period of evading capture revealed the often tangled boundary between criminal justice and military action. There was little doubt that the two Bosnian Serbs were notorious criminals, but there were no law enforcement agencies available or willing to apprehend them. That mission fell to the military, and it proved to be an almost impossible task.

The military is often better at *recording* lessons observed than at *learning* those lessons. If we had absorbed the lessons of hunting individuals from Bosnia, we might have been better prepared in 2001. Late that year, a very similar situation played out in the mountains of eastern Afghanistan and the autonomous tribal areas just across the Pakistani border. After the 9/11 attack, the United States and its allies had toppled Afghanistan's Taliban and sent their al-Qaida allies into flight. Many—including top leaders like Usama bin Laden and Ayman al-Zawahiri—sought and received asylum, most likely from the tribal councils of Waziristan near Pakistan's Khyber Pass frontier with Afghanistan. Once again, tracking the movements of a few wanted men hiding amid thousands of loyal partisans, especially in such difficult terrain, proved a difficult mission.

On Thursday, October 12, 2000, I was asleep in our quarters at Fort Myer, just north of Arlington National Cemetery. My phone rang before dawn, usually a bad sign. There had been a serious explosion aboard the USS *Cole*, a *Burke*-class guided-missile destroyer transiting the Red Sea en route to the Persian Gulf. The ship had made a routine refueling stop in the Yemeni port of Aden at the southern tip of the Arabian Peninsula.

At the Pentagon that morning, details on the situation came in slowly and were confusing and contradictory—what we expected from first reports on a badly damaged vessel in a remote location. But by noon in Washington, we were able to assemble a fairly clear picture of events in Aden. While the *Cole* was moored at a fueling buoy, an open boat disguised as a garbage scow passed near the ship and then veered sharply into the destroyer's port side to detonate a massive explosion.

The powerful blast obliterated the scow, killing the two suicide bombers and blasting a gaping forty-by-forty-foot hole in the ship's hull, almost vaporizing the galley. The attack had occurred at 11:18 A.M. local time, just as sailors were lining up for lunch. Seventeen sailors were killed instantly, and at least forty others were seriously injured, many of these with terrible burns. The *Cole* was dead in the water, barely able to keep its pumps working as the surviving crew fought to save their ship.

CENTCOM commander Gen. Tommy Franks, scheduled to leave his Tampa, Florida, headquarters for the region that morning, had ordered rapid response teams to Aden. French Navy ships from their nearby base in Djibouti on the Horn of Africa and British Royal Navy ships cruising nearby sped to the port to help with medical evacuation.

For the moment, the U.S. military had done as much as possible. Over the coming days and weeks, FBI forensic investigators determined that the scow had been laden with powerful military-grade explosives. Obviously, a well-organized and highly motivated terrorist organization had been involved. And the most likely suspects were al-Qaida and its leader, Usama bin Laden. We had seen their work before.

In February 1998, al-Qaida, which had several thousand adherents and at least several hundred active operatives in sixty countries, had issued a religiously based fatwa calling on all Muslims to do their utmost to kill Western civilians and military. This fatwa targeted the United States, its allies, and Israel for a campaign of unrelenting violence. In effect, al-Qaida had declared war on the West—but few in the West took notice.

Our intelligence community had worked long and hard to acquire a reasonable understanding of al-Qaida and its principal leaders, especially the once wealthy Saudi exile Usama bin Laden (commonly referred to as "UBL" in intelligence reports) and his key deputy, Egyptian fugitive doctor and Islamic revolutionary Ayman al-Zawahiri. But we still did not have enough actionable intelligence to allow us to strike an effective blow against the group.

Usama bin Laden had spent part of the 1980s in Afghanistan struggling against the Soviet occupation. With a perseverance grounded in fundamentalist Muslim zealotry, he eventually built a small but fanatically loyal inner circle. In 1988, he and several close associates had broken away from other primarily Arab fundamentalists in Afghanistan and formed al-Qaida, literally the "Base" or the "Foundation."

Al-Qaida's guiding doctrine was grounded in a dogmatic Salafism, which sought to recreate in the modern world—beginning in Arab and other Muslim nations, and then spreading across the globe—the glory of Islam's first three generations following the Prophet Muhammad in the sixth century A.D. Salafism was a rigid belief system contending that the contemporary world was decadent, due to the sinfulness of non-Muslims—particularly Jews, Americans, Europeans, and Russians.

For Usama bin Laden's radical Salafists, the first order of business was dominating what they saw as wayward Arab states such as Saudi Arabia and secular countries such as Egypt. Salafism was puritanically Sunni Muslim in its dogma and viewed the smaller Shiite branch of Islam as heretical. Once the Salafists of al-Qaida had dominated the Muslim world, they would turn their attention to areas where Islam had once held sway, including Spain, the Balkans, and Central Asia. They would eventually undermine the West, in particular the United States. An al-Qaida internet website showed a series of world maps that charted this inexorable progression toward the twenty-first-century Caliphate, which incorporated spiritual and temporal authority and reflected the glory of the seventh-century Caliphate.

The al-Qaida map revealed Africa, Western Europe, most of Russia and Central Asia, large areas of China, and, of course, North and South America under the dominion of Salafist Islam. Rather than be discouraged by the monumental challenge of their mission, al-Qaida's leaders embraced it—all the more so because of the promise of martyrdom inherent in the struggle, which attracted zealous young volunteers to the cause.

The war that al-Qaida had declared was not going to be a short, easy struggle.

———————————

On returning to Saudi Arabia from Afghanistan, after the Afghan war with the Soviets, Usama bin Laden sought the violent overthrow and destruction of his enemies, no matter who or where they were. And the United States was high on the list of his foes.

His hatred of America and our Western allies intensified in 1990 when the Western Coalition stationed large numbers of troops in Saudi Arabia to liberate Kuwait from Iraqi occupation. Under growing pressure from the Saudi royal government in 1992, bin Laden shifted al-Qaida operations to Khartoum, the capital of Sudan, which he hoped to convert into a suitable launch pad for his global extremist Islamic revolution while continuing to chastise the Saudi monarchy. The Saudis reacted by demanding the Sudanese confiscate bin Laden's passport and pressured his family to cut off an annual multi-million-dollar stipend to him. In effect, Usama bin Laden was now an impoverished, stateless refugee. But he relished this role, which brought him a tinge of righteous martyrdom and a closeness to his indigent warriors.

In 1996, Usama bin Laden led the al-Qaida exodus from Sudan back to Afghanistan, which was in the grip of a civil war among tribal factions and religious extremists for control of the war-ravaged country. Meanwhile, money poured into al-Qaida's coffers from a wide spectrum of extremist Muslim sources, which included the original Arab mujahideen supporters and the Pakistani Inter-Services-Intelligence branch. Partially shielded from outside scrutiny by the factional struggle in Afghanistan, Usama bin Laden established camps and a fortified headquarters near the border with Pakistan.

The civil strife in Afghanistan had ushered in the rule of the Taliban, a group of fundamentalists even more extreme than bin Laden and al-Qaida. The Taliban were almost totally composed of ethnic Pashtun tribesmen from the east and south of Afghanistan, who made up more than 40 percent of the country's population. Led by a ruthless zealot named Mullah Mohammed Omar, the Taliban overwhelmed their rivals among the principal ethnic minorities: the Tajik, Hazara, and Uzbeks.

After capturing the capital, Kabul, the Taliban unleashed the most repressive form of sharia (Islamic law). Music, movies, and other forms of popular entertainment were banned. As the Taliban consolidated their power, their prohibitive edicts increased: dancing, artistic or photographic depictions of humans, even kite flying were added to the list of forbidden distractions from the pursuit of pure Islam.

Girls were restricted to only three years of education. Most women were not allowed to work outside their homes and were required to wear a head-to-toe burqa with just a narrow slit for vision. Unless accompanied by a male relative, women had to be treated by female doctors, who were rare at best.

The Taliban leadership replaced all Hazara, Tajik, and Uzbek civil servants, many with technical or Western education, with Pashtun loyalists, mostly educated in madrassa religious schools. The ethnic tension became severe when Taliban militias swarmed north to the city of Mazar-e-Sharif and massacred more than eight thousand Hazara and Uzbek civilians.

This slaughter and the Taliban's relentless drive to control all of Afghanistan helped spark the creation of the Northern Alliance, a confederation of Tajik, Uzbek, and Panjsheri tribesmen, all veteran guerrilla fighters from the Soviet occupation. Ahmad Shah Massoud, a university-educated Panjsheri, had been one of the fiercest and most successful anti-Soviet leaders. Under pressure from the Taliban, he brought the Northern Alliance together in well-defended mountain redoubts, a bastion from which they repulsed repeated Taliban attack. By 1998, there was a stalemate. The Northern Alliance were probably the better fighters, but the Taliban had more troops, weapons, and equipment.

The Taliban's Islamic Emirate of Afghanistan had become a failed state whose only diplomatic recognition came from Saudi Arabia, Pakistan, and the United Arab Emirates. This situation suited Usama bin Laden well: Landlocked Afghanistan had a very porous eastern border with Pakistan's semiautonomous tribal districts. It seemed unlikely that al-Qaida's enemies would reach the organization in its Afghan sanctuary. Meanwhile, bin Laden and al-Qaida forged a tight bond with the Taliban. Not only did al-Qaida train Taliban guerrillas in techniques such as sabotage and battlefield communications, bin Laden supplied his Afghan hosts with funding and modern weapons. In return, al-Qaida now had both the protection of Afghanistan's geographical isolation and the military shield of large Taliban armed forces.

Further, the undeniable fact that the Taliban and al-Qaida had equally rigid ideologies ruled out any possibility of negotiation or reasonable discourse with them. Both groups had embraced jihad and would gladly accept martyrdom rather than compromise.

As our national security establishment slowly came to grips with the seriousness of this situation, none of us considered the struggle in Afghanistan—or al-Qaida's intentions—a major threat to our national security. Many, myself included, saw this more as a tactical than a strategic challenge for our country. Further, this was a new kind of problem for the United States. We had fought nation-states; we had been engaged in long guerrilla wars and insurgencies. But we had never struggled on a global scale with ruthless, shadowy groups motivated by religious zealotry that were hard to define as enemy formations under standard criteria. At that time, the closest we could come to defining the problem was the inadequate term "non-state players" that were engaged in "asymmetric warfare" against us.

And most Americans did not understand the true nature of the threat these groups represented, which, in any case, did not seem a danger to our daily life.

But in 1998, soon after bin Laden issued his jihad fatwa, al-Qaida terrorists in East Africa bombed our embassies in Kenya and Tanzania, killing twelve Americans and 212 foreign civilians. The United States reacted, launching cruise missile attacks. These very attacks, however, made us appear weak, desperate, and inept to our adversaries. One attack destroyed the al-Shifa pharmaceutical factory near the Sudanese capital of Khartoum, which the CIA estimated was being used to produce chemical weapons for use by al-Qaida. The second cruise missile strike was against known al-Qaida training camps around Khost and Jalalabad in eastern Afghanistan. U.S. warships launched seventy-five cruise missiles against the three major Afghan camps, destroying many of the tents and buildings. But, overall, the results of these strikes were meager: Our intelligence sources could find no hard evidence that the Khartoum factory had in fact been producing chemical weapons, and after the attacks on the Afghan camps we learned that Usama bin Laden and his senior associates had left the Zawhar Kili training center only hours before the cruise missile strike.

Even after the *Cole* attack, I, along with most Americans, did not grasp the true gravity of the threat violent international extremism posed. The African embassy bombings had been tragic—but almost all of the dead had been Kenyans and Tanzanians—and the Americans who were killed had volunteered to serve abroad. The death toll on the *Cole* was also tragic, but like our Foreign Service personnel, those sailors were voluntarily serving in dangerous waters. The important question seemed to be whether the American people would be willing to approve a major military response once we could definitively prove al-Qaida had attacked the *Cole*.

Largely out of public view, however, the Clinton administration vigorously pursued options to strike al-Qaida and Usama bin Laden.

But al-Qaida's Afghan sanctuary remained virtually immune from direct attack. First, Afghanistan was a sovereign country, a member of the United Nations and other international organizations. The country's isolated, landlocked location also protected al-Qaida from "boots on the ground" Special Operations Forces raids because airborne or helicopter-borne missions would require overflight permission from neighboring countries. Even without overflight permission, detection of incoming aircraft could have jeopardized operational security. Further, there never was the exact intelligence needed for a precision air strike (assuming we could get overflight permission).

Nevertheless, planners in the U.S. Special Operations Command (SOCOM) worked hard on scenarios in which our elite units could be inserted to capture or kill Usama bin Laden and his chief lieutenants. No matter how carefully our military planned, however, each proposed operation included a relatively large logistics support "tail" and was considered too risky, with too little chance of reward.

As the former SOCOM commander, Hugh Shelton understood full well how difficult and potentially unfeasible these plans were. They only highlighted how hostile Afghanistan was as an operational environment and the difficulty of carrying out military operations without a solid logistics base somewhere nearby. Although al-Qaida could move freely back and forth between Pakistan and Afghanistan, American SOF units could not and would almost certainly be detected and attacked. But—despite the policy dilemma President Clinton faced—if we *had* been able to present him viable options, I'm convinced he would have approved military action.

Defense Secretary William S. Cohen, the sole Republican in the Clinton cabinet, was a former congressman and three-term U.S. senator from Maine, and a good man to work for—supportive of the military, decisive, and willing to listen to our advice. Although the Clinton White House was leaning on him fairly hard to pull some kind of Special Ops rabbit out of his hat and snatch bin Laden in Afghanistan, Cohen listened to the professionals in uniform.

There was consensus among the professional military that we couldn't use SOF in a small "surgical" manner and expect success. If we went into Afghanistan after bin Laden and al-Qaida, we would most probably also have to engage the Taliban. Although America had no diplomatic relations with Afghanistan, we did acknowledge the existence of the Taliban government and communicated with them—mainly about humanitarian relief efforts. Even small special operation ground units would require air support ranging from helicopters to AC-130 Spectre gunships, and perhaps fighter-bombers carrying Precision-Guided Munitions. In effect, we would be launching an undeclared war that would require overflight of Pakistan or Central Asian republics, and would probably be viewed by our civilian leaders as a politically dicey act in the 2000 election year.

———————

Probably the strongest indication that Usama bin Laden and the other al-Qaida leaders feared a significant American reprisal for the *Cole* bombing was the fact that they waited until 2001 before claiming responsibility for the attack. Then, al-Qaida circulated a recruitment video obliquely citing its own role. Although bin Laden appeared throughout the hundred-minute tape, he never accepted personal responsibility. Instead the video showed masked terrorists training in an Afghan camp as a rousing song chanted in Arabic, "We thank God for granting us victory the day we destroyed *Cole* in the sea." Another image showed a blazing explosion with Arabic script superimposed: "The destruction of the American destroyer *Cole*."

This was very persuasive evidence of culpability. But the evidence was not sufficient for a criminal indictment against Usama bin Laden, who *had* been indicted for al-Qaida's involvement in the African embassy bombings. Instead the Justice Department named Usama bin Laden as an "unindicted coconspirator" in the attack.

By mid-2008, more than twenty al-Qaida members convicted in Yemeni courts of conspiracy in the *Cole* bombing had either escaped from prison or been released as part of a Yemeni government amnesty.

———————

Like our fellow Americans, those of us serving in uniform on the Pentagon E-Ring watched fascinated as the results of the 2000 presidential election finally reached a conclusion in the Supreme Court. Most of us did not know President-elect George W. Bush personally. But during the campaign he had continued to stress the importance of transforming the military. Now he would have the chance to try implementing those ideas, a task made more difficult by the hair-thin Republican majority in both houses of Congress. My colleagues and I were frustrated by the lack of nuanced military options for dealing with al-Qaida. And we had a shared sense of urgency about transforming our military so we could offer the President viable alternatives.

The service chiefs and senior officers on the Joint Staff met the President when he came to a Pentagon briefing soon after his inauguration. We found a leader who was knowledgeable about military matters, who knew when to ask questions and—equally important—when to listen. As to the accusation that he was inarticulate, President Bush freely admitted with a grin that he occasionally "murdered the English language." (He would sometimes mischievously throw in a "strat-ter-gery" or "nu-cu-lear" at National Security Council meetings just to lighten the atmosphere.)

This sense of humor and self-deprecation made the personal interaction between the President and the military more pleasant. But even if he had been unfriendly, our overall acceptance of the central principle underpinning our service—adherence to civilian control of the military—would have remained constant.

The new Vice President, Dick Cheney, was familiar in the Pentagon, having served as Secretary of Defense during the Gulf War. A former Wyoming congressman and chief of staff of the Ford White House, he had earned a reputation as a politically astute government official and successful corporate executive who kept the news media at arm's length. I had briefed Cheney several times when he was SecDef and found him to be a good listener and very logical in his decisions.

Secretary of State Colin Powell was the administration's senior cabinet member and fourth overall in the presidential line of succession. Having served as National Security Adviser to President Ronald Reagan and as Chairman of the Joint Chiefs of Staff under President George H. W. Bush, Powell was very familiar with defense processes. He was not hesitant to share his views in any forum, always put his cards on the table, and examined issues from a well-balanced worldview.

Dr. Condoleezza Rice was a true professional with great respect for the military. She had been special assistant to the director of the Joint Chiefs of Staff in the 1980s. As an academic, she was a recognized expert on the Soviet Union and Eastern Europe before eventually being appointed provost of Stanford University, the youngest person, the first woman, and the first African

American to hold that position. In addition to her other accomplishments, such as fluency in Russian and French, Condi Rice was a talented classical pianist.

Her deputy, Stephen Hadley, was my counterpart on the National Security Council Deputies Committee, composed of the second-ranking people from the NSC, the State Department, the CIA, and the Defense Department. We met frequently to discuss the same topics as the NSC principals. I found Steve an ideal public servant, experienced, hardworking, never seeking the limelight, just results. Steve had a Yale law degree and had served in the Clinton Defense Department as a NATO and missile defense policy expert, where I had some contact with him when I was assistant to the Chairman.

My only regret as the new NSC team came on board in January 2001 was that Condoleezza Rice canceled the participation of the non-political-appointee members of the deputies committee at the informal lunches that we had held during the Clinton administration. This meant that the Vice Chairman of the Joint Chiefs of Staff and the deputy CIA director would not attend. I pushed back on this decision on a couple of occasions—to no avail. These meetings had been very helpful, allowing the deputies to exchange ideas freely in an informal setting. In my view, Washington needs more such interaction to augment the formal process. My experience was that this provided the grease to get the hard issues solved.

Donald H. Rumsfeld, the incoming Secretary of Defense, had the most varied résumé of any recent cabinet secretary. He began his public service as a naval pilot and flight instructor following graduation from Princeton University. Like Cheney, Rumsfeld had been a congressman, serving four terms in the 1960s from a suburban Chicago district before resigning to work in the Nixon White House. While serving as U.S. Ambassador to NATO in Brussels, he was called back to Washington to direct the transition team of President Gerald R. Ford. Rumsfeld went on to become Ford's chief of staff and then became Secretary of Defense in 1974, at forty-three, the youngest person to hold that office.

After his service in the Ford administration, Rumsfeld spent the next twenty-two years in the private sector, rising to become chairman of a worldwide pharmaceutical giant. He transformed the company from a financially troubled institution into a global leader in the field. He went on to head another leading pharmaceutical firm and a high-technology company. While engaged in this successful business career, Rumsfeld found time to chair the bipartisan U.S. Ballistic Missile Commission and the U.S. Commission to Assess National

Security Space Management and Organization and a number of other national security advisory boards. I was Vice Chairman when I met Rumsfeld, who was then heading the Space Commission.

I found him to be an insightful and incisive leader. As Rumsfeld monitored the discussions of the scientists and military space leaders, he watched closely through his polished rimless trifocals, and I got the impression that very little if anything escaped his attention.

That initial impression was confirmed during Rumsfeld's initial weeks as Secretary of Defense. If the cliché "hit the ground running" applied to anyone, it was Donald Rumsfeld. Although at sixty-eight he was the oldest person to be sworn in as Secretary, Rumsfeld had greater intellectual curiosity and energy than people decades younger. He questioned everything and took very little at face value. We quickly learned that "this is just how we do business here" was *never* the appropriate answer for the new Secretary of Defense.

His immediate response would be, "Why?"

Because his curiosity was so insatiable, Rumsfeld devoured information, peppering OSD staff and officers on the Joint Staff with an avalanche of memos that quickly became known as "snowflakes" because they were typed on plain white paper devoid of seals of office. The blizzard of memos from the SecDef's stand-up desk in his large third-floor office might only be a dozen on a quiet Wednesday, but could number fifty or more the next day. Some were only a few lines; others contained several pages, each one listing multiple questions.

The subjects of the snowflakes also varied widely and were seldom predictable. Rumsfeld often used the memos to capture his thoughts, sometimes dictating the memo into a pocket tape recorder or jotting the text onto a note card to be transcribed later. This was a management tool he had developed earlier in his government service, one that he took with him into the private sector. He might work on snowflakes early in the morning at the stand-up desk or record them in the backseat of his official sedan en route to a meeting.

A memo could curtly address the staff's apparent tardiness in answering an earlier query. I remember one in the winter of 2001 that chided us for not replying to his questions in what he considered a timely fashion:

". . . Almost two weeks have passed.

"Have you been thinking about this?

"Thanks."

Even when he was exasperated he was always polite.

It took me several months to realize that the Secretary habitually exaggerated for emphasis or to spark a debate. The skepticism with which he customarily greeted reports and requests from subordinates did not necessarily mean that Rumsfeld disagreed with us but rather that he was pushing back to test the strength of our own commitment to a position. That was a management style very different from what many of us in uniform had encountered in our careers.

Above all, the memos were meant to stimulate, to jar us out of business-as-usual inertia that could easily grip the Pentagon bureaucracy—an obstacle that threatened progress of the President's goals for military transformation. Some snowflakes addressed fundamental, far-reaching strategic questions such as the ideal mix of "heavy" conventional ground forces and "light" (but lethal) Special Operations Forces on the future battlefield. But the next memo might be limited to one terse sentence on the size of the paperclips he wanted on the draft communications we sent him. (We learned that Secretary Rumsfeld considered *all* communications reaching his desk as drafts for him to edit, clarify, and sharpen, and documents with stapled pages disrupted this process.)

One incident in the Pentagon lore that grew around Rumsfeld concerned a combatant commander who brought in a *finished* draft operational plan for the SecDef to review, a procedure that had been considered almost an automatic process in the past. These were the type of plans that would sit on the shelf until needed.

"Mr. Secretary," the officer said, handing over the thick ring binder, "I'm here to have you approve my OPLAN."

Rumsfeld hefted the heavy document, eyes twinkling. "No, General. You're here to have me *improve* your plan."

You might think it was inappropriate for a civilian to say he'd improve a military commander's plan. But the most critical elements in any operational plan were the assumptions that went into it. Many of these assumptions were political or geopolitical in nature, and therefore the Secretary would normally have great insight into their appropriateness. On the other hand, I never saw Secretary Rumsfeld try to tell an operational commander how many troops to put where or how to organize combat formations.

And not all his dismissive comments were that lighthearted. In fact, the Secretary could be stern if you showed up at his office door unprepared. And he had little patience when material presented to him was repetitive or simplistic. If it looked as if he was being spoonfed an answer, Rumsfeld would interrupt. "Please slow down so we can think this over."

The drive to improve all aspects of Defense Department operations, civilian and military, and make them more relevant in the twenty-first century was what motivated Secretary Rumsfeld to be such a prolific memo writer and such a rigorous taskmaster. Some of his critics—both in and out of uniform—would disparage Rumsfeld as a compulsive, needlessly abrasive control freak. He could be all these things at times. But he had been in Washington far too long to entertain illusions that any single official or office would ever actually gain *control* over the twenty thousand people who worked each day in the Pentagon. In fact, Rumsfeld knew he would have to get buy-in from the service chiefs, the Chairman and Vice Chairman, and the senior civilians in the Pentagon to accomplish anything. If the DoD went to Congress without everybody on the same page, there was no chance of making the changes so badly needed in national defense.

The best he could hope to achieve with the blizzard of snowflakes and by focusing presentations was to prod some of these people to think of fresh ways of achieving success.

In those early weeks and months, he did not make many new friends in the Pentagon. That was not his goal. But those of us who worked directly for Rumsfeld soon grew to respect him and gained a sense of his priorities, including the primacy of transformation. In any event, I told my colleagues, we had no choice. On the E-Ring, authority flowed from the Secretary to us. We worked for him, not the other way around.

Secretary of Defense Donald Rumsfeld soon realized that the flag officers around him appreciated that simple truth. He lost any lingering misgivings about serving with the "Clinton Generals" (a simplistic term popular in some think tanks) who purportedly filled the Joint Staff, and mutual trust began to spread. Rumsfeld came to realize that professional military officers owed allegiance to the Constitution, not to any individual President who had the power to send men and women out to risk death in combat. Mutual trust was essential.

Those of us in uniform also understood that civilian control of the military was essential in a democracy.

Certainly none of us was insubordinate. This was as it should be. But we weren't robots, mindlessly following orders. The Joint Chiefs of Staff were always compelled to give Secretary Rumsfeld our best military advice, and we didn't shy away from difficult arguments or hard questioning. The principle of civilian control of the military was engrained in the Constitution, and was sacrosanct among my peers.

However, the relationships among the Defense Department, the State Department, and the Central Intelligence Agency sometimes involved bureaucratic squabbling. Secretary Rumsfeld tried to get us to "think" as opposed to just accepting things as they were. Early in his tenure, he gave us some blunt advice: "Be careful of CIA assessments. Challenge them." His tone was stern. The SecDef did not expand on his views, but he *had* made his point. He respected the job the men and women at the CIA were doing, but wanted us all to think for ourselves. This was consistent with the lessons I'd first learned in Vietnam. There was no school for senior officers on how to critically assess intelligence.

Rumsfeld's relationship with State was always professional, and I never saw him view an issue as "them and us." He might indicate he didn't support a certain State position, but was much more interested in getting the Defense Department's arguments in order and taking policy disputes to the deputies, principals, or the full National Security Council to be settled. This was about providing the President the best policy choices and not about personalities or dwelling on the positions of others.

When Secretary Rumsfeld had just arrived at the Pentagon in January 2001, he stirred things up by creating nineteen panels of outside experts to investigate and report on a wide spectrum of defense issues. These "Rumsfeld Review" panels included nuclear and conventional force strategies; ballistic and theater missile defense; modernizing intelligence collection and space operations; crisis management; removing unproductive equipment and weapons; streamlining financial planning; developing "metrics" that realistically focused on the output of major military and DoD organizations; restructuring the Office of the Secretary of Defense; and an honest appraisal of cost versus benefit in all the areas examined. One of the more important panels examined morale and quality of life of military families, who are the foundation of our national defense. Each panel followed the principle of a "baseline" study: where we were, and where we wanted to go.

The arrival of the panels was not universally welcomed at the Pentagon. Many of the experts were retired military officers or came from the private sector, prepared to impose business efficiency models on military structures that had existed unopposed for decades. The active-duty generals and admirals might grumble, but the SecDef wanted old assumptions to be challenged. If you could defend your position, you prevailed. If not, Secretary Rumsfeld won the round.

He reminded the service chiefs that the process was flexible: "Nobody gets cut out of this process. You all have the opportunity to pick up the phone, call the panel leaders, and give them your opinion."

I reinforced this point to my colleagues on the Joint Chiefs: The Secretary had assured us that we would all have a voice, separately or individually, in the decision-making process arising out of the review panels' work. The panels continued their tasks, ultimately feeding their work into the development of the Quadrennial Defense Review (QDR). But many officers continued to feel threatened by the unfamiliar process of outside reviews. I often found myself acting as their spokesman and was glad that the Secretary did not belong to the shoot-the-messenger school.

———————

That summer, Rumsfeld's probing curiosity continued to make waves on the E-Ring. He wanted the Chairman's opinion on a proposal to combine a number of important Joint Staff military offices with their civilian equivalents in the OSD. Rumsfeld proposed merging the Joint Staff Public Affairs, Legal, Legislative Affairs, and Protocol offices under a civilian roof. He also recommended combining military and civilian mess dining facilities.

Hugh Shelton and I were opposed to mingling military and civilian messes. It wasn't as if we would be forgoing five-star restaurants. The attraction of a senior officer dining facility was that we could adjourn for lunch and continue discussions of classified material without fear of inadvertently compromising sensitive information in a more public setting. Also, as I had learned while serving on the Air Staff, a military mess was a great place to renew contact with your peers, discuss professional issues, and generally improve camaraderie. Secretary Rumsfeld accepted our argument.

But convincing him to abandon his position on combining the functional military and civilian offices was not that easy. Hugh Shelton pushed back first, writing the Secretary a strongly worded letter indicating that he didn't think the merging of the offices was a good idea. Hugh showed me the draft because, whatever the outcome, I would have to live with it for at least several months until my two-year term as Vice Chairman ended after he retired on October 1, 2001.

The letter was well reasoned: In order for us to provide the Secretary of Defense and other civilian leaders with our best military advice—a key provision of the Goldwater-Nichols Act—the Joint Chiefs of Staff needed military lawyers. We couldn't rely on the OSD General Counsel (a political appointee) who would by definition have to view issues, at least in part, from a political perspective. As we would put it, "Their spectacles have different lenses."

This same argument applied to Public Affairs: It was our duty to deal with the news media in an open and honest manner, untainted by political overtones. Neither Hugh Shelton nor I had ever received political guidance on what we should tell the public. When we spoke or wrote for public consumption, no one in the OSD provided us talking points.

Equally, we felt it was essential that the Joint Chiefs' Legislative Affairs office remain a military operation. This function had to be separate so as not to lose focus on preparing the combatant commanders, service chiefs, and the Chairman and Vice Chairman for congressional testimony. And Congress wanted to deal with us on military matters, not as flag bearers for any particular administration. The Secretary went along with our reasoning, and the offices of the Joint Chiefs that he had proposed merging with the OSD remained military operations.

In those early days of Rumsfeld's tenure it was hard to tell where I stood with him. One incident was typical of our relationship at that time. That spring, the Secretary was railing against the Pentagon's procurement process, which he described as disorganized, wasteful, and obsolete. Even though I was beginning to recognize his habit of exaggerating for emphasis, I thought his comments went too far and I couldn't let them stand without speaking.

I had been undergoing a twenty-four-hour blood pressure check with an automatic cuff on my arm periodically inflating. As Rumsfeld was provoking us, I figured I might set a new record for blood pressure checks. "Mr. Secretary," I interrupted, "we've got the best weapons and equipment in the world. Everybody wants them, so we must be doing *something* right."

Donald Rumsfeld silently looked at me over his rimless glasses. This discussion moved on without any telltale sign of how he took my comments. The JROC, responsible for approving operational requirements, was a new process to him, and the position of Vice Chairman was also new since he had served as Secretary in the 1970s. He was attempting to bring efficiency to the acquisition process, I realized, not trying to amass dictatorial power.

He did not comment on my interruption and remained an enigma.

While the Secretary and the Joint Chiefs were taking each other's measure, Rumsfeld shared with us a view that was central to his thinking about transformation of the military.

In late March 2001, he had told us: "This is a moment in time when we have an opportunity that we must not squander." He added that for the first time in decades, the country faced no major strategic challenge abroad, so achieving success, while difficult, was clearly possible. "We don't have to wake up every morning thinking something terrible is going to happen."

There would be no superpower confrontation because the United States was the world's sole superpower and could afford to take risks preparing our force for the twenty-first century. But, he cautioned, our most reckless course would be to dwell on old threats. I think all of the senior military leaders felt the same way: Now was the time to make the hard decisions that could shape the course of the Defense Department for the better.

The first military crisis of George W. Bush's administration came unexpectedly on April 1, 2001.

Early that morning I received a terse classified message forwarded through the Pentagon's National Military Command Center: A Navy EP-3E Aires electronic surveillance plane had collided with a Chinese fighter and been forced to make an emergency landing at Lingshui Air Base on the southern island of Hainan. Although there was no word on the fate of our twenty-four crewmembers, reconnaissance satellite images clearly showed the big aircraft on the runway.

Bad, I thought, rushing to dress. The EP-3 was a military version of the 1960s-era Lockheed Electra airliner. Even with four powerful turboprop engines, the aircraft was painfully slow. But it did carry a heavy payload and had a long range, an ideal combination for a recon aircraft—provided it wasn't harassed by hostile jet fighters. In the past, however, Chinese jets had played an increasingly hazardous game of intercepting our EP-3s as they lumbered along in international air space.

The first day of the crisis we learned that a Chinese J-8 Shenyang "Finback" supersonic fighter had struck the EP-3's left wing. The J-8 broke in half; the nose radar cone of the EP-3 had been torn away, and the propeller of the outer left number-one engine had been badly chewed up. The Chinese fighter pilot, Wang Wei, had ejected, but disappeared in the South China Sea. Even though the EP-3 had suffered massive damage, the aircraft commander, Navy Lt. Shane Osborn, had somehow managed to keep the plane flying. His Mayday calls announcing the intention to attempt an emergency landing at Lingshui Air Base on Hainan were among the last messages received from the aircraft. But we did learn that the crew had "set condition five," attempting to destroy the multiple racks of highly sensitive radar and electronic surveillance equipment in the plane's long cabin.

The next news of the crew we received was a complaint from the Beijing government to our embassy that the EP-3 had illegally entered Chinese air space and maneuvered in such a way as to cause the collision. This was obviously nonsense: The crews of EP-3s were among the most highly trained in the Navy, and their multiple radars and electronic navigation equipment gave them precise position readouts at all times. Moreover, it was impossible to imagine a big, slow plane like an EP-3 suddenly veering off its steady track to hit a smaller, much more maneuverable J-8 interceptor. There could be little doubt that the fighter was flying too close, had lost control, and had hit our plane.

But now the Chinese government was demanding an official apology from Washington and insisted on conducting their own "investigation" of the incident before they would consider releasing our crew.

We did not want the crew subjected to harsh interrogation, and we wanted them released quickly. Fortunately, our Ambassador in Beijing, retired Adm. Joseph Prueher, had been commander of U.S. Pacific Command before taking over the embassy in 1999. Joe Prueher, my boss when I commanded Pacific Air Forces, had a solid understanding of Chinese politics and their military and realized open confrontation with their leaders would be counterproductive. Prueher was in constant contact with the White House, the State Department, and the Pentagon, working on the best course of action to resolve the situation.

This was the first chance I had to observe Donald Rumsfeld during a major crisis. As I expected, he was cool, incisive, and productive. Chinese President Jiang Zemin was on a long diplomatic mission to Latin America. Given the rigidly centralized nature of Chinese leadership, this wasn't good, as he was essentially out of the decision loop. And when he was back in contact, his military probably wouldn't tell him the full story of the incident.

Within forty-eight hours, Ambassador Prueher had prevailed on the Chinese to allow our defense attaché, Army Brig. Gen. Neil Sealock, to visit the EP-3 crew at the Hainan hotel where they were staying as "guests." He confirmed what we had suspected: Our plane had been flying on autopilot at 22,500 feet on a straight and steady course at an airspeed of 180 knots, seventy miles south of Hainan, well outside Chinese territory. The J-8 had approached nose-high near stall speed and slammed into the propeller of the number-one engine. As Lieutenant Osborn and his cockpit crew had fought to keep the plane in the air, the reconnaissance specialists in the rear of the plane had struggled to destroy the sensitive instruments and computer drives while the aircraft shook and staggered.

This task was made very difficult because the EP-3 had spun violently and plunged several thousand feet before Osborn regained control. With the plane virtually falling out of the sky, the crewmembers pulled on their parachutes, only to remove them when the pilots recovered control and the aircraft leveled off and made its lurching descent toward Hainan.

In Washington, our interagency crisis managers agreed with Joe Prueher's assessment: The Chinese wanted a solution to the situation that would allow them to save face. Their government was eager for admission to the World Trade Organization and almost desperate to have Beijing named the site of the 2008 Olympic Games. But the U.S. government would *not* apologize for an accident that the aggressive attitude and inept airmanship of the Chinese pilot had caused.

Instead, we reached a compromise. Ambassador Prueher delivered a letter to the Chinese Foreign Minister that stated our government was "very sorry" their pilot had been killed and apologized for making an emergency landing on Hainan without first receiving permission to enter Chinese air space. Significantly, the letter was in English, and we did not include a translation. The English word "sorry" could be rendered to imply varying degrees of responsibility, and we let the Chinese draw their own conclusions.

Ten days later, the EP-3 crew returned to their home base on Puget Sound, Washington. Lieutenant Osborn was awarded the Distinguished Flying Cross; he and the crew posed for pictures with President Bush in the Oval Office.

But there was more to the story. During extensive debriefing of the crew, we learned that not *all* the sensitive equipment and classified documents had been destroyed or jettisoned during the wild descent toward Hainan. The crew had tried their best to follow standard operating procedure, but this had been a terrifying, disorienting incident. Back in the States, some of the electronic reconnaissance specialists from the rear of the plane detailed what part of the SOP checklists they had actually completed and which might have been neglected. This meant that the Chinese might have gained an insight on our electronic intelligence gathering and would take measures to shield themselves.

Sitting with Secretary Rumsfeld through most of this crisis, it was obvious that we were not providing him with the critical information he needed. He asked lots of questions pointing to a "system" that couldn't respond in a timely manner. Moreover, he also asked penetrating questions on why we got into this situation: Was it absolutely necessary to fly planes loaded with sensitive hardware and the intelligence information they had "swept" so close to hostile territory? Just as important, should the Department of Defense have anticipated this crisis and devised foolproof methods—other than swinging fire axes and dumping weighted sacks of classified material overboard—*before* an aircraft was forced down?

"This place just isn't *sharp*," Secretary Rumsfeld said, shaking his head. Valuable intelligence had almost certainly fallen into the hands of the Chinese, but the Defense Department had no way to determine how much. To Rumsfeld, and all of us, this was an intolerable situation.

This opened an unexpected door to transformation. Rumsfeld requested a full review of our sensitive reconnaissance operations. He noted that the approval process for collection operations had become a "habitual" Cold War endeavor. We were "rubber-stamping" everything, he said, and this would have to stop.

With the Secretary's persistent urging, we fundamentally changed long-standing processes and procedures.

After the crisis subsided, the pressure of daily work resumed. By early summer 2001, the services and OSD were deeply engaged in drafting the administration's first Quadrennial Defense Review. This was a relatively new exercise, required by Congress, that asked the department to conduct a comprehensive examination of defense strategy and the modernization of existing and future force structures. By statute, we would also have to create budget projections related to strategy for the next twenty years.

The office of the Chairman of the Joint Chiefs of Staff had a major responsibility in this huge assignment, which had to be coordinated closely with the services, the Secretary, and the OSD. But the timing of the task was bad: Rumsfeld still hadn't been able to fill all his top civilian jobs and therefore didn't have the advice and counsel of many senior civilian political appointees.

An expression we often heard from the Secretary at this time typified his frustration: "I don't know what I think," he'd say. "I need to *know* what I think."

The exacting task would normally have taken us months of coordinated effort. But we did not have the luxury of months in the summer of 2001.

As the muggy Washington summer spread haze above the Potomac, I couldn't help but think about my future in the military. Hugh Shelton would step down on October 1, after serving a total of four years as Chairman. I was only the fifth Vice Chairman to hold the position since Goldwater-Nichols created it, and no Vice Chairman had ever become Chairman of the Joint Chiefs of Staff—even though GNA had cited the possibility. If I were nominated, I would be the first.

But I doubted Rumsfeld would nominate me. I felt that we had clashed too many times on too many issues for him to want me in the job. After explaining all this to Mary Jo, I went down to Nordstroms in the Pentagon City shopping center to buy two civilian suits at the annual summer sale. Come March 2002, I'd probably be out there looking for a job. After thirty-six years in uniform, I had learned a lot about commanding and managing large military organizations, but had a much vaguer understanding of the corporate world or how to catch a bass. *Well,* I thought, *you're about to find out.* Mary Jo and I also talked about where we might settle down. We both liked Colorado Springs. The location was central, so our children and grandchildren could visit.

But these retirement plans were interrupted when I learned that the Secretary and the President had me on their short list to replace Hugh Shelton. The list of candidates soon narrowed down to two people: Adm. Vern Clark, Chief of Naval Operations, and me. Vern and I got along very well. In fact, we'd often meet in the Secretary's outer office as the interview process continued and brief each other on the particular subject of the day.

As the final decision approached, I had lunch with Secretary Rumsfeld and Hugh Shelton in late June.

"I want you to know that I don't interpret candid advice as disloyalty," Rumsfeld assured me. "Always give me your best candid advice. And once a decision is made, I expect the Chairman to salute and carry out instructions."

The most important interview in the selection process, of course, was with President George Bush. I met with him and Vice President Cheney in the Oval Office in mid-July.

"Tell me, Dick," the President said, getting right to the point. "Why do you want to be Chairman?"

Rather than answer this question, I recast it. It ran counter to my ethos as a professional officer to see the Chairmanship as an end in itself. *I only want to be*

Chairman, I thought, *if you and the Secretary of Defense determine I'd be your best military adviser.* So I did not reply directly and instead summarized my joint and Air Force experience, offering my thoughts on how to provide the best military advice to my civilian superiors.

The President pushed harder, seeking to learn if I were inflexibly tied to any particular strategy, military doctrine, or weapon system. How would I, a senior Air Force general, react if it became necessary to cancel expensive new aircraft such as the F-22? He wanted some confidence that I'd be an ally in his signature effort to transform the military.

On the morning of Thursday, August 23, I was in my office when my secretary, Mary Turner, ushered in CNN Pentagon correspondent Jamie McIntyre.

Grinning, he gave me a CNN souvenir coin and shook my hand. "Congratulations, General. You've just been chosen to be the next Chairman of the Joint Chiefs of Staff."

I'd heard nothing about this, not a whiff.

"Where'd you get the news?" I asked.

"Directly from my White House colleagues, General. The word is out that you're the nominee."

"Thanks for the heads-up," I said. I'd have to wait for Secretary Rumsfeld to confirm the information. It appeared that McIntyre was surprised—and maybe a little rattled—that I hadn't heard the news myself from some inside source.

An hour later, Rumsfeld's secretary called to say he wanted to see me in his office.

"General," he said with a warm smile, "the President has picked you to be the next Chairman. Congratulations."

This was firm confirmation, not speculation.

"It's a great honor, sir," I said. If only Mom and Dad had lived to see this day. I knew that Mary Jo and our children would be proud, but I also know we all had mixed emotions about my assuming such a challenging position.

The Secretary got on to pressing business. "I've been looking at potential Vice Chairman candidates and have narrowed the field down to two, one Army, one Marine. I wanted your input because obviously you'll be working closely with the new man."

He handed me a piece of paper with the names and brief service summaries of both candidates. The name of Marine Gen. Peter Pace, at Southern Command stood out in my mind. Pete had been my deputy commander in Japan, and I'd found him to be one of the brightest, most energetic, well-rounded officers I had ever served beside.

"I thought it appropriate that we balance the backgrounds of the two top military officers," Rumsfeld added.

I thought hard, weighing the strengths and weaknesses of the two men. Neither had obvious faults. However, I knew Pete Pace better and admired him for his leadership talent and skill. "Mr. Secretary," I said, "I would choose General Pace."

Rumsfeld gave me one of his probing looks. "Is he tough enough?"

What he meant was, could Pace stand the heat of the E-Ring or interagency "pressure cooker." As a young platoon leader, Pete had served in Vietnam during the heavy combat of 1968–69. He'd been the deputy commander of Marine forces in Somalia in 1992 and more recently been the J3 Operations Officer on the Joint Staff.

"He's definitely tough enough, sir," I said. He was also a genuinely nice man, but that only meant that he'd smile when he went in for the kill. I'd seen him conducting long, hard negotiations with the Japanese, which could be a rough bargaining environment. And he'd almost always been successful in getting everything we wanted for U.S. troops in Japan. "Mr. Secretary," I continued, "I'd like a Vice Chairman who treats people respectfully but firmly. Pete is the guy I want and is the one who'll help me advise you and the President the best."

He made a quick note to ask Pete Pace and his wife, Lynne, to join us the next day at the Summer White House in Crawford, Texas, where President Bush would announce our nominations.

"Myers," Secretary Rumsfeld said, "would you be interested in seeing how I came to pick you?"

"Definitely, sir."

He went to his desk and retrieved a large folded paper, which he spread open on the round table of his office.

This paper covered most of the table and contained a "matrix" that had a detailed, almost three-dimensional layout. On one axis, Rumsfeld had listed the qualifications and skills he and others thought a Chairman ought to possess in the twenty-first century. On another axis he had listed multiple names—people he knew and didn't know, but would know at least some of the candidates. They were civilians, retired military, in government, out of government—people with a wide variety of backgrounds. Rumsfeld then had the handful of original Chairman candidates listed. He had called all the contacts listed on the matrix, he explained, asking them to comment on each of the candidates' attributes as compared to the list of qualifications and skills on the main axis. This must have been very time-consuming, but the process was typical of the way he built "conviction"—especially when he didn't know most of us very well at that point in his tenure. Of course he wouldn't let me see what various people had said about me or any of the other candidates.

"Very interesting, sir," I observed.

"I thought so," he said.

When I read in the next few weeks articles by the pundits stating why I was chosen I had to laugh at their inaccuracy. They had absolutely no insight into Rumsfeld's meticulous process, yet were freely opining about this or that rationale. Several said I was chosen because I had a "space" background that fit well with the Secretary's transformation agenda. The President and Secretary had never mentioned that in any of the interviews and Rumsfeld, and I had never talked about my SpaceCom experience in the almost seven months I had worked with him.

On August 24, 2001, Rumsfeld, Pete Pace, and our wives met the President at his Prairie Chapel Ranch near Crawford, Texas. Pete's wife, Lynne, had rushed to Texas from Florida and just managed to join us with minutes to spare. We adjourned to meet the news media at the Crawford Community Center. President Bush strode up to the microphones and addressed the traveling White House press corps.

"Secretary Rumsfeld and I thought long and hard about this important choice," he said. "And we enthusiastically agree that the right man to preserve the best traditions of our armed forces while challenging them to innovate to meet the threats of the future is Gen. Richard B. Myers." He turned to grin at me. "General Myers is a man of steady resolve and determined leadership. His is a skilled and steady hand."

I would still have to pass muster in the Senate Armed Services Committee, but no one foresaw any problems there. The Joint Chiefs' Legislative Affairs Office was already scheduling my preconfirmation courtesy calls on the Hill, which would be completed the second week of September. That period after Labor Day was usually a quiet time for Congress.

And there was nothing to indicate that September 2001 would be any different.

PART III

ATTACK AND COUNTERATTACK: SEPTEMBER 11, 2001– OCTOBER 1, 2005

8

DEFINING MOMENT
Vulnerable on Our Own Soil

M y driver, Dan Downey, braked hard at the Pentagon River Entrance, and we jumped from the car. The steps were crowded with men and women fleeing the building, many still coughing from the smoke inside. Col. Matt Klimow, my executive assistant, stood near the door, waiting calmly with a notebook. As we entered, my senses were assaulted: People moved quickly through the smoky corridors toward the exits. Speakers in the ceiling blared repeatedly, *"Evacuate the building! Evacuate the building!"*

We ran against the flow of the crowd to the National Military Command Center off the D-Ring. The NMCC has been portrayed in many fanciful ways in Hollywood films and television dramas, usually with overly dramatic lighting and stadium-size screens projecting the flow of distant battle on land, at sea, and in the air. Although there is a certain *Star Wars* flavor to the Command Center, in reality the facility is a communications hub, a switchboard connecting the Pentagon, the civilian government, and the combatant commanders. Horseshoe-shaped computer cubicles dominate the Current Actions Center, which is about the size of a basketball court. At one end is the NMCC deputy director of operations' office, a windowless room with several desks, a conference table, and lots of telephones.

When we entered the Command Center, all the officers on duty were working calmly at their stations, despite the smoke wafting in through the ventilation system, the fact that the Pentagon had just been struck, and the distracting blast of the evacuation alarm.

Army Brig. Gen. Montague Winfield was the duty officer in charge of the center that morning. The smoke wasn't as bad inside his closed office where he was participating in a conference call linking the NMCC, North American Aerospace Command (NORAD), and the White House, which had been under way since just before we arrived at the Pentagon.

We learned that there was apparently a fourth hijacked aircraft, United Airlines Flight 93 out of Newark, bound nonstop for San Francisco. Like the other planes, it had switched off its transponder, making it much harder if not impossible to track on ground radar.

A military aide in the White House relayed an important message. "NORAD estimates the aircraft is headed toward Washington," Winfield said. "Vice President Cheney has forwarded the President's authorization to go Weapons Free if that plane is confirmed hijacked and threatens the White House or the Capitol."

Weapons Free, I thought—permission to shoot down the hijacked plane.

There were U.S. Air Force and Air National Guard fighters up as we spoke, searching for that Boeing 757 widebody, heavily laden with fuel. No one in the Pentagon knew how many passengers were on board, but I realized the President had made the right decision in authorizing fighters to shoot down the aircraft before it reached Washington or another city. I also thought of those fighter pilots who would be ordered to kill their fellow Americans along with the hijackers. Many of the Air National Guard pilots also flew for the airlines, which would make obeying the shootdown order that much harder. But as a young pilot myself, I'd learned that war was an unforgiving business that tested moral strength as well as physical courage.

General Winfield was doing a good job of managing the information flow and keeping the chain of command plugged in, linking the President (the National Command Authority), the Secretary of Defense, the combatant commanders, and the other relevant military and civilian organizations. So I went to find Secretary Rumsfeld. As I left the Current Actions Center, CNN showed the south tower of the World Trade Center collapsing in an avalanche of smoke and debris. The announcer said something about a possible death toll of ten thousand.

The smoke was thickening on the E-Ring corridor. And it was almost as bad in the Secretary's office suite. One of Rumsfeld's aides told me he was "outside," helping with the wounded. I left word that I was returning to the NMCC.

When I got back there was a period of confusion about the flight numbers of the hijacked aircraft known to have crashed and the one still airborne. This was exacerbated by a communication glitch making it impossible to speak directly to the Federal Aviation Administration on the secure conference call, but we did confirm that the FAA had grounded over twenty-one hundred airborne civilian aircraft by then and had diverted all inbound overseas flights. Even though we still could not communicate directly with senior FAA officials on this secure circuit, we were confident they were working as fast as possible to clear U.S. air space. There was no alternative, however: Terrorists who could hijack aircraft so readily could probably also eavesdrop on unsecured phone lines. At this time, it was tough to judge the full scope of the danger we were facing, so the conference call had become an "air threat" call, which followed priorities and protocol that I knew well from my days in command of NORAD in Colorado Springs.

One of those priorities was guarding the President of the United States aboard *Air Force One*, which was en route from Florida to an air base in Louisiana. NORAD had scrambled a fighter escort for the plane and now ordered a wide-area AWACS airborne radar surveillance plane up on the West Coast to search for intruding or hijacked aircraft in that sector.

I also recommended that all American military commands and units worldwide go to THREATCON Delta, the highest alert level. Officially, this meant, "A terrorist attack has occurred or intelligence has been received that action against a specific location is likely." Terrorists had staged major attacks in New York and Washington. Although we did not yet have reliable intelligence on when and where they would strike next, it seemed likely that they would.

After 10:00 A.M., an Air Force officer working in the White House told us that Deputy National Security Adviser Stephen Hadley had requested the implementation of "continuity of government measures." These were taken only in the gravest of emergencies, and most recently had been expected to meet the Cold War threat of nuclear attack. But those had been training exercises; this was real.

The measures included establishing a survivors' core of key federal government members. A rotating staff of around 150 senior officials from every cabinet department would be sent to two secure underground bunkers within driving or helicopter-flight distance of Washington. Their families and loved ones could only contact them through a "sterile" toll-free phone number.

Another element of the emergency plan was launching the National Airborne Operations Center. This was a high-technology command, control, and communications center carried aboard a converted Boeing 747 jumbo jet. Some in Washington considered it an expensive, unnecessary relic of the Cold War, but with the capital itself now under imminent threat, it was clear that NAOC was still a useful part of the inventory. I asked Matt Klimow to verify that the plane was airborne.

NORAD now confirmed that there was an Air Force combat air patrol over Washington. If ordered to do so, the fighters would shoot down any hijacked airliner threatening structures and people in the city.

While the conference call proceeded, the CNN picture showed another horrible telescopic image: The north tower of the World Trade Center collapsed from the upper floors, the tall building's sides billowing out like a flimsy cardboard box on a bonfire. The mushrooming cloud of smoke and dust evoked a nuclear explosion. I wondered how many thousand people trapped in that burning tower had just died.

Information reached us by a variety of routes—NORAD updates, National Security Council and FBI intelligence reports, and forwarded FAA data, which was still slowed by our lack of a direct secure channel to the agency leadership. At 10:17 A.M., we got word that the blip image of the aircraft that the FAA had assumed to be United Flight 93 had just disappeared from the radar, eastbound over southcentral Pennsylvania. This could mean several things. Was it flying so low that radar couldn't see it? If so, was the plane still a threat to Washington? At this point we didn't have answers to these questions.

A report from the Military District of Washington announced that almost every government office in the capital had been evacuated and that many people were leaving the city on foot. The CNN image of this flood of evacuees soon appeared on our TV screens.

This was a nightmare, and we didn't know when it would end. But at 10:21 A.M., United Airlines confirmed that its Flight 93 had crashed near Shanksville, Pennsylvania. Unless there was another hijacking before all the flights still airborne landed, this first phase of the terrorist attack had apparently ended. But we couldn't be certain what was happening overseas or if the terrorists had held more aircraft, large or small, in reserve for a second wave—or if they had options other than airplanes in the execution stage.

Confusion rose and fell. Fractured, unconfirmed reports reached us from the intelligence community and the Secret Service: A civil aircraft was down near Camp David (false report) . . . a car bomb had exploded near the State Department, raising the question of where the nearest biochemical protection team was located (false report) . . . three commercial aircraft were "squawking" Mayday distress calls (false report) . . . the fighters responding to the situation that were not under NORAD control did not have a clear understanding of the Rules of Engagement (ROE) for hijacked planes. In other words, the country was at war again, and the fog of war was descending.

Added to this situation, acrid smoke started filling the operations floor of the NMCC and was thickening to the point that it was potentially hazardous.

But we now had a secure video teleconference scheduled, linking the Defense Department's civilian and military leadership with the rest of government. The NMCC facility for secure teleconferences was a tiny room with a thick, airtight door. This protected us from the smoky operations floor, but the space was severely cramped. Somehow we found room for Secretary Rumsfeld and Steve Cambone, Rumsfeld's lanky special assistant, myself, Assistant Secretary for Public Affairs Torie Clark, General Counsel Jim Haynes, and Vice Adm. Ed Giambastiani, the Secretary's military assistant, with Matt Klimow jammed into a corner, taking notes. By now, Deputy Secretary Paul Wolfowitz had reached Site R, from where his image appeared in a small box at the upper righthand corner of our screen.

Again, the main issue under discussion was Rules of Engagement for NORAD to follow should there be more hijackings. The civilian leadership had their experts and a lawyer, we had ours. Some of us were developing bad headaches from the deteriorating air quality.

Back in the NMCC director of operations' office, Ed Giambastiani, a veteran submariner with years spent submerged, announced, "There's no clean air in this center. It's filling up with CO_2." He told Matt Klimow to find a firefighter with an air monitor, while he searched out an alternative place to meet.

The doomsday bellow of the fire alarm, *"Evacuate the building!"* had finally stopped. Our eyes were starting to sting, some streaming tears, and Secretary Rumsfeld was hacking because he had breathed thicker smoke helping to evacuate the wounded earlier.

"Sir," I told him, "I'm worried about the people outside this office supporting us, because the air is worse out there."

Rumsfeld nodded. "We're going to stay in here as long as we can."

We tallied the preliminary casualty and damage to the Pentagon estimates—well over one hundred killed or missing, scores wounded, including many terribly burned—and the complete destruction of a large wedge on the western, "Navy Side" of the building.

"We need to have the press on board, to keep them up to speed," I told Torie

Clark. "It's important for historical reasons and to get the word out. Don't leave them behind."

Secretary Rumsfeld asked loudly enough for everybody to hear, "What *else* could the enemy do?"

He was thinking ahead, engaging in Rumsfeld's well-known outside-the-box speculation.

"NBC," I said. I didn't mean the National Broadcasting Corporation. I meant nuclear, biological, and chemical—weapons of mass destruction.

At noon, Vice Adm. Tom Wilson, Director of the Defense Intelligence Agency, confirmed what everybody at the conference table had already surmised: The attacks had undoubtedly come from al-Qaida.

Usama bin Laden and his al-Qaida leadership were dug in deeper than ever in Afghanistan, still protected by the Taliban. Afghanistan was in the Area of Operations of Gen. Tommy Franks's Central Command. Like Hugh Shelton, Tom Franks was overseas. Franks's plane was on the ground at the Navy base in Suda Bay on Crete.

"Ask him to get back to CENTCOM headquarters in Tampa, Florida, as soon as possible," I told Matt Klimow. "I want General Franks to start looking at options for al-Qaida."

If the President and the Secretary ordered us to go to war in Afghanistan, we were going to have to do it before winter, and that didn't leave us a lot of time in the foothills of the Hindu Kush.

With that responsibility in Tom Franks's hands, I turned to the others. "We need to keep asking, 'What's next?' " In the face of such a concerted attack, we couldn't fall behind. I assured Secretary Rumsfeld that General Franks was now examining all options for al-Qaida.

Reports from the combatant commanders around the world were coming in. Their bases and facilities were sealed tight at the highest possible alert status. No unidentified aircraft, vessel, or vehicle could approach any American military installation. At least our troops were protected. There wouldn't be another USS *Cole* today.

But it was too late for many in this building. Matt Klimow arrived with an Arlington County firefighter in tow. The report was not good: The concentration of CO_2 in some corridors was 88 percent, near deadly. The level in the NMCC was 32 percent. Oxygen in the NMCC was still a breathable 16 percent, but falling. When it hit 13 percent, the fireman urged us to evacuate. Ed Giambastiani brought some good news. He'd found a smoke-free shelter, "OSD Cables," a communications hub near the Office of the Secretary of Defense complex. We relocated there.

It was from here that I passed on the Secretary's authorization for a partial Reserve call-up, including fighter pilots, aerial tanker crews, and communications specialists. With the country suddenly at war, we would need all the help we could muster, and much of that help was in the Reserve and National Guard.

After noon, *Air Force One* landed at Barksdale Air Force Base in Louisiana, where President Bush broadcast a brief message to the nation. The Department of Defense, he said, was taking all appropriate security measures, including putting the military at the highest alert level worldwide. The President asked for prayers for the thousands who had died and for their families.

"Make no mistake," he said. "The United States will hunt down and punish those responsible for these cowardly acts."

At 12:40 P.M., I updated the SecDef. The FAA reported that five airliners inbound from the Far East had come too far to return due to low fuel. One, Korean Air Flight 85, was squawking a hijack code on its transponder, which might have been authentic or more likely a pilot error. We couldn't take a chance. Fighter interceptors were scrambled to escort all five flights. Air Traffic Control requested the Korean plane land at an isolated field in western Canada. NORAD had contacted us requesting an additional Reserve call-up of Air Defense units. The request would be routed through the Secretary's office to the President. Just so we were all reading from the same page, I reminded Secretary Rumsfeld that Air Defense and Air Sovereignty were primarily Air National Guard missions. The commandant of the U.S. Coast Guard had given his commanders authority to challenge any inbound vessel. The Coast Guard was completing its own Reserve call-up.

"Mr. Secretary," I said, "I've got the final recommended ROE from General Eberhart at NORAD. If our fighters intercept an aircraft obviously heading for a runway, they will let it land. But if a plane is on a glide path toward a possible government target or civilian installation, they will shoot it down. Our pilots will have to exercise great discipline and judgment. If that aircraft veers off, it will be too late."

Clearly, shooting down a civilian airliner with innocent men, women, and children on board was not a good option, but given the circumstances, it was really the only course of action to minimize the death and destruction planned by the hijackers.

Secretary Rumsfeld approved our ROE. This was not a time to be indecisive. Rules of Engagement were a deadly serious matter.

Pentagon Police Chief John Jester reported on damage. The lower-floor fire had not yet been contained, and the fire on the fifth floor that had spread through three of the building's concentric rings was still raging. There could be as many as twenty victims trapped in the burning rubble of the B-Ring. It was still too early to estimate who had been killed when the almost fully fueled jet had hit the building. "Most of them were in Army and Navy offices on that side, sir," Jester said.

Secretary Rumsfeld contacted the President by secure video teleconference at 3:15 P.M. The FBI had just forwarded a report of a possible hijacked USAir flight. "We've sent fighters up to intercept," Rumsfeld said.

The President looked grim. We all knew what the outcome of an F-15 intercepting a hijacked airliner would be like.

At one point, the President chided us. "Get the facts first. And clean up your language!" Earlier, several unprofessional epithets had strayed in, the result of stress and tension. But President Bush was reminding us to stay focused. "I want everyone hearing this teleconference to know that no faceless thug will hold our country at bay. I want you to find out who did it, seek them out, and *destroy* them."

I finally called Mary Jo around 2:30 that afternoon. This obviously was way too late. Fortunately, she had called the office just after the Pentagon attack and my secretary had reassured her that we were all okay. That must have indeed been reassuring, because the noise of the exploding airliner had rattled the windows of our house at Fort Myer, a mile from the Pentagon. She then headed for the Army Community Center on post to help answer the large volume of calls from desperately worried family members of Pentagon employees.

Just before 5:00 P.M., I joined Secretary Rumsfeld outside the building for an inspection of the crash site. The sooty gouge of the airliner's belly across the concrete helicopter pad was obvious. The walls and roof on a wide section of this western Pentagon sector had collapsed into a heap of still-smoldering rubble.

Pentagon Police Chief Jester explained how "lucky" we'd been that the plane had struck the building where it did. This was the only section that had been refurbished and had new reinforced steel supports and new windows, which were absent in the rest of the building. The steel and windows had held for thirty minutes before collapsing, allowing hundreds of people to escape the flames.

Next, I met with the Secretary and Senators Carl Levin and John Warner in OSD Cables. The senators were due to join us for a press conference at 6:20 P.M.

Warner and Levin looked even more somber than the President. Levin advised the Secretary on retaliating against al-Qaida. "Use all the resources available, even those we haven't drawn on before, like Russia and the former Soviet Republics."

Five minutes later, Secretary Rumsfeld called Russian Defense Minister Ivanov to request his country's cooperation.

At 5:40 P.M., the Chairman, Gen. Hugh Shelton, having just returned from his aborted flight to Europe, arrived in the NMCC, which now had breathable air because the worst of the fires had been extinguished. Hugh Shelton was as lanky and taciturn as ever, but his craggy face was grim as I briefed him. Air National Guard and regular Air Force combat air patrols were flying above our major cities under AWACS control. The entire American military was on THREATCON level Delta. Joint Forces Command was sending headquarters units to New York and Washington.

Shelton turned to Vice Adm. Tom Wilson of the DIA and Rear Adm. Lowell "Jake" Jacoby, the Director of Intelligence of the Joint Staff. "Have we had any intel 'squeaks' on an attack like this—anything at all?"

Tom Wilson spoke up at once. "The only possible hint of this coming was several months ago when we got a single intercept requesting jumbo jet training. Since then, there's been nothing."

He was referring to the vast electronic signals data-mining operations of our intelligence community that targeted known terrorist networks, such as al-Qaida and their allies.

Over the years since September 11, 2001, there has been considerable, often persistent, speculation that the White House had received detailed warning of the al-Qaida terrorists' plans for the attack involving hijacked airliners. This is not true. Those who make a case for this advance warning usually cite the CIA's Presidential Daily Brief (PDB), which he received on August 6, 2001.

The PDB noted that al-Qaida had at least one active "cell" of terrorists in the United States and that Usama bin Laden often planned his attacks well in advance. There was no reference to a specific threat in the briefing. However, the CIA did report the following in the briefing: "We have not been able to corroborate some of the more sensational threat reporting, such as that from a Redacted service in 1998 saying that Bin Laden wanted to hijack a U.S. aircraft to gain the release of 'Blind Shaykh' 'Umar 'Abd al-Rahman and other U.S.-held extremists."

Then Condoleezza Rice testified to the 9/11 Commission that the August 6, 2001, PDB contained "historical information based on old reporting. There was no new threat information." This gives a glimpse of the uncertainty and ambiguity that often surround our intelligence "products."

The Presidential Daily Briefing of August 6, 2001, is cited in some detail in the National Commission on Terrorist Attacks Upon the United States report.

I told Hugh that the Secretary had spoken directly with Russian Defense Minister Ivanov. He promised "solidarity" and said Russian military and naval forces were immediately canceling TU-95 bomber training exercises near Alaska. Ivanov also recommended a G-8 summit on terrorism.

I then got word that the Deputies Committee of the National Security Council would have a secure teleconference at 6:30 P.M. to prepare for an afternoon meeting of the NSC in the White House Situation Room on Wednesday. Secretary Rumsfeld had already announced that the Pentagon would be back on a regular work schedule in the morning.

During the planning video teleconference, I spoke from the Pentagon; Steve Hadley was at the White House; Assistant Secretary of State Rich Armitage was at the State Department, and several representatives of the intelligence community joined from their offices. Everyone was tired, but we recognized the urgency of the matters at hand.

We verified that counter-NBC decontamination units had been called out and deployed, standing by in case al-Qaida decided to follow up with WMD attacks on our cities.

Then we spoke of terrorist target lists. The President had ordered us all to seek out and destroy those responsible for these attacks on our people and our nation. We did not want a repeat of August 1998 after the al-Qaida bombing of our embassies in Kenya and Tanzania. Then, the U.S. response of firing waves of cruise missiles on suspected terrorist facilities in the Sudan and several al-Qaida training camps in Afghanistan had done little significant damage and obviously nothing to deter the terrorists. Now it was clear that our response to the World Trade Center and Pentagon suicide attacks had to be more proportionate and, most important, more effective.

Paul Wolfowitz took the lead. "This is an act of war," he said, jaw clenched. He then spoke slowly, emphasizing each word. "And . . . we . . . are . . . at . . . *war.*"

Now CIA Deputy Director John E. McLaughlin spoke about our response to the attacks. "After today, we need to see clearly who is with us and who is not with us." His message was obvious: Afghanistan, al-Qaida's home base, would not be an easy target. This landlocked country had vast deserts and high, trackless mountains bisected by steep gorges.

The Soviet army had virtually fallen apart trying to subdue the Afghan mujahideen in the 1980s in spite of having been able to launch a conventional invasion over a good road system through the southern Soviet republics of Turkmenistan, Uzbekistan, and Tajikistan. We had no such guaranteed access. Further, Iran, to the west, was a rabidly anti-American Islamic republic. We might be able to work with the Pakistanis, but the operative word there was "might." Military-to-military relations had suffered as a result of Pakistan's development of nuclear weapons and the ending of funding for training Pakistani military personnel in the United States by Congress.

The discussion swirled around potential allies and enemies in the region, and how the attacks on our soil had changed the calculus of these relationships.

Once more Paul Wolfowitz tried to focus the issue in a dramatic manner. "We should be thinking whether we should declare war," he said. ". . . And then against whom?"

Armitage, the senior diplomat in the teleconference, spoke from his perspective. "Well, what should our declaratory policy be?"

We now discussed the draft National Security Presidential Directive on Combating Terrorism that had been presented on September 4, 2001. Its principal objective was to eliminate the al-Qaida network, using all elements of our national power to do so—diplomatic, military, economic, intelligence, information, and law enforcement. After today, we agreed, these concepts would have to be focused more sharply against both al-Qaida and the Taliban in Afghanistan.

When the teleconference ended, I summarized the work facing the American military. We had to frame our objectives in a realistic manner; choose among a classic conventional operation, a Special Operations campaign, and a surgical strike.

"Remember," Hugh Shelton said, "we have to look at everything and think broadly."

"That means we don't just focus on terrorists," I added, "but also on those who harbor them."

At 8:30 P.M. I joined my colleagues to listen to the President speak to the nation. Despite the tension and fatigue I then felt, certain key phrases of his address have continued to resonate.

"Today, our fellow citizens, our way of life, our very freedom came under attack in a series of deliberate and deadly terrorist acts. The victims were in airplanes, or in their offices; secretaries, businessmen and women, military and federal workers; moms and dads, friends and neighbors. Thousands of lives were suddenly ended by evil, despicable acts of terror.

"The pictures of airplanes flying into buildings, fires burning, huge structures collapsing, have filled us with disbelief, terrible sadness, and a quiet, unyielding anger. These acts of mass murder were intended to frighten our nation into chaos and retreat. But they have failed; our country is strong.

"A great people has been moved to defend a great nation. Terrorist attacks can shake the foundations of our biggest buildings, but they cannot touch the foundation of America. These acts shattered steel, but they cannot dent the steel of American resolve."

Late that night I left the building by the River Entrance, which it seemed I had entered a long time before. My uniform reeked of smoke. As I walked down the steps to the car, I heard a sound that was both unusual and familiar—the snarl of military jet engines. Over recent years, I'd become accustomed to hearing commercial airliners flying much more quietly as they followed FAA noise-abatement procedures into and out of Reagan National Airport. But the jets crossing above the Pentagon at medium altitude were F-15s whose noise was pure, raw power.

This was the sound of a nation at war.

9

TAKING THE WAR TO
THE ENEMY IN AFGHANISTAN

Operation Enduring Freedom

The next day the full National Security Council met in the White House Situation Room to review America's options. Hugh Shelton asked me to attend the meeting because he wanted us "joined at the hip" for the final two weeks of his term as Chairman. Seated shoulder to shoulder around the table, I was aware of the smoky odor of my uniform. Before leaving home that morning, I had decided to wear the same jacket that had hung inside the Pentagon to remind me and perhaps others that we were at war. That was not necessary.

Normally, President Bush opened White House meetings with a little light repartee. Not today. The President, grim but calm, sat at the head of the table and flatly reminded us that America had been attacked in "an act of war." We would hunt down the enemy and *destroy* them. Protecting America and eliminating her enemies had become the "number-one priority" of his presidency. The full power of the United States, civil and military, would be devoted to achieving this goal. He wanted those of us in this room, the American people, and the entire world to understand this.

The task would undoubtedly prove more difficult than any of us could imagine, he added. But no matter how hard or how expensive it was in terms of blood and treasure, we would not shirk the challenge.

"This time," the President said, "we're not just going to pound sand." He may have been referring to the 1998 cruise missile retaliation strikes in Afghanistan and Sudan after the African embassy bombings. "The terrorists started this war, but we will finish it. We'll do *whatever* it takes to win. We're probably going to have to do a lot of things that are unpopular. If that means this will be a one-term administration, then so be it. We have to do what's right."

He could not have made his intentions any clearer than that. And obviously we had to win. But the definition of winning eluded us in the early parts of our campaign against the terrorists. In fact, the definition of what it meant to win would vex me and the rest of government throughout my tenure. This was a very different type of conflict, one that didn't easily yield to conventional definitions of victory. It most likely would not be a victory in the traditional military sense. Of course, if we were not able to define winning, we all knew the American people would be reluctant to show the appropriate will, resolve, and especially patience.

President Bill Clinton's two administrations had dealt with terrorism much differently. The early emphasis had been on apprehending and bringing to justice terrorist suspects. Although Usama bin Laden had declared war on the United States in 1998, the country as a whole did not take the threat seriously. Before the 9/11 attacks, the strategy was primarily to go after Usama bin Laden. Now a broader strategy was our only option.

On September 14, Congress passed a joint resolution authorizing the President to use "all necessary and appropriate force against those nations, organizations, or persons he determines planned, authorized, committed, or aided the terrorist attacks that occurred on September 11, 2001, or harbored such organizations or persons, in order to prevent any future acts of international terrorism against the United States by such nations, organizations or persons."

The next day, a tape of Usama bin Laden appeared on Al Jazeera television. "I would like to assure the world," he said, "that I did not plan the recent attacks, which seem to have been planned for personal reasons."

We had good evidence by then that it was indeed al-Qaida that had planned and executed these attacks, and I thought it out of character for Usama bin Laden not to take credit. What could possibly be his motive for denying involvement? Could it have been fear that the Americans were about to show serious resolve?

Since the hectic days immediately following the 9/11 attacks, some of those who helped shape the strategy for what came to be known as the "Global War on Terror" have portrayed the early decision making as sharply focused and decisive. But I was deeply involved at the strategic military level, and to me that period was often clouded by confusion and ambiguity. Although the President defined the enemy and those who harbored them as the terrorists, to translate that definition into military action would take much more thought. This would be one of the crucial jobs that General Shelton and I would have to coordinate with the Joint Chiefs, the Joint Staff, and the combatant commanders. In the end, the Secretary of Defense and President would want our military advice. It would take time before we saw a clear path ahead.

Certainly we all understood the *need* to develop a practical strategy that would meet the President's national objective of locating and destroying the enemy. This strategy would definitely involve Afghanistan, but it was obvious from the beginning that this course of action would be a complex, frustrating challenge.

Our strategy began to take form very slowly on the weekend of September 15–16 at the presidential retreat of Camp David in the cool Catoctin Mountains west of Washington. The principals of the National Security Council, important CIA counterterrorism deputies, and Bush's close White House advisers took part in the wide-ranging discussion. Hugh Shelton and I were the only members of the military present. Clearly some of the earliest and most visible action would be by the U.S. armed forces, and we were included in all deliberations.

These talks were more loose brainstorming sessions than the structured policy presentations that some present later described. Almost all of us favored a military campaign against the violent extremist groups responsible for the 9/11 attacks, starting with al-Qaida in Afghanistan and the Taliban regime that harbored them.

Rumsfeld knew the President would be impatient for our recommendations, but warned us after 9/11 not to give in to pressure and promise more than we could deliver. "Think four or five moves ahead." He also cautioned us to be decisive in our recommendations. "I'm from Chicago," he said. "I learned a long time ago that if you cock it, [a pistol], you'd better be prepared to use it."

Hugh Shelton and I knew that our job was to advise the civilian leadership, not to create national policy. So, during the give and take of the Camp David discussion, we outlined broad choices for the National Security Council. Shelton emphasized that the Defense Department had no off-the-shelf operations plan (OPLAN) for Afghanistan, but presented three options that escalated in terms of the degree of force used and the risk to our forces. Since no objectives for the use of force were yet agreed to, these options just presented an opportunity for the senior leadership to indicate where they were leaning. The possible courses of action to consider were: (1) a quick Tomahawk Land Attack (TLAM) cruise missile strike against al-Qaida training camps, which by now were almost certainly empty; (2) a larger TLAM and air-launched cruise missile attack paired with manned-bomber strikes against these and other targets; (3) a much more robust combined air-ground campaign with Special Operations Forces followed by regular ground troops—a large commitment of America's blood and treasure. This option could take weeks to develop and certainly would require overflight as well as basing and staging rights from some of the countries surrounding landlocked Afghanistan as well as from friendly nations in the Persian Gulf.

As we had expected, nobody at the Laurel Lodge conference table thought much of options one and two. But the President seemed interested in option three, which he said we'd discuss further during the coming week. As we fleshed out the strategic concept and campaign objectives, they would quickly be handed over to CENTCOM Commander Gen. Tommy Franks, so he and his staff could do the military operational planning. This would be an "iterative" process.

Secretary of State Colin Powell described preliminary efforts under way to build a coalition, using the United Kingdom and our NATO partners as its core and calling on the Russians for support with the former Soviet republics of Central Asia, which still had close ties with Moscow.

Deputy Defense Secretary Paul Wolfowitz commented that Afghanistan might prove to be too hard but we might be able to crack the same nut by bringing down Saddam Hussein's regime, which had possibly been involved in 9/11. His approach did not receive much support. President Bush pointedly said that he didn't want speculation on Iraq to continue.

Rumsfeld stressed that any military operations would have to be conducted with unprecedented speed of execution and draw on everything DoD had developed in terms of advanced battlespace Command-Control-Communications and Computers and Surveillance technology (C^4) as well as Precision-Guided Munitions (PGMs). We knew that this would be a new type of war, as the enemy had few assets that amounted to hard targets, which brought the often-discussed concept of asymmetric warfare into much sharper focus. It also meant that my concept of transformation's being more between the ears would be tested quickly in this new environment. Afghanistan had been fought across for decades, but the Taliban did value the few aircraft, tanks, and artillery pieces it still possessed. Of course al-Qaida had few tangible assets, except financial, so this would mean going after individuals and small groups. Success against the Taliban would also require countering their ideology.

CIA Director George Tenet said that his agency had officers in contact with the leaders of Northern Alliance tribal militias in their isolated redoubts, which the Taliban and al-Qaida had been besieging for months. Unfortunately, al-Qaida had been able to insert a suicide assassination team into the headquarters of Alliance leader Ahmad Shah Massoud on September 9, just two days before the 9/11 attacks. Posing as Belgian television journalists, the assassins detonated a powerful bomb, killing Massoud and virtually decapitating the Northern Alliance. As the CIA's most productive contacts had flowed through Massoud, the Agency would have to scramble to re-establish effective relations with the "tribals." But we had no other option: The Northern Alliance remained the best organization through which to gain a foothold in Afghanistan.

We reviewed the problems with conducting a military operation in landlocked Afghanistan. Inserting an amphibious Marine unit would not be possible, so we might have to win Pakistani support for a helicopter or fixed-wing assault across the country's southern Baluchistan panhandle. We would also certainly need support from countries such as Uzbekistan that bordered northern Afghanistan.

One of the problems, as I've mentioned, was that in the case of Pakistan, our military-to-military relations had come to a virtual halt in 1990 when the congressional Pressler Amendment cut off all training and arms funding following the refusal of the Islamabad government to stop working on nuclear weapons. This funding is always an easy target for Congress when it's displeased, but such action often has negative consequences for many years. The Pakistani military no longer knew the American military and we didn't know them. For many Pakistani officers, their view of the Americans was often based upon the shrill rhetoric of extremists, since they no longer were able to come to the United States for training and have the chance to see our country firsthand.

Also, the Taliban were an internationally recognized government. To enhance the legitimacy of our cause should we go to war, it would be best to offer their leaders the chance to avoid a conflict that would unleash the destructive power of America's modern arsenal. So we discussed the possibility of giving the Taliban a two-day ultimatum to turn over bin Laden and the other al-Qaida leaders once we were ready to strike, but before beginning operations against Afghanistan. Therefore, the Bush administration might initially have to pursue parallel diplomatic and military options, hoping to persuade the extremist government in Kabul to extradite Usama bin Laden and his followers to us, while simultaneously preparing for a major military—and paramilitary—operation. Those were among the many unresolved options on the table at the end of the Camp David meeting.

The President formally approved the simultaneous diplomatic-military approach at an NSC meeting on Tuesday, September 18, 2001. This gave official authority to proceed with the planning already under way at Gen. Tommy Franks's CENTCOM headquarters at MacDill Air Force Base in Tampa. Since 9/11, both Secretary Rumsfeld and President Bush had been leaning on Tom Franks pretty hard to build a "meaningful" operations plan that would execute the strategic concept under which the U.S. committed major forces inside Afghanistan, going far beyond what the President had disparaged as "pounding sand."

Gen. Tommy Franks seemed to me an excellent commander to meet this complex and demanding challenge. At this point I hadn't had much of a chance to get to really know Tommy, but that was changing quickly. Although he could adopt the role of a folksy West Texas boy and spit tobacco juice with the oil field roughnecks and quail hunters from his hometown of Midland, Tom Franks was a worldly, professional soldier. He also had a talent for diplomacy, which stood him in good stead among the *retired* generals running many of the countries in CENTCOM's Area of Responsibility (AOR), which stretched from the Horn of Africa, across the Arabian Peninsula and Iraq, through the Central Asian "stans," and all the way to Pakistan. We would need support—implicit or explicit—from those countries if we were going to succeed in Afghanistan.

During the week after the 9/11 attacks, it became obvious that at a minimum we would require overflight permission from Pakistan for any operation in Afghanistan. But obtaining that cooperation would not be easy, due to the absence of military relations with Pakistan. The Joint Staff assigned the problem to the J5 Director of Politico-Military Affairs for the region, Air Force Brig. Gen. Kevin P. "Chili" Chilton, a former space shuttle astronaut. Because Pakistan seemed unlikely to welcome our presence, Chilton originally explored the idea of approaching India with a cooperation request. But this solution was problematic, because India and Pakistan were bitter enemies, and we did not want to sour relations with the large Muslim population of South and Central Asia. Chilton took his concerns to Army Lt. Gen. John Abizaid, the Director of the Joint staff J5, the office of Strategic Plans and Policy, who told him to try to assemble an interagency team to travel to the region and find a solution.

"Go over and meet someone," Abizaid said, leaving Chilton a wide range of independence.

In the end, quickly assembling a diplomatic team proved impossible, because qualified interagency officials had already committed to urgent meetings in Washington that week. So Chilton and Air Force Lt. Col. Jeff Paulk flew Pakistani Air Lines to Islamabad, the State Department having cabled our Ambassador, Wendy Chamberlain, that they were coming. She was a very enterprising Foreign Service officer and immediately arranged a meeting with Lt. Gen. Mahmud Ahmed, head of Pakistan's shadowy but powerful Inter-Services Intelligence Directorate (ISI). Ambassador Chamberlain told Chilton that Mahmud was the man to see to get decisions.

Mahmud opened the first meeting trying to evade the issue by claiming the Taliban "aren't the problem." Wendy Chamberlain would not accept this. She wrote a note with a single, direct question and handed it to Mahmud: "Are you with us or against us?"

The feared intelligence chief caved in. "We are with you." He then quickly excused himself.

The next morning, Chilton and service attachés from the embassy met with senior Pakistani officers. By the end of the day, the Pakistanis had agreed to our request for a Combat Search and Rescue (CSAR) base near Afghanistan (the Jacobabad base in Baluchistan was later selected). Chilton suggested—and the Pakistanis agreed—that the best way to prevent alarming the local population would be for Pakistani forces to provide security on the base's outer perimeter, while we guarded the inner. He had also asked the American officers to list the needs of each of their services: For example, the Navy wanted to operate inside Pakistan's twelve-mile territorial limit. The Pakistanis agreed. And so it went.

Satisfied with his work, Chilton called Abizaid and said he was coming home.

"I'm afraid you're not, Chili," Abizaid told him. "You're going to Tashkent to meet with John Bolton from State. We definitely need Uzbekistan."

Bolton was Undersecretary of State for Arms Control and International Security. He knew the lay of the land in Southwest Asia.

Chilton flew to Tashkent where he and Bolton started the tough negotiations with President Islom Karimov—a Soviet-style politician who played very hard to get. But we had to have an air base in Uzbekistan, so Chilton and Bolton kept pushing. Although they did not return with an agreement, their visit opened the door for further negotiations.

During late September, CIA Director George Tenet kept us informed on the Agency's progress with the Northern Alliance, elaborating on a proposed operational concept discussed at Camp David. The CIA would form the initial American presence, bolstering the tribal militias. The effort would have to be conducted with the militia forces still leaderless after the assassination of Ahmed Shah Massoud. The CIA would be dominant in the initial phases of the operation, but later Agency paramilitary teams would coordinate their work with Army and Air Force Special Forces.

One big advantage the Special Forces would bring to the fight was the combat air controllers, highly trained Air Force enlisted personnel who accompanied each team to precisely locate enemy troops, vehicles, or fortifications and transmit exact target coordinates to aircraft dropping precision-guided weapons like Joint Direct Attack Munitions. This gave the small Special Forces teams the heavy striking power of much larger conventional units. Moreover, the teams could move fast and adapt to the irregular tactics of guerrilla militias. The CIA also had MQ-1 Predator Unmanned Aerial Vehicle (UAV) reconnaissance drones available to stalk the Taliban and al-Qaida. As operational planning proceeded, the CIA would complete upgrades to the Predator to arm the drone to launch Hellfire missiles.

At some point early in the process, we needed a decision from the President on who would be in charge, the CIA or CENTCOM and the Department of Defense? In other words, would the CIA's small, previously clandestine assistance to the Northern Alliance remain the dominant thrust of the campaign, or would a much larger operation under Pentagon command supplant it? The CIA knew the Northern Alliance personalities and capabilities best, but the DoD had the warfighting assets and logistics needed for a campaign. It was decided that, as the Afghanistan operation expanded, the U.S. Central Command would organize and execute it, with the CIA playing a supporting role to Gen. Tommy Franks.

Afghanistan would be a campaign in a larger conflict with violent extremism. Unless the Taliban obeyed our ultimatum to neutralize al-Qaida, we could proceed with our most robust military option—combining precision air strikes and SOF teams operating beside CIA paramilitary, and eventually moving on to larger conventional forces. Bush requested an operational concept to be followed by a detailed OPLAN that included "meaningful" target sets as well as an execution timetable.

Tom Franks would quickly become busier than he already was—so would all of us on the Joint Chiefs of Staff.

––––––––––

Franks and his J3 Operations Director, Air Force Maj. Gen. Gene Renuart, flew up to Washington on September 20 to brief Hugh Shelton and me on CENTCOM's operational concept for Afghanistan. That afternoon, Franks and Renuart were scheduled to brief Secretary Rumsfeld before we took the concept to the White House the next day for the President to review. In the previous week, we had contributed our ideas to Tom Franks, and I was impressed with the progress CENTCOM had made in that short period.

"We see the operation as having four phases," Franks began. He pointed to an easel chart: "Phase I, Set Conditions and Build Forces to Provide the National Command Authority Credible Military Options." Franks expanded on this complex military and diplomatic challenge. While the Department of Defense decided exactly what forces would be needed, the State Department and CIA would assist us in cementing basing and staging accords with the countries bordering Afghanistan, especially Uzbekistan to the north and Pakistan to the east. Because of its geography and tribal affiliations inside Afghanistan, Pakistan was particularly important and would be a critical ally if we were to succeed. This was why General Chilton had made the initial approach to Islamabad. In addition, our negotiators continued to reach out to other countries, such as Uzbekistan, for overflight and basing rights. Although the United States had policy differences with many of these countries, we needed their support at this critical juncture.

The CIA's paramilitary officers already in Afghanistan were trying to build the confidence and assess the willingness of the surviving Northern Alliance leaders to work with us as well as to learn their practical needs and capabilities. The Tajik general, Mohammed Fahim Khan, as well as Abdul Rashid Dostum, who led an Uzbek militia, would be important players. The Agency's paramilitary operators were was also working to gain the support of militia leaders Mohammed Attah, a Tajik, and Mohammed Mohaqeq, an ethnic Hazara Shiite, to prepare the operation.

Even if the CIA were able to build enough goodwill (and spread enough money) among the tribal militias to persuade them to join us in the fight against the Taliban and al-Qaida, these guerrillas still needed major logistical support. Short of most war-fighting essentials, they were particularly low on weapons and ammunition, and boots, winter uniforms, as well as saddles and feed for their horses and mules. This would be an army that traveled through the high passes of the Hindu Kush in saddles, trailing pack animals, an anachronism in the twenty-first century.

"Phase II," Tom Franks continued, "Conduct Initial Combat Operations and Continue to set Conditions for Follow-on Operations." Ideally, Phase II would follow Phase I without pause. Speed and flexibility would be critical in this battle. The idea was to hit the enemy hard and give him no time to recover. I recognized the key transformational elements of CENTCOM's plan. No country had ever fought a military campaign quite like this. Once "kinetic" operations began, Tomahawk cruise missiles would decapitate the Taliban's rudimentary integrated air defense systems and B-2 stealth bombers would arrive overhead in darkness to drop tons of precision-guided JDAMs. As these initial combat operations proceeded, Army Special Forces teams would cross into Afghanistan and begin to link up with their Northern Alliance counterparts.

The 7th Fleet aircraft carrier USS *Kitty Hawk* would steam from Japan to international waters off the Pakistani coast and become a "lily pad" from which SOF helicopter assaults into southern Afghanistan would be launched. Other aircraft carriers in the Arabian Sea would launch fighter-bomber strikes, providing around-the-clock tactical air support for the SOF teams and our Afghan allies. The heaviest air punch would be delivered by B-1s and B-52s flying from the British base on the Indian Ocean island of Diego Garcia. Armed with JDAMs, these bombers could loiter above the battlefield for hours, dropping their ordnance on targets the SOF combat air controllers selected. No matter how fanatical the resistance, no enemy force caught out in the open—or in trenches—could withstand the destructive power of such bombardment.

It goes without saying that JDAMs were a dangerous weapon: As we had learned in the Balkans, they hit their aim-points precisely. So the forward air controllers always had to make certain those targets were the enemy, not friendly forces.

In the 1980s, of course, the Soviet Union had conducted a brutal air campaign during its war against the Afghan mujahideen. But the Soviets did not have laser- and GPS-guided target-designating equipment or JDAMs. A B-52 orbiting unseen miles above the ground, unleashing numerous Precision-

Guided Munitions, would be far more destructive, both physically and psychologically, than a SU-25 fighter-bomber screaming low over the ridge tops to drop "dumb" bombs. Also, the tactics CENTCOM would employ were far more sophisticated than the heavy-unit bludgeon with which the Soviets had tried to crush the Afghan mujahideen militias. The long Soviet campaign had often depended on armored vehicles and had been restricted to Afghanistan's primitive road network, susceptible to ambush. CENTCOM's battle plan would exploit the country's mountainous terrain, taking the rapidly evolving war directly to the Taliban and al-Qaida.

Tom Franks moved on to Phase III, Conduct Decisive Combat Operations in Afghanistan, Continue to Build the Coalition, and Conduct Operations AOR Wide. America's NATO partners, as well as Australia, were already lining up to contribute forces and logistical support to a coalition. France had also offered combat aircraft and Special Operations Forces. The United Kingdom under Prime Minister Tony Blair had assured our government that British troops and planes would be available for the fight, however long it lasted.

The President had directed the military to think beyond Afghanistan and begin planning how we could disrupt terrorism and violent extremism around the world. This presidential thinking was in line with ours on the Joint Staff, although disrupting terrorism and violent extremism would require more than military force. As Franks correctly noted, much of that extremist activity was centered in CENTCOM's Area of Responsibility (AOR): the Middle East and Central Asia. But much of this threat was not susceptible to direct military operations, even the type of transformational campaign that Franks and Renuart outlined. That would probably have to be the purview of CIA paramilitaries and our Special Forces working with locals. Again, our effectiveness would be directly proportional to the precision of our intelligence and its integration with the other instruments of power.

Phase IV of CENTCOM's operational concept was still the most nebulous: Establish Capability of Coalition Partners to Prevent the Re-Emergence of Terrorism and Provide Support for Humanitarian Assistance Efforts. Franks had planned very early for emergency humanitarian assistance, working with the Air Force's Air Mobility Command to prepare for multiple loads of rations to be airlifted from Ramstein Air Base in Germany aboard huge C-17 transports and dropped to refugees displaced by the fighting. An extended food air-drop operation, however, would not meet the needs of the tens of thousands of refugees we anticipated. So it was important to open "land bridges" from Uzbekistan and Pakistan for aid workers and trucks carrying tents, blankets, flour, and cooking oil—all that would be necessary to sustain a refugee population through the first post-Taliban winter. This humanitarian aid was also meant to build goodwill between the people of Afghanistan and our Coalition forces.

Preventing the re-emergence of terrorism in Afghanistan would be a tough challenge, however. At Camp David and after, the White House had made it clear that America would not engage in "nation building" in Afghanistan. Our mission was to topple the Taliban regime and destroy al-Qaida, not nurture civilian institutions. Having been through these discussions before, I wasn't at all sure that we could topple the Taliban and eradicate al-Qaida and then simply leave. I hoped that other nations, international organizations, and non-governmental organizations (NGOs) would take up the postconflict effort. President Bush's aversion to nation building was certainly strong enough at this point that he wanted stability and reconstruction efforts to depend mainly on international donors and NGOs.

CENTCOM, working closely with the CIA, had developed a solid operational plan, which satisfied Hugh, me, and George Tenet. However, we weren't the only people Tom Franks would have to please before we briefed the President the next day. He did not look at all happy when Hugh Shelton announced that the Joint Chiefs would join us in the "Tank"—the JCS conference room—early that afternoon for Secretary Rumsfeld's briefing. The Tank got its name from the World War II meeting place of the service chiefs. It was in the basement of a building in Washington, D.C., near the water tank for the steam heating system. Although Tom was obviously disgruntled at this news, there was no way to avoid briefing the Joint Chiefs of Staff even at this conceptual stage of the OPLAN's evolution; Goldwater-Nichols made that obligation clear. Although Gen. Tommy Franks would command the operation, the armed services, as represented by the Joint Chiefs, would provide the necessary troops and materiel. As the saying went, they definitely "had a dog in this fight."

The Tank briefing with the Joint Chiefs of Staff was not a happy occasion. Franks had hoped this session would inform the services on CENTCOM's preliminary concept, not become a detailed critique of his initial thinking. When Hugh Shelton asked the Chiefs' opinions that afternoon, they weren't shy about offering them. Army Chief of Staff Gen. Eric Shinseki, Chief of Naval Operations Vern Clark, Marine Commandant Jim Jones, and Air Force Chief of Staff John Jumper, all had something to say. But they all spoke in a tone of constructive criticism. The operation was too light, too dependent on SOF; heavier forces were needed—but such units would be too difficult to sustain. Others recommended more airpower. One suggested that helicopter-borne Marines, deployed in sufficient force, could get the job done. These were the nation's senior military leaders, who had been involved in war before, and were looking for a paradigm for a conflict with a failed state and stateless terrorists.

Tommy Franks's war-fighting concepts were new and mostly unproven, and the Joint Chiefs had to be fully informed on the CENTCOM plan. We all had a legal obligation to provide military advice to the President and National Security Council, and this advice had to be based in part on the details of the operational plan. No President or Secretary of Defense would approve a war plan without getting the Joint Chiefs' opinion. And there was another reason for this briefing, if asked about Afghanistan events during congressional testimony or media events, they would have to be informed.

Secretary Rumsfeld had let the animated discussion among Tommy Franks and the Joint Chiefs proceed at its own pace. No doubt Rumsfeld thought it was important for him to judge how the senior military viewed a potential complex combat operation thousands of miles away.

I was sure that America would be going to war following the CENTCOM plan, and when I became Chairman of the Joint Chiefs of Staff in ten days, one of my most important jobs would be to keep Tom Franks and the Joint Chiefs talking to each other and pulling together.

On the evening of September 20, President Bush addressed a joint session of Congress and, via live television, the world to describe the response America planned to the 9/11 attacks. He singled out Usama bin Laden and al-Qaida's affiliates, Egyptian Islamic Jihad and the Islamic Movement of Uzbekistan, as well as the Taliban. (I watched from a hospital bed after undergoing surgery on my right knee. The surgeon said the operation had to be that day to save the cartilage. I had torn the cartilage just by standing up from my conference table. I hoped this reflected an earlier sports injury and not just the hazards of staff work.)

"By aiding and abetting murder," Bush said, "the Taliban regime is committing murder. And tonight, the United States of America makes the following demands on the Taliban: Deliver to the United States all the leaders of al-Qaida who hide in your land. They will hand over the terrorists, or they will share their fate."

Watching the speech, I remembered Donald Rumsfeld's statement that the

United States should never issue a warning unless we were willing to act on it. The President's speech was rousing. Would the military be ready in time to meet his demands?

The President explained that America's response would involve "far more than instant retaliation and isolated strikes." America should not expect one battle, but a "lengthy campaign, unlike any other we have ever seen."

He proclaimed that "every nation, in every region, now has a decision to make. Either you are with us or you are with the terrorists."

Bush then announced the creation of a new cabinet-level organization: the Department of Homeland Security, which would coordinate the efforts of dozens of federal, state, and local law enforcement agencies. He nominated former Pennsylvania congressman and governor Tom Ridge, a Harvard graduate and Vietnam veteran, as the first Secretary of Homeland Security.

Concluding, President Bush spoke with real conviction. "I will not forget this wound to our country or those who inflicted it. I will not yield; I will not rest. I will not relent in waging this struggle for freedom and security for the American people."

It was a good speech that addressed all the necessary points and helped prepare the public for the coming campaign. But words alone did not win wars. Now the Department of Defense had to prepare the President for the military operation we envisioned.

On Friday afternoon, September 21, Secretary Rumsfeld, Hugh Shelton, Army Maj. Gen. Dell Dailey, commander of the Joint Special Operations Command (JSOC), and I met President Bush and Vice President Cheney in the White House, in a study off the living quarters on the second floor. Discussing CENTCOM's concept of operations, Tom Franks was much more relaxed than he had been in the Tank. Although the President's time was tightly booked with phone calls and appointments during this crisis period, his staff had scheduled two hours for the meeting.

Even so, Bush was not in a hurry. No sooner had Franks begun describing Phase I than the President asked about our progress in securing host-nation basing and overflight support in the region. Franks had the answers the President wanted. Sultan Qaboos of Oman had offered air bases and logistical support for our fleet. Our Air Force AC-130 gunships would fly from Oman and Dell Dailey's JSOC special operators—including Navy SEALs, Army Rangers, and the Delta Force—would stage from there, flying long-range MH-47 Chinook helicopters out to the USS *Kitty Hawk* in transit to a lily pad station off the Pakistani coast.

As the briefing continued, we outlined the efforts we were working on to put in place workable airlift and air-drop operations in northern Afghanistan. Fortunately, we had discovered a wonderful interlocutor in the Uzbek Minister of Defense, Kodir Ghulomov. Uzbekistan was beginning to respond to Pentagon and State Department overtures to gain access to the former Soviet air base at Karshi-Kanabad (K-2). Secretary Rumsfeld was using his considerable influence to cultivate the minister and help win over President Karimov. Rumsfeld planned on touring the area to convince the regional leaders that cooperation with us was in their own best interest. As a byproduct of our operations in Afghanistan, we would do our best to destroy the Islamic Movement of Uzbekistan guerrillas operating with the Taliban in Afghanistan and help Uzbek forces with needed military equipment. We also intended to pay Karimov's government well for the use of the remote K-2 air base, which could accommodate heavy airlift planes and both SOF and Combat Search and Rescue (CSAR) helicopters.

Pakistan's leader, Gen. Pervez Musharraf, remained more leery of open cooperation with the American military for two important reasons. He faced a stubborn fundamentalist Islamic opposition, particularly in the northwest tribal districts bordering Afghanistan. In addition, many officers in Musharraf's own Inter-Service Intelligence Directorate were Taliban supporters who had a lot at stake in its survival: If India, Pakistan's intractable enemy, ever invaded and pushed Musharraf's forces west over the Khyber Pass, they could fall back on the miles of desert and gorges that Afghanistan's "strategic depth" would provide. So Musharraf had to be sure of his footing among his own military before he agreed to cooperate with the United States.

Maj. Gen. Dell Dailey outlined where his SOF operators would initially concentrate. They had already begun rehearsing for "takedown" strikes against enemy leadership targets, including the fortified compound of Taliban leader Mullah Mohammed Omar. Dailey's forces were also planning rescue missions for foreign aid workers in Kabul whom the Taliban could possibly take hostage once the operation began.

Another potential target for the special operators was a fertilizer plant that the Soviets had built near the northwestern city of Mazar-e-Sharif. Although the factory had apparently cut back large-scale fertilizer production, reconnaissance revealed that the Taliban had ringed the grounds with guard posts and set up checkpoints on the surrounding roads. Even more interesting, intelligence agents reported that known members of al-Qaida regularly visited the plant, which might be producing chemical and biological weapons. However, the plant might just be making common fertilizer, and the guards and checkpoints might merely be protection from Northern Alliance raids. But it was well known among chemical weapons experts that a facility that could make fertilizer could also produce poison gas such as sarin. And none of us sitting that September afternoon in the President's comfortable White House study doubted that al-Qaida would use weapons of mass destruction if they managed to obtain them.

When our special operators were finally able to search the plant that fall, they found no traces of nerve gas or specialized equipment for making it. However, this did not prove that the factory had *never* done so. That was the insidious side of such "dual-use" facilities: A pharmaceutical plant could simultaneously produce antibiotics and biological warfare agents; a chemical factory both fertilizer and nerve gas.

We obtained at least a partial verification of al-Qaida's quest for WMD ten months later when an Afghan sold a trove of videotapes to CNN correspondent Nic Robertson in Kabul. The man said the tapes had come from a house Usama bin Laden and other al-Qaida members had once occupied. The tapes were quickly verified as authentic, and several had a direct bearing on the WMD issue. The most stark showed a young mongrel dog tied to the wall of a concrete room. The dog rises expectantly as two men in baggy Afghan trousers appear in the camera frame. "Let's do this fast," one man says in Arabic. Wispy gray fumes begin to rise as they dash out. The dog trembles and then falls against a wall, where it shakes violently, moaning and whimpering, until it dies. The tape also records the gassing of two more young dogs, dying in the same agonizing spasms, which are characteristic of sarin gas.

David A. Kay, who would later lead the search for WMD in Iraq, commented that the tapes demonstrated al-Qaida had succeeded in either producing or obtaining "primitive" chemical weapons. "The terrible racking sound of the dog in death throes," he said, "is a classic sound of a nerve agent like sarin."

I remembered the deadly nerve gas used in the Tokyo subway terror attack in March 1995, when the Aum Shinrikyo doomsday cult had unleashed sarin in the trains and tunnels. The religious zealotry of al-Qaida made it even more fanatical and ruthless than Aum Shinrikyo.

Although Tommy Franks and his CENTCOM staff were fine-tuning their plan, it was clear to Hugh Shelton and me that a number of inevitable delays had to be overcome before kinetic operations started. Basing and staging remained unresolved issues for longer than we would have preferred. Finally it was decided that Secretary Rumsfeld would fly to the region and personally consult President Karimov and the Saudi Arabians to ensure we would have access to essential bases: the large K-2 field in Uzbekistan and the Combined Air Operations Center (CAOC) at Prince Sultan Air Base. Gaining Pakistani consent for bases had been easier because we would not be operating large combat aircraft from their territory, but rather planned to stage CSAR helicopters from the Shahbaz Air Base in Jacobabad on the border between Sindh and Baluchistan provinces—a dusty locale evocative of Rudyard Kipling.

The Pakistanis moved their aircraft out to make room for our operations. When I visited, the airfield was not up to U.S. standards and needed lots of work by our troops, but the hospitality of our new Pakistani friends was superb and the local base commander very cooperative. This unlikely location started the rebuilding of U.S.-Pakistani military-to-military relationships that had atrophied so badly over more than a decade, and that in my view was a good thing.

As the basing arrangements moved ahead later in September, we still faced the unresolved problem of identifying worthy targets in Afghanistan. Like Somalia, Afghanistan was a failed state, its infrastructure ruined by years of war with the Soviets and the civil strife that followed. The surviving roads and bridges were of little strategic value and we certainly didn't want to further destroy Afghanistan's fragile transportation system and the ability to carry on economic activity after the conflict. Both the Taliban and al-Qaida were basically light infantry forces susceptible to air strikes only if they massed to fight the Northern Alliance or we could catch them moving through choke points such as mountain passes.

The Taliban's armed forces did possess a rudimentary integrated air-defense system that combined a few obsolete radars and Soviet-built surface-to-air missiles. They also flew a handful of old MiG fighters, as well as a few battered Mi-8 and Mi-17 helicopters and Antonov-26 turboprops. Collectively these meager assets barely represented the "meaningful" target sets the President had asked us to identify. The Taliban also had other dangerous air-defense weapons that would be much more difficult to target for long-range air strikes. In particular, their ZSU-23mm multibarreled cannons, towed behind trucks, and heat-seeking, shoulder-fired missiles posed a danger to our helicopters. Once our SOF combat air controllers were on the ground, laser-designating the Taliban's mobile antiaircraft artillery for strikes by Precision-Guided Munitions, that danger would no doubt be quickly eliminated.

But, as we on the Joint Staff and CENTCOM saw the problem, there would probably be a difficult lag between the start of air operations and the insertion of the SOF teams. Part of the problem would be overcoming impatience in the White House and the Secretary's office. Once the missiles and bombs began to fall, President Bush and Secretary Rumsfeld would have to convince the American people that this was not just another exercise in pounding sand. That was one of the reasons we needed visible American "boots on the ground." At NSC meetings, the President was calm and seemed comfortable with our planning progress to date. I felt his urgency when he spoke to the need for "defining pictures": U.S. troops and their Afghan partners occupying former Taliban and al-Qaida strongholds, for example. Although the planned operation would be far from a publicity stunt, any photographs and videos of American special operators fighting side by side with their Afghan allies—or B-52s circling overhead battering the enemy with JDAMs—would go a long way to assure the American people, our allies, and the enemy that this time we were serious.

Another complication of the targeting process was the need to minimize civilian casualties, "collateral damage" (CD) in military parlance. Once the kinetics began, we wanted to be very careful to follow the Law of Armed Conflict, and by so doing, help win over the Afghan people to our side. And, finally, this would show the world that U.S. military might was not used indiscriminately, in contrast to our adversaries' use of terror. During our many discussions, the President, the senior military officers, and the civilian officials involved determined that the first wave of attacks should avoid all urban areas to minimize collateral damage. Bush made sure we understood that whatever action was taken in Afghanistan would be against the Taliban, *not* the Afghan people. We would use all the tools at our disposal—humanitarian ration drops, strategic communications, and psychological warfare leaflet drops—to get that message across.

But above all, President Bush stressed, this would be a coordinated operation. "Everyone must have a sense of progression," he told us. "One bombing raid is not the entire mission." Bush worried that the American people might become discouraged when they saw the first air attacks did not cause rapid enemy capitulation. So the President wanted to show the world a *continual* tempo of operations, that we were not a one-trick pony—always considering the needs of operational security. When the ground SOF operation began, Bush said, we would try to capture or kill Usama bin Laden. We should never forget that he and his top lieutenants were our principal targets.

Meanwhile, both planning and dealing with unexpected contingencies continued at an exhausting pace. There was a complex set of variables. As we expected, the Taliban were not interested in reaching a compromise with the United States following the President's speech. Instead, they attempted to stall by vaguely offering to identify those responsible for the 9/11 attacks and try them at an "Islamic tribunal."

So there remained little doubt that we would be fighting in Afghanistan, probably sooner rather than later. At least we were securing tangible support from Saudi Arabia, the United Arab Emirates (UAE), Uzbekistan, Kyrgyzstan, Pakistan, Oman, and Bahrain. Our cruise missiles would be launched from ships and planes in the Arabian Sea; some helicopter-borne SOF operators would fly from the *Kitty Hawk*; others from the K-2 air base in Uzbekistan.

The big question at this point was whether the CIA paramilitary officers could convince the Northern Alliance militias to join the battle, and if so, how hard would they fight?

During the frantic planning the last week in September, we still had not decided on a name for the operation. Some favored Infinite Justice—until we learned that in Muslim theology, only God could dispense infinite justice. Another candidate name for the operation was Freedom's Light—but it was quickly observed the name sounded like Freedom Lite. Finally, on September 24, General Franks proposed Operation Enduring Freedom, which the SecDef liked and sent over to the White House for approval. The name stuck.

There was the usual friction between the executing command, CENT-COM, and the supporting commands as they tried to mesh gears smoothly. Transportation Command, for example, was impatient to receive General Franks's final Time-Phased Force & Deployment List—the TPFDL, which was the Holy Grail of all military logisticians. On some days it seemed that dozens of such problems erupted, which had to be resolved in sit-down meetings or via teleconferences. One difficulty concerned the increasing tension between Georgia and Russia, which threatened to become a hot war. Another difficulty was that a meeting on proposed worldwide staff cuts in headquarters had a direct impact on CENTCOM's ability to plan and execute Operation Enduring Freedom. Another was the establishment and support of a "Coalition Village" (for allied liaison officers) at CENTCOM's headquarters on MacDill Air Force

Base. What department would pay for the humanitarian assistance we were going to air-drop to Afghanistan's internal refugees—DoD or State? What about refining the size and mission of the Air National Guard and Reserve Combat Air Patrols protecting our cities and nuclear power plants? All these concerns occupied our days—and nights.

On other days, fewer issues arose. But they always arose. Business as usual for the Joint Staff after 9/11.

In the middle of this detailed work, I asked the Joint Staff to work with Rumsfeld's special assistant Steve Cambone to map out new responsibilities for the U.S. Special Operations Command. One of the major changes would be to implement the planned shift of SOCOM from a supporting to a supported role with global responsibilities. This seemed a simple enough undertaking; after all, SOCOM already had people and assets based worldwide. But our reorganization went beyond people and facilities. If it was approved, the very way SOCOM was organized and its worldwide responsibilities would change dramatically. This had the potential to change the fundamental way SOCOM interacted with the other combatant commanders and would be controversial. But in my view it was essential to have one command that could look globally, since we were facing a global threat and an adversary that didn't much care about our precise combatant command AOR boundaries.

Among the countless details we were working on, I addressed the concerns of Torie Clark, the Assistant Secretary of Defense for Public Affairs. She was absolutely terrific to work with and very good at her job. We were helping her develop needed policy guidance on how to provide appropriate media coverage for the operation. We all understood that the President and the Secretary wanted the most complete and accurate coverage possible—we also had the vital issue of operational security to address. So we could not give the media *any* advance notice on this operation. A breach in security might well cost lives: of our helicopter crews and SOF troops, and of CIA paramilitary officers. And the whole issue of leaks had an international dimension: Gen. Joe Ralston called from Europe to report a the French were "very frustrated," and their chief of staff Gen. Jean-Pierre Kelche was peeved that France had not been involved in the planning. He was demanding a lot more information and proposed a campaign-planning committee. He even grumbled that France might have to reconsider its commitment if it did not receive this accommodation. The French had important capability and, just as important, they were willing to use it. We needed to keep them on our side.

Meanwhile, among all the distractions, Hugh Shelton and I worked with the Secretary and his subordinates, Deputy Secretary Paul Wolfowitz and Undersecretary for Policy Doug Feith. We had to consider how Operation Enduring Freedom would "decrement" other war plans we had for Korea and the Middle East—everywhere we had planned for contingencies around the world. The Department of Defense was a gargantuan organization, but our roster of people and our inventory of ships, planes, munitions, and equipment was not limitless, nor was all of the force able to do all things. Whatever forces and equipment we shifted to the Afghanistan operation, the change would inevitably affect our strength elsewhere to some degree.

But our priority was Afghanistan, and we were going to war.

I was sworn in on Monday, October 1, 2001, in Conmy Hall at Fort Myer. I was still on crutches from arthroscopic surgery on my right knee a couple of weeks previously, and it hurt like hell as I stood at attention on the platform and for hours in the receiving line at the reception afterward. So much for following doctor's orders to keep my leg elevated. But the war was going to start in seven days. Our troops were going into harm's way, and some would soon be hurting a lot worse than this.

I felt great pride on this occasion and it should have been a special time to be with family and friends. Of course it was, but I was far more concerned that the nation would shortly be sending our blood and treasure to war, and there was still lots of work to do. I remember my children asking after I was nominated whether all the press coverage about the "new Chairman" would last through my tenure. I assured them that as soon as I was sworn in "you won't hear about the Chairman at all." Then after 9/11, I realized that we were about to enter a time of intense media exposure and scrutiny. The Chairman would indeed be a very busy person and I wanted to get on with it. But for the moment I was smiling and shaking hands with the well-wishers—friends, diplomats, military personnel, and foreign military attachés—at the reception.

This moment of transition was also a good time to review my professional and personal priorities. The foremost was the Global War on Terror, potentially an issue of national survival. Then came continued transformation of our military: It would be easy to lose our perspective amid all the pressing operational matters. Another critical concern was the need to maintain decent pay, medical care, and housing for our service members and their families. They were the essence of our national security, and we couldn't afford to shortchange them. I made these the priorities for the Joint Staff during my tenure.

———————

Before becoming Chairman of the Joint Chiefs of Staff, I had often reflected on the often-complex civil-military relationship. Fortunately, I had met Dr. Dick Kohn during my year at the Army War College in 1980. He's now a professor at the University of North Carolina Chapel Hill and has given much thought to this topic. He sent me a couple of chapters of Eliot Cohen's then-upcoming book, *Supreme Command*. Eliot, the director of the Johns Hopkins Paul H. Nitze School of Advanced International Studies, had also given rigorous consideration to civilian control of the military. The first time I read Eliot's manuscript I felt that he leaned much too far toward civilian control, to the detriment of the military. After I had thought about it for a while and read the material a second time, however, the military's role in our society became crystallized for me. In essence, the senior military officers' role is to vigorously provide the best professional advice possible to our political leaders. The Commander in Chief or the Secretary of Defense makes the decisions. And unless they are illegal or immoral, the military must carry out the orders of the President or the Secretary. To do otherwise would be to impose our own military judgment on what are political decisions, an action that's fundamentally inconsistent with our Constitution or the laws of the land.

In the event of disagreement, resignation is rarely an option either, in my view. The very act of resignation would be seen as a political statement, drawing the armed services into political debate. The ultimate danger is a politicization of the military. It could lead to the military's inappropriately influencing national events. In the end, it's not the military that judges the decisions the President or Secretary of Defense make, it's the other two branches of government. And we have seen that play out in the past few years.

———————

The personal side of the transition to the Chairman's position was tough. Mary Jo and I had been married thirty-six years and had shared many adventures— her trips up to Udorn as I flew combat missions . . . our tiny house at the end of the Futenma runway on Okinawa, with roaring cargo aircraft or typhoon wind and rain rattling the roof and walls . . . eating fugu blowfish in Japan . . . moving our children around the world and sending them to dozens of different schools. Throughout all those years, we had shared our life and love daily. But now I realized that was going to change. There simply would not be enough hours in each day to spend the time with her that I would want.

As October 1, 2001, approached, I told Mary Jo, "We won't get our lives back for four years, but we will do this as a team as we have for the last thirty-six years." We both looked upon this time not only as a great responsibility but as a great honor to represent the men and women in uniform and their families. Although there is no official role, many responsibilities and opportunities are presented to the spouses of the Chairman and other senior leaders. Her agenda was a full-time job as well. She was able to travel with me all over the world, but there was not much quality time together. On the plane, we both had our own homework and preparation to do, as we were on separate itineraries. Her feedback was invaluable as she often learned things from the families that never reached my ears.

In all the services, up through the chains of command, spouses play a vital role in unit cohesion and provide the sense of family and support that is missing when family members are far from home. This support system becomes especially critical during times of war.

In fact, it wasn't long before she would wait outside the shower before dawn with a pad and ballpoint pen, reviewing issues that had arisen the previous day so we could make our routine daily decisions. Then, she would ask questions and take more notes on upcoming important events. She realized that this brief encounter might be the only chance we'd have to speak face-to-face before late that night.

There are also many representational duties as Chairman, and you could spend almost every evening at one social or diplomatic event or the other. You had to place a limit on such activities. A free evening without social or professional obligations meant that Mary Jo and I went to the fitness center or to Walter Reed or Bethesda to visit wounded troops and their families.

I was determined not to let the job grind me down physically or emotionally. I exercised by either running the mile and a half to or from the Pentagon with my security detail in tow (wondering how they got so lucky to get to run so slowly with this general), on my home treadmill in the morning, or stopping by the Fort Myer fitness center in the evening. Regular meals were also important, and I found that I could combine exercise with eating by walking down the long corridor to the Pentagon Subway shop for a turkey-and-Swiss on whole wheat. Getting adequate sleep was not a problem: I cut way back on my caffeine consumption and let Pete Pace handle the more *routine* emergencies that came in the middle of the night. That had been my job when I was Vice Chairman; now Pete could carry the load. The duty couldn't have been in more capable hands.

Pete Pace's responsibilities were heavier than mine had been as Vice Chairman, because the country was now at war. Fortunately, a very capable Joint Staff backstopped him on military matters, and the civilians in the Office of the Secretary of Defense were innovative and energetic in helping him handle the new challenges. I told Pete to make Doug Feith his new best friend. Undersecretary of Defense for Policy Doug Feith worked closely with Pete on the Campaign Planning Committee (CAPCOM) that was essentially a traffic cop breaking up jammed policy matters before they blocked the door of Rumsfeld's office. Doug and Pete were the CAPCOM cochairs, and they worked tirelessly and effectively to smooth the seams between the military and civilian sides of the E-Ring. To keep the voluminous paperwork and many decisions flowing, I authorized General Pace to approve anything he felt comfortable approving, and just keep me informed of the more important decisions. There was certainly enough work for the two of us and I didn't want the Joint Staff or OSD to be frustrated waiting for my signature.

The countdown to the start of Operation Enduring Freedom now proceeded without major incident. In the Arabian Sea, our TLAM "shooters" were ready to launch; our long-range bombers in Missouri prepared for their first strikes. Special Mission Unit troops rehearsed their missions before moving to staging sites in Oman to link up with the *Kitty Hawk*. Army Special Forces teams were leaving for Germany, en route to the K-2 base in Uzbekistan, as a battalion of the 10th Mountain Division prepared to deploy from Fort Drum, New York, to join them as a security and rapid reaction force.

Then, a new threat emerged. On Thursday, October 4, Bob Stevens, a photo editor at the *Sun* tabloid in Boca Raton, Florida, fell gravely ill after exposure to a suspicious white powder found in an envelope. Two days later he was dead. Law enforcement technicians identified the powder as granulated anthrax bacteria spores, which, if inhaled, are often fatal.

Over the next several days, letters containing anthrax spores were mailed to a number of Washington offices, including those of Senate Majority Leader Tom Daschle and his Democratic colleague Senator Patrick Leahy, as well as NBC News anchor Tom Brokaw. These letters were addressed in childish block letters and bore a return address of "4th Grade, Greendale School" in Trenton,

New Jersey, a nonexistent school. The letters to the senators contained taunt-
ing computer printout messages dated 09-11-01: "WE HAVE THIS ANTRAX
... YOU DIE NOW ... ARE YOU AFRAID? ... DEATH TO AMERICA ...
DEATH TO ISRAEL ... ALLAH IS GREAT."

The anthrax in the letter to Senator Daschle was highly concentrated and
"weaponized" grade, a feared biological warfare agent. Postal workers in the
capital area began to get sick, and two died. The Hart Senate Office Building
had to be sealed and decontaminated. Before the attacks ended, five people
were dead and seventeen infected, and others suffer after effects to this day.

Was this the work of a homicidal amateur or the first wave of a new al-Qaida
terror campaign? We simply didn't know and had to wait to see if the mailings
continued and what clues our intelligence community could provide. Meanwhile, the sense that America was under siege and, with it, the pressure to find
the enemy overseas and capture or kill them continued to mount.

And because the anthrax spores in several of the letters had undergone sophisticated drying and processing, government experts considered the poison
almost certainly had come from a weapons laboratory.

It was not until almost seven years later—after a convoluted FBI manhunt—
that the Justice Department abandoned its conviction that Steven Hatfill, a researcher at the Army's biological weapons laboratory at Fort Detrick, Maryland,
was responsible and focused instead on another of the facility's scientists, Bruce
E. Ivins. In July 2008, Ivins committed suicide on learning he was about to be
indicted in the crimes. The FBI considered DNA evidence linking him to the
anthrax-tainted letters overwhelming.

Early on Sunday, October 7, less than a month after the 9/11 attacks, Tommy
Franks called to report that we had all the pieces in place. The Tomahawk missiles and the JDAMs from the B-2 stealth bombers would begin striking the
Taliban's air-defense system after sunset in Afghanistan. And America's military would start the cycle of strikes, battle damage assessments from reconnaissance, and restrikes if required. Again the problem was the small number
of targets worthy of attacking in Afghanistan. So beginning the most important part of the operation would require patience.

I was in my office that morning to review the initial strike reports when the
President addressed the nation. "On my orders," he said, "the United States
military has begun strikes against al-Qaida terrorist training camps and mili-

tary installations of the Taliban regime in Afghanistan." The strikes were "carefully targeted actions" designed to disrupt the use of Afghanistan as a terrorist base and to destroy the Taliban military.

Once the President approved the operations, the Joint Staff prepared the Execute Order, Secretary Rumsfeld signed it, and I sent it to all the combatant commanders and to all involved departments and agencies.

Careful targeting was in fact the hallmark of the operation. The missiles and Precision-Guided Munitions had struck their targets, and our B-2s remained invisible to the Taliban radar as they dropped their JDAMs. From a planning perspective, the stealthiness of the B-2 virtually ensured we wouldn't have to deal with the issues surrounding captured aircrews. It looked as if the enemy air defenses would be quickly destroyed, but I was afraid that running out of meaningful targets would become an issue.

That afternoon, Secretary Rumsfeld and I gave our first briefing in the packed Pentagon press room. I followed the SecDef in on my crutches. Rumsfeld spoke in a calm, confident manner. "We support the Afghan people against al-Qaida, a foreign presence on their land, and against the Taliban regime that supports them. . . . We hope to create conditions for sustained antiterrorist and humanitarian and relief operations in Afghanistan."

He commented on the aircraft and weapons used and cited the contribution of the "dozens of countries" that helped with transit and landing rights, basing, and intelligence support. I stressed that we were in the "early stages of ongoing combat operations," adding that the first target was hit at approximately 9:00 P.M. Afghan time (12:30 P.M. in Washington). "And operations continue as we speak." I also highlighted the initial humanitarian assistance airdrops of some thirty-seven thousand prepackaged meals, as well as badly needed medicine. In the question-and-answer period that followed, the correspondents were inquisitive, polite, even upbeat, which was reflected in their stories.

I hoped that the positive news media mood would continue.

———————

That proved to be a futile hope.

As we had expected, freelance news media crews and a few foreign network correspondents managed to convince the Taliban authorities to allow them into Afghanistan. The videotape they sent back across the Khyber Pass often showed bombs from unseen planes striking distant, seemingly empty ridgelines against the backdrop of snowy mountains. It was impossible to see the camouflaged Taliban trenches or bunkers. From our perspective, the scattered media coverage of ragged, poorly armed and equipped Northern Alliance troops holed up in their medieval mud brick fortifications was even worse. The impression was that we had backed the losing horse in the race.

Correcting inaccurate media coverage remained as difficult as it was necessary. The facile video image, lifted from an edited correspondent's report, was often accepted as the truth. Sometimes press stories were no more substantial than rumors. When Operation Enduring Freedom expanded in Afghanistan during 2002, for example, there were media accounts of *reckless* Coalition bombing killing hundreds of innocent civilians. But before we could respond, we needed time for CENTCOM to verify what actually had happened. In more than one case, our forces had attacked villages where Taliban leaders were meeting, and regrettably there had been civilian casualties, although not the hundreds that some newspapers reported. We were often unable to correct the misperception in a timely manner and the erroneous reports frequently took root with the public.

Getting the accurate story out would plague me and the DoD (and the administration, for that matter) for the rest of my tenure. As the old saying has it, "A rumor goes around the world twice before truth can get its boots on." In this case, the strategic effect of wrong information can be devastating, sometimes for the perception of the United States that it creates and sometimes in an operational way—costing lives. A few years later, it was falsely reported that guards at the Detainee Detention Center in Guantanamo Bay, Cuba, had flushed copies of the Koran down the toilet. The ensuing riots in the Middle East resulted in over two hundred deaths, and of course the report reinforced the perception that the United States was anti-Islam. We couldn't refute the report until we had done a complete and thorough investigation of the allegation, and this took several weeks. By then the damage had been done.

United States military forces weren't organized, trained, or equipped to deal with the information technology revolution, and in many respects our system and processes were "steam-driven." Field commanders just wouldn't make this issue a top priority. I put a lot of emphasis on our ability to be relevant in this new information age, and this situation got somewhat better during my tenure. However, we had much more work to do to be able to compete with an adversary for whom the truth didn't matter and who understood very well the value of winning the "war of perceptions." Given that we were fighting an insurgency and winning the hearts and minds of the populace was a necessary condition for victory, our inability to keep the record straight was not helpful. And this wasn't just an issue for the military; the responsibility concerned the whole government. The President often asked who was in charge of getting the appropriate messages out to our many constituencies. The answer was never satisfactory.

———————————

One reason that we wanted to provide uniforms for the Northern Alliance militiamen was that we sought to correct the impression that our Afghan allies were ill-disciplined and disorganized. We wanted the world to know that, unlike the enemy, our forces complied with the Law of Armed Conflict.

So we were confident that the tone of the media coverage would improve once the Special Forces teams had infiltrated Afghanistan and linked with their CIA paramilitary colleagues. Further, the picture would brighten as we provided the Northern Alliance with air support and funneled the tons of uniforms and munitions that were stacking up at the K-2 base to them. Our original plan had called for the Special Forces to be quickly inserted in six-man elements among our militia allies aboard the CIA paramilitary's vintage Mi-17 transport helicopters after the air attacks began.

The bombing and missile raids had started on October 7, but the Special Forces teams remained at K-2, grounded for a variety of valid reasons, including nagging mechanical problems with the Mi-17s—but mainly the terrible weather of the Afghan mountains. Although lower than the Himalayas, the western Hindu Kush range had passes above sixteen thousand feet that would have to be negotiated.

There were also Northern Alliance political considerations involved: For example, it would probably provoke animosity among the rival warlords if one appeared to receive his promised American support well in advance of another. Therefore Tommy Franks and his Special Forces task force commander Col. John Mulholland had to be as much diplomats as war-fighters. This especially applied to Northern Alliance Uzbek Gen. Abdul Rashid Dostum and his militia south of Mazar-e-Sharif. Their contribution would be pivotal to the overall success of the operation, but Dostum could be difficult and had often changed sides during the years of struggle with the Taliban. Now we needed to keep him on our side. That necessity also applied to Gen. Fahim Khan, who had inherited leadership of the Tajik forces from the assassinated Ahmad Shah Massoud. Once we inserted our teams among these militias, their followers would come on board, if for no other reason than to receive the new or refurbished

East Bloc weapons and ammunition, warm uniforms, and winter boots that we provided.

Finally, by October 13, Franks got word that the Special Ops MH-53 Pave Lows, MH-47 Chinooks, and smaller MH-60 Pave Hawks had been airlifted into K-2 and would be ready to fly their first insertion within twenty-four hours. Secretary Rumsfeld was pleased but still impatient for tangible results. He had been calling Franks daily with the same question: "What's the status of the teams?" I knew Rumsfeld's impatience stemmed in part from the White House questions we heard at every National Security Council meeting. The President was eager to demonstrate progress beyond air operations. He wanted what the news media called "good visuals" to reassure the American people we weren't just bombing rocks and sand. The period between the start of the air campaign and October 19 became known at CENTCOM as "the ten days from hell": Nothing seemed to be going right, and the weather was only getting worse.

Whenever a big MH-47 Chinook or MH-53 Pave Low helicopter lifted off, the mountain passes became socked in with cloud, freezing rain, snow, and sometimes zero-visibility dust storms mixed in with the precipitation. The Chinook and Pave Low pilots from the Army's 160th Special Operations Aviation Regiment and the Air Force 1st Special Operations Wing were among the most skilled in the world. Their aircraft had been modified for high-altitude flying, but there was nothing they could do to defeat the weather conditions in these mountains.

But late on the night of October 19, two MH-53s flew a Special Forces team to Gen. Abdul Rashid Dostum's fortified militia site south of Mazar-e-Sharif. It was as if the dam had broken. As the good weather held, the Special Operations aviators lifted in more SOF detachments to other sites.

Our Green Berets and their combat air controllers loaded up their horses and got to work. The troops had earlier received an overly abbreviated *crash* course in staying aboard a stubborn Tajik mountain pony. This was not a skill that was covered in our tactics, techniques, and procedures. Within hours they were calling down the first heavy air strikes against Taliban and al-Qaida targets. But the team operating with Dostum was hampered by his fear they would move too close to the enemy and be killed or captured. Navy and Air Force fighter-bombers were joining the operation to provide close air support. Dostum's reluctance to risk American lives soon evaporated. The initial strike reports were promising: To say the Northern Alliance was impressed would be an understatement. The militias were stunned, in awe of the accuracy and destructive power of the JDAMs and laser-guided bombs. Obviously the surviving enemy forces were also impressed. They began to retreat in disarray, leaving hundreds of dead behind.

On the afternoon of Saturday, October 20, the United States made a very important statement to our enemies and to the world. Four Air Force Special Operations MC-130s flying out of Oman crossed into Afghanistan in darkness and dropped 199 men of the 75th Ranger Regiment onto Objective RHINO, a desert airstrip southwest of the Taliban stronghold of Kandahar. This airstrip was part of a hunting camp belonging to United Arab Emirates Sheik Mohammed Bin Zayed, who had alerted Tommy Franks to its existence.

As this air drop progressed, I sat in a closed facility in the National Military Command Center watching video screens with the Predator "real-time" night images of Kandahar as several MH-47s flew from the deck of the *Kitty Hawk* carrying Dell Dailey's special operators. Their target was Taliban leader Mullah Omar's sprawling mud-walled compound. Planning the operation, our intelligence said it was doubtful that Omar himself would be at the site, but we expected to recover valuable tactical intelligence material. At both RHINO and Kandahar, a big AC-130 Spectre gunship droned overhead in the darkness ready to unleash its massed firepower on the enemy. A few guards in the compound resisted and were killed. Our Special Operations Forces took those who were captured back to the *Kitty Hawk*.

Above all, however, we had intended to send a clear message to the enemy: America was willing to take risks and put boots on the ground. We would strike anywhere in Afghanistan, not just in the north. And we would be returning.

During the assault, one branch of the armed services at the Pentagon began giving tactical directions to those involved in the operation in the theater. Tactical direction came from field commanders, but the Pentagon's role was to provide strategic direction. I asked my staff to make it clear to all the services that, while we could watch the operations as they unfolded, it was absolutely unacceptable to twist the "seven-thousand-mile screwdriver" on our tactical forces.

Someone advised Donald Rumsfeld that he could have this real-time video from our UAVs in his office if he wanted it. He was not interested. "That's not the job of the Secretary of Defense," he said. "That's General Franks's job and the job of our field commanders."

The importance of the operation in Afghanistan was brought home to us at the NSC meeting on October 23. President Bush told us that bin Laden "may have a nuclear device" that could destroy half of Washington, D.C. Our intelligence community was still working out whether al-Qaida had enough fissile material for the weapon. There were credible reports of a Pakistani nuclear expert working closely with Usama bin Laden, and also evidence of a larger group of Pakistani experts assisting. Whether this intelligence was accurate in every detail wasn't my concern. It was potentially so devastating that we had to take it seriously and continue our pursuit of al-Qaida with as much speed and aggressiveness as possible.

This was a deeply troubling and complex puzzle. We had clues but no definite answers. There was enough Russian weapons-grade fissile material unaccounted for to provide al-Qaida with a bomb. Once they had assembled a weapon, we were not sure how difficult it would be to smuggle it into the United States. The Pakistani piece of the riddle was critical: The CIA was in contact with a key Pakistani scientist who talked about the planned al-Qaida weapon and emphasized the severity of its potential blast damage.

Vice President Cheney looked pale at the news, which he had heard just before our meeting.

"We have to intensify the hunt for Usama bin Laden," he said.

———————————

Certainly our intelligence community was hunting bin Laden. The United States had raised the reward for his capture or killing to $25 million. But no one had stepped forward with hard information on his whereabouts. The best estimate, however, was that he and his most loyal colleagues were holed up in fortified cave complexes in eastern Afghanistan, especially in the area of Tora Bora south of Jalalabad on the border with Pakistan's Federally Administered Tribal Areas near the Khyber Pass. This was very difficult terrain for combat: It had helped defeat foreign armies from the time of the British Raj to the Soviets. And bin Laden's Muslim fanaticism appealed to the local tribes, who would probably never be tempted by the huge cash reward. Indeed, the reward might have been incomprehensibly high to many Afghans; some in Washington suggested a string of fresh donkeys might have worked better.

So, if we were going to capture or kill bin Laden, we would have to do it before he slipped across the border into Pakistan. We had a relative handful of the right type of American troops available in Afghanistan, but we could not afford to wait weeks to bring in a larger force of light infantry to conduct an operation at Tora Bora. It would not only have taken weeks or months to increase our force three, four, or even tenfold (as some critics suggested), but might well have alienated the Afghans we had just liberated.

The more we evaluated the mission, the harder it became. Beyond the steep, freezing gorges, the resistance of the al-Qaida forces in these mountains proved to be the fiercest we had yet encountered. They were fanatical and had skillfully positioned their trenches and bunkers to provide interlocking fields of fire. Although we had two Special Forces teams in the fight, they were thin on the ground and could offer only limited support to the local anti-Taliban commander, Northern Alliance leader Hazrat Ali.

His troops were willing, but nowhere nearly as skilled as their al-Qaida opponents. The basic light infantry tactics of fire and maneuver were alien concepts to Ali's men. They seemed to believe in firing off huge amounts of ammunition and then pulling back for the night, thus having to advance over the same ground in the morning. Our Special Forces teams were able to coordinate devastating air strikes from observation posts on both sides of a narrow canyon where the al-Qaida troops had sought safety. Still, the enemy would not abandon their positions, even though hundreds were killed. This could have indicated that they were a suicidal rear guard protecting the retreat of Usama bin Laden over the ridges into Pakistan. The seesaw fight continued for eight days. Once the surviving al-Qaida force finally abandoned the ground, leaving behind some of their wounded, the "battle of Tora Bora" was over.

We had won the tactical fight but had not captured bin Laden. Just as in Bosnia, hunting for individuals was a very difficult task. We would continue to work aggressively over the next several years to improve our intelligence and operational capabilities.

Meanwhile, we had to destroy the Taliban and convince the Northern Alliance they had joined the winning side. Destroying the Taliban would send a message to other state sponsors of international terrorism.

A victory in the Afghan struggle would also persuade the world that our operations weren't bogged down in a "quagmire," as some in the news media suggested. On October 31, for example, *Time* magazine reported that Donald Rumsfeld had to explain at length why *quagmire* was a misnomer for the situation in Afghanistan. Rumsfeld was responding to the "steady rumble from the media, politicians, Afghanistan experts, and even some U.S. allies that the operation has the hallmarks of a classic political and military quagmire." Even as that issue of *Time* reached newsstands, the situation in Afghanistan changed dramatically.

On November 9, Mazar-e-Sharif fell to the Northern Alliance, followed two days later by Herat. The Taliban were obviously crumbling. On November 13, less than two weeks after *Time's* "quagmire" article, the Northern Alliance captured the capital, Kabul. Twenty-four hours later, Northern Alliance forces overran the al-Qaida stronghold of Jalalabad. In the southwest, Northern Alliance troops surrounded the Taliban power center of Kandahar. The city fell on December 7.

The successful campaign had involved a few thousand American and allied Special Operations Forces and airmen using advanced communications and reconnaissance equipment linked to Precision-Guided Munitions. In the 1980s, the Soviet Union had tried to pacify Afghanistan with hundreds of thousands of troops—and their effort had ended in failure. For the United States, Operation Enduring Freedom in Afghanistan stands as a model for a transformed military force and strategic doctrine.

Meanwhile, there were breakthroughs on the political front. At a December 2001 U.N.-sponsored conference in Bonn, Afghan participants called for the creation of an interim administration and named the anti-Taliban southern Pashtun leader Hamid Karzai to head it. During the post-9/11 fighting, he had worked with the CIA's paramilitaries and then linked up with one of our Special Forces teams.

Karzai was dedicated to defeating the Taliban, who had assassinated his father. Although he had spent several years in exile, he retained good contacts among the southern tribes. So Karzai was spirited out of the country to Bonn. Dressed in his colorful tribal attire and speaking fluent English, Hamid Karzai accepted the Bonn conference's appointment as chairman of the Afghan interim government. The United Nations also created the International Security Assistance Force (ISAF) to provide Afghanistan well-trained and disciplined foreign troops to secure Kabul. ISAF was initially under the command of a British general. This step prevented the country's descent into internecine strife among the splintered militia groups.

After the September terrorist attacks, President Bush had spoken urgently about the need for "defining pictures" from Afghanistan to raise the morale of the American people. In my opinion, the images that best met this description were the photos of our Special Forces on horseback, charging across the dry grass slopes of the Hindu Kush foothills with their Northern Alliance partners. The photos were dramatic, depicting American troops engaged in a twenty-first-century cavalry charge.

But the pictures provided far more than colorful images. Those of us who understood what we saw recognized the laser target designators, the GPS receivers, and the satellite communications equipment carried in their distinctive cases among the bags of feed and the blankets lashed to the saddles. The images were striking . . . the centuries-old military technology of saddles, stirrups, and feedbags . . . connected via satellite to jet aircraft dropping precision munitions from the edge of the stratosphere.

This was transformation made tangible. Not only was the equipment innovative, the strategy of our leaders and the tactics of these brave and resourceful troops were truly revolutionary.

We had developed a new way to fight wars. Perhaps out of necessity, we had dared to use it. And in three months we had overthrown the Taliban and liberated millions of Afghans.

10

A NEW PLAYING FIELD

*WMD and Operation Iraqi Freedom, Detainees,
the Geneva Convention*

As widespread Taliban and al-Qaida resistance crumbled across Afghanistan that winter, our Coalition was faced with a new problem: what to do with the thousands of enemy prisoners captured on the battlefield. Some Northern Alliance militiamen simply took few prisoners until their leaders reasserted discipline. But among these tribal fighters, hatred for the Taliban and those the al-Qaida fighters referred to as "the Arabs" remained intense.

The situation was very fluid as Hamid Karzai was inaugurated in Kabul and began the hard job of hammering together national security forces. Refugees choked the cities, and there was at least one large and active pocket of enemy resistance along the mountainous border with Pakistan.

On December 16, Donald Rumsfeld flew to Bagram Air Base north of Kabul to confer with Hamid Karzai and Gen. Mohammed Fahim, who had just been named Afghanistan's new Minister of Defense. Rumsfeld congratulated the two Afghan leaders on their victory. But he was characteristically realistic when addressing American troops and airmen at the base. "The Taliban is not running the country at the moment," he cautioned them. But Rumsfeld added, "There still are al-Qaida and Taliban . . . in the mountains, hiding in the cities, in the caves and across the borders. There are a lot of fanatical people. And we need to finish the job."

At least emergency food supplies were finally flowing into the country again over the Khyber Pass and the Friendship Bridge connecting Afghanistan and Uzbekistan. The Russians had also set up a hospital in the capital, and the international donor community was beginning to fill the most critical humanitarian assistance needs. There would be no mass famine or epidemics among the internal refugees.

But the problem of the enemy prisoners remained unresolved. The Northern Alliance swept up thousands on the battlefields and in the trench lines that American airpower had shattered. Most were taken to the Bagram base and housed in temporary barbed-wire enclosures inside cavernous, bomb-scarred hangars. Although the hangars' roofs and walls provided shelter from the wind and snow, there was no heat or running water. But the prisoners were issued plenty of blankets and had the same oil-drum field toilets as our own troops. They were adequately fed food that met Muslim dietary restrictions, and they received good medical care.

The collection point quickly became crowded, however, creating a potentially dangerous situation. No one had forgotten the bloody prisoner uprising that had exploded in late November at the Northern Alliance's improvised prison compound in a mud-brick fortress called Qala-i-Jangi near General Dustum's headquarters at Mazar-e-Sharif. About three hundred Taliban prisoners from the northeastern city of Konduz—including Pakistanis, Chechens, and Arabs—were held in the fortress. On the morning of November 25, the prisoners overpowered their guards and attacked the two CIA officers, Johnny "Mike" Spann and his partner, Dave Tyson, who had come to interrogate them. The Taliban killed Spann, overran the compound, and stole AK-47s, rocket-propelled grenades, and mortars from the armory.

That afternoon, American and British SOF arrived and called in precision air strikes from Coalition planes circling overhead. Even under this relentless bombardment, the Taliban refused to surrender. Hundreds were killed. The survivors booby-trapped the bodies of their comrades and retreated to a basement, still refusing to surrender. Only when the basement was flooded did they come out. More than three hundred Taliban had arrived as prisoners, but only eighty-six survived.

In December, CENTCOM requested that the Defense Department establish a permanent detention-and-interrogation facility outside Afghanistan to relieve the potentially dangerous overcrowding at Bagram. Their plan was to conduct an initial triage of the prisoners and release those who posed no obvious threat to our forces or had no clear value as intelligence sources. Hundreds of naïvely zealous madrassa students who had volunteered to serve with the Taliban were in fact expelled to Pakistan. Afghan peasant prisoners with no connection to al-Qaida were also paroled and allowed to return to their home villages. With each release, the chances that we were holding people of no intelligence value decreased. Equally, however, as the "hard core" of enemy detainees became more concentrated, the danger of another revolt also rose.

The detainees' unique potential as intelligence sources made them valuable. This was especially true of the several hundred al-Qaida detainees. One, Usama bin Laden's personal driver, Salim Hamdan, was picked up near the border with Pakistan and turned over to the U.S. military. Not only would their captivity keep them off the battlefield, their successful interrogation might yield important intelligence. We knew, for example, that some highly placed and knowledgeable al-Qaida leaders had fought in Afghanistan. In November 2001, Usama bin Laden's key military commander, Mohammed Atef, an architect of the 1998 American Embassy bombings, had been killed in a CIA Predator strike that had targeted his Kabul home with a Hellfire missile. But we did not know how many other senior al-Qaida combatants there had been on the ground, or how many we had captured. Did we already have in our custody terrorists with knowledge of the next 9/11 attack or al-Qaida's WMD program? Only patient, expert interrogation would answer those questions.

During the decades of the Cold War, we could gather critical intelligence through remote means, in particular satellite imagery and electronic eavesdropping. But al-Qaida and other violent extremist groups were not as vulnerable to this type of intelligence collection. The critical information lay in their minds.

Fighting this type of warfare against such an adversary was not at all like the conventional warfare we were used to planning for—at least at this scale. The ambiguity surrounding the detainees' true identity and their intelligence value would be just the first of many uncertainties surrounding the conflict with violent extremists.

Because of the lack of adequate facilities, the interrogations needed to be conducted outside Afghanistan. CENTCOM estimated that after preliminary screening there might be several hundred detainees to move out of Afghanistan. Now we had to choose a remote, secure facility to prevent escape or a rescue attempt by terrorist comrades. The requirements virtually excluded the entire Middle East. Lawyers from the White House, OSD General Counsel, and the Justice Department recommended that the prisoners not be housed on sovereign American territory to prevent their possible habeas corpus petitions, and to prevent giving them the full range of options criminal defendants have in U.S. courts. Eventually, the NSC designated the U.S. Navy base at Guantanamo Bay in southeastern Cuba as the best site.

As this process developed, Secretary Rumsfeld repeatedly told me how unhappy he was that the department had been saddled with the responsibility of housing and caring for these detainees. At the outset, he also told senior OSD staff that running the Guantanamo Bay detention facility would probably be the "source of more trouble and more criticism" than any of us could foresee. But Rumsfeld also realized that in early 2002 we did not have secure facilities in Afghanistan to hold large numbers of prisoners. Continuing to keep them at Bagram could spark a Taliban rescue attempt.

And we did need intelligence: We all remembered the October NSC meeting when we were told that al-Qaida might have obtained nuclear weapons designs from Pakistani scientists and was actively searching for Russian fissile material. If in fact al-Qaida had laid its hands on enough enriched uranium to make a bomb, we were facing a threat that would make the 9/11 attack look pale in comparison.

In early 2002, the U.S. Southern Command submitted a preliminary plan for the Guantanamo Bay detention center large enough to house over two thousand prisoners. Secretary Rumsfeld was not happy. That plan, he said, was too grandiose. If we built the facility, the military would feel obligated to fill it up. Instead, he wanted the commanders in the field to make the hard decisions on sorting through their detainees and releasing all those they didn't have compelling evidence to hold. That would relieve burdens all around. We did not want the United States to squander the goodwill generated after the 9/11 attacks, he said, by seeming to have suddenly become "the world's jailer." And with fewer prisoners, a smaller group of our most skilled interrogators, including those few who were language-qualified and culturally aware, could concentrate on the most likely intelligence sources.

Eventually, ten thousand detainees would be screened and freed and fewer than six hundred sent to Gauntanamo. The number that did reach the detention center was further reduced as the interrogation process determined that some of the prisoners did not possess valuable intelligence and were no longer likely to pose a threat to Coalition forces, and their home countries agreed to their repatriation, further agreeing to treat them humanely.

On January 27, 2002, Secretary Rumsfeld and I flew to Guantanamo Bay with a delegation headed by Senators Daniel Inouye of Hawaii, Ted Stevens of

Alaska, Dianne Feinstein of California, and Kay Bailey Hutchison of Texas, all experts on defense matters. The purpose of the trip was to inspect the site and see the facilities where the initial 158 detainees from Afghanistan were housed. Camp X-Ray, the first detention unit, was hot and stark, surrounded by double fences of razor wire. But a sea breeze blew through the compound day and night. Cells were temporary cyclone-fence enclosures with metal roofs and roll-up canvas sides that provided shade and fresh air. The prisoners slept on thick foam-rubber mattresses and had sheets and blankets.

As an interim solution, I thought these arrangements were acceptable. Given that there were security concerns with these temporary facilities, and we had no idea how long we might have to hold the detainees, we needed to get permanent facilities constructed quickly. We would use federal prison standards as a basis for constructing the cells we would build. There were Navy medical facilities set up just for the detainees. I remember thinking that for most of them this would be the best medical care they had ever received. While at the base, Rumsfeld and I spoke with representatives of the International Committee of the Red Cross (ICRC), who said they didn't have any problems with the provisions for, or treatment of, the detainees. Rumsfeld told the reporters traveling with us that the detainees here and in Afghanistan "are not POWs" and characterized them instead as "unlawful combatants," but emphasized they were receiving humane treatment. The United States had arrived at this policy after careful deliberation.

"Don't forget," he said, "we're treating these people as if the Geneva Conventions applied."

But we needed to interrogate the detainees for the important intelligence known to a few of the al-Qaida leaders about possible plans for renewed threats to the United States and our allies. We had field manuals governing legally permissible techniques of prisoner interrogation. Waterboarding was *never*—was not then and is not now—a technique in our interrogation manual and was never authorized for use by the military interrogators. Any service member who exceeded these methods was subject to disciplinary action, including court-martial. In fact, there has been disciplinary action taken where detainee abuse was found to have occurred.

However, the strict security rules in place at Camp X-Ray were warranted. Rumsfeld called the detainees at Guantanamo "among the most dangerous, best-trained vicious killers on the face of the earth. This is very, very serious business."

I certainly agreed. These men were especially dangerous in transit when an uprising among fanatics could disable a military transport plane's exposed control cables and hydraulic lines or break open emergency exits, causing explosive decompression and a crash. Therefore, the prisoners were chained, shackled, and blindfolded during their long flights from Afghanistan to Cuba until they were secured in individual cells.

Unfortunately, the images of blindfolded and flex-cuffed detainees in orange jumpsuits, kneeling in a fenced holding area as military guards processed them into their cells, overnight became the image of the alleged brutal treatment we gave the captives. These pictures were prominently featured in the European press and on al Jazeera television. Rumsfeld's unease about America's becoming branded with the stigma "the world's jailer" was being justified sooner than any of us imagined.

Back in Washington, Senator Inouye, a World War II Medal of Honor recipient who had lost an arm in combat, told the media that our military guards at Guantanamo "went out of their way to be considerate to the detainees." They received fresh food and first-rate medical attention and had spiritual care from two Muslim chaplains. "I'd rather be detained there at Guantanamo than in Kabul."

In late January 2002, I heard that executive branch lawyers had met with the President on January 18, a Friday, at the White House to reconsider the prisoners' status. My understanding was that they had convinced the President that the 1949 Geneva Conventions, a treaty to which the United States and Afghanistan were signatories, did not apply to our fight with either the Taliban or al-Qaida. I disagreed with this decision and gave Secretary Rumsfeld my judgment that this was an important national security matter. Moreover, this decision had been made without NSC deliberations, and without the advice of the Joint Chiefs and the Secretary of Defense. Rumsfeld agreed that the issue merited a full discussion and asked Condoleezza Rice to put the question of the detainees' legal status on the NSC docket.

There were really two issues here. The first was whether the Geneva Conventions applied to our conflict with the Taliban. (At this point it was accepted by most everybody involved in the discussions that the Geneva Conventions did not apply to al-Qaida.) The second issue was whether the Taliban had the right to prisoner of war (POW) status under the Geneva Conventions. My thoughts on the first question were clear: Afghanistan was a party to the Geneva Conventions, so they applied to our conflict with Afghanistan, whether or not the Taliban were entitled to POW status. It was inappropriate to try to weasel out of our obligation to apply the treaty, despite the Department of Justice lawyers' arguments to the contrary. During the long Vietnam War, I would have been one of the thousands of American aircrew facing brutality or even execution at the hands of the enemy if captured. Along the Ho Chi Minh Trail, the fate of a prisoner could be especially gruesome. But even in North Vietnam's capital, Hanoi, the enemy routinely tortured prisoners to extract propaganda statements. Although North Vietnam is a party to the Geneva Conventions, they classified American captives as "air pirates" not entitled to the protection of Geneva or to be treated as prisoners of war. The North Vietnamese government had made a subjective judgment that the Geneva treaty didn't apply to these air pirates. That's the kind of name-calling that could always be used to rationalize a refusal to follow the laws of war. I didn't believe the United States should be looking for creative ways to set the Geneva Conventions aside.

My rationale was threefold. The Geneva Conventions were a fundamental part of our military culture and every military member was trained on them. In addition, our military personnel were trained to treat detainees and prisoners humanely. Objectively applying the conventions was important to our self-image. It would continue to make the U.S. armed forces the "gold standard" of the world's militaries and would increase our ability to get other countries to work with us. The second part of my rationale concerned reciprocity. I wanted any Americans who might fall into enemy hands anywhere in the world to be protected under the Geneva Conventions. I didn't naïvely believe that al-Qaida or the Taliban would treat Coalition prisoners humanely out of the goodness of their hearts (there wasn't much goodness there, as we saw with beheadings of captured U.S. servicemen by al-Qaida in Iraq), but I did think that our respect for the Geneva Conventions could give us support around the world that might translate into pressure on our enemies—in this war or any future war—to give proper treatment to any of our forces unfortunate enough to be captured. Finally, in this new War on Terror, showing the humanity of American culture was more important than ever. It was part of the crucial psychological dimension of the conflict.

However, this issue had confusing elements that required both an astute legal mind and insight into the often-competing policy considerations involved. Donald Rumsfeld asked Undersecretary of Defense for Policy Douglas Feith to review the question. Feith had a Georgetown law degree and had worked extensively on Geneva Convention matters during the presidency of Ronald Reagan. If anyone in the Office of the Secretary of Defense could unravel the confusing legal web surrounding the detainees' status, it was Doug Feith.

Responding to Secretary Rumsfeld's request, the President scheduled a February 4, 2002, NSC meeting to determine whether the Geneva Conventions applied to the detainees captured in Afghanistan. Several days before that meeting, I was waiting in Donald Rumsfeld's outer office to discuss the subject when Doug Feith arrived. My opinion had only strengthened since the Guantanamo trip: If the White House did not agree that the Geneva treaty applied to our fight with the Taliban, we would be no better than the North Vietnamese in selectively applying the convention. So I was resolved to share my opinion with the Secretary.

I wasn't sure where Doug stood on this issue. "I want you to know," I told Feith before he had a chance to speak, "that I feel very strongly about this. And if Rumsfeld doesn't defend the Geneva Convention, I'll contradict him in front of the President!"

This was more than a matter of personal feelings. Under the Goldwater-Nichols Act, I was legally obligated to provide the President my *best* military advice—not the best advice as approved by the Secretary of Defense. Although I would never undermine Secretary Rumsfeld's authority, as Chairman I had my own obligations to the President as well as the National Security Council. Doug Feith, with his mild, scholarly manner, looked shocked, as much by my tone as by the fact that I had ignored the Secretary's title.

The meeting with Donald Rumsfeld was a frank exchange. I argued my points, and as usual, he pushed back, but I did not give any ground. For me this was a question of fundamental principle, not a theoretical opinion. I didn't think Rumsfeld felt strongly, but instead wanted to test our own depth of commitment and fully understand the positions we presented.

Doug Feith supported my views strongly and broke the potential stalemate, noting that the United States had no choice but to apply the Geneva Conventions because, like all treaties in force for the country, they bore the same weight as a federal statute. He delineated points that government lawyers and the public often overlooked. Accepting the fact that the Geneva Conventions applied to the war in Afghanistan did *not* mean that Taliban detainees were entitled to the status of prisoners of war. He argued the treaty was clear that combatants had to earn that protected status by wearing uniforms, carrying weapons openly, and operating within a chain of command and conducting their operations in accordance with the laws and customs of war.

The Conventions, Feith stressed, effectively separated lawful and unlawful combatants. POW status was a privilege granted to lawful combatants. Because the Taliban did not follow the LOAC, he noted, they did not merit prisoner of war status, even though the Geneva Conventions governed our war in Afghanistan. In addition, the Taliban often fought beside their al-Qaida allies, further confusing the issue.

Rumsfeld seemed satisfied and asked Feith to join us at the February 4, 2002, NSC meeting. Feith drew up a list of talking points based on the rationale we used with the Secretary (Feith called me at home to clear these talking points before our White House meeting): The Geneva Convention was a worthwhile treaty; we trained our armed forces always to follow it with enemy prisoners—on pain of court-martial. He also emphasized that the essence of the Geneva Convention was the distinction between military and civilians. "Terrorists are reprehensible," Feith wrote, "precisely because they negate that distinction by purposefully targeting civilians." Conversely, the Convention protected civilians by requiring military combatants to wear uniforms. In effect, the treaty provided an incentive system for combatants to act in a legal manner to obtain prisoner of war status if their members were captured.

In the White House meeting, Secretary Colin Powell and I seemed to be on the same page, but not everyone in the Situation Room was convinced. Looking around the long table, I noted the government attorneys sitting along the walls behind each of their principals. When it was my turn to speak I said, "Mr. President, you'll notice that everybody's here with a lawyer. I don't have a lawyer with me; I don't think this is a legal issue."

The President smiled and said, "Go on."

I made my points that this was principally a moral and a military question more than a legal question: The U.S. must maintain the moral high ground and do what was required by the law, which was to apply the Geneva Conventions to the Taliban; this was consistent with our military culture and training; and we wanted our own people to receive fair treatment, should they fall into enemy hands. But the basic issue was respect for the Geneva Conventions. Asked by Secretary Rumsfeld to present our talking points, Feith reinforced my argument to the President.

Attorney General John Ashcroft detailed the legal theory behind not applying the Geneva Conventions to our conflict with the Taliban. Afghanistan could be viewed not as a nation, but as a failed state, and therefore the Taliban prisoners had fought for an illegitimate government, he said, adding that the Taliban and al-Qaida were a "coalition of pirates."

But President Bush did not seem convinced by this reasoning. "Would you apply the Geneva Convention to Iraq?" he asked Ashcroft.

The Attorney General nodded. "Yes, Mr. President."

"But you can say that Saddam Hussein is a pirate, too," George Bush said, quickly seeing the danger in using a subjective standard for applying the Geneva Conventions.

The President said he would take all of this on board and think about it. That ended our discussion of the detainees and the Geneva Conventions. While the President was deliberating, the press coverage of the issue continued.

Three days later, White House spokesman Ari Fleischer announced the President's decision on the Guantanamo detainees. "President Bush," Fleischer said, "has today decided that the Geneva Convention will apply to the Taliban detainees, but not to the al-Qaida international terrorists."

However, Fleischer added that the United States would continue to treat both categories of detainees humanely. He noted that even though the Taliban government of Afghanistan was a party to the Geneva Conventions—and the Taliban detainees were entitled to protections under the treaty—they did not qualify as POWs. Nevertheless, all the detainees would be provided with many POW privileges as a matter of policy. "They will continue to receive three appropriate meals a day, excellent medical care, clothing, shelter, showers, and the opportunity to worship." And they were given the right to private visits by the International Committee of the Red Cross. Of course, there were some prisoner-of-war privileges they wouldn't receive due to practical security concerns. The Conventions outline numerous privileges, such as canteens where POWs may procure foodstuffs, soap, tobacco, and ordinary articles in daily use and being allowed to receive scientific equipment and musical instruments. Many of these detainees were ruthless and very dangerous. They would kill their guards if given the chance.

Although Fleischer did not explicitly say so, the policy offered some protection to prevent mistreatment of American POWs in the future. The War on Terror was not envisaged when the Geneva Convention was signed in 1949. But in 2001, he emphasized, "Global terrorists transcend national boundaries and intentionally target the innocent. The President has maintained the United States' commitment to the principles of the Geneva Convention, while recognizing that the Convention simply does not cover every situation in which people may be captured or detained by military forces, as we see in Afghanistan today."

Because the subject involved legal technicalities and the administration's policy could be easily misconstrued, at the Pentagon press briefing the next day, Secretary Rumsfeld further clarified DoD's policy. "When the Geneva Convention was signed, it was crafted by sovereign states to deal with conflicts between sovereign states." The current war on terrorism was not a conflict envisioned by the framers of the Geneva Convention. But our forces had been ordered to treat all Taliban and al-Qaida detainees humanely.

Rumsfeld explained why the Taliban did not qualify for POW status: "A central purpose of the Geneva Convention was to protect innocent civilians by distinguishing very clearly between combatants and noncombatants. This is why the Convention requires soldiers to wear uniforms that distinguish them from the civilian population." The Taliban did not wear distinctive insignias, symbols, or uniforms, but instead sought to blend into the population. "Indeed," the Secretary noted, "al-Qaida forces made up portions of their forces." Although I was concerned about the potential for lingering ambiguity in our policy, I was somewhat satisfied with this outcome. The President had agreed with the key points I stressed: The Geneva Conventions *did* apply to our conflict with the Taliban. And though he determined that no detainees were entitled to POW status, they would receive humane treatment. As I understood it at the time, this meant that the Taliban detainees would be given the proper treatment they were due under the Conventions. And the al-Qaida detainees would also receive the proper treatment they would have been entitled to if the Geneva Conventions had applied to our conflict with them. Clearly, dealing with this new enemy would require policy nuance as well as force.

The way this issue developed and the manner with which subsequent detainee issues were handled was interesting. In the early days of the War on Terror these challenges were treated as narrow legal issues with only intermittent input from the senior military officers, military legal counsel, or the policy specialists at the Defense Department. This changed over time. In those early discussions over sensitive detainee topics, the issues deserved wider debate. There were much broader strategic matters here that needed more than simply legal analysis.

By relying so heavily on just the lawyers, the President did not get the broader advice on these matters that he needed to fully consider the consequences of his actions. I thought it was critical that the nation's leadership convey the right message to those engaged in the War on Terror. Showing respect for the Geneva Conventions was important to all of us in uniform. This episode epitomized the Secretary's and Chairman's different statutory responsibilities to the President and the nation. The fact that the President appeared to change his previous decision showed that the system, however imperfect, had worked.

In February 2002, reconnaissance revealed that Taliban and al-Qaida units approximately two hundred strong were operating from the high, isolated Shah-i-Kot Valley in the Arma Mountains close to the Pakistani border southeast of Kabul. Signals intelligence indicated that Usama bin Laden and his highest surviving lieutenants might be among the enemy. Gen. Tommy Franks informed me that CENTCOM intended to attack using conventional and Special Operations troops and air assets already in its Area of Responsibility. The planners for this Operation Anaconda had to work fast because they wanted to catch the enemy before it slipped across the frontier into Pakistan. If properly executed, Anaconda could finally crush al-Qaida's leadership and a stubborn Taliban remnant—possibly even ending organized anti-Coalition resistance in the country.

Maj. Gen. Franklin L. "Buster" Hagenbeck of the 10th Mountain Division was the overall Coalition commander for the operation. Buster was a terrific officer and had worked for me on the Joint Staff before going to the 10th Mountain Division. In addition to the SOF teams from four countries, Hagenbeck would deploy about one thousand Afghan troops from the newly formed pro-Kabul military, as well as seventeen hundred Americans drawn from the 10th Mountain and 101st Airborne divisions. This would be the first "maneuver"-unit combat in Afghanistan, as opposed to the actions involving small SOF teams working with the Northern Alliance forces.

Almost from the outset there were problems. Before dawn on March 2, several trucks in a convoy carrying the Afghan forces and their SOF team advisers broke down or overturned on the steep, mountainous track leading to the valley's entrance. The Afghans turned on headlights to avoid disastrous accidents, alerting the enemy on the surrounding ridges that a Coalition force was approaching.

But the enemy did not inflict the first casualties. Patrolling overhead, an AC-130 Spectre gunship, call sign *Grim 31*, spotted trucks from the strung-out convoy creeping up the rough terrain toward an over-watch site selected to provide the Special Forces a good view of the valley. The gunship's navigation equipment malfunctioned, causing the crew to believe the vehicles they saw below through the night-vision scopes were enemy trucks. This suspicion was reinforced because the trucks' cabs were not marked with the distinctive "glint strips" that would have reflected the infrared searchlight the circling plane shined down. The AC-130 opened fire with its 105mm howitzer. Green Beret Chief Warrant Officer Stanley L. Harriman was killed, and other Special Forces and Afghan soldiers were wounded.

Friendly fire incidents are totally unacceptable. The unfortunate fact is they happen in war, although at a decreasing rate over the last century. Our job is to ensure we have the right tactics, training, and procedures to help eliminate this tragic outcome as well as employ technology where it can help. The Blue Force Tracker used in Iraq was one such technology; it displayed the exact GPS coordinates of friendly vehicles and troops. But given human frailties, even "foolproof" technology can sometimes be fooled.

The confusion deepened. When the main SOF-Afghan element of the convoy reached its assigned line of departure near the head of the valley, they expected a fifty-five-minute bombardment from a B-52, a B-1B, and F-15E Strike Eagles to clear the way ahead. But a weapon on the lead B-1B hung up after it had dropped only six bombs. The plane received permission to jettison the bomb. As the radio calls were relayed—some from CENTCOM's Combined Air Operations Center in Saudi Arabia—the remaining bombers orbiting at holding points heard what they thought was a general recall order and also departed. The planned heavy bombardment to soften up the enemy had consisted of just six bombs. Hunkered down, the Coalition forces were discouraged—especially because it was obvious that the enemy firing mortars and heavy machine guns from the heights above had known they were coming and had set their weapons to strike precise aim-points on the rough track below. The numbers of dead and wounded mounted among the Afghan militiamen, and the force retreated in frustration, as much from the casualties as from the inexplicable disappearance of the promised American air cover.

Things got worse. Intense fire struck the infantrymen unloading from their CH-47 helicopters at the designated blocking positions on the eastern ridges. As the confusing combat unfolded on that first day, one fact became clear: Al-Qaida and Taliban forces in the area numbered many more than the two hundred of the original intelligence estimate. There were extreme difficulties in estimating enemy strength—both in Afghanistan and later in Iraq. Beyond the anticipated AK-47s and Rocket-Propelled Grenades (RPGs) the enemy was much better armed than expected, equipped with mortars, heavy machine guns, and even Soviet-made 122mm artillery pieces. I was surprised to learn that their clothing and footwear were also first class. Further, the al-Qaida and Taliban troops were well concealed and well protected within caves, bunkers, and stone weapons pits. And they stayed to fight rather than melting away. The 10th Mountain and 101st Airborne troops had six AH-64 Apache helicopter gunships for close air support; the aviators were courageous, delivering rockets and cannon fire into enemy bunkers and caves.

The Apaches were mauled by ground fire, but continued their mission. In addition, communications and operational procedure problems delayed the timely arrival of fixed-wing air support. This battlespace was small when seen from high above, and there were friendly helicopters darting back and forth, which made deconflicting weapons drops a priority—sometimes delaying attacks. Even with these problems, however, the supporting aircraft inflicted heavy losses on the enemy and slowly drove them back to the protection of caves.

Just after dawn on March 4, two groups of Navy SEALs flying on MH-47 Special Operations Chinooks headed toward the shoulder of Takur Ghar, a mountain with a panoramic view of the valley and all surrounding terrain.

An RPG hit one Chinook, badly damaging the helicopter. As the MH-47 lurched away down the mountain, SEAL Petty Officer First Class Neil C. Roberts was thrown off the open tail ramp into the snow. When courageous troops attempted to rescue Roberts, they, too, were taken under heavy fire. Fighting up and down the ridge was often close-in, savage. By the end of a long day of combat, seven more Americans had died.

The enemy clung stubbornly to their caves and bunkers and eventually had to be blasted out by relays of bombers. Only after CENTCOM scrambled to smooth out the kinks in the command-and-control system did the ground forces have adequate air cover in the coming days. What had been planned as a seventy-two-hour operation lasted seventeen days. Coalition casualties totaled fifteen American and Afghan dead and scores wounded.

It was hard to estimate the al-Qaida and Taliban dead because our bombs and aerial cannon fire had ripped many bodies apart or sealed those still alive into collapsed caves. The closest figure we reached was between five hundred and eight hundred, with an unknown number fleeing across the border into Pakistan. Judging from the abandoned weapons recovered on the battlefield, the higher figure was probably more accurate.

From my perspective in Washington, I was frustrated and angry to see Anaconda start off in such a confused, unintegrated way. Our soldiers, airmen, and special operators had shown great courage and determination. As the disasters mounted in the first few days, however, I told the Joint Chiefs, "We're turning people into heroes who don't have to be."

The enemy had massed for the second time (Tora Bora was the first), thus making itself vulnerable to sustained air and ground attack. If CENTCOM had insisted that Hagenbeck build a truly joint operations plan that tightly welded the ground, air, and Special Operations elements—and if the command in Afghanistan had had the ability to execute a more thorough reconnaissance—our Special Forces and conventional troops might not have been surprised by the large, determined, and well-armed enemy.

I had visited General Hagenbeck's headquarters at Bagram Air Base only three weeks before Operation Anaconda was scheduled to begin. The plan that Hagenbeck was working up seemed reasonable at that time. He was assembling enough troops, with seasoned Afghan militiamen providing the bulk of the Task Force Hammer force that would push the enemy up and out of the valley into the American positions of Task Force Anvil. Hagenbeck told me he was expecting a "tough fight," but was confident. His Bagram staff was lean, but I assumed they were working closely with their CENTCOM air component counterparts in Saudi Arabia.

Still, I was uneasy about what I had seen at Bagram: The Army had equipped Buster Hagenbeck's Tactical Operations Center so that it looked like something out of a World War II movie, with paper maps instead of interactive digital plasma screens. His Predator feed was around the corner, away from the commander. The Special Ops shop was in an entirely separate building. CENTCOM had not provided Hagenbeck the facilities that he needed to command and maneuver his forces in a rapid and flexible manner.

This headquarters isn't integrated in a modern way, I thought. *Still, the plan itself looks okay.*

That proved to be an inaccurate assessment. In fact, the plan had mainly been built from an Army and Special Operations perspective, with the air component brought in far too late. It was almost as if our commanders had ignored the concept of the integrated joint-service force that had matured so well since the Goldwater-Nichols Act was passed. In the first week of Anaconda, the air-ground-Special-Ops components were poorly coordinated. Even though the aircraft carried modern targeting equipment and Precision-Guided Munitions, given the poor level of integration, the force as a whole was fighting as if it were in Grenada in 1983.

Our forces in the Anaconda operation had *tried* to employ innovative tactics against the enemy, but had failed to integrate all the ground, air, and Special Operations resources available.

There was a sense of urgency in the operation. We knew where the enemy was massing and had to go after him in the Shah-i-Kot Valley before he slipped away—either back into Afghanistan or over the border into Pakistan. Although our forces eventually prevailed, Operation Anaconda was definitely not a model of integrated joint operations to emulate.

Despite the operation's success, I couldn't let go of the fact that brave Americans had lost their lives because of things we could control. We had paid an unnecessarily heavy price for our ultimate victory. When I spoke to Tommy Franks after the operation, I was not diplomatic: "Tom," I said, "this lack of air and ground integration was absolutely unacceptable."

"Got it, Chairman," he said, chagrined by my blunt tone. I did not have to repeat that message. General Franks immediately went to work with his component commanders, re-emphasizing the necessity for joint-service integration in all operations. CENTCOM's air component commander, Lt. Gen. Michael "Buzz" Moseley, called an emergency theater-wide conference to address the problems that had emerged during Anaconda. If CENTCOM had to conduct another conventional battle, I was confident that its forces—in the air and on the ground—would be much better integrated.

After Operation Anaconda In March 2002, I called all of my Joint Staff directors to a Saturday meeting in the Pentagon. The press of daily issues made doing any real "thinking" during the week almost impossible—that was just reaction time spent putting out fires or spent in endless meetings. Saturdays and Sundays provided the time needed to reflect and think through the complex issues facing our military.

The enemy's ability to fight a sustained asymmetric battle, despite severe losses in Afghanistan, still posed a significant threat to the United States and our allies. The intelligence pointed to al-Qaida's having the patience, will, and resolve to continue the fight, and not just in Afghanistan. I was worried that with our attention so intensely focused on Afghanistan we would lose sight of the larger fight, and of the fact that al-Qaida would continue its mission despite the outcome there. Although it was not the place of the Joint Staff or Joint Chiefs of Staff to conduct operational planning, we did have the responsibility to do strategic planning. We had to find ways of making America and our friends and allies safer from the al-Qaida threat.

I looked around the table at the faces of these experienced flag officers, the cream of America's military leadership.

"Who in this room thinks we have a strategy to defeat al-Qaida?"

No one raised his hand or spoke. We had been thinking tactically after 9/11. In fact, most of Operation Enduring Freedom in Afghanistan had been conducted on the tactical scale. Now we needed to plan strategically.

"Okay," I said. "Put your best people to work on it. Obviously, this is important. We'll meet again next Saturday."

While the Joint Staff worked that week, I conferred with CIA Director George Tenet. I wanted any global strategy and supporting operations to be complementary, not inadvertently in conflict. This was an especially important consideration because of the high degree of secrecy that would be required for success. The military and the intelligence community undoubtedly had to work together, but we had to avoid leaks. Each side brought its own strengths and resources to the table. The CIA had language specialists, case officers with productive agent networks, and keen analytical capability. The military had unequaled reconnaissance and surveillance capacity, elite Special Operations Forces, and firepower. So any strategic offensive against al-Qaida would have to combine military force and intelligence assets to succeed.

At the meeting the next Saturday Rear Adm. Lowell "Jake" Jacoby, the J2 Intelligence Director, reported that, as a first step, his officers recommended a concerted effort to neutralize al-Qaida's senior leaders and planners, specifically Usama bin Laden and Ayman Muhammad al-Zawahiri, plus seven leading planners and operational commanders. This list of names became the basis for the "Two Plus Seven Strategy" because by capturing or killing them, we hoped to cripple or seriously disrupt al-Qaida's planning and operations. We carefully coordinated this list with the CIA.

That Saturday strategy session was codified in a plan approved by the President and the National Security Council. Over the next thirteen months, that cooperation paid off: Some of the high-ranking al-Qaida members on our strategic list were either killed or captured in Pakistan, the Middle East, or North Africa. In March 2002, senior al-Qaida planner Abu Zubaydah was one of the first terrorists the Pakistanis captured and turned over to the CIA for interrogation (later to be transferred to Guantanamo Bay). The American pressure continued. In September 2002, Pakistani police raided a Karachi apartment and captured senior al-Qaida member Ramzi bin al-Shibh after a gun battle that killed several of his colleagues. On November 4, 2002, a Hellfire missile launched from a CIA-controlled Predator over the Yemeni desert killed Ali

Qaed Sinan al-Harthi, one of planners of the *Cole* bombing. Mustafa Ahmed al-Hasawi, the main financial coordinator behind the 9/11 terrorist operation, was arrested in Rawalpindi, Pakistan, in March 2003. The pressure on al-Qaida's leadership remained relentless.

Probably the most important al-Qaida terrorist on the Two Plus Seven Strategy list to be captured was Khalid Sheik Mohammed, generally acknowledged as the organization's third-ranking leader. On March 1, 2003, Pakistani security seized him during a raid on a house in Rawalpindi, Pakistan. He was one of the principal planners of the 1998 U.S. Embassy bombings, the attack on the USS *Cole*, and, his most notorious act, the September 11, 2001, attacks on the World Trade Center and the Pentagon that sparked the Global War on Terror. The report of the National Commission on Terrorist Attacks Upon the United States later described Khalid Sheik Mohammed as the "principal architect of the 9/11 attacks."

His capture underscored the increased cooperation and determined effort, especially between the Pentagon and the CIA, that had emerged since 9/11.

Two years after al-Qaida had launched its surprise attack on America and its allies, we were conducting a successful counterattack. Certainly, the terrorists would continue to strike when and where they could, and it was way too soon to say we had crippled their organization. Al-Qaida had lost much of its centralized operational coherence. However, I remained uneasy. We needed to ensure that it did not reinvent itself in such a way that it would be as strong as, or even stronger than, before 9/11. This was a key strategic issue I had begun to grapple with three months after the attack on the United States.

The United States and its allies continue to use advanced surveillance and reconnaissance techniques and a rebuilt human intelligence capability to hit key al-Qaida targets. In July 2008, for example, a U.S. warplane dropped a precision-guided bomb on a house in Pakistan's tribal region that had been identified from combined intelligence techniques, killing Midhat Musir al-Sayid Umar, the leading al-Qaida chemical weapons expert.

Today, the Taliban continues to use Pakistan's tribal areas on the Afghanistan border as a haven and has again begun to spread its influence in Afghanistan.

The day before Thanksgiving, 2001—while the last Taliban- and al-Qaida-held cities in Afghanistan were falling—Secretary Rumsfeld came back to the Pentagon from a White House meeting.

"Dick," Rumsfeld said, "the President wants to know what kind of operations plan we have for Iraq."

I had been so preoccupied with Afghanistan in the two months after the 9/11 attacks, I hadn't had much time to think about Iraq. But since Desert Storm I had followed Iraq closely. I was always aware that our airmen and British and French airmen were in harm's way daily patrolling the northern and southern no-fly zones that the Coalition had established in Iraq in 1991. By 2001, Iraqi air-defense forces regularly fired on the American and British aircraft enforcing the two zones. Indeed, it always amazed me and the Joint Chiefs that America would let Saddam's regime fire at our aircraft and aircrews literally for years with few repercussions. Military aviators by definition operate out of public view—but I always wondered what the government's tolerance level would have been if these had been American ground forces being shot at several times a week.

For years, I had also been concerned that terrorists would somehow acquire Iraq's WMD. This concern was heightened considerably after witnessing the ruthlessness of our adversary on 9/11.

"The plan for Iraq is badly out of date," I told the Secretary. "It's based on 1990s assumptions and doesn't reflect current degraded Iraqi strength or our expanded inventory of Precision-Guided Munitions and command-and-control systems."

Rumsfeld said he figured as much. "The President and I want to dust off that plan, bring it up to date. Let's schedule a call to General Franks for early next week."

The President's interest in a possible military operation in Iraq did not surprise me. Even before the 9/11 attacks, the behavior of Saddam Hussein's Baathist government had become unacceptable. President Bill Clinton had signed into law on October 31, 1998, the Iraq Liberation Act, passed by the House with a vote of 360–38 and the unanimous consent of the Senate. Identifying the need to support a "transition to democracy in Iraq," the act cited Iraq's continued violation of international law and resistance to United Nations inspectors searching for weapons of mass destruction. Earlier in 1998, Iraq conceded that it had possessed an offensive biological warfare capability including thousands of gallons of botulinum, two thousand gallons of anthrax, twenty-five biological-filled Scud missile warheads, and 157 aerial bombs with biological agents—but claimed to have destroyed this deadly arsenal.

President Clinton chided the Iraqis for evading international inspectors searching for a secret atomic weapons program. The international inspectors,

Clinton said, believed that, while admitting to some WMD, Iraq was undoubtedly disguising "stockpiles of chemical and biological munitions, a small force
of Scud-type missiles, and the capacity to restart quickly its production program and build many, many more weapons."

Since 1998, Iraq had continued to evade the efforts of the United Nations
weapons inspectors while feigning cooperation. U.N. weapons inspections in
Iraq were suspended in November 2000 after sharp disagreements over access
to suspect sites. In the months after the 9/11/2001 attacks, we began to consider
possible military operations to defeat Saddam Hussein's regime if it continued
to hamper the U.N. weapons inspectors. Our planning also took place in the
shadow of the October 2001 anthrax attacks and mounting intelligence that
al-Qaida possessed deadly chemical weapons.

But Iraq's existing weapons of mass destruction arsenal was not our only, or
indeed, our major concern with Saddam Hussein's regime. Since the Gulf War,
we had been committed to patrolling the two no-fly zones in order to protect
Shiites in the south and Kurds in the north. However, no one knew if that protection could continue much longer without the presence of our combat aircraft triggering a military confrontation. On July 27, 2001, Secretary Rumsfeld
wrote a memo to Colin Powell, Condoleezza Rice, and Vice President Cheney.
We could simply abandon the no-fly zones "before someone is killed or captured," he said, or we could "acknowledge that sanctions don't work over extended periods and stop the pretense of having a policy that is keeping Saddam
'in the box' when we know he has crawled a good distance out of the box and
is currently doing the things that will ultimately be harmful to his neighbors in
the region and to U.S. interests—namely developing WMD and the means to
deliver them and increasing his strength at home and in the region month-by-
month. Within a few years the U.S. will undoubtedly have to confront a Saddam
armed with nuclear weapons."

Rumsfeld suggested in this memo the possibility of asking "our moderate
Arab friends" if they would be willing to "engage in a more robust policy." He
even suggested we might try contacting Saddam Hussein directly to see
whether he was "willing to make some accommodation" that would defuse the
hostility of the United States and the West.

And then the 9/11 attacks occurred, and the problem of Iraq was temporarily shelved—but only temporarily.

On Tuesday, November 27, 2001, I flew to Tampa for a visit to CENTCOM headquarters, and Tommy Franks and I spoke to Secretary Rumsfeld on the secure video teleconference link. Rumsfeld explained the President's interest in the options for potential operations in Iraq.

OPLAN 1003, Tom Franks agreed, was outdated, basically "Desert Storm II," and did not reflect changes in the force levels in the region. The Iraqi military was less than half as big as it had been in 1991, and its capabilities were much less lethal—discounting possible use of chemical or biological weapons. The American military, on the other hand, was not only much more lethal than our Desert Storm force in terms of precision-guided weapons, our upgraded C^4 (Command-Control-Communications and Computers and Surveillance system) now connected individual aircraft, combat and logistics vehicles, and ground units into nearly seamless digital networks that would have seemed like science-fiction fantasy when our forces had last fought the Iraqi Army in 1991. Space-based and aerial overhead reconnaissance had made quantum advances since the Allied Coalition expelled Iraqi forces from Kuwait. Our latest recon satellites and upgraded aerial platforms, like the Joint Surveillance and Target Attack Radar System (JSTARS) gave us the "God's eye" situational awareness and ability to see through bad weather and battlefield smoke that commanders had sought for generations. This was the framework for our new digital-display Blue Force Tracker system through which we could precisely locate our own forces day or night, in any weather, and we could target our opponents with precision weapons striking exact GPS coordinates.

Franks emphasized that we had learned a lot about precision-weapons capabilities during Operation Enduring Freedom in Afghanistan. And we were still learning more.

"Fine, General," Secretary Rumsfeld said. "Please dust off your plan and get back to me next week."

I realized one week was not giving Tom and his staff much time to sharpen the OPLAN, but he and his officers had proven they were up to tough challenges. This was our first clue that the Secretary wanted to be in on the "take-off" of a new war plan for Iraq.

On December 4, 2001, Tommy Franks gave us a preliminary "Commander's Concept" for the revised Iraq OPLAN 1003. The President's instructions were to keep the exchange extremely close-hold, so only Rumsfeld, Vice Chairman

Marine Gen. Pete Pace, Doug Feith, and I were at the Pentagon video teleconferences terminal, with Franks and his J3, Air Force Maj. Gen. Gene Renuart,
in Tampa.

Any well-structured operations plan begins with assumptions about the potential adversaries' strengths and weaknesses, the character of the conflict, and
the operational objective. Updating an OPLAN consisted only of addressing its
transportation and logistics aspects every couple of years. (This process was
inadequate in the 21st-century security environment and would change during
my tenure.) But totally restructuring the OPLAN 1003 for Iraq was a much
more substantive undertaking, so Rumsfeld asked Franks to address the assumptions first: Was the military balance of forces the same as when the plan
was last revised (1998)? Were the objectives the same? For example, in the Desert Storm operations plan, the objective had been the expulsion of Iraqi military forces from Kuwait, *not* the toppling of Saddam's regime. Ten years later,
that supposition had changed. Referring to the first slide of his presentation,
ASSUMPTIONS, Franks stated what he believed to be the case in December 2001:
The objective of initiating military operations in Iraq would be to remove the
regime of Saddam Hussein.

Rumsfeld agreed with that assumption, but added, "The President will ultimately make that decision."

Franks continued with his second assumption: If we carried out military
operations, another important mission would be to remove Iraq's military
threat to its neighbors from either conventional forces or weapons of mass destruction. In other words, we would destroy Iraq's *offensive* capability.

And then Tom raised doubts that the existing plan had kept pace with the
situation in Iraq. He jumped ahead to the last slide, END STATE, pointing to two
sets of bright-red block letters: REGIME CHANGE and WMD REMOVAL.

But because the situation in Iraq was so unpredictable, it was best to understand our existing capability to execute the current plan if forced to do so. Further, in late 2001, the possible link between the Iraqis and terrorist organizations
was poorly understood at best. From the week of the September 2001 terrorist
attacks onward, the President had been very hesitant to link Saddam Hussein
to al-Qaida in general and to 9/11 in particular. I never saw any convincing
evidence linking Iraq to the 9/11 attacks. But we did know that at least one
al-Qaida leader, Abu Musab al-Zarqawi, who had been wounded in Afghanistan, was then hospitalized in Baghdad. After his medical treatment, Zarqawi
had set up some sort of terrorist training center among the fundamentalist

Sunni Kurds of Ansar al Islam in a well-defended area of northern Iraq called Khurma.

Given Saddam's elaborate internal security apparatus, it was almost certain the Iraqis knew the facility existed. But whether the Iraqi regime was actively supporting the operation in Khurma was never known.

Secretary Rumsfeld and I went to the President on several occasions to try to get approval to strike these facilities in northern Iraq in 2002. We desired an air strike or cruise missile attack or a small ground force that could conduct an exploration of the site. The latter would have required the help of Turkey for staging helicopters and would have involved ten to twenty airlift aircraft. We didn't know the full extent of what was going on there and wanted to ensure that whatever they were doing with chemical, or possibly biological weapons wouldn't be "exported" to al-Qaida in other locations. Besides, the CIA had reported as many as two hundred al-Qaida fighters had fled there from Afghanistan. Others argued that unless we could get in on the ground for site exploitation, we shouldn't strike it. My view was, attacking al-Qaida was always a good thing and that site exploration should be secondary. We never got the President's approval, probably because he was concerned we might trigger a war with Iraq before our diplomatic efforts played out.

The possible nexus of weapons of mass destruction and international terrorism was even more ominous: If Iraq supplied any WMD to al-Qaida, Usama bin Laden would undoubtedly use the material. With the United States still reeling from the shock of the earlier anthrax attacks, this was a threat no one could ignore.

Rumsfeld, the Joint Chiefs, and I wanted a fresh strategic approach to Iraq, and that was what Franks provided. Before starting this review, we agreed on a key assumption that it was possible to safely conduct lightning-fast, near-simultaneous air and ground operations once the "kinetic" phase began. The emphasis on "lightning-fast" would mean fewer military and civilian casualties, less danger of regional instability, mass starvation, refugees, and sabotage of oil fields—a very good thing.

That was the foundation of Franks's concept. But exactly what size force *would* be required was yet to be determined; there were many factors involved in this decision. We did not want to push the Iraqis into an unnecessary war by massing troops on their borders in unmistakable offensive formations, or give away any tactical surprise we might otherwise have. On the other hand, we could not afford to go in too light and have our troops mauled by heavy Iraqi

Republican Guard armored units. There were also a number of other preliminary requirements to consider: the eventual timing and sequence of deployment orders; overflight, staging, and basing options; integration of our resources (air, ground, naval, and SOF); as well as allied support. And all this had to be done while maintaining strict operational security.

Thus began an almost year-long series of often frustrating—for CENTCOM at least—iterations of the OPLAN 1003. Although Tom sometimes became exasperated with the process, I understood that Rumsfeld was not getting too deep down "in the weeds." The President had given the Secretary of Defense and CENTCOM's commander a very serious responsibility: preparing for a war with Iraq that we hoped would be prevented by diplomatic means but that we intended to win decisively if war became necessary.

Tommy Franks's tolerance for the process increased dramatically—over time. After one of these early Saturday meetings, Franks stormed into my office and threw his cap across the room. He was visibly upset, and I was surprised, as he had been calm in front of the Secretary. He said, "Chairman, if these sessions continue like this, I'll quit. I don't need the hassle." As he was venting and stomping about my office, Secretary Wolfowitz opened the door and walked in. He looked on in some puzzlement, wondering what was going on. Franks and I finished saying good-bye and he headed back to Tampa.

After Franks left, I told Wolfowitz that Tom really chafed at the many questions Rumsfeld asked him about the plan. This was a two-sided issue; Rumsfeld's style of rigorously intellectually challenging assumptions, and oversensitivity on Franks's part. We both decided to make the Secretary aware of Franks's reactions to the planning sessions, and I chose that I would work with Tommy, and my staff with his staff, to help prepare them to brief Rumsfeld periodically. I wanted to be able to support Franks appropriately, but needed to know the areas he considered important. Both Rumsfeld and Franks modified their approach to the sessions, and things started to smooth out immediately.

This friction between combatant commanders and Secretaries of Defense is natural in many ways and has existed for as long as the positions have. This tension also exists between the combatant commanders and the Joint Chiefs because of their different statutory requirements. As Franks admitted at the end of the process, the repeated trips to Washington to review the OPLAN with the Secretary and Joint Chiefs resulted in a better plan than he and his staff would have developed working alone.

Tommy Franks tackled the job with energy and imagination. To help us all follow the logic of his planning process, he had created a "Lines-and-Slices" matrix—a gridwork of vertical and horizontal columns that represented the tools at our disposal to achieve specific missions. The seven horizontal "Lines of Operation" were the types of forces or tactical approaches available. Across the top of the grid were the nine mission objectives or targets for CENTCOM's forces.

As Franks's staff filled in the working matrix it proved especially helpful in showing the overall scope of the possible operation and in breaking the task down into manageable pieces. It displayed sixty-three boxes: nine slices of the Iraqi regime's structure multiplied by seven operational lines. The matrix revealed opportunities where we could be especially effective: Operational Fires against Leadership, Internal Security, WMD Infrastructure, and so forth. But, equally important, the graphic illustrated that there were *no* kinetic operations directed against civilians or the commercial sector.

When disassembled into its logical components, the matrix demonstrated that conducting a major military operation in Iraq could be a manageable task. I, along with the other Joint Chiefs, agreed with Tom Franks that we could conduct a successful operation with a much smaller, more capable and flexible force. The important question to address, however, was how we would handle the postconflict stability and reconstruction phase.

In Afghanistan during 2002, Hamid Karzai was pursuing his duties as the chairman of the Transitional Administration that had been established following the Bonn conference in early December 2001. The country was in bad condition, with hunger rampant and starvation held at bay only through the efforts of donor organizations like USAID, the World Food Program, OXFAM, and a variety of nongovernmental agencies (NGOs). Although the administration had initially sought to leave the "nation building" challenge of Operation Enduring Freedom to others, it had become clear that we would be needed for the indefinite future.

The military picture was better, but not ideal. Following the battle of Tora Bora, elements of the 10th Mountain Division and 101st Airborne Division garrisoned Bagram Air Base northeast of Kabul. U.S. Marines controlled the airport at Kandahar, while NATO's international security force maintained order in Kabul. But our intelligence showed pockets of Taliban holed up in the mountains north of Kandahar and al-Qaida remnants remaining in the Spin Mountains of the east.

On December 28, 2001, President Bush and Tommy Franks conducted a secure video teleconference with Vice President Dick Cheney, George Tenet, Condi Rice, Andy Card, Secretary Rumsfeld, and me. Bush and Franks were at the Western White House in Crawford, Texas; Cheney and Rumsfeld were at their vacation homes in Wyoming and Taos, New Mexico; I was with Tenet, Rice, and Card in the White House Situation Room. Since 9/11, we had all become completely accustomed to these geographically divided teleconferences, and no one felt the distance separating participants.

The main order of business was a possible military operation against the Baathist regime in Iraq. CENTCOM presented the Commander's Concept of the updated 1003 operations plan, which contained the Lines-and-Slices matrix.

Working on the assumption that regime change and WMD removal would be the overall objectives if the President decided war was necessary, Franks again emphasized that speed would be one of the most critical assets we would bring to a campaign centered on these objectives. Most important, speed was essential to taking the enemy capital without confronting a "Fortress Baghdad." He assumed that overwhelming the city quickly would not only win the campaign, it would defeat the enemy with a minimum loss of civilian life and infrastructure damage.

As we were talking about speed, Secretary of State Colin Powell asked what type of "deployment timelines" Franks foresaw. Before Operation Desert Storm, when Powell was the Chairman of the Joint Chiefs of Staff, it took the Allied Coalition almost six months to deploy the massive ground force and position it to attack the enemy.

Tommy Franks pictured a much different type of operation, with a rapid buildup of Army and Marine units in Kuwait and Turkey, followed by an even faster air-Special-Operations-ground campaign. The idea was to throw the Iraqis completely off balance, to strike hard, advancing with unprecedented speed toward Baghdad. We had Precision-Guided Munitions and the sensor systems for their targeting that would combine to annihilate the most dangerous Iraqi formations. Our fastest "spear-tip" advancing units could bypass remaining enemy forces, leaving them for follow-on forces to deal with.

Maj. Gen. Gene Renuart then presented the four specific phases of CENTCOM's operational concept: Phase I (Preparation); Phase II (Shape the Battlespace); Phase III (Decisive Operations); and Phase IV (Post-Hostility Operations). As in Operation Enduring Freedom in Afghanistan, the phases of the new operation would themselves be subdivided. The phases would follow sequentially, but their boundaries might overlap. In this new construct operational flexibility would be critical.

Franks discussed the variables governing the number of U.S. forces involved. If we could simultaneously advance into Iraq from Jordan, Saudi Arabia, and Kuwait, as well as move south toward Baghdad from Turkey—and if we could base and stage forces in the friendly Gulf States—we could begin the operation with as few as 105,000 troops. Over the following sixty to ninety days—which would encompass the first three phases of the operation—we could increase our ground forces to approximately 230,000 troops. In fact, one of the unique features of the plan was the concept of "off ramps." The idea was to have forces flowing and ready to flow into Kuwait as hostilities began. If the smaller force was successful, then the forces in reserve would be "off ramped" and turned around or not deployed. If progress was stalled, Franks was sure he could protect the deployed force as more forces arrived in theater. In the end, there were several hundred thousand troops available if needed. Later, when Saddam Hussein's regime fell, Franks had determined that additional forces were not required for the transition to Phase IV.

As Franks outlined CENTCOM's various Phase III options, I studied the wide arrow on his chart representing the final Phase IV (Post-Hostility Operations). It was the longest on the graphic; its duration "UNKNOWN." I agreed that the duration of this phase was probably an unknowable factor. Although some in the administration were confident of a smooth, short transition to Phase IV, few military professionals were comfortable predicting what would happen in Iraq once we defeated the Baathists. Further, Tom Franks, Secretary Rumsfeld, and I consulted some of the world's leading academic experts on Iraq. They were all confident of their predictions, but their opinions differed widely. Since there was no consensus, we had to prepare for a variety of contingencies.

As the video teleconference wrapped up, President Bush addressed us, trying to bolster our morale as he usually did. "We should remain optimistic that a combination of diplomacy and international pressure will succeed in disarming the regime." He paused while we all nodded agreement. "But if this approach isn't successful, we have to have other options. That's why I asked Secretary Rumsfeld and General Franks to work on this concept. The worst thing that could happen to America would be a combination of WMD and terrorism." There had been no U.N. weapons inspectors in Iraq since 1998, and we didn't know what Saddam might have developed since then. But we *did* know he had used WMD on the Iranians and on his own people. "I will not allow weapons of mass destruction to fall into the hands of terrorists."

Over the next two months, Tommy Franks and Gene Renuart became regular commuters between CENTCOM's Tampa headquarters and the Pentagon as the iterations of OPLAN 1003 continued to evolve. Secretary Rumsfeld knew that the President wanted the best plan the military could deliver, and that was what Rumsfeld and the Joint Chiefs insisted Franks produce. Secretary Rumsfeld also wanted the Commander in Chief to get to know and have confidence in his combatant commander. To this end, Rumsfeld had Franks brief the President on his planning effort from time to time at the White House.

As the planning evolved, Secretary Rumsfeld insisted that Tommy Franks and his CENTCOM planners—now assisted by a small cell of Joint Staff planners—work through that spring and into the summer to produce a draft "Hybrid" operations plan. This would compress Phases I through III by reducing the number of ground troops required to start the operation, while maintaining the level of our combat aircraft and cruise missiles. In other words, we could start smaller, but then enlarge the force as needed. The Hybrid plan could be adapted from what Tommy Franks had begun calling the "Running Start" option: Once our airpower and SOF had shaped the battlespace inside Iraq, ground forces from the Allied Coalition would cross into Iraq and move rapidly toward their objectives.

The Running Start option was bold and had other interesting attributes: Kuwait was a tiny desert country with a small population, and, unlike Saudi Arabia, had a limited port capacity for the "drive-on, drive-off" ships that would carry our trucks and armored vehicles. During Operation Desert Shield/Desert Storm in 1990–91, the big Saudi Arabian network of seaports had made possible the buildup of the Coalition forces to over 560,000 troops. As CENTCOM and the JCS refined OPLAN 1003 in 2002, we did not have the option of building up such a huge force. One reason was that there was limited space in tiny Kuwait for a large force. Another was that a large force could give the impression that our diplomatic efforts were not sincere. But even if we *had* managed to jam hundreds of thousands of troops into compressed encampments on

Kuwait's border with Iraq, their presence would have quickly stripped us of any hope of tactical surprise.

I had trouble that fall getting Franks to focus on Phase IV planning for any iteration of the OPLAN. The plan called for the military to be in charge of this stability and reconstruction phase until such time as responsibility was passed to civilian authority or to the Iraqis. There were no dates associated with these changes from military to civilian or Iraqi authority. Despite several phone calls and personal messages to Franks, CENTCOM's planning for Phase IV never improved.

But there was extensive Phase IV interagency planning going on in Washington starting in summer 2002. We established a cell of people on the joint staff to link the planning in Washington and Tampa for the stability and reconstruction of Iraq. Later, the National Security Council took leadership of this planning. Frank Miller, a longtime civil servant in the Pentagon, was now on the NSC staff and led the Executive Steering Group that focused on the interagency Phase IV planning. In January 2003, retired Army Lt. Gen. Jay Garner was brought in to integrate and develop much of this interagency work. He would go forward to Iraq once major combat was over to lead the effort to rebuild Iraq. Garner had served in northern Iraq after the first Gulf War, administering the humanitarian efforts to aid Kurdish refugees.

I also directed that a Combined Joint Task Force (CJTF-4) be stood up to focus on postconflict efforts. This task force was led by an Army one-star and trained for their mission by Joint Forces Command. (They deployed to Kuwait and were placed under the Land Component Commander, Army Lt. Gen. David McKiernan.) CJTF-4 should have been assigned to the military commander in Iraq after major combat to help execute our Phase IV planning. Unfortunately, it was never employed as intended, most likely because the Coalition Provisional Authority (CPA) assumed civilian control in May. However, people from this task force were used individually to man the CPA and other military organizations in Iraq. The difficulty of moving rapidly from military to civilian operations was a tough lesson learned about the critical transition from Phase III to Phase IV.

Surprise lay at the heart of any operations plan we might employ in Iraq. We did not want to force Saddam Hussein into starting a conflict until we had our forces in place. If he felt threatened, he could trigger the conflict by using chemical or biological weapons on our forces just a few kilometers south of the Iraqi border. Or he could set the oil fields on fire, as he had in Kuwait in 1991, or blow many of the bridges over the rivers or break the Euphrates dams, slowing our advance and making the reconstruction phase much more difficult and costly. But equally important, we did not want our military planning to interfere with the intense diplomatic effort under way to reach a settlement short of war.

Tommy Franks had successfully brought in Gulf States as Coalition supporters; the President and Colin Powell had solidified tacit support of Saudi Arabia. Jordan's King Abdullah was not in a position to grant our conventional units transit through his country from the Red Sea port of Aqaba to Iraq's western desert, because of his large and restive Palestinian population. But Abdullah was committed to providing staging and basing for Coalition SOF who would cross the wide, virtually unguarded frontier into Iraq and play havoc with enemy lines of communication. Franks worked the Jordanian relationship, as he and King Abdullah were close friends. I would work the Saudi support.

While we had the tacit support of Saudi Arabia, any large footprint in the country would be a serious problem for the Saudi government. The Saudi population didn't want the kingdom to host too many Americans. Yet, for our Iraq plan to succeed, we would need Saudi basing for both air and SOF assets, at least through major combat. On January 11, 2003, a Saturday, the Vice President, Secretary of Defense, and I met with the Saudi Ambassador to the United States, Prince Bandar. I had known Bandar for many years and we had our Air Force fighter pilot experiences in common. The purpose of our meeting at the White House was to reveal the basics of our plan for major combat in Iraq, convince Bandar that the United States was serious about war if diplomacy failed, and give him a sense of what support we needed from his country if we went to war. We decided that approaching the Saudi Ambassador was better than working directly with Riyadh.

Following this White House meeting Bandar called me, wanting to meet in the Pentagon. We set up a meeting on January 22 for late afternoon. As the Prince walked into my office he asked if he could smoke a cigar. The Pentagon had been smoke-free for over a decade, and even VIPs were expected to go outside to designated areas to smoke. I thought that we were about to ask Saudi Arabia for a lot of support for our operations, and this would be very unpopular in the kingdom. If a cigar was what the Prince wanted, then he should have it. He threw us for a loop when he asked for an ashtray. I hadn't seen one around the huge Pentagon complex for a very long time. An ordinary plate sufficed.

I had asked Franks for everything that he wanted from the Saudis, and I went through the list with Bandar. What we desired included conducting the air war from the Combined Air Operations Center at Prince Sultan Air Base, overflight to and from the base, fuel for our aircraft, and the staging of SOF out of a small base in northern Saudi Arabia near the Iraq border (this was potentially the most contentious issue with the Saudi population). Bandar was a real gentleman and agreed to work our requests with the Saudi government. In the end we got all we asked for. But to assuage Saudi concerns, we closed down the northern staging base (Ar'ar) about the time major combat was over, and were out of the kingdom totally, including relocating the CAOC to Qatar, by August 2003.

The situation in Turkey was not so clear—and was far less promising. CENTCOM's Hybrid plan, which the SecDef and the Joint Chiefs had endorsed, called for staging a major combat force centered on the heavy 4th Infantry Division and the 3rd Armored Cavalry Regiment—a force totaling sixty-two thousand—to stage in southeastern Turkey and flow south into Iraq when kinetic operations began. In that manner, Baghdad (the enemy center of gravity) would be threatened by powerful Coalition forces advancing from two directions and would be obliged to divide its Republican Guard divisions to protect the capital. This idea originated from Marine Corps Commandant Jim Jones during one of Franks's briefing to the Chiefs.

By February 2003, Turkey's National Security Council had introduced a bill in parliament authorizing this deployment. But the political situation in the country was strained. Although the moderate Islamic-based Justice and Development Party had been voted into power in November 2001, its senior politicians were widely considered to be temporary placeholders waiting for permanent, more seasoned leaders to take over. Those in power in early 2003 lacked a team of foreign policy professionals and were themselves apparently too inexperienced to master the parliamentary negotiations required to pass the bill approving the Coalition troop deployment.

I had a good relationship with the Turkish Chief of Defense, Hilmi Ozkok. We met often at NATO meetings, and I had hosted his wife and him in Washington and we had been hosted in their home in Ankara. I wanted to ensure that in the internal Turkish debate, where Ozkok would have a voice, they understood a "no" voice would *not* keep the United States from going to war in Iraq. "If our President directs, we're going to war whether or not Turkey allows our forces to move through your country," I told him.

Vital political and military discussions with the Justice and Development government in Ankara puttered on into the spring of 2003, but were eventually abandoned. During the later phase of the negotiations, the ships carrying 4th Infantry Division cruised back and forth off the Turkish Mediterranean coast, waiting for authorization to land that never came, and they eventually off-loaded in Kuwait. But their frustrating experience was not wasted: Intelligence sources revealed that the Iraqis believed they *were* eventually going to disembark in Turkey and move south across the border to threaten Baghdad. So they kept their northern forces—including two Republican Guard divisions—in place too long to aid in the defense of Baghdad.

But by summer 2002, I was getting concerned about having enough time to do the necessary detailed planning on OPLAN 1003V. This would open the plan to thousands more people. Secretary Rumsfeld had insisted on the strictest possible security for our planning, so details to this point had been kept to an absolute need-to-know basis, but now the small group of those familiar with the plan had to be expanded: It had become imperative to alert U.S. Transportation Command to coordinate the planning of our airlift and sea shipments for thousands of troops and tens of thousands of tons of cargo and equipment. Before we could start moving those troops and supplies into Kuwait, brigade by brigade, we would have to coordinate closely with the services, Pacific Command, European Command, Special Operations Command, Space Command, and Joint Forces Command, because they would provide many of the forces or would participate in preparing the deployment orders. They would also have to secure overflight and arrange for basing in transit.

I made the case with Secretary Rumsfeld that it was past time to begin enlarging the planning circle. In summer 2002 he authorized me to bring the services and appropriate combatant commanders into the process. We could have the best war plan in the world, but if we didn't bring in Transportation Command to figure out how to get the forces halfway around the world, we wouldn't be able to complete the mission.

As the OPLAN had matured, it had become more solid and substantive. The series of iterations was paying off. Most of us on the Joint Chiefs, in the combatant commands, and in OSD were convinced that our forces would win a lopsided victory when the President gave CENTCOM the order to execute the operation. But none of us knew when or *if* he might give that order.

In November 2002, General Franks hosted a final runthrough of the plan with his component commanders. This exercise revealed the need to totally change the transportation planning that had gone on for months. In effect, the order of the many units arriving in theater was changed around by Franks and his commanders so they would arrive in the order in which they would be required on the battlefield. Usually this type of replanning effort would take many months to complete. We weren't sure if or when the President would give us the go-ahead, but we had to be ready as quickly as possible.

Redoing the transportation plan turned into a coordination problem. Gen. John Handy, commander of Transportation Command, was our best logistician, and he was having trouble getting the services and combatant commanders to cooperate. I was very confident that operationally Franks had a handle on the execution of the plan. But I wasn't as confident that the logistics planning was moving as efficiently as it should. After all, we were taking our troops and equipment seven thousand miles, unloading in a couple of relatively small ports or airports in the region, then traveling hundreds of miles to Baghdad. That's a very long supply line; no other nation in the world could expect to move the equivalent of several midsize cities halfway around the world and have the forces ready for combat.

After discussions with John Handy, I decided to host secure video conferences once or twice a week for the next two months. I met with representatives from the services and combatant commanders and tried to help resolve the multiple issues that arose from this need to completely redo the transportation plan. Despite the frustration that many had, they were not willing to display it with the Chairman present. It was certainly unusual for the Chairman to get involved in this level of detail, but I saw the logistics issue as being the only one that could possibly lead to a failed mission. And that wasn't going to happen.

But we had to maintain the delicate balance of increasing our forces in the region publicly enough so that Saddam and his inner circle would feel the pressure, while not believing war was inevitable and abandoning the possibility of the peaceful settlement that we were working toward through diplomacy.

This was an unusual situation: The United States had very rarely chosen to attack. We had almost always responded to attack. Preparing for a preemptive war was a new experience for our force.

———————

As the flow of our forces to the Middle East slowly continued, it was time to strengthen international support for possible military operation against Iraq. The United Nations General Assembly always met in September, and President Bush used the occasion to seek that international backing. On September 12, 2002, almost exactly one year after the 9/11 attacks, Bush addressed the hundreds of General Assembly delegates, once more cataloging the Iraqi regime's long record of stubborn rejections of U.N. demands for greater cooperation on WMD disclosure.

News media reaction to the speech was largely positive. The major newspapers all noted the President had focused not only on Iraq's WMD policies, but also on its support for terrorism, and on the repressive nature of Saddam's regime. If Iraq's regime defied the world community again, he said, "the world must move deliberately, decisively to hold Iraq to account."

Both houses of Congress passed the Authorization for Use of Military Force Against Iraq Resolution of 2002 in the early morning of October 11, 2002, exactly thirteen months after the 9/11 attacks. The vote had the support of a strong majority of members of both parties in both houses. President Bush signed the bill into law on October 16.

A key provision of the law authorized the President to use the military "as he determines to be necessary and appropriate" in order to "defend the national security of the United States against the continuing threat posed by Iraq; and enforce all relevant United Nations Security Council Resolutions regarding Iraq."

———————

On November 8, 2002—as Coalition combat units were entering camps in Kuwait—the United Nations Security Council passed Resolution 1441 by unanimous vote with no abstentions. The resolution detailed Iraq's past material breaches of U.N. demands for a full accounting of weapons of mass destruction programs and insisted that Baghdad cooperate fully with the United Nations Monitoring Verification and Inspection Commission (UNMOVIC), which had been created to broaden the base of Security Council pressure. Even Iraq's supporters on the Security Council, including Russia, France, and Syria, voted for the measure, which passed 15–0.

The Iraqi response was not satisfactory. On December 7, 2002, Baghdad turned over a twelve-thousand-page weapons of mass destruction declaration to UNMOVIC's chief inspector, Dr. Hans Blix, and Mohammed El Baradei of the International Atomic Energy Agency. It was soon apparent that much of this material was shuffled, rehashed reports—what some in Washington dismissed as "a pile of old phone books."

Without question, Saddam Hussein and his inner circle were feeling the heat, which was exactly what we wanted. We were now entering that delicate phase where combined military pressure and bare-knuckles diplomacy might just achieve our goal of regime change in Iraq short of war. But my daily discussions with Secretary Rumsfeld and regular conferences with President Bush made it clear to me that the United States would have to ratchet up both sides of our policy toward Iraq before Saddam Hussein would relinquish power voluntarily. Those of us in the military remembered that Saddam had waited to begin withdrawing his forces from Kuwait during Operation Desert Storm until the Coalition was bombing Iraqi troops day and night, and about to cross the Saudi border to destroy the surviving units. Vice President Dick Cheney had been Secretary of Defense then, and Colin Powell the Chairman of the Joint Chiefs of Staff. This administration had a long institutional memory about Saddam's Iraq.

In January 2003, the Joint Chiefs of Staff and all the combatant commanders met with the President in the cabinet room of the White House. The President wanted to know how each person around the table felt about the preparations for war and the war plan itself, and, if he were to decide to go to war, whether they had any reservations about our preparedness. Each service chief and combatant commander spoke in turn. The consensus was that the U.S. military was ready, and everyone agreed there were no show stoppers if the President were to commit to war.

After the meeting, the President and the First Lady hosted the Joint Chiefs and the combatant commanders and their spouses for dinner in the Blue Room. This dinner in late January or early February had become an annual affair, starting with President Clinton. Given what we had just discussed, however, the mood was serious and somber.

Colin Powell addressed the United Nations Security Council on February 5, 2003, making a detailed presentation on Iraqi weapons of mass destruction. Dr. Hans Blix of UNMOVIC had set the stage by reporting to the United Nations that "Iraqi appears not to have come to a genuine acceptance—not even to-day—of the disarmament, which was demanded of it and which it needs to carry out to win the confidence of the world to live in peace." To illustrate his point, he added that Baghdad seemed unable to account for about "one thousand tons" of VX nerve agent—a few drops of which on exposed skin would kill a human being. On hearing his words, I once more envisioned the Tokyo subway attack and the fear that haunted the city's residents for months after the sarin gas nerve agent had been released.

Before speaking to the Security Council, Colin Powell went to CIA headquarters to review the details on all the intelligence we had accumulated on Iraq's WMD program. This was slightly unusual, but Powell thought he could ensure we were on solid ground before he went to the United Nations. On this matter, Powell did not seek advice from the Defense Department or the White House, insisting rather on sticking to the Agency's substantive position. To dramatize CIA support for the presentation, Powell got George Tenet to accompany him to the Security Council chamber and sit right behind him.

Colin Powell described Saddam Hussein's efforts since 1998 to "reconstitute his nuclear program" by acquiring "sufficient fissile material to produce a nuclear explosion. . . . Saddam Hussein is determined to get his hands on a nuclear bomb." Powell described in detail what our intelligence community was convinced were Iraq's efforts to import high-strength aluminum tubes for "centrifuges used to enrich uranium" to weapons grade.

Seated before the television cameras that carried his message to the world, Secretary of State Colin Powell continued to present a litany of evidence against Iraq, which he said was "deeply troubling." He read a series of communications intercepts that revealed a pattern of deceptive behavior among Iraqi military units intent on hiding "forbidden ammo" and other illegal material. Powell continued to detail strong evidence that Iraq was evading its obligations to reveal thoroughly its entire WMD program—just as Hans Blix had stated.

Early in his presentation, Powell riveted the audience by holding up a tiny glass vial of white powder representing about "one teaspoon" of dried anthrax spores. That was the amount that had crippled the U.S. Senate in October during the attack that had killed five innocent people and forced several hundred more to seek emergency medical help.

Finally responding to the demands of the international community, he said, "Iraq declared 8,500 liters of anthrax," but added that U.N. weapons inspectors estimated "Saddam Hussein could have produced 25,000 liters." This was a somber assessment, and Secretary Powell had produced a convincing case.

Having Powell spend a weekend at the CIA satisfying himself that the intelligence was solid and watching his convincing presentation at the United Nations reinforced my instincts that we had a solid case.

In September 2005, however, Colin Powell told Barbara Walters of ABC News that learning his 2003 presentation to the Security Council on Iraqi WMD had been based on flawed intelligence was "painful." "It's painful now," he said, adding that he felt "terrible" about his statements. Worse, he continued, it was "devastating" to later discover that certain unnamed intelligence officers had known the information he received from the CIA was unreliable but had not come forth to warn him.

At the time, I was personally much less convinced that removing the Saddam Hussein regime would be the key to the spread of peace and democracy in the Middle East. Some experts thought that a stable, democratic government in the region would become the catalyst for similar positive change throughout the area. But the WMD issue was enough of a concern to me, and I felt that the objective of removing Saddam from power would justify putting our men and women in harm's way if directed by the Commander in Chief.

Three weeks after Powell's Security Council presentation, it was clear that our military pressure on Iraq was reaching a critical point. The Senate exercised its oversight rights to be certain we were heading in the right direction. On February 25, 2003, the service chiefs were called before the Senate Armed Services Committee to comment on the probable war with Iraq.

Michigan Democratic Senator Carl Levin pressed Army Chief of Staff Eric Shinseki on the size of the occupation force needed to stabilize Iraq "following a successful completion of the possible war." Levin's question put Shinseki in a difficult position. This was a matter that came within the purview of CENTCOM's combatant commander, Gen. Tommy Franks.

So Ric was hesitant to give in to Levin's pressure and reiterated that force size was a decision for Franks.

Levin continued to press: "How about a range?"

When a senator or congressman asked for personal views during testimony, all officers understand their fundamental obligation to provide it. Senator Levin's question required Shinseki, as it did all members of the Joint Chiefs of Staff, to provide this personal view. But Ric did not want his testimony to limit CENTCOM's options in any way. He had to think about the wider implications of his words.

"I would say that what's been mobilized to this point—something on the order of several hundred thousand soldiers is probably a figure that would be required." There were approximately 170,000 Coalition ground forces either deployed in the war theater or en route to it in February 2003, with the capacity to go 300,000 plus using the "on/off ramps."

The matter might have ended there if Deputy Secretary of Defense Wolfowitz had not jumped in after the hearing to publicly rebuke Shinseki for making this estimate. Wolfowitz told the news media the figure had been "far off the mark." Journalists—and their editors—find nothing more attractive than a possible rift within an administration. The deputy secretary's comment bolstered the impression that Rumsfeld's senior team was unfairly stifling dissent. In a subsequent letter to Rumsfeld after he retired, Shinseki said he didn't believe there was a right answer at that time to Senator Levin's question. "I gave an open-ended answer suggesting a nonspecific larger, rather than smaller, number to permit you and General Franks maximum flexibility in arriving at a final number."

I told Wolfowitz that his remarks about Shinseki's testimony were inappropriate. Ric Shinseki was a combat-experienced Army leader with great integrity.

Wolfowitz agreed that his reactions had been unwise. Most military advice to the senior civilian leadership is never revealed publicly. Likewise, if senior civilians have an issue with a statement made by a senior military officer, they should meet with the officer in a private setting to discuss the difference in their views. Trust in relationships is a two-way requirement and there is no quicker way to destroy that trust than to take the differences public. This is especially important when the people involved are the seniormost civilian and military leaders in the country.

———

On Tuesday, February 18, 2003, Franks had his last meeting in the Pentagon on the Iraqi war plan with the Secretary and me. After the meeting, Rumsfeld asked Franks and me to stay behind. The Secretary said that we had done a lot of work together and asked Franks if he was confident we would be successful. Franks said that he was. Rumsfeld then soberly said, "Well, we're all in this together now, Tommy. You can count on our full support here in Washington, no matter how it turns out." The Secretary meant it, and I'm sure Tom Franks was happy to have the support. Any time you're responsible for leading American men and women in combat, it is a lonely position. This poignant moment was just what Franks needed as he left for his headquarters in Qatar.

By mid-March 2003, Gen. Tom Franks reported that all the units needed to initiate "G-Day"—our invasion of Iraq—were positioned in their forward camps. These forces were so close to the Iraqi border that it was virtually certain enemy intelligence had detected their presence. If the Iraqi military were half as good as we believed, they would have estimated the size and intentions of the Coalition armored force maneuvering just south of the gravel berm and barbed-wire barrier marking the actual frontier with Kuwait. Our advanced units could move at any time.

But before they did, President Bush decided to give Saddam Hussein and his two sons one last chance to save themselves and spare their country from the suffering of a new war. At 8:00 P.M. EST on Monday, March 17, 2003 (4:00 A.M. in Baghdad), the President addressed the nation from the White House.

He stressed that "it is too late for Saddam Hussein to remain in power. It is *not* too late for the Iraqi military to act with honor and protect your country by permitting the peaceful entry of Coalition forces to eliminate weapons of mass destruction. Our forces will give Iraqi military units clear instructions on actions they can take to avoid being attacked and destroyed. I urge every member of the Iraqi military and intelligence services, if war comes, do not fight for a dying regime that is not worth your own life."

On the afternoon of Wednesday, March 19, 2003—a full twenty-four hours before the simultaneous ground and air campaign was scheduled to begin—CIA Director George Tenet requested an urgent meeting with Secretary Rumsfeld and me at the Pentagon. Tenet arrived with his deputy, John McLaughlin, and several Agency officers specializing on Iraq who had been running an agent network, code name ROCKSTAR, which had provided fairly accurate human intelligence on Saddam and other key Iraqi leaders. Now those agents reported that Saddam, and probably his two sons, were scheduled to attend a meeting at the family estate known as Dora Farms on the banks of the Tigris south of central Baghdad. The sources also reported that Saddam was due at the meeting about 3:00 A.M. local time, just after the sons arrived. If in fact that information were true it would put the Hussein family into a very tight "target ring" for us to strike. Rumsfeld decided this was important information to discuss with the President and a few other principals of the National Security Council.

We piled into several vehicles and raced toward the Memorial Bridge and the White House. There, we conferred with President Bush, Vice President Cheney, Chief of Staff Andy Card, Condi Rice, and Colin Powell. In the small private dining room adjoining the Oval Office, Tenet laid out several detailed maps of Baghdad and gave a succinct report on the situation. It was possible, Tenet said, that the agents near Dora Farms could actually confirm that Saddam and his sons were in the compound and get word out. But if they could not, was it worth the risk to strike the target, thus upsetting CENTCOM's intricate timetable? Further, we all pondered the repercussions if we did strike, and Saddam and his sons were already complying with our ultimatum and were on their way out of the country? Beyond these points was the major question of avoiding serious collateral damage—killing or injuring a large number of innocent civilians whom the cynical dictator might have with him in the Dora Farms compound.

If either of these elements of the pending decision turned against us and we appeared to be breaking the terms of our own ultimatum and killing innocent civilians in the process, the goodwill of the world that we had established to date would quickly disappear. Further, CENTCOM had already inserted Special Operations Forces into Iraq. Would a strike on Dora Farms blow their cover? But most important, what would be the impact of this precipitous attack on the overall operational security shield we had so carefully constructed? We would certainly lose the vital element of tactical surprise that we hoped to maintain.

The President was faced with a complex and exceedingly difficult decision. Rumsfeld asked me to get Tommy Franks on the secure Red Switch phone to CENTCOM forward headquarters. Franks sounded groggy, as if he hadn't slept for days and nights, which I'm sure was the case. But, alerted by his staff's CIA liaison officer, Tom had already prepared for the Dora Farms contingency. His TLAM cruise missile shooters aboard naval vessels in the Persian Gulf and the Red Sea were already "spun up" and ready to fire on receipt of the Execute order. I told Tom we would get back to him as soon as we knew more.

But a report had just arrived that there was a *manzul*—Arabic for "shelter" or "bunker"—inside Dora Farms. If that were true, conventional TLAM missiles would be ineffective. The CIA in Langley, Virginia, was trying to refine this information. As we waited, the late-winter dusk deepened, and the headlights of commuter cars streamed along Constitution Avenue toward the suburbs. Confirmation from Langley that an underground bunker, probably containing a secure conference room, did exist at Dora Farms would change our planning variables. The only weapon we had in the war theater that could strike them was the F-117 Nighthawk Stealth fighter dropping two-thousand-pound GBU-27 "bunker buster" bombs that penetrated deep underground and through reinforced concrete before exploding. There were major limiting factors on using the F-117s, however. Invisible to radar, the planes could be easily seen in daylight and targeted by antiaircraft fire, missiles, or fighter interceptors. So if they were going to strike Dora Farms to supplement the TLAM mission, the Stealth fighters would have to leave Iraqi air space before sunrise at around 6:00 A.M. local time. And if an F-117 were shot down and the pilot captured, what would that do to the plans to start the campaign in less than a day?

While we debated the pros and cons of a strike on Dora Farms, the President said the decision would be a lot easier if we were positive that Saddam was at that location. George Tenet had been coming and going from the Oval Office where we now conducted our discussion to use a secure phone at the translator's desk outside the door. Now when he returned, Tenet reported that one of the ROCKSTAR sources passed on the information that Saddam had just arrived at Dora Farms, riding in a taxi to deceive spies. This had been verified by an elaborate electronic security system that tracked the Iraqi President's movements, so that his bodyguards would always know his whereabouts.

Now the only question was whether the F-117s uploaded with the bunker-busting bombs would be able to take off from Qatar, hit the target, and exit Iraqi air space before the sun rose. It would be very close. I tried calling Tom Franks again to get an update, but he was not up to speed on the need to change munitions. It was almost 6:00 P.M. in Washington, 1:00 A.M. in Iraq and Qatar. We couldn't waste time. I called CENTCOM's Air Component Commander, Lt. Gen. Buzz Moseley, directly. He was on top of the situation and had already issued the orders to arm two F-117s with bunker busters. An aerial refueling tanker had been launched and was flying its oval track over Kuwait to rendezvous with the Stealth fighters inbound and outbound.

"The one-seventeens are on the ramp and will be ready for takeoff within an hour," Buzz reported.

"I'll let you know as soon as we have a decision," I said.

As I re-entered the Oval Office, the President was asking those present, including the senior CIA officers, for their opinions. When it was my turn, I carefully considered my position: acting decisively in war involved balancing risks and rewards. We now had a TLAM package of twenty-four missiles targeted on Dora Farms and sixteen more aimed at Iraqi C^4 sites elsewhere in Baghdad. The Stealth fighters were being armed. Sunrise over Baghdad would be at 0609 hours local time, 2309 in Washington. The flight north from Qatar took at least three hours, and two more back to Kuwait air space with aerial refuelings. So the planes had to launch soon or they would lose their cloaking darkness.

"I recommend we launch, Mr. President," I said. All of the other advisers in the room came to the same conclusion.

Only moments later, George Bush reached his decision. The mission would proceed. America and her Coalition partners would, as events turned out, be at war with Iraq before sunrise.

11

LEADERSHIP IN TIME OF WAR

The Coalition, the Growing Insurgency, Abu Ghraib, Reshaping the Military

A detailed military narrative of the Operation Iraqi Freedom (OIF) campaign has been well documented in other books and in the news media. In this chapter, I cover my role in the war as Chairman of the Joint Chiefs of Staff as well as the many other responsibilities I had during my tenure.

At 11:00 P.M. Washington time on March 19 (6:00 A.M. March 20 in Iraq), the two F-117s, *Ram 01* and *Ram 02*, radioed that they were out of the Baghdad Missile Engagement Zone, southbound for their final aerial refueling and Qatar. The sun had been rising above a broken overcast just as the pilots saw their bombs strike the aim-points. Although I had never flown an unarmed Stealth aircraft in heavily defended enemy territory, I had sweated out a few tanker rendezvous flying "on fumes" after a combat mission.

Steve Hadley called my home from the White House for an update on the mission and to learn if the F-117 pilots were out of harm's way: The President knew we were cutting it close with the daylight issue and wanted to know if the airmen were safe. I reported that the two Stealth pilots were fine and returning to base, and Steve passed on the good news to the President.

I managed to get a few hours of uninterrupted sleep the night we attacked

Dora Farms. However, the next morning the CIA reports from Dora Farms were not all that good: Initially, the Agency's source sent an eyewitness account of Saddam Hussein being pulled from the rubble, his skin appearing "blue" and hardly breathing with the aid of an oxygen mask as he was hustled to an ambulance. By the end of the morning, however, it seemed that not only had Saddam and his sons survived, but they might never have even been at the Dora Farms estate the night before.

This was a good example of the difficulty of developing reliable human intelligence in a dictatorship like Saddam's Iraq—and of organizing military operations based on such intelligence. The shortage of good human intelligence (HUMINT) plagued us not only from the start of the war in Iraq, but also throughout the first several years of the Global War on Terror. That was because we were still trying to rebuild HUMINT capability that had been decimated in the 1990s through shifted priorities following the end of the Cold War and because of the view that our overhead space reconnaissance systems could do the job by themselves. The challenge to get reliable intelligence on Iraq persisted until I retired.

At this opening stage of the operation, Army Lt. Gen. David McKiernan's Coalition Ground Forces Component had a total of 183,000 soldiers and Marines, including 41,000 British troops, 4,000 Australians, a battalion of Spanish soldiers numbering 1,300, and a Polish contingent of Special Operations Forces that had the mission of capturing a large offshore oil platform complex near the Gulf port of Umm Qasr and protecting it from enemy sabotage.

All told, there were forty countries providing contingents of troops, naval units, or logistic support to the Operation Iraqi Freedom. With the British and Australian forces making such a significant contribution, the Commonwealth represented our staunchest allies.

By May 1, 2003, forty-nine countries from around the world were participating in the Coalition, some with combat forces, others with medical units, support, or engineering troops. A number of our NATO partners—Spain, Denmark, Norway, and Italy—had contingents of varying size. Japan and South Korea sent forces. Smaller Eastern European countries such as Estonia, Georgia, Lithuania, and Latvia had also sent units. Although small in population, El Salvador stationed combat units in Iraq.

Earlier, overhead imagery had shown Iraqi tanks and artillery of the 51st Mechanized Division moving through the Rumilyah Oil Field. Capturing that vast complex of wellheads and pumping stations near Basra before Saddam Hussein ordered his army to sabotage it—just as they had set ablaze more than seven hundred wells in Kuwait's Burgan Oil Field before retreating from the emirate in 1991—would be essential.

Now, if Coalition ground forces did not move quickly to protect Iraq's oil infrastructure, the country's legacy would be in jeopardy. Overhead reconnaissance and human intelligence revealed several wellheads had already been set ablaze. When it had become obvious that the Rumilyah Oil Field was in imminent danger, CENTCOM revised the operations plan to advance the scheduled start of the ground invasion (G-Day) by almost nine hours to the night of March 20. This meant that the strategic air strikes (A-Day) would occur well *after* our ground forces were inside Iraq and speeding north—and displayed the great flexibility of our field commanders and the forces under them. This "rescheduling" also had the advantage of surprising the Iraqis: They would expect massive air attacks before our troops crossed the frontier. The President, Secretary Rumsfeld, Franks, and I had discussed the new timing by video teleconference and agreed that Franks had made the right call.

In Washington, we knew that Tom Franks had a robust plan to deal with complex Coalition operations. At myriad meetings with Secretary Rumsfeld, the Joint Chiefs, and General Franks, we had undertaken an exhaustive planning process. Now that the operation had commenced, we trusted Franks to execute the plan and felt no need to lean over his shoulder and micromanage. Trust up and down—and sideways—along the chain of command would be a critical element in success. So we gave Tommy Franks considerable autonomy as he started the drive toward Baghdad.

Although I was confident that Coalition forces would defeat organized Iraqi military opposition more quickly than many in the news media and the public predicted, I remained uneasy about the state of planning and support for Phase IV (Post-Hostility Operations). In December 2002, I had found it necessary to issue Modification 6 ("Mod 6") to OPLAN 1003V, stating in great detail CENTCOM responsibilities for stability and reconstruction. These included the planning for law and order, protecting infrastructure, and our public information operations after major combat. I had to lean on Tommy Franks fairly hard to make sure he assigned enough people from his J5 section to focus on detailed posthostility planning. I asked for a briefing from Franks by mid-January, but he requested it be slipped to February, and I agreed. When the President made the decision to go to war, Franks had to exercise an even more laserlike focus on Phase III—Major Combat. This presented a dilemma: I didn't want to overburden Tom and his key staff just as they were fine-tuning the complex OPLAN 1003V. On the other hand, Secretary Rumsfeld and I certainly did not want to see CENTCOM invade Iraq without a practical solution to what the Joint Staff foresaw as potential major challenges.

On the eve of the invasion, however, I had encountered few American officials or military officers who foresaw a protracted occupation or nation building in Iraq. At that point, most thought that Iraqis would be eager to take and be capable of taking charge of their own destiny. Additionally, Iraq's basic oil infrastructure, road networks, industrial sector, and electrical grid would not be targeted. We couldn't be certain how much work (and money) would be required to make needed improvements, but we saw the task as readily manageable—by the Iraqis themselves, with a relatively small number of Coalition troops providing security. Further, American economic experts envisioned the new Iraq having tens of billions of dollars readily available through postembargo oil exports and the use of Iraqi assets currently frozen abroad to pay for all this.

The President directed the creation of the Office for Reconstruction and Humanitarian Assistance (ORHA)—led by retired Army Lt. Gen. Jay Garner. And the command's Civil Affairs staff would have plenty of work in the immediate posthostility period. Though many of us in Washington knew that the future of post-Saddam Iraq was uncertain and risky, we did not expect it to be as violent and challenging as it turned out to be.

Although still notional, CENTCOM's latest Phase IV timeline called for a steady drawdown of forces in the war theater at the end of major hostilities all the way down to a small peacekeeping and military training team totaling five thousand within forty-five months. I thought these troop strength numbers were overly optimistic; however, there were so many uncertainties that we couldn't be sure. But the Phase IV timeline and troop numbers were flexible. Further, as we prepared for Operation Iraqi Freedom, the State Department was exploring negotiations with several Arab and Muslim countries, including Bangladesh, Pakistan, and Morocco, to provide troops to the Coalition in Iraq once major combat had ended. We were also making preliminary overtures to the Turks, to help either with posthostility troops or with logistics support in the north. I spent a lot of time working with our allies trying to get their commitment to help.

The public knew nothing of the Dora Farms disappointment in late March 2003 because we provided no details to the news media. Intelligence operations and sensitive tactical maneuvers always had to remain secret while they were unfolding, but as soon as A-Day began, newspaper reporters and television crews were jolting along in Coalition Humvees and armored personnel carriers as our forces moved into Iraq. They were part of the unique media program that had "embedded" over 770 (more than 500 with ground forces) American and international news professionals with our combat and support units pushing north toward Baghdad.

In January 2003, my public affairs officer, Navy Capt. Terry "T" McCleary, came to me to suggest we have the news media members "embedded" beside our forces in the war zone. He said that Torie Clark, the Assistant Secretary of Defense for Public Affairs, was for it. I asked how CENTCOM and Franks felt. Franks was concerned with the logistics and safety problems when adding so many reporters to combat formations, but said he was willing to do what the Secretary directed. General Franks also worried about operational security with so many reporters so closely integrated with our forces. His view was important, as he would be responsible for ensuring the reporters would be properly trained and that they would be as safe as possible. (Eventually twenty-five percent of the embedded journalists were non-American.)

I didn't think the problems were insurmountable, especially when weighed against the embedded program's potential benefits. During World War II, correspondents had worn uniforms and been subject to military discipline; even though their material had been carefully censored, they brought a sense of reality from the global war fronts to the home front. In Vietnam, the military had tolerated the media, but animosity between the reporters and the senior command often developed, driven to a large extent by the divisive political debate back home. The Coalition during Operation Desert Storm had not satisfied the press because it had limited reporters to pools (small escorted groups representing the larger press contingent) or formal news briefings. The experiences in Vietnam and Desert Storm had left a mutual "credibility gap" between the military and the media. It was time to try to correct that, and I was convinced that if the reporters got to know our military, they would come to admire these warriors and their professionalism and discipline. Of course, I also knew we would have to accept the good, the bad, and the ugly reporting that would flow from the battlefield.

We were trying a completely new approach: the Embedded Media Program would have hundreds of reporters and correspondents from large and small news organizations living and moving with our forces, sharing the danger, discomfort, and terror of the modern battlefield as they filed their stories or footage by satellite links.

Torie Clark and I went to see Secretary Rumsfeld with the recommendation to go ahead with the embedding program. It took the Secretary about ten seconds to decide it was a good idea. This was a potentially risky policy because no one could be certain going into the operation that all the media members would obey the ground rules and not divulge sensitive information that jeopardized operational security. However, since the reporters themselves would be embedded with the units, this disclosure might also put them at risk, so we were confident the danger was manageable. Further, media members in training were already showing signs of bonding with their assigned units while retaining their journalistic independence.

As the campaign progressed, a handful of journalists did break operational security. Some were taken off the battlefield by their management, which determined they weren't following the rules. Others were quickly sent home, without any questions, when we informed their superiors that they had failed to comply with the ground rules.

When it did begin, the military campaign itself was less dramatic than we expected. Coalition ground forces encountered little initial resistance as they moved into Iraq. In the west, Special Operations Forces had entered the country early from advanced bases in Jordan and Saudi Arabia and, along with airpower, quickly took control of vast sections of desert, which the Iraqis would have needed had they intended to launch Scud missiles against their neighbors. But those medium-range missile attacks never happened; instead, the Iraqis fired a few much-shorter-range missiles at our bases in Kuwait, which our Patriot air-defense batteries destroyed. The question remained, however: When would Saddam decide to use his WMD?

To be sure, there were areas of intense combat. But the Iraqi Shiite conscript units that we initially encountered offered only light opposition. They had nothing to gain by sacrificing their lives for Saddam Hussein. Watching the Blue and Red Force Tracker icons that followed the GPS positions of ground units and aircraft on the plasma screens, we saw that the Baghdad and Medina Republican Guard divisions were still dug into concentric defensive positions around the capital. *They're not eager for a fight,* I thought. Or they had some clever countermove planned. Either way, at some point they were going to come face-to-face with our forces, and we would to destroy them.

The A-Day bombing operation began after dark on March 21 in Baghdad. The international news media were set up in hotels along the bends of the Tigris in the center of the capital. Their cameras caught the whole terrifying spectacle of cruise missiles striking Saddam's command apparatus in presidential palaces and military ministries across the river. One by one, these buildings—but *not* a single nearby civilian structure—exploded in dazzling clouds of flame. Meanwhile, more TLAMs struck, and F-16s flew Wild Weasel missions targeting SAM and radar sites surrounding the city. By the next day, the Iraqi integrated air-defense system around Baghdad had been rendered combat ineffective.

The final iteration of OPLAN 1003V was about as good as any I'd seen—but OPLANs seldom survive the first contact with the enemy. The unexpected always seems to happen. From the first day of the operation, I waited for the enemy to unleash WMD attacks, especially as we pushed aside or destroyed the Iraqi regular army units and closed in on the Republican Guard divisions. From the first day, all Coalition ground forces wore hot and clumsy protective suits. Inexplicably, at that time at least, the Iraqis never did use the WMD that we were convinced they had secretly stockpiled.

Instead, they hit us with an unexpected weapon: irregular forces, including the Fedayeen Saddam and Baath Party militia, who fought with fierce, often suicidal determination as our soldiers and Marines of the I Marine Expeditionary Force moved around the southern cities to bypass them. The well-armed Fedayeen came out to confront us, packed into open pickup trucks. Although no match for our armor, these Saddam loyalists were willing to die to slow us down. They died, but so did our troops.

After sunset on March 23, a column of trucks and Humvees from an Army maintenance unit lost its way near Nasiriyah and was ambushed by Iraqi forces. Several soldiers were killed or wounded. PFC Jessica Lynch was badly injured when her vehicle collided with another, and she was captured. She was later rescued.

On March 23 twenty Americans and two British were killed, and several of our troops were taken prisoner. It had been a very bad day from the standpoint of casualties. When I came home late that evening, Mary Jo, who had been watching the news all day, met me at the front door of our quarters in tears.

She asked, "Are these the type of losses we're going to have as this conflict continues?"

Of course, I didn't have a good answer; precisely predicting events during war is never easy. I did tell her that I would be surprised if our losses continued at this level. In fact this was the worst day of the Phase III war in terms of casualties.

The enemy defenses around Baghdad were battered but intact as our bombing continued. We were pounding them hard, however. Because our supply routes were rapidly lengthening, it was important to have complete control over our long resupply lines, and the Eighty-second Airborne Division was assigned the job. The only break we got in accomplishing this task was that the Iraqi irregulars always fell back on the local Mukhabarat or Baath Party headquarters to rearm and receive new orders. When our UAVs observed this pattern, CENTCOM targeted these buildings.

Then Coalition meteorologists detected ominous conditions brewing in the Mediterranean, with the cold front from a deep low predicted to sweep gale-force winds across Iraq, churning up a blinding *shamal* sandstorm.

When the sandstorm struck on the night of March 25, it was even fiercer than predicted. Visibility dropped below one hundred meters in daylight, much less in darkness. Helicopters and close air support fighters were grounded. The storm continued unabated. During the *shamal*, Fifth Corps commander Lt. Gen. Scott Wallace was asked by a *New York Times* reporter about the situation. "The enemy we're fighting," he said frankly, "is a bit different than the enemy we wargamed against because of these paramilitary forces," so we had been obliged to take a "strategic pause."

His honest statement was shaped into a *Times* story headline, "A Gulf Commander Sees a Longer Road," which implied we were bogged down yet again in an operational quagmire.

Security constraints permitting, Scott Wallace could have described the intense engagement then under way against the Republican Guard formations trying to maneuver north of Karbala Gap through the blinding *shamal*. Following their best transformational thinking, CENTCOM had quickly devised a brilliant plan to strike these heavy enemy units as they tried to move under what they thought was the protective blanket of the sandstorm. With the dense clouds of brown dust choking out daylight, the Iraqis assumed their maneuvers were hidden. In fact, we could track their movements right down to individual tanks, APCs, trucks, and artillery pieces, using a variety of sensors on overhead reconnaissance platforms in space and on aircraft (including the upgraded JSTARS tactical radar plane that I had helped deploy in Operation Desert Storm).

In Washington, the Joint Staff briefed Rumsfeld and the Joint Chiefs daily on these events and discussed them at the regular meetings with the President and the rest of the National Security Council. General Franks, however, continued to run the war.

———————

The enemy units had moved south of their previous defensive positions around Baghdad to dig in north of the Karbala Gap between the city and the swampy edge of Lake Razzaza. With their new GPS coordinates plotted, we could prepare to crush them. That devastating strike began on the night of March 25, as the *shamal* was rising to its full intensity. We used B-1 and B-52 strategic bombers dropping JDAMs, carrier-based fighters and Air Force fighter-bombers, and a variety of Army battlefield missile systems dispensing clouds of destructive bomblets. The Iraqis were stunned, unable to comprehend how we had targeted their elite units.

We kept up this fierce bombardment for thirty-six hours. The sand and dust billowed; the munitions rained down. When the air cleared, our Predators revealed that the Medina and Hammurabi Republican Guard divisions had become blackened hulks strewn among the date groves or tipped into the irrigation canals. The doorway to Baghdad was open.

Our ability to crush enemy formations trying to cloak themselves in near-zero visibility was a good example of "Network-Centric Warfare." In this still-emerging concept, a technologically advanced power combines reconnaissance sensors, such as the synthetic aperture radar on the JSTARS or the Predator UAV's thermal-imaging cameras, to identify and track enemy units. Precision-Guided Munitions from aircraft, ground-based missiles, or artillery are then employed to destroy the enemy. This can be safely accomplished because of the enhanced "situational awareness" inherent in systems such as the Blue Force Tracker, which assigns and displays precise GPS coordinates for all friendly vehicles and aircraft, thus greatly reducing the persistent battlefield danger of fratricide. Network-Centric Warfare allows commanders virtually to see through the traditional "fog of war" and employ forces with superior tactical effectiveness.

Meanwhile, Tommy Franks still had the problem of how to continue pinning down the Iraqi forces north of Baghdad along the Green Line established
after Desert Storm designating the predominately Kurdish area of Iraq. There
were several Iraqi divisions on the Green Line and we were worried they might
cross over and attack the Kurds. Pinning them down would have been much
easier if we had received permission to bring the 4th Infrantry Division through
Turkey, but that wasn't to be. After consulting the Secretary and me (and the
Joint Chiefs of Staff), Franks put together an operation that combined elements
of tactical feint with substantive strategic maneuver. On the night of March 26,
2003, fifteen giant C-17 Globemasters dropped almost one thousand paratroop-
ers of the Army's 173rd Airborne Brigade from Vicenza, Italy, on the short,
muddy Bashur airstrip in northern Iraq. Within hours, the C-17s were back, dis-
gorging M1-A1 Abrams main battle tanks. The Airborne troops linked up with
Special Operations Forces already scouting the area with Iraqi Kurd Peshmerga
guerrillas. After a few short, sharp engagements, our Bashur airhead was secure,
a portal for troops and supplies flowing into northern Iraq. We had just enough
force in the north, along with airpower, to hold the Iraqi divisions in place.

With organized Iraqi resistance crumbling both north and south of the capital,
our forces advanced cautiously, convinced that the time was near for the enemy
to strike with WMD. That conviction had increased when Marines in the
southern town of As Samawah discovered an arms cache behind the padlocked
steel door of a warehouse. Dozens of boxes marked in Arabic "Special Republican Guard" contained more than three hundred brand-new WMD protective
suits complete with masks and gloves. The Marines also found hundreds of
syringes preloaded with atropine, the antidote for nerve gas exposure. British
soldiers near Basra had found a similar but smaller trove.

The Iraqis knew that *we* didn't have WMD, so why did they need this protective equipment?

Whatever the answer to that riddle, chemical weapons attacks never came,
even when advanced units of the 3rd Infantry and the I Marine Expeditionary
Force penetrated the capital's outskirts and probed toward the city center. On
April 7, as our armor pushed toward central Baghdad, Iraqi Minister of Information Mohammed Saeed al-Shaf—"Baghdad Bob" to the jaded press corps—

proclaimed there were no living American troops in Baghdad, but added that "hundreds" had committed suicide at the city's gates. As he spoke, the windows of the press center shook from the treads of our tanks and Bradleys rumbling by a few hundred yards away.

The heavy enemy divisions had been destroyed well south of the capital, much of the destruction coming from precision weapons used during the week-long *shamal*. So the feared battle for Fortress Baghdad never happened.

Two days later, an exuberant, mainly Shiite, crowd swarmed into Firdos Square in central Baghdad and used a U.S. Marine Corps armored engineer vehicle to drag down a monumental statue of Saddam Hussein.

Phase III of Operation Iraqi Freedom, Major Combat Operations, had ended.

Phase IV Post-Hostility Operations—which still continues—proved to be more difficult than the Major Combat phase. First, although Saddam Hussein's monumental statues lay in heaps around the country, CENTCOM found no trace of the dictator or his sons. On the positive side, there had not been significant civilian casualties or damage to civilian structures or infrastructure. The feared immediate exodus of refugees didn't materialize. Preparing for a long battle, Saddam Hussein had issued a three-month supply of state-subsidized rice, flour, cooking oil, and beans. Jay Garner and ORHA did not have to solve a refugee or food crisis.

This did not mean, however, that the country was calm and stable. After a few days of joyous outbursts at the overthrow of Saddam's regime, crowds of looters took to the streets. Small-scale looting by "couch pushers" stealing furniture from government buildings quickly gave way to organized bands of vandals stripping anything of value they could lay their hands on in ministries and hospitals—even museums. Coalition forces should have done more to stop this.

The search for Iraq's missing weapons of mass destruction was also proving to be an unexpected problem. The U.N. weapons inspectors had left Iraq in March 2003 and were replaced the next month by the Iraq Survey Group (ISG). This was an organization of over one thousand American, British, and Australian experts that the Department of Defense, the Central Intelligence Agency, and the Pentagon's Defense Intelligence Agency assembled to track down WMD. It drew a virtual blank on chemical and biological weapons but found that Iraq had in fact preserved its intention and ability to produce chemical and biological weapons rapidly and even unearthed a few old chemical munitions.

On May 1, 2003, President George W. Bush flew on a Navy jet to land on the flight deck of the USS *Abraham Lincoln* off the California coast.

I was pleased that the President acknowledged the sacrifice and valor of the soldiers, sailors, airmen, and Marines, who, he noted, had liberated an oppressed people and driven a dangerous tyrant from power. Listening to the President's speech, however, I felt a pang of uneasiness: The Iraqi people *seemed* to have welcomed us as liberators, but it was far too early to predict that this initial sentiment would last. On close examination, Iraq's previously state-run industrial base lay in serious disrepair—not from war damage but from neglect and corruption under the regime of Saddam Hussein. In addition, the country was beset with unemployment while tens of thousands of bitter, well-armed former Iraqi troops, many still loyal to Saddam, had melted away from their crumbling combat units and were watching in their towns and villages, waiting to see what impact the Coalition occupation would have on their daily lives.

I thought that the newly created CENTCOM Combined Joint Task Force-7 (CJTF-7) in Iraq might temporarily need to maintain a force of combat and support troops equivalent to the approximately 160,000 then in the country. Later, we could adjust levels to CENTCOM's "troop to task" analysis, an established military formula. How many would be needed and for how long was hard to judge, and at this point the U.S. government still believed that a significant number of those troops would come from friendly Arab or Muslim nations that had not contributed forces to the major combat operation, but might be willing to help with the stability and reconstruction phase.

By the summer of 2003, it became clear that we had inherited a political-sectarian problem of large proportions in Iraq, which the Sunni extremists of al-Qaida were working viciously to aggravate. Saddam Hussein and his Baath Party inner circle had ruled though a fear-and-reward system. The Shiite majority were brutalized and only allowed to prosper through allegiance to Saddam and the Baathists.

One result of the sudden decompression that followed the arrival of Coalition forces was that persecuted and oppressed Iraqis lashed out, and not just by looting, but also against members of the old regime and those who represented it. The police fled, taking their weapons with them to protect their families. The outraged mobs resorted to arson when it became clear that Coalition troops would not turn their machine guns on rampaging civilians as Saddam's forces would have done.

Jay Garner's ORHA team did not face the anticipated humanitarian crisis, but they did encounter hundreds of would-be local officials clambering for positions as mayors or provincial governors. Garner tried to address the issue of democracy by organizing a large meeting of Iraqi leaders at the ruins of Ur, one of civilization's oldest cities. He hoped that the assembled Shia, Sunni, Arabs, and Kurds alike would cooperate in the spirit of Iraqi nationalism.

That was a noble ambition, but it did not work out. The scene under the wide tent near the flat-sided ziggurat at Ur was not one of harmony and trust. It dramatized that Iraq had been badly traumatized by decades of Baathist tyranny. The Shiite exiles—ranging from Westernized political and financial leaders such as Ayad Allawi and Ahmad Chalabi, to leaders of secular anti-Saddam resistance groups, such as Ibraham al-Jaafari—whom we had flown to Iraq demanded "immediate" democracy (which would empower them, of course), and refused to speak to the Kurd or Sunni delegations, who worried about Shiite domination. L. Paul Bremer eventually confirmed seven of the returned exiles as the nucleus of a larger effort to help the head of the Coalition Provisional Authority (CPA) Administrator govern the country until the restoration of sovereignty in 2004.

It was soon obvious that creating a democratic Iraq was not going to be a straightforward process. Mutual distrust and open sectarian hatred ran deeper in the country than we had anticipated.

As retired Army Gen. Gary Luck reported after the Secretary and I sent him to Iraq to review our strategy in early 2005, living decades under the Saddam Hussein regime had removed any incentive to show initiative. By dint of three decades of brutal oppression, Saddam had temporarily robbed the Iraqi people of their legendary ability to improvise and invent. The consequences could be drastic. There were few Iraqis, other than those who ruled under Saddam, who had the experience to take charge and help restore the functions of civil society to Iraq.

The original plan had been for the CENTCOM commander to be the Coalition Provisional Authority until the responsibility to administer Iraq could be transferred to a civilian or the Iraqis. Right after major combat, the situation in Iraq was relatively calm, and the President decided that the CPA would be transferred to a civilian to direct the complicated process of building Iraqi democracy. The White House recommended former Ambassador L. Paul "Jerry" Bremer III, once a manager at Henry Kissinger's consulting firm and an experienced foreign policy and counterterrorism expert, and Secretary Rumsfeld and the National Security Council concurred.

On May 12, 2003, I gave Bremer and his senior team a ride out to Iraq aboard the C-17 that carried me and a few support staff to Baghdad via Kuwait. As our transport took evasive maneuvers, spiraling down to the Baghdad airport to avoid ground fire, it was a sure sign we were in hostile territory.

The nature of Bremer's all-important "reporting channel" was at times ambiguous. Although he was officially designated President Bush's personal representative in Iraq, Bremer was directed to coordinate his actions with Secretary Rumsfeld and would have to work closely with Army Lt. Gen. Ricardo Sanchez, who assumed command of CJTF-7 in June.

We all recognized that Bremer would be the person in charge of the U.S. presence in Iraq. The Secretary and I also directed that Ric Sanchez be in "direct support" of Bremer, although Sanchez would report to CENTCOM. It was clear to me that close coordination between the military in Iraq and the CPA staff would be critical to successful mission accomplishment. We were still operating in Phase IV of a complex military operations plan; most of our people in Iraq were military, and in May and June 2003, at least, most of the money and support structure for the Coalition occupation came from the Department of Defense budget. Leaving CENTCOM as the CPA, with ORHA working the stability and reconstruction challenges, seemed to me to be reasonable. But I also understood that the President saw a chance to capitalize on our victory when the level of violence was low—and we had the opportunity to be seen as liberators—by appointing a civilian CPA. All of us hoped the initial unrest following the collapse of the Iraqi regime would soon quiet, as the CPA's civilian advisers helped the Iraqis stand up their post-Saddam institutions.

Indeed, early on the security situation was relatively quiet from a military standpoint. Certainly there were sporadic attacks on Coalition troops during the first months of Phase IV, but most were random incidents involving hit-and-run snipers or hastily fired RPGs or mortars. Overall, security seemed fairly stable. The intelligence consensus at the time was that this was harassment by

Baathist "dead-enders" conducting desperate acts of revenge. The terms "insurgency" and "improvised explosive device" did not come into wide usage until fall 2003. CENTCOM's new commander, Gen. John Abizaid, was the first senior officer to speak of an "insurgency." The use of the word "insurgency" was not quickly embraced by our civilian leadership, but after some discussion it came to be the word that everyone used to describe the situation in Iraq.

Our "all-source" intelligence was weak, however. We did not have enough experienced case officers in the country, and those we did have often had weak language skills. It was also nearly impossible for a Westerner to penetrate the convoluted webs of tribal and clan loyalty that made up Iraqi society. Moreover, the priority for much of our intelligence effort in 2003 and early 2004 was focused on whether Saddam Hussein's regime had in fact hidden huge caches of WMD that could proliferate to violent extremists.

The result was a murky intelligence picture at best. I can recall scores of frustrating meetings at which we'd ask the intelligence officers around the table, "What are the characteristics of the enemy we are facing? What are their numbers?"

The answers were a long time coming.

I should have recognized that there was another issue as well. At the end of major combat in May, Tom Franks had expressed his intention to retire as soon as possible. His official retirement date wouldn't come until July, but as time went on his focus naturally shifted from the situation in Iraq. Even though Gen. John Abizaid, his deputy, would move up to replace Franks, I'm sure we paid a price in the quality of our decisions on organizational structure by having Franks distracted.

Physical isolation and poor communications infrastructure were two of the problems Bremer and the CPA and CJTF-7 faced. The CPA headquarters was in the mammoth domed Republican Palace located in a walled compound on the west bank of the Tigris in central Baghdad. This "Green Zone" was spacious and secure, but it was cut off from most Iraqis and CJTF-7, which was based miles to the west in camps around Baghdad International Airport. Further, the CPA was never adequately manned with enough civilians to help re-establish the Iraqi government. Either our U.S. government departments and agencies didn't have the manpower, or people just weren't that interested in serving in a dangerous assignment (people still tended to covet the assignments that historically had been beneficial to career advancement). Over time, the CPA's chronic personnel shortage became emblematic of our country's inability to focus *all* instruments of national power on a critical security problem. And there was no mechanism to require them to go. Many who did come served on short temporary duty assignments.

The gap between Bremer and Sanchez had other causes than the problem of traveling back and forth on the increasingly dangerous Airport Road (what later became "IED Alley").

Jerry Bremer frequently made decisions without consulting Ric Sanchez. This often meant that the first time CENTCOM commander Gen. John Abizaid, Sanchez's boss, would hear of a Bremer decision was when the Secretary and I mentioned it in a video teleconconference. It was clear as 2003 wore on that the disconnect between the CPA and CJTF-7 was growing wider.

———————————

Even from the distant perspective of Washington, it was clear that our joint civilian-military effort in Iraq was not meshing well. Retired Lt. Gen. Jay Garner, who originally worked for CENTCOM, melded his remaining ORHA people into the CPA. After working with Ambassador Bremer for a short time, Garner became frustrated with the relationship and quietly flew home. In Washington, he remained a valuable asset due to his hard-won personal knowledge of the Iraqi personalities with whom he had worked, the Iraqi culture, and the situation on the ground.

I also recognized that the disconnect between the civilian and military sides of the effort was due in part at least to the inadequate size and perceived missions of CJTF-7. Our military presence was basically a multi-division corps headquarters, augmented by people from all the services, commanded by a three-star officer. Ric Sanchez was a strenuous worker, but he had to work at both the strategic level, with Bremer, and the tactical level to deal with the slowly developing threat. This was a broad mandate for the staff that supported him.

In the critical months from mid-2003 until the end of the year, armed resistance to our presence began increasing in an insidious manner. This required Sanchez to divert his attention from the strategic issues to the tactical problem. As the developing situation worsened, the key military leadership saw that CJTF-7 was not properly organized or manned to deal with the complexities and challenges they faced.

From the beginning there had been some critics calling to increase our troop strength. The belief was that if we had virtually flooded the country with

troops, saturating the larger cities and the provincial capitals with combat bri-
gades with their organic armor, helicopter, and reconnaissance assets, we might
have been able to stifle the rising insurgency that came into the media parlance
by spring 2004.

That might have been the case. But General Abizaid believed, from his experience in Iraq and the region, that more U.S. forces could actually have the
opposite effect; that more "infidels" in Iraq would look more like occupiers and
incite more violence. Abizaid and I talked about this frequently and I concurred
with his assessment. As the conflict in Iraq wore on this was a subject that
would be debated frequently by the Secretary, the Joint Chiefs, General Abizaid and Gen. George Casey (the four-star officer who took over for Ric Sanchez). We always understood that there is a fine line between too many troops
and too few. And while we were mindful of the strain on overall armed services force levels that sending more troops to Iraq would bring, that was not
the deciding factor. Our goal was always to provide the troop strength that the
commanders in the field thought they needed. And troop strength by itself
wasn't the only issue in achieving progress in Iraq. Political and economic
progress were also needed to help bring the insurgency under control, and that
remained very problematic until the new Iraqi government formed in early
2006. Ensuring simultaneous security, political, and economic progress is still
a problem today, although the situation in Iraq is dramatically better since the
2007 surge.

As the frequency of the attacks with improvised explosive devices (IEDs)
slowly rose, Coalition forces were not the only people suffering. Suicide bombings began to target Iraqi civilians shopping in neighborhood markets or re-
cruits lining up to report for duty with the new Iraqi Army or police force.

However uneven, there was progress. On July 22, 2003, soldiers of the 101st
Airborne Division surrounded a large house in the northern city of Mosul
where Saddam's two sons, Uday and Qusay Hussein, were hiding with Saddam's
fourteen-year-old grandson Mustapha. The Hussein brothers refused to surrender, and a firefight ensued. By the end, everyone inside had been killed, and
the bodies of Saddam Hussein's two heirs lay on bagged ice in a hospital morgue
in Baghdad. Very few mourned them. They had been responsible for the massacre and torture of thousands of their fellow Iraqis. And their deaths, we
hoped, would help Sunni insurgents recognize that their cause was hopeless.

That did not happen. On August 19, 2003, a huge suicide truck bomb exploded just outside the Baghdad headquarters of the United Nations mission. Sergio Vieira de Mello, the top U.N. envoy, and twenty-one others were killed in the blast, which demolished the solid three-story building. The crime went far beyond planting an IED mortar shell beneath the carcass of a dog or donkey. The truck bomb was the work of skilled and audacious terrorists. While there is still some speculation on who carried out the bombing, it was certainly the act of violent extremists. Abu Musab al-Zarqawi, al-Qaida's top operative in Iraq (later killed by U.S. forces) at the time claimed responsibility for this act. But many other extremist groups were thought to be responsible as well. Zarqawi said, "We destroyed the U.N. building, the protectors of Jews, the friends of the oppressors and aggressors. The U.N. has recognized the Americans as the masters of Iraq. . . . Do not forget Bosnia, Kashmir, Afghanistan, and Chechnya." This was the evidence that what we were facing was a global problem and not just an insurgency in Iraq or Afghanistan.

Coalition troops were still being killed almost every day as they patrolled Iraq's city streets, highways, and village lanes. However, while many sectors of the country were quieter than others, several regions verged on open rebellion. One of the most fractious was the "Sunni Triangle" that spread west along the Euphrates from Baghdad and its southern suburbs and included the city of Fallujah, a concentration of solidly pro-Saddam sentiment. The enemy here was predominantly composed of former regime elements, disaffected Sunnis, and al-Qaida.

Some of this emotion cooled on December 13, 2003, when patrols of the Fourth Infantry Division and Joint Special Operations forces discovered the bearded, disheveled former Iraqi dictator hiding in a well-concealed "spider hole" in the yard of a small farm near his hometown of Tikrit.

Saddam was captured just before I flew out to the Middle East for the annual USO Christmas tour on Sunday, December 14, 2003—in the company of actors/comedians Robin Williams, Blake Clark, and Leeann Tweeden, among others. Visiting the troops was always important, especially around Christmas. These USO-sponsored entertainers put politics aside and had only one objective: bringing a little bit of home and relief from their dangerous duties to our deployed troops. They would go until exhaustion entertaining and talking with our forces if you let them. When I boarded the plane at Andrews Air Force Base, the news of Saddam Hussein's capture had just been released. Our USO entertainers were overjoyed: They had been searching for a theme for their comedy on this trip, hoping to find humor that would cheer up the troops. Williams quickly thanked me for capturing Saddam and created a shtick about Saddam Hussein entering jail and meeting his new cellmate, the hulking "Bubba." "We-all gonna become *real* close friends, Saddam ole buddy . . ."

Still, the insurgents' terrorism against the Coalition and the new Iraqi security forces continued. From captured intelligence documents, we learned that those who opposed us in Iraq—from former regime elements, to Shiite extremists, to irredentist Sunni Arabs, to al-Qaida and its foreign supporters—were convinced that the American-led Coalition lacked the will, resolve, and patience to remain in Iraq if they killed enough of our troops. To achieve this they adopted some of the classic methods of asymmetrical warfare against the military. IEDs were particularly effective for committing random acts of violence against Coalition forces. This tactic was relatively cheap and easy for the enemy and extremely costly for us, in terms of blood and treasure. Simultaneously, the insurgents, especially among al-Qaida's foreign fighters and the Sunni Arabs in Baghdad and central Iraq, believed that extremely violent acts of terrorism against civilians would undermine the slowly spreading public confidence in Iraq's future. The enemy believed that through ruthless violence and indiscriminately killing innocent men, women, and children, they could undermine the CPA's efforts to establish good governance, political progress, economic stability, and rebuilt infrastructure.

From my perspective, 2004 was a turning point in the American perception of our efforts in Iraq. I saw this coming as I testified before Congress over the first half of 2004. Early in the year you would get a question from someone in Congress that would go like this: "General, I didn't vote for the war, but now that we're there we have to be successful. So tell me General . . ." In the middle of the year, as the presidential race heated up, the questions turned much more partisan. This was affecting public opinion about U.S. efforts in Iraq, and the hyperbole made getting the facts out and understood much more difficult. Both parties shared the responsibility for letting the rancor of the debate get out of hand. Earlier I had discussed with the Secretary the need for the President to use his bully pulpit to explain the importance of patience, will, and resolve for our efforts in the Middle East. The President agreed, but we had started too late and with too little focus on this message for it to be heard. I naïvely thought that after the presidential election we could return to a more nonpartisan debate and good public discourse that would put our commitment in Iraq and

Afghanistan into a larger, longer-term national security context. Unfortunately, that has not happened to this day. In the next chapter I will argue that we can best do this by understanding and countering the global terrorist campaign that is being waged against the United States and its friends and allies.

By early 2004 it was obvious that our military structure would have to adapt to the growing insurgency and the fact that the CPA would go away and we would have an Ambassador to the Interim Iraqi Government. Things had changed to the point that no one person or organization, such as CJTF-7, would be able to handle the growing complexities in Iraq. In addition, our early efforts to organize and train Iraqi security forces were under-resourced, and these early Iraqi forces proved not to be very good. This was partly because we had used a "national guard" concept, recruiting and training forces where they lived. When trouble arose, these "local" forces were reluctant to fight their friends and neighbors. I spent time with Abizaid and others looking for different models of success in terms of building both an Iraqi National Army and an Iraqi National Police Force. We looked for lessons learned from Lebanon and Gendarmes in France and Carabinieri in Italy among other things. All this was folded into the strategy for training Iraqi Security Forces.

Ric Sanchez had done a terrific job, given that the environment changed dramatically during his tenure, that he had to work get Bremer's approval for his priorities for Iraq, and that he didn't have the staff resources to keep up with the unfolding challenges. Secretary Rumsfeld and I vigorously supported him for a fourth star, but the fact that he was the commander in Iraq when the abuse at Abu Ghraib took place (even though he had no culpability) made his nomination for a fourth star contentious on the Hill and made the White House reluctant to forward his nomination to the Senate.

To show how the situation in Iraq had changed in one year, in July 2004 we replaced Ric Sanchez with two senior officers, a four- and a three-star. Gen. George Casey would work the strategic problems with our new Ambassador to Iraq, John Negroponte, while Lt. Gen. Tom Metz would command the tactical forces dealing with security issues.

To invigorate the training of Iraqi security forces we tapped the former commander of the 101st Airborne, David Petraeus, who was promoted to three-star rank and led the newly created Multi-National Security Transition Command Iraq for training, mentoring, and equipping Iraq's new military and public security forces. His task was difficult and always frustrating. But he was persistent, and he gradually achieved results. Later, Petraeus compared his command's mission to "repairing an aircraft while in flight—and while being shot at."

One of the biggest problems he faced was that he was training a military and national police force for a nation still being born. The Iraqi units were not certain as they were "stood up" what leader or authority they were serving— indeed risking their lives to defend. It would be two full years before Iraq had a constitutional government in place to which its new military and police could pledge their full allegiance.

By the time General Petraeus turned over the command in 2005, a force of one hundred thousand Iraqi military, police, and security personnel had been trained and issued modern weapons, body armor, vehicles, and communications equipment.

Petraeus was a natural choice for the training mission as he commanded the 101st Airborne in the Mosul area after major combat. He had refined the counterinsurgency techniques he would later disseminate though much of the Coalition in Iraq: Work hard to earn the trust of local civilian leaders, both civil servant and tribal; use reconstruction money as a military tool; do not promise more than you can deliver.

The Secretary and I thought Petraeus would be best used at the Army's Combined Arms Center, which focused on innovative doctrine and training, when he returned home in 2005. He and Marine Lt. Gen. James Mattis supervised the publication of the ground-breaking Field Manual 3–24, *Counterinsurgency*, to which a widely diverse body of military strategists and academic foreign policy professionals contributed. The document and its implementation were truly transformational, stressing imaginative thinking and new approaches to old problems. The techniques and procedures that evolved from this fresh look at means to win unconventional war would go a long way toward eventually turning the corner in Iraq.

Our overall strategic objective was simple; increase the size and competency of the Iraqi forces so they could eventually replace U.S. and Coalition forces. We assumed that this military initiative, in combination with political, economic, and security progress, would lead to a stable Iraq. To accelerate the development of Iraqi security forces, Casey came to Washington and convinced the Joint Chiefs that we needed to embed eight to ten American servicemen in Iraqi units down to battalion level. They would help the Iraqi units train and teach them the tactics, techniques, and procedures they would need to be operationally successful. This was a tough sell to the Chiefs, as it stretched the

Army and Marine Corps, especially, to their limits as they provided the more than one thousand midcareer officers and NCOs that the effort demanded. This would also be dangerous duty, as these small teams would live side by side with their Iraqi counterparts and would not have the normal support that a larger U.S. unit would have. This program is still very successful and a big reason that Iraqi security forces have developed as quickly as they have. After a lively debate, the Joint Chiefs became convinced that embedding our trainers with the Iraqis was the best course of action.

Although many in the public and the news media attribute the success in 2007 to the troop "surge" (the significant increase in American forces), the seeds for success were planted well before large numbers of new troops arrived.

Unfortunately, the public revelation of the abuses at Abu Ghraib prison in April 2004 spurred a backlash against U.S. operations in Iraq and around the globe. General Abizaid had called in January, alerting me and the Secretary that there had been illegal treatment of detainees at Abu Ghraib prison. But we did not yet know the details. The images that eventually emerged were shocking, showing American guards from a night shift of the 372nd Military Police Company abusing, punching, and humiliating Iraqi detainees, many of them hooded with sandbags, bound, and nude.

The few photographs that I had seen were so disgusting that, if made public, they could: undermine efforts to form an interim Iraqi government, which had reached a critical point in the difficult negotiations; place a number of Western hostages at risk; and disrupt the Army's continuing comprehensive criminal investigation of detainee abuse at the prison, under the direction of Maj. Gen. Antonio Taguba.

The Taguba Report was still working its way through the military justice system in April 2004 when I learned that the CBS news program *60 Minutes II* had obtained the Abu Ghraib photos and planned to air them in a segment on the scandal. On April 14, I called the show's anchor, Dan Rather, and asked him to delay the broadcast due to the precarious position of hostages and continuing critical military operations in Iraq; he agreed. Then a week later, I requested another delay. Once more, he agreed.

I had always tried to be open and honest with the news media. If I did not know the answer to a question reporters asked in a press briefing, I said that I would get back to them, rather than hiding behind "no comment" or being deceptive, and I always followed through. In so doing, I endeavored to earn the media's trust. From my perspective in the Pentagon, I rarely knew all the details of events happening overseas, but as soon as I did have accurate information, we shared it to the greatest extent possible within the constraints of operational security. And I also went beyond this by hosting off-the-record background sessions for the Pentagon press corps and hosted lunches for the anchors of the three leading networks in New York. Developing and maintaining credibility with Peter Jennings, Tom Brokaw, and Dan Rather was vital. They were the three of the most influential television journalists in America, and making sure they understood the complexities and nuances of our fight against violent extremists would allow them to better inform the American public of the nature of the threat we faced. In the process, it would also enhance the mutual trust between the media and the military. The media are so important to our democracy that I believed I had to go to extraordinary lengths to keep them informed the best I could.

I was drawing on that trust when I asked Dan Rather to sit on this blockbuster story. But he worked for a commercial network that had competition. When CBS learned the *New Yorker* magazine was about to publish an article on Abu Ghraib by Seymour Hersh, *60 Minutes II* then proceeded with the show. That broadcast and Hersh's article ignited an outcry of indignation, both at home and around the world.

Secretary Rumsfeld, Army Chief of Staff Pete Schoomaker, and I were called to testify to the Senate Armed Services Committee on Abu Ghraib in May. Rumsfeld told the senators that those seen in the graphic photographs would face military justice. He added that the images were part of a continuing criminal investigation and were never intended for public release. Rumsfeld emphasized that he and I had not seen the full collection of photographs until the previous week, but because the scandal had broken "on my watch . . . I am accountable . . . I take full responsibility." Rumsfeld also said he felt awful about what happened to the prisoners and offered them compensation. "They are human beings, they were in U.S. custody, our country had an obligation to treat them right. We didn't. That was wrong."

There would eventually be a total of fifteen separate investigations of treatment of detainees. None found *any* evidence of high-level DoD or senior military involvement in authorizing any detainee abuse.

After the scandal broke, Rumsfeld told me President Bush called and asked him, "Should I fire Myers?"

Donald Rumsfeld said, "No, you'd be firing the wrong guy, Mr. President."

Rumsfeld felt intense loyalty down the chain of command and great empathy for those members of the military who had not done anything wrong but had seen their careers blighted by a connection to the Abu Ghraib scandal. He often went out of his way at Pentagon press briefings to preface his answers with a statement that he accepted full responsibility for what had happened in the prison. He offered to resign more than once, but the President wouldn't accept his resignation.

I, along with everyone who wore the U.S. military uniform, felt shamed of what our fellow servicemen and women did at Abu Ghraib.

That exchange between the President and Secretary Rumsfeld about my future exemplified the importance of trust among high-level leaders. As the principal military adviser to the Secretary and the President, I always knew it was essential that we all be completely honest with each other. There must never be a breach of trust between senior military officers and their civilian superiors. In 2001, when I served as Vice Chairman, I wasn't always sure that I would have a position of mutual trust with Secretary Rumsfeld. But we got to know each other better, especially after that terrible September day in the Pentagon with all of us coughing on the acrid smoke of the fires. Donald Rumsfeld would always share important information with me, just as I would with him. I can't remember the number of times that the Secretary asked me to stay back after a meeting, or called later to ask, "Dick, do you fully agree on where we are on this matter?" During the four years of my tenure, he never made an important decision without consulting either me or Pete Pace.

We could not have secrets when our national security or the lives of our men and women in uniform were at risk. I took this very seriously, and so did Secretary Rumsfeld. It would have been easy to be "friends" with the Secretary and the President. But to ensure we adhered to the fundamental principle of civilian control of the military, I always strove to keep a professional distance in the relationship. In one of my first meetings with our new Secretary, Rumsfeld said, "Just call me Don," as was the custom in the business world and most other professions. That would have been inappropriate; he would always be

"Secretary" Rumsfeld. I wanted to ensure that friendship never got in the way of providing my best independent military advice.

Despite the trust, there was always some tension in the relationship with our civilian superiors, as we had different statutory responsibilities. One of those areas of tension was the Strategic Risk Assessment that the Chairman was required to deliver to Congress each March. This was my assessment of our military's ability to carry out our National Military Strategy. I would rigorously work this assessment with the Joint Chiefs, but the Secretary could only put a cover letter on the document. I was proud of these classified assessments and thought they fairly presented the current and future strategic risk associated with executing our military strategy. During my tenure, as the wars in Iraq and Afghanistan continued, our military risk increased. This was not always the message our civilian leadership wanted the Congress to hear.

At a dinner in Washington in the middle of my time as Chairman, I sat next to retired Air Force Lt. Gen. Brent Scowcroft, Ronald Reagan's National Security Adviser. "Dick," Scowcroft said, "you're doing a good job."

"Thank you, General," I said. "Yes, we have a very good team between the Joint Staff and the Chiefs."

Scowcroft leaned forward. "No, *you're* doing a good job."

I went through my teamwork explanation again, but I must have looked puzzled because he continued.

"I've known Rumsfeld for forty years," Scowcroft said. "He is the most complex man I've ever known, and I can never totally figure him out. And from what I see you're doing a very good job working with him." Coming from someone of Scowcroft's stature that little comment meant a lot.

———————

Although Donald Rumsfeld always expected his subordinates to be well informed on professional matters, he realized that no one officer or civilian could know everything. So he placed great emphasis on collaboration. Meetings in the Secretary's office were usually crowded with people representing all sides of an issue. He liked to examine important questions from a 360-degree perspective as he developed conviction on a particular matter. As always, Rumsfeld would ask tough questions—right up to the limit, and sometimes past the limit, of reasonableness. At such times, the tension in the meetings became palpable. He wanted us to *think*, not merely voice platitudes. But when the atmosphere in the room became especially tense, I learned that a little well-timed humor could be an important relief valve for everyone. If I could get Rumsfeld to smile, or at least put a crack in his stern demeanor, he would quickly relax and we could move on with the meeting.

Although people outside the Chairman's office often thought that Iraq was my only responsibility during this period, to execute my Title 10 responsibilities properly, I always had to be mindful of my many other duties as the nation's senior military officer. In fact, I would use the daily and hourly changes to the little white schedule card I carried everywhere as an indication of just how busy, and at times chaotic, my life was. My wonderful executive secretary, Mary Turner, had been with me since I came to the Pentagon in 2000 as the Vice Chairman. She was remarkable and always kept me on track and on time. But, as I responded to requests from the nation's executive and legislative leadership or to international crises, such as the Asian tsunami, I remember on some days Mary would have to redo the card five or more times just to keep up with all the changes to my schedule.

One of the things that never stopped was our transformation activities to reshape our military. This could not become sidetracked because we were at war. During my entire tenure as Chairman, I had been leading the effort to make the services more relevant to our twenty-first-century challenges. One of the major transformational efforts I supervised was the melding of two large combatant commands: Strategic Command and Space Command. Both dealt with high-technology systems and weapons, and each had a global perspective and responsibility. Given their similarities, it made sense to consider meshing them. This idea had been discussed before, but never adopted. After considerable thought and discussion, the Joint Chiefs and I recommended to the Secretary that SpaceCom (located in Colorado Springs) be melded into STRATCOM (located in Omaha). STRATCOM had been responsible for our nuclear deterrent arsenal and had a fairly robust capability in global command and control and communications. So we developed a comprehensive plan to disestablish U.S. Space Command and take its pieces over to the "new" STRATCOM. During the integration we were particularly mindful of protecting the nation's strategic nuclear deterrent. We assessed that this could best be accomplished by creating a new combatant command that integrated our nuclear deterrent, the space mission, and other new mission areas, including intelligence, surveillance, and reconnaissance; missile defense; and information warfare (including cyber defense). All of these mission areas were interdependent and the integrations just made sense.

Both of the previous commands had been burdened with too many vertical command and decision "stovepipes," so we needed a new commander with an agile and flexible mind. Secretary Rumsfeld and I chose Marine Gen. Jim "Hoss" Cartwright—nicknamed after the *Bonanza* character. Cartwright was working for me on the Joint Staff at the time and was a thoughtful officer, and agile in his dealings with new problems. Again, flexibility and broadness of perspective were key in this new command. For the foreseeable future, the United States was the world's sole superpower, and it was imperative that our military leaders be able to think and act globally.

———

Mary Jo and I had many traditional responsibilities outside the Pentagon itself, but none were more important to us than trying to bring comfort to our military wounded and their families.

Stationed in Washington, D.C., we were fortunate to be in close proximity to Walter Reed Army Medical Center and the National Naval Medical Center at Bethesda. We had the privilige of visiting our wounded servicemen and women every three or four weeks. I remember the trepidation that Mary Jo and I both felt before our first visit. I was especially concerned about her, as she could hardly bear to look at the cuts and scrapes that children get in growing up. She baked cookies for the first visit with the thought that that would be an icebreaker when meeting the patients. One might think that visiting the wounded who have lost limbs or have life-affecting injuries would be difficult and depressing, but we came away time and time again feeling incredibly heartened and humbled by their brave spirit, their optimism, and their fortitude. We quickly learned that even though the purpose of our visit was to encourage them and increase their morale, they raised ours. I was reminded of a phrase from Adm. Chester Nimitz about the battle for Iwo Jima during World War II: "Uncommon valor was a common virtue."

Their faces were often very young. Much of life was in front of them, but now they faced challenges in their futures that they had not contemplated only days before. But they weren't looking back. When they were given convalescent leave, they often expressed a desire to go back to Iraq to rejoin their unit. There was no self-pity.

Instead I often heard, "Sir, I have no regrets. I don't want my children to be fighting terrorism. I just want you to tell the American people that we are volunteers, that we wanted to be there doing the job that we are trained for. We know why we're there, and we know how important it is to the future of our country."

A young Ranger, who had just had his leg amputated, said, "Sir, I lost my leg, but I was prepared to give my life."

One injured soldier, when I asked if there was anything I could do to help him, answered, "Sir, can you help me become a citizen of this country?"

We were also touched deeply by the strength and the sacrifice of the family members who came to be by the bedside of their loved ones. I especially remember one mother, a small, demure woman, whose son had lost a leg. When she asked if she could speak with me in the hall, I wasn't at all sure what to expect. She wanted to know if her son could still fulfill his childhood dream and be an Army Ranger. It was most heartening to see the support that these men and women had from friends and family. And many organizations are developing programs to integrate our wounded back into their communities.

The strength of purpose and the resilience exemplified by these brave men and women in uniform is making a difference around the world.

During my tenure as Chairman I also spent about a week a month traveling around the globe to strengthen our military relations with our many friends and allies. It was important to meet with my counterparts in their home countries and to show respect for their customs and culture. For instance, I was the first Chairman ever to visit Mongolia, and they constantly reminded me of how much it meant to them that I would take the time to come to their remote country. I don't know whether it had anything to do with my visit, but they are still providing troops to our Coalition in Iraq.

In return, I would entertain several of my counterparts on visits to the United States each month. The last part of their American trip would be in Washington, and Mary Jo and I would host them in our spacious quarters at Fort Myer. We would have thirty-five to forty guests, including the appropriate Ambassador, folks from the Hill, and the media. I would memorize the name of every guest so that I could introduce each one personally. It was hard work after a long day at the Pentagon, especially when our guests' names were Chinese or Turkish. But the effort paid dividends in goodwill. Our terrific enlisted aides presented impressive meals; Mary Jo and I wanted our guests to feel at home, to gain a true sense of American hospitality.

At the end of each evening I had the Army Chorus for entertainment.

But it was more than amusement. Without any prompting from me, the program would always include at least one song in our guests' native language—Latvian, Korean, even Mongolian. I've seen the tears in our guests' eyes as they listened to this wonderful male chorus. We built many lasting friendships at those dinners.

My goodwill toward the French military did not always sit well with Secretary Rumsfeld, however. He liked the French as individuals, and appreciated the French military's contribution to our War on Terror efforts, but was disdainful of their government. So, when I proposed presenting the Legion of Merit decoration to the chief of their General Staff, Gen. Henri Bentégeat, Rumsfeld sat on the recommendation letter for an inordinately long time—just as I knew he would.

After a morning staff meeting he asked that I stay behind. He tossed the recommendation package across the table to me and said, "Are you serious about this?"

"Yes, sir, I am."

The French had supported us well in Afghanistan and the Balkans, and Henri and his wife Chantal were good friends as well.

He dashed off his signature and shoved the letter back.

———

Despite my hectic schedule, I needed a way to decompress from the unrelenting pressure of the Chairman's office. I also thought it was important to bond with my only grandchild at the time and tried to steal a couple of hours every Sunday to spend with little Sophie, child of Nicole and her husband, Wade Little. She was just one year old, and we would often drive town to Gravelly Point on the Potomac near Reagan National Airport. She loved pointing out the airplanes and I hoped that the roar of the jets flying just above our heads wouldn't frighten her—as I had been frightened as a toddler. But Sophie was engrossed by the huge machines in the sky and liked to kick the soccer ball around, chase the ducks or birds, or just watch the boats coming and going at the boat ramp. I suppose knowing we would always stop for a treat, against Nicole's firm orders, also heightened her enthusiasm for our outings.

There was something wonderful about being with an innocent young child, holding her tiny hand, when my nation was at war. It certainly made it clear why we were devoting so much effort to keeping our country safe.

———

Secretary Rumsfeld and the top Pentagon military officers and officials met regularly in a new forum established by the Secretary, the Senior Leadership Review Group (SLRG). It was composed of the Secretary, deputy, under and assistant secretaries of defense, the Joint Chiefs of Staff, and the service secretaries, and others who had something to contribute to the topic at hand. We addressed very important strategic policy issues—manpower levels, budgets, recommendations on base closings, quality of life, and the Quadrennial Defense Reviews mandated by Congress. We often met weekly, sometimes more frequently, and everyone had a say and was expected to speak up. The SLRG was very much like a board of directors of a public company. I had served many years in the Pentagon, and this was the first "corporate board" activity, combining senior civilians and military, I had ever seen at this level.

A big part of my responsibilities as Chairman was to keep the Joint Chiefs as well informed as possible, so that they could participate in important decisions and offer the best possible advice, either through me or directly to the President or the Secretary. Beyond the SLRG policy meetings, I gathered the JCS in the Tank at least twice weekly. We worked through operational issues very thoroughly and were always able to achieve consensus. I was the principal military adviser to the national leadership, but I was also required by law to always give the advice of the Chiefs, if it differed from my own. During my tenure as Chairman I never once had to tell the President, "This is *my* advice, but here is how the Army (or the Air Force) feels about it. . . ."

There are no doubt many misconceptions about how the Chairman provides advice. Providing advice is not a single event or a single moment. Rather it's a cumulative process, usually the result of many hours of discussion on the important issues. Through that process and the back and forth, the give and take, a common perspective normally emerged. My goal was to be sure to take the time to work through the issues with the Joint Chiefs so we could agree on the way forward.

The process was the same with the Secretary. We could usually achieve agreement on whatever the issue was and present a unified position in NSC or Principals Committee meetings. In the rare instances we couldn't agree, I was always free to, and did, voice my opinion.

———————

Meanwhile, the military situation elsewhere in Iraq had become critical. The predominantly Sunni Arab city of Fallujah, lying on the Euphrates west of Baghdad, had become a hive of insurgents. Sunnis resisted the Iraqi Governing Council and the Coalition—often sniping at our troops or attacking Iraqi police stations—and seemed intent on following the dead-end aim of re-establishing Baathist control.

In late March 2004, Sunni insurgents ambushed two SUVs of the American military-support contractor Blackwater. The rebels dragged four Americans from the vehicles, beat and stabbed them to death, then hanged the charred corpses from the steel beams of a bridge.

Our Marines launched an offensive operation to clear Fallujah of insurgents, but the Iraqi Governing Council vigorously objected. The Marines were ordered to pull out after twenty-seven men had been killed in action and more than ninety wounded. Insurgent losses were much higher.

The suspension of offensive operations in Fallujah gave the Iraqi Governing Council the political breathing room they needed to make progress on an interim constitution, the Transitional Administrative Law. On June 28, 2004, after Interim Prime Minister Allawi was sworn in, Jerry Bremer left Baghdad.

The same month, the men and women of Afghanistan went to the polls to elect a president, despite widespread violence and threats. Women in particular were the targets of threats. In Bamian Province, the women were warned that if they went to the polls to vote, they would be killed. This was a serious threat, as just recently in the province, people had been dragged off a minibus and killed on the spot if found to have voter registration cards.

But women in Bamian Province, where the Taliban had been especially harsh, would not be intimidated. Before dawn on election day, thousands rose, bathed, and put on their best clothes, as if preparing their own bodies for a funeral. They then went to the polls and voted.

Despite setbacks, overall political progress in both Afghanistan and Iraq moved further and faster than the pessimists had predicted.

In January 2004, Afghan men and women voted to ratify the constitution that the traditional Loya Jirga assembly had drafted in June 2003. Hamid Karzai was elected president in October 2004 and sworn in for a five-year term that December. Parliamentary elections for a National Assembly took place across Afghanistan in September 2005.

After the initial combat of Operation Enduring Freedom ended in 2002, I realized that Afghanistan would need a robust peacekeeping and stability force to maintain order. NATO members had performed well in that capacity in the Balkans. So I supported NATO stabilization and security forces for Afghanistan, commanded by a rotation of alliance partners, that would eventually also play a major role in rebuilding the economic framework necessary for the country to advance beyond the war-shattered, tribally divided ruin we found when the Taliban and al-Qaida were defeated in 2003.

By 2006 the NATO–International Security Assistance Force (ISAF) was able to assume much of the responsibility for security across Afghanistan from the American-led Coalition. Today, NATO-ISAF forces in the country total over fifty-two thousand troops and police. They serve in a variety of combat, combat-support, training, and reconstruction roles. Although there has recently been a resurgence of Taliban and al-Qaida guerrilla activity in Afghanistan, the American and NATO-ISAF forces have so far coped with it, while continuing to protect and foster reconstruction and humanitarian assistance.

However, I am convinced that the Taliban extremists and their al-Qaida allies will continue to fight our effort to work toward a democratic and prosperous Afghanistan. It is our responsibility to keep up the pressure on the enemy, while we continue to support the government of Afghanistan. In addition, as Ambassador Zalmay "Zal" Khalilzad said to me during a visit to Kabul, "Afghanistan's success will ultimately depend on how successful they are in dealing with the drug issue." The struggle will be long and hard, but the alternative is not acceptable.

My relations with Congress were generally very good. I met frequently with the Chairman and ranking members of both the Senate and House Armed Services Committees. Senators Warner and Levin and Representatives Hunter and Skelton knew me well and we had developed a high level of trust between us. I was very mindful of the importance of the statement all three- and four-star officers signed before being confirmed to their new positions that we would provide our personal opinion on a given matter when asked, even if it differed from that of the administration. I would be tested on this more than once.

After 10:00 P.M. on a weekend in late October 2004, I received a call from Duncan Hunter, Chairman of the House Armed Services Committee. He was in a joint Senate-House Armed Services conference committee that was considering a bill on intelligence reform, which would create the new office of the Director of National Intelligence. What concerned Chairman Hunter was that it would remove the Secretary of Defense from the budget process for all the Defense Department's intelligence agencies. These agencies instead would forward their budgets directly to the National Intelligence Director. That would have been a management nightmare. The Secretary would have retained responsibility for the Defense Intelligence Agency and the other offices, but would have lost the budgetary power needed to control them.

Chairman Hunter wanted me to send him a letter outlining where I stood on the matter. Working by phone with the Joint Staff Director of Intelligence, Army Maj. Gen. Ron Burgess, we crafted a letter and faxed it to Hunter late that night. I informed Rumsfeld of the request and that I was responding. He saw the letter for the first time after it was delivered to Hunter. In my letter I said that good management required that if the Secretary was to properly oversee the defense intelligence agencies, he should also have budget authority. Given that these defense intelligence agencies were critical to war-fighting, I believed the Secretary had to have control.

The White House was not amused, as it had a different opinion. Within a couple of days, I got a call from one of the President's inner circle. "I hope you know, General, you just cost the President the election."

The days before a national election are always tense for the White House, and this official's outburst was a typical display of pre-election nerves. He was convinced that the news media would try to use my letter to Duncan Hunter against President Bush.

So be it, I thought. When asked, I had a legal obligation to give my best military advice to Congress as well as to the President and the NSC.

It would have been gratifying to watch the situation in Iraq settle into a peaceful transition toward stability and democracy. That, of course, did not happen. Insurgents continued to explode IEDs, car bombs, and explosive suicide vests in crowded markets. Hundreds of Iraqis were killed each month. Numbers of Coalition killed and wounded remained high. But our forces continued to take the fight to the enemy.

The largest assault was a combined Marine-Army-British-Iraqi operation launched on November 7, 2004, to finally capture Fallujah from the insurgents, who had used the months since April to fortify the city into a bastion. Fighting house to house, Coalition forces suffered heavy casualties as they squeezed the enemy relentlessly inside a tighter perimeter. This time there was no politically necessitated compromise.

However, despite threats of insurgent violence and Sunni militant calls for a boycott, Iraq's first free elections took place on January 30, 2005, as the Iraqis elected an interim assembly to draft a national constitution. More than eight million men and women stood in line for hours on rain-swept streets, guarded by Coalition and Iraqi police and troops, and entered five thousand polling places in schools, clinics, and government offices. The percentage of those voting was highest in Kurdish areas and lowest in provinces dominated by Sunni extremists, who realized the election meant the end of their traditional power.

Iraqis emerged from the polls holding high their right index fingers stained with indelible purple ink, the proud symbol that they had voted.

I described this image as a "finger in the eye of extremists like Usama bin Laden and his ilk . . ." and added, "we saw these Iraqis stare down intimidation, stare down insurgents, and say, 'Our vote is going to count.'"

The Iraqi people ratified their new constitution in October 2005. In December 2005, Iraqis elected the first constitutionally stipulated National Assembly. Violence continued in both Iraq and Afghanistan, but the spirit of democracy remained stubbornly alive.

I couldn't think of a more fitting tribute to the sacrifice of the Coalition troops who had fought to free Iraq from tyranny.

During that period, the combatant commanders would come to Washington frequently to meet with me, the Joint Chiefs, the Secretary, and often the President (the Secretary thought it a good idea for the President to know the people in the chain of command). Given the importance of Iraq, Generals John Abizaid and George Casey came back to Washington quite often. They would regularly meet with the Congress as well. The President had great trust in both Casey and Abizaid and was the one who kept extending Casey's tour of duty. (He served almost three years in Iraq—a hardship for his whole family.) I was struck by a comment that Abizaid would often make, "You know everyone here in Washington is so negative. I just came from Iraq and our troops and leadership are fired up, and they're making a difference. It seems we're on two different planets."

The fighting continued in Iraq as Coalition forces hunted the terrorists and our training command worked tenaciously to form new, multisecular, multiethnic military and police units.

In 2005, the goal of bringing into existence a democratic new Iraq often seemed impossible to achieve or no longer worth the cost in lives or dollars—or both—to many critics in America or abroad. Television commentators and editorial writers called for the President to set a timetable for withdrawal of our forces that would leave Iraq to the tender mercies of extremists like Moqtada al-Sadr and Abu Musab al-Zarqawi. (Moqtada al-Sadr was a violent anti-American shiite militant, who hungered for power.) When President Bush or Secretary Rumsfeld asked me about this idea, I always answered that abandoning Iraq would have a direct negative impact on our security and the security of the region. We had achieved a lot in Iraq, but it was still a big challenge and we needed to stick with it.

Secure in his second term, however, President Bush held firm, even though his popularity dropped steeply. The American public became understandably impatient as Iraqi politicians in the new interim government seemed incapable of finding ways to share power among the factions. While the politicians in Baghdad squabbled, the spring and summer of 2005 brought repeated insurgent attacks against Iraqi security forces and civilians: Thousands were killed between March and October alone. Coalition casualties continued at about the same level as they had the year before.

However, Coalition troops were hurting the enemy while simultaneously helping Iraqi civilians build and repair infrastructure. Although I recognized that our forces and the Iraqi civilian reconstruction efforts were in fact making progress, a new village school, a rural clinic, or an irrigation culvert could not compete with lurid video footage of the aftermath of ambushes and car bombs.

The question on my mind was whether the American people would have the courage and persistence needed to see this conflict end in victory.

I still did not know the answer as my second term as Chairman of the Joint Chiefs of Staff ended on September 30, 2005.

That bright Indian summer Friday morning was the last time I wore my country's uniform. Honor guards from all the armed services stood at attention in ranks on the Summerall Field parade ground at Fort Myer. Vice President Cheney, Secretary of State Condoleezza Rice and former Secretary Colin

Powell, as well as my other National Security Council colleagues, were in chairs beneath a marquee tent opposite the reviewing stand where Mary Jo and I sat to President Bush's right. Secretary Rumsfeld was at the President's left with Vice Chairman Gen. Pete Pace beside him.

I had carefully reviewed the details of the retirement ceremony, but somehow sitting there and listening to Donald Rumsfeld's description of my "extraordinary career," his words acquired an air of unreality. "It occurred to me," Rumsfeld said, "that there will be a time, some years from now, when troops and families will walk through the corridors of the Pentagon. Children will likely gaze up at portraits of Marshall, Eisenhower, and Arnold. And they will see a portrait of Richard B. Myers, with a word or two about the War on Terror he helped lead, and the two brutal regimes he helped U.S. forces eliminate, and the fifty million people they liberated. What else might we tell them? We might tell them about the general whose responsibilities encompassed countries, oceans, and even outer space, but who never forgot that he came from a small town in Kansas."

I thought of my parents and Mary Jo's and my children listening across the parade ground. I hoped they were as proud of me as I was of them.

The Secretary continued, describing the doubts of the critics who were convinced that the *shamal* sandstorm had halted our advance on Baghdad back in 2003. "At one of our tumultuous press conferences, General Myers leaned into the microphone and the maelstrom of criticism and said of the second-guessers: 'They either weren't there, or they don't know, or they're working another agenda. . . . I will stick by my statement that this is a great plan . . . one I've signed up to . . . one all the Joint Chiefs signed up to, and it's one we're going to see through to completion.' That day folks learned two things. They underestimated our troops. And they underestimated General Dick Myers."

I was especially pleased and proud that the Secretary singled out Mary Jo for praise. He thanked her for her "heartfelt support for the troops" during scores of visits to military hospitals here and overseas and to families of service members. As a mark of that appreciation to her, the Secretary had just presented Mary Jo with the Defense Department Public Service Medal.

When President Bush spoke, he noted that every Chairman has faced "difficult tests, yet none took up his duties under more demanding circumstances than Dick Myers. In his first week as Chairman, we launched strikes on terrorist training camps in Afghanistan. By the middle of December, American troops and our allies had driven the Taliban from power, put al-Qaida on the run, and freed more than twenty-five million people." The President continued to describe my leadership in helping to forge the Coalition against terror that toppled Saddam Hussein's regime.

When it was my turn to speak, I did not focus on my own career, but rather on the American military it had been my privilege to lead. Our country had the best fighting force on the planet, I said, but it was not enough to be warriors: Our men and women in uniform also took the values of America with them wherever they went.

Our service members defeated two brutal regimes and brought freedom to millions of Afghans and Iraqis, "people who now vote for their government officials, people who can express their opinions and chart their own hopeful futures, the same rights our predecessors fought for in 1776." Directly addressing the men and women of our armed forces I said, "I'm so honored to have the privilege to wear this uniform alongside you."

The parade ground shook with the sound of low-flying military helicopters passing overhead. Then there came the deeper thunder of Air Force fighters. Squinting into the bright autumn sunlight, I saw an F-15, an F-16, and in the center of the formation the thick fuselage and angled wings of an F-4 Phantom.

Mary Jo gripped my hand as the emotion almost overcame me.

A whimsical Christmas card from Hawaii (1998). Our first Christmas as empty-nesters, except for Taisho, our Old English Sheepdog. (This was the third motorcycle that I owned, but not the last.)

My last flight in a fighter aircraft in my Air Force career at Hickam AFB (July 1998). My children Rich and Erin were ready with the traditional "Finis Flight" fire hose and a wet-down.

Nominated by President Clinton, I was sworn in as Vice Chairman of the Joint Chiefs of Staff on March 1, 2000, at Conmy Hall, Fort Myer, Virginia, by Secretary William Cohen. Mary Jo is holding the Bible, and our children, Rich, Nicole, and Erin, are looking on.

The Myerses, Secretary Cohen, Chairman of the Joint Chiefs Gen. Hugh Shelton, and outgoing Vice Chairman Gen. Joe Ralston with his wife, Dede (March 1, 2000). We count the Ralstons among our closest friends.

Dinner at the White House hosted by President and Mrs. Clinton for the combatant commanders and Joint Chiefs of Staff (January 1999).

President Bush announced my nomination as Chairman of the Joint Chiefs at his Crawford ranch on August 24, 2001. When I asked Mary Jo to step forward and stand beside me, she snapped a salute. I detected a bit of irreverence in this, since she was never one to take orders.

…was sworn in as Chairman in Secretary Rumsfeld's office with Mary Jo …lding the Bible while Jim Haynes, the OSD General Counsel, gave the …th (October 1, 2001).

…special lunch day for Papa with granddaughter Sophie Marie …tle, age two, in the Chairman's office (July 2004). A reminder …about what we are fighting for.

The locker room of the Kansas City Chiefs (October 2003). I enjoyed maintaining ties with my hometown and its football team. The members of the team have shown great support for the members of the military in their region.

A visit to our troops in the Gulf (December 2002). These visits were the most energizing and rewarding part of my job.

A pre-Christmas meal with deployed troops in 2004. Each holiday we teamed up with the USO and visited about eighteen locations, most of which were combat bases in the Gulf, including Djibouti, Africa.

At the Crawford ranch (August 2002). Secretary Rice, Vice President Cheney, the President, Secretary Rumsfeld, Barney—the Bushes' Scottie—and me. When the President was working at his ranch, it was customary for the Secretary and me to visit and discuss wide-ranging defense issues.

It has become a tradition for the President to host the Joint Chiefs of Staff and combatant commande at the White House during their conference (January 2005). Front row, left to right: Gen. Pet Schoomaker, Chief of Staff of the Army; Gen. John Jumper, Chief of Staff of the Air Force; Ge Peter Pace, Vice Chairman; Paul Wolfowitz, Deputy Secretary of Defense; Vice President Richa Cheney; President George Bush; Secretary of Defense Donald Rumsfeld; myself; Adm. Vernon Clar Chief of Naval Operations; Gen. Mike Hagee, Commandant of the Marine Corps. Second Row: Adm Edward Giambastiani, Joint Forces Command; Gen. John Handy, Transportation Command; Ge Jim Jones, Supreme Allied Commander, Europe; Adm. Tom Fargo, Pacific Forces Command; Ge John Abizaid, Central Command. Back row: General Craddock, Southern Command; Gen. Ji Cartwright, Strategic Command; Gen. Doug Brown, Special Operations Command; Adm. Timot Keating, Northern Command; Gen. Leon LaPorte, U.S. Forces, Korea.

Secretary Rumsfeld and me in the press briefing room at the Pentagon (May 2003). During combat operations we usually did weekly press briefings; I thought it important to keep the public informed while the nation was at war.

The White House Situation Room (Memorial Day Weekend, 2003). From left, Condoleezza Rice, the President, Secretary Colin Powell, me, General Pace, and CIA Director George Tenet. We would meet several times a week in the Situation Room with the Principals Committee or the National Security Council.

Flying in the Gulfstream G-5 business jet. One of the pleasures I had as Vice Chairman and Chairman was to stay pilot-qualified and be able to sometimes fly on my required travels.

Camp Pendleton, California (May 2004). Nearly every one of these Marines had been deployed at least once or was facing deployment. In trying to encourage them and keep their morale up, I got back more than I gave.

The President graciously hosted us at the White House during my last week as Chairman (September 2005). From left to right: our son-in-law, Wade Little; me holding our grandson, Cole Little; our daughter Nicole Little holding their daughter Sophie; our daughter Erin Voto; the President; Mary Jo; our son, Rich; Mary Jo's sister Jan Ballard; our son-in-law Mike Voto; and brother-in-law Bob Ballard.

My retirement (September 30, 2005). I'm seated next to President Bush, Secretary Rumsfeld, and Gen. Peter Pace. The four of us had been through so much together at a critical time in the security of our nation.

The naming of the Military Science Building at Kansas State University (November 2007). President Jon Wefald his wife, Ruth Ann; Joyce Rumsfeld and Secretary Rumsfeld on the left. This honor was the culmination of the great support I received from my alma mater throughout my career.

Mary Jo and me on Summerall Field, Fort Myer, Virginia, September 30, 2005. The traditional flowers were hardly sufficient thanks to her for the forty-plus years of being a military spouse. Her love, companionship, and ability to keep me grounded were especially important to me in my last years of service.

PART IV
OUR NATIONAL SECURITY FUTURE

12

THE ENDURING THREAT

Violent Extremism

If the last four years of my service taught me anything, they've taught me the seriousness of the threat we face as a nation. For that matter, it's the same threat that our friends and allies also face. When I speak in public on this subject, I call it "World War X"—not X as in the Roman numeral "ten," but X as in the unknown in a mathematical equation. That's because the conflict we are engaged in is not like any past conventional struggle, it's not like the Cold War, and it's not like any counterinsurgency that we have fought before.

Usama bin Laden declared war against the United States, and essentially against all Western civilization, in 1998. We were pretty slow on the uptake. We experienced the East African bombings in Tanzania and Kenya. They killed hundreds of people, including U.S. citizens and State Department workers as well as third-country nationals that were working in our embassies. Then we had the bombing of the USS *Cole* in Aden Harbor, Yemen. In previous chapters, I described our response to those events, or in the case of the *Cole*, the lack of a response. It wasn't until the events of September 11, 2001, that we received a real wake-up call. It was then that we understood how dangerous and ruthless this enemy could be. An enemy without armies, air forces, or navies and small in number but one that could strike on our soil. September 11 also showed us how determined they were to influence events on the world stage.

My personal view is that the threat from violent extremism is more dangerous to our way of life than anything we have faced going way back to our Civil War. Why do I say that? It has to do with how violent extremists use terror to create fear. They're ruthless, and often suicidal, deluded into thinking they are pleasing their god if they die for their cause. So the terror they inflict causes fear that affects the way we think, the decisions we make, and how we perceive our government's ability to deal with the terrorist threat, especially if weapons of mass destruction are involved. Fear of course distorts logic, as the economic crisis of fall 2008 demonstrated.

Indeed, the darkest days in the White House Situation Room were those in October 2001 when there were reports of al-Qaida's having possibly obtained fissile material. I remember how ashen Vice President Cheney's face looked at a meeting after one such report. Fissile material could be used to produce a nuclear device that could result in a nuclear explosion, or the material could be used to produce a radiological device, which might not kill many people, but might render large areas of major cities uninhabitable for decades due to the residual radiation. Just think of the fear that would be created if large sections of a major U.S. city or a large city somewhere else in the world were rendered uninhabitable for decades while we waited for the area to "cool down." That would inevitably have some impact on how we dealt with matters, our logic in business decisions, our logic in personal decisions, and in our confidence in our government's ability to protect us. And there should be no doubt that if al-Qaida and their associates obtain fissile material, they will use it to produce real tragedies here in the United States or somewhere else in the world. The impact, of course, no matter where the event occurred, would be felt globally. There is a lot at stake, and we can't simply wish this threat away.

So what have we done to combat this threat from violent extremists? First, we realized we needed both a defensive strategy for protecting the United States and our friends and allies as well as an offensive strategy for defeating the enemy. You can never build your defenses so strong that dedicated, ruthless, violent extremists can't get through them, especially in free societies. There's no wall you can build that's high enough, and there's not enough barbed wire in the world to stop determined murderers. If we want to keep living a free life we have to understand that defense alone will not be enough; there has to be an offensive component to our strategy.

Since the 9/11 attacks, many organizational steps have been taken to enhance our defenses. The major steps included standing up the Department of Homeland Security and creating an entirely new military combatant command, Northern Command in Colorado Springs, as well as a new intelligence organization, the Office of the Director of National Intelligence. These were major undertakings involving both the executive and legislative branches of our government in the decision making.

The Department of Homeland Security combined several existing organizations into one in which greater focus of effort could be brought to ensuring the domestic security of the United States. Its leadership has certainly brought focus and unity of effort to our many security challenges and has definitely made us much safer here at home. The department has concentrated on protecting our transportation infrastructure, airports, seaports, and other points of entry into the United States. They are safer today than they have been in years, despite the continuing threat of international terrorism. Also, the American public is much more aware of this threat, thanks in large part to the admittedly imperfect color-coded system of threat-level warnings that DHS maintains. Overall, I think this has been a success, and while there are still growing pains associated with the relatively new Department of Homeland Security, it has matured steadily.

Looking back from my perspective as a former commander, it's hard to believe that before the creation of Northern Command, no unified command was responsible for the entire defense of the United States. The United States and Canadian militaries operated NORAD, and this command was concerned with the air and missile threat to North America, but did not have the responsibility to defend the maritime or land approaches to America. Here again Northern Command brings the focus and unity of effort that the threats of the twenty-first century pose for the United States.

In addition, Northern Command became the Defense Department's instrument for helping the Department of Homeland Security and FEMA deal with man-made or natural disasters in the United States. The first test of this new responsibility was Hurricane Katrina, which hit Louisiana and Mississippi in 2005. Northern Command indeed fulfilled its envisioned statutory responsibilities to support the Department of Homeland Security and other organizations, by coordinating the DoD and the military's efforts as the nation struggled to bring order out of the chaos in the aftermath of Hurricane Katrina.

Obviously, this unprecedented disaster demonstrated that there was still plenty of room for improvement in coordinating the response of the states' National Guard units (which had the primary disaster relief duty) and that of the regular U.S. military. However, it is equally clear that the Katrina death toll would have been far higher if helicopters and transports from active duty and reserve component units had not saved hundreds of victims from drowning and medically evacuated almost four thousand patients to hospitals outside of hard-hit New Orleans.

The new office of the Director of National Intelligence (DNI) was created to bridge the gap between domestic and foreign intelligence gathering and analysis. It was also seen as a way to break down the "stovepipes" restricting information-sharing that existed in our intelligence communities. As you will recall, there were scattered bits of information about the pending attacks on 9/11 in domestic intelligence channels including the FBI, and a few bits in the foreign intelligence channels. But these pieces of information never made it to a place where any analysis could take place and determine whether there was an attack pending, or what the objective of that attack would be. The office of the DNI was structured to help make up for that deficiency and encourage the integration of the many pieces of our intelligence apparatus. The new organization was also to make "all source" intelligence analysis easier by encouraging better collaboration between the many disparate intelligence organizations in the U.S. government.

But the failure to share intelligence extends beyond our borders. One example of the damaging lack of openness among allied intelligence agencies is the notorious case of the Iraqi defector agent the German Federal Intelligence Service (BND) code named Curve Ball. The man was a chemical engineer who claimed to have worked on mobile biological weapons laboratories disguised as tractor-trailers to hoodwink U.N. weapons inspectors. Although the Germans had serious concerns about the Iraqi defector's veracity and mental stability, the BND did not allow the CIA to debrief Curve Ball directly, nor did it warn the United States about the defector's questionable reliability. The result was that Colin Powell based part of his February 5, 2003, presentation to the United Nations Security Council on the dubious Curve Ball intelligence.

This episode illustrates the obligation of moving beyond the Cold War "need-to-know" principle to a "need-to-share" requirement among friendly intelligence agencies, foreign and domestic, particularly in this new security environment where the threat is global.

The most obvious part of our offensive action occurred in Afghanistan less than a month after the attacks of 9/11. We went after the perpetrators, al-Qaida, in the country where they had planned the attacks. We wanted to capture or kill al-Qaida's leadership. A year and a half later we went into Iraq, where, as I've discussed, the issue was the nexus of violent extremism and the weapons of mass destruction Saddam's regime was thought to possess. The United States, its friends and allies, and the United Nations thought that Iraq had WMD. And while there wasn't an alliance between the Iraqi regime and al-Qaida, the latter had the financial resources, and could conceivably have bought the weapons of mass destruction—the chemical, biological, and fissile material—that it desired from a regime such as Iraq. Therefore, we can consider Coalition intervention in both Afghanistan and Iraq as important offensive actions undertaken with the intent of stopping violent extremists from operating in their havens and protecting the United States from weapons of mass destruction.

Those were two of the more obvious offensive elements. There were other offensive pieces, such as undermining the Abu Sayyaf Group, operating mainly in the Philippines. There was also an effort to shut off the money flow that al-Qaida used to fund its various initiatives. And, of course, the military and the CIA were going after al-Qaida's senior leadership wherever in the world they were located. That campaign was later modified to hunt the senior leaders of the loosely organized al-Qaida network as it became less hierarchical and more a "franchised" operation in the years after 9/11.

Clearly we are in a much safer position today than before 9/11. But given the determination of our adversary, I am surprised that the United States has not been attacked since then—very pleased, but surprised. I think there's no question that our defensive and offensive efforts are the reasons we have not been attacked in the last eight years. We have worked hard to protect our infrastructure and transportation systems, and we have taken the fight to the enemy, hunting al-Qaida and its allies in their sanctuaries. Since the 9/11 attacks, the United States and its allies have killed or captured hundreds of violent extremists, often disrupting operations on the verge of execution. In August 2006, for example, British authorities upset an alleged conspiracy to blow up airliners on transatlantic flights using liquid explosives. Although a jury eventually found only three of the eight men tried guilty of conspiracy to commit murder, British antiterrorism experts remain convinced they uprooted a major extremist plot before it could be executed.

However, the rest of the world has not been so lucky. There have been more than thirty major terrorist attacks around the world, outside Afghanistan and Iraq, since 9/11. So our adversary hasn't given up and this threat remains very serious. The recent audacious and well-coordinated attack against Western interests in Mumbai, India, is a good example of the type of destabilizing violence we can expect from Muslim extremists in the future.

While both offensive and defensive actions are needed, neither is sufficient to deal with the threat that we face in the twenty-first century. The real question is: Do we have an appropriate overarching strategy for dealing with this daunting adversary?

On this issue we have much work to do. We have failed to adequately define our adversary and, therefore, lack an appropriate strategy for dealing with that adversary. What we've been doing is waging the tactical fight and not looking at the long-range strategic struggle before us. Of course, Iraq and Afghanistan are serious issues and form a big part of the overall fight against violent extremism. But when you step back and look at those questions—adequately defining the enemy, developing an appropriate strategy, and articulating what it takes to win—we didn't spend as much time as we should have at the national level on those issues. The military and the Defense Department pushed this hard, but more immediate, urgent issues always prevailed. I can count on two hands the number of times at a National Security Council meeting we talked about these long-range strategic issues. In contrast, we met literally hundreds of times on the problems in Iraq and Afghanistan, on the more tactical aspects of this struggle with violent extremism.

These tactical issues were certainly important to our overall strategy. But we had the capacity to go beyond the tactical to the strategic if we had wanted to. It was one of my frustrations as Chairman that we never devoted the time to the "larger insurgency" that it deserved.

This issue of the broader strategy is not unlike the quandary the United States found itself in after World War II when communism seemed to be sweeping the globe. That ideology was gaining favor in France, China, and other parts of the world. It took us several years to come up with a strategy of containment for confronting communism. The containment strategy guided our policy and actions for the next five decades during the Cold War until eventually most communist regimes collapsed.

As others have discussed, it's time for this nation to devise a long-range strategy for dealing with violent extremism. There has been much thought both inside and outside government devoted to the subject, but it has not resulted in major policy decisions; now we need to take the lead and, together with the international community, develop a strategy for dealing with this enemy and the terror that they seek to strike in the hearts and minds of people around the world. This strategy will likely take decades to succeed. However, we have to reach the point where men and women don't want to join jihad in the numbers that they do today. I doubt that we'll ever totally eradicate violent extremism just as we can't totally eradicate any of the scourges, such as slavery, that afflict the Earth. But we can diminish the threat sufficiently so that our children and our grandchildren can travel, experience the richness of other cultures, and do so without the threat of being blown up on an airplane, in a ship, in a hotel, or on a bus. Fundamental to this strategy will be properly defining our adversary.

Have we defined our adversary correctly? I don't think we have done so in our "official" papers and government documents, treating this issue. This is a difficult problem because the struggle is unlike any other conflict we've fought, and certainly doesn't fit any mold that this world has ever seen. In 2004, I created a small team, headed by two of my special assistants, Lt. Col. Chris Cavoli and then Col. Paula Thornhill, to take a broad strategic look at defining our adversary and the threat. I specifically asked them to explore the possibility that the United States was an unwitting target in a global insurgency currently led by al-Qaida. If this hypothesis proved true, this would recast the existing conception of terrorism as a significantly larger and more dangerous threat. Testing this hypothesis, we found that it created a paradigm for defining our enemy and crafting a comprehensive strategy for confronting it. As we presented this paradigm informally to the DoD leadership, it was continually refined, but in general we found the idea of a global insurgency resonated.

Under this paradigm, a global insurgency, inspired by international terrorists, is aimed at limiting America's power in large swaths of the planet so that alternative forms of government, such as an Islam-based global Caliphate, can reign. This existential struggle unfolds as part of the long history of two civilizations, Islam and the West. However, the conflict is *primarily* a struggle within Islam to capture the direction of a continuing quest for an Islamic resurgence. It pits a vision of a pure marriage of Islam and the Muslim state against the imperfect form that marriage has thus far found in the modern world.

Fundamentally, this is a struggle for legitimacy to rule between usurpers (embodied in such global terrorist movements as al-Qaida) and existing authorities—the definition of an insurgency. Because of the movement's goals, its conception of the entire world as a legitimate field of battle, and the wide reach of its methods, the insurgency is global in scope. Although the fight is not primarily about the United States, we cannot avoid it. We must win, and we must win on our terms.

This global insurgency carries within it a contradiction that might lead to its destruction. It is driven by an extremist element that wants to co-opt the struggle to pursue violently its own radical vision. These global insurgents seek to galvanize the Muslim world into action, but the majority of the world's Muslims do not agree with all aspects of the extremists' approach, in particular their use of indiscriminate violence. These disagreements are difficult to reconcile. Forced to face them, the insurgency will ultimately collapse, overwhelmed by a more moderate direction in the Islamic resurgence. But we have nothing to lead us to believe that the path to this point will be short or bloodless, and it will require the constant attention of the United States and the international community.

The global insurgents have tapped into a broad movement, the longing for a reformed Muslim world. The movement is not monolithic; it is divided by its adherents' attitudes toward the ends of the struggle (the vision) and their attitudes toward the use of violence in achieving them (the means). Adherents share a view that the Muslim world has fallen from an exalted position, and they seek to return Islam to a position in the world that coincides with their understanding of the religion's superior nature.

This desire for an Islamic resurgence has existed for many decades, but the end of the Cold War accelerated it. The demise of the Cold War international political order, and the subsequent destabilizing economic, social, and informational influences pushed the Muslim world into crisis. A far-ranging debate ensued within the Islamic world over how to recast more secular Muslim governments like that of Egypt to realign with the traditions and teaching of Islam; how to "purify" Muslim societies linked too closely with the West; and how to redress the relative weakness of the larger Muslim world. The debate represents a rejection of the secularized Western forms of authoritarian and socialist governance, which Islamic countries tried in the twentieth century. In that sense the resurgence is a struggle between the "old Islamic order" currently in power and alternative visions of the future.

Within the common vision of a restored Islam, significant variance of scope and scale exists: Some global adherents—al-Qaida and its allies—wish to re-establish a governing Caliphate, whether in the physical sense or virtually, by reuniting religion and government. Some local groups—such as Abu Sayyaf in the Philippines or Jemaah Islamiyah in Indonesia—wish to rid themselves of corrupt local governments or "apostate" regimes they consider insufficiently Islamic. Some seek to effect change on a global scale; others merely seek revolution in the traditionally Muslim lands, or only within their own country. Some seek the establishment of traditional Islamic (sharia) law; others wish to roll back what they see as a tide of non-Islamic practices and institutions. Uniting all these visions, however, is the urgent collective sense that true Islam must be restored, that Western forms must be re-evaluated and reconciled or replaced with an "Islamic way."

Two essential strains run through the Islamic resurgence. One seeks an accommodation with modernity. It encompasses adherents of a range of political thought in the Muslim world—secularists, conservatives, and even many traditionalists. They seek to renew Islamic governance and society in a way that rejects the perverse version of "Westernism" that the Muslim world experienced in the twentieth century, while preserving its essential liberal qualities. Some would argue, for example, that Recep Tayyip Erdogan's government in Turkey is currently working to balance these factors.

The other strain in the resurgence has less to do with modernity. The adherents of this strain, such as the violent extremists operating in Pakistan's Federally Administered Tribal Areas (FATA), tend to be traditionalists or religious fanatics and admit no possibility or desirability of accommodation between Islam and the modern world; this is where the insurgency begins.

Within this trend, there exist various visions for the future of Islam. They share significant areas of ideological common ground, and these overlaps give the global insurgency force beyond what its seeming lack of cohesiveness would imply.

In addition to areas of ideological commonality, local movements like the Taliban give the global insurgents a way to tap into powerful emotions, sentiments, and attitudes. Thus, apocalyptic global extremists such as al-Qaida, Palestinian radicals, Chechens, and Kurdish extremists can find common cause, using each other's violent movements to advance their own, despite divergent final goals.

These violent extremist groups likewise differ in their attitudes toward the West. Some are concerned with the West because it props up the forces they seek to overthrow within the Muslim world. Others see the West as a morally corrupting force whose influence must be expunged from Muslim lands. Still others blame their failures on the West and seek to convert, eliminate, or destroy it. However, in this, too, there is an area of convergence: the idea that Islamic resurgence depends on limiting Western influence by undermining the nation-state model of geopolitics. This overlap gives strength to the movement and makes the West an inevitable target of the insurgency's actions and designs.

Those who want Western influence to be eliminated in order for Islam to be restored differ widely in their attitude toward violence. Their attitudes cover a spectrum. The most extreme consider violence against any and all whose death might advance the cause to be a legitimate and necessary means to advance their ends.

The insurgents at this far end—those who view the insurgency most globally, who view the Western and Islamic worlds as mutually exclusive, and who are most committed to violence—represent the greatest threat to the United States and its interest. These groups are best epitomized by al-Qaida, which has chosen a strategy of attacking America and its allies as the primary means of achieving its goals. Inspired by a puritanical, and utterly impractical, Salafist interpretation of Islam, al-Qaida and its allies hope to spread Islamic governance throughout the world. This grouping itself is amorphous, and while Salafists are currently the vanguard, they will morph over time. They work in close concert with like-minded members of the Sunni clerical establishment and Sunni community. This loose grouping of Salafist imams, mullahs, and organizations provides an ideological grouping and a physical network for the global insurgents. Thus a global group such as al-Qaida can join regional local groups such as the former "Salafist Group for Preaching and Combat" (GSPC) in Algeria (now called the "al-Qaida Organization in the Islamic Maghreb"). The resulting symbiotic relationship gives energy to the attempt to drive the Muslim resurgence in the direction of insurgency. Their combination of terrorist tactics and expansive goals makes this loose alliance of global insurgents a powerful adversary of the United States.

The bulk of the Muslim world does not actively support the methods of the violent extremists aimed at America and the West, just as the majority does not share their far-reaching vision of the future. Nevertheless, the widespread sense in Islamic populations that Western influence is repressing Islam and blocking its resurgence creates broad sympathy for them in the Muslim world.

Converting that sympathy into support or acceptance of terrorist methods and Salafist goals is the basis of the insurgents' strategy. At the heart, they are fighting a war of persuasion.

The global insurgents seek to win the support of the majority of Muslims and to drive the rest closer to acceptance or at least tolerance of their extreme goals and methods. To this end, local struggles provide the global insurgents extremely useful points of entry. Local insurgents operating in the ungoverned areas inside weak nations such as of Yemen and Somalia welcome the global insurgents because they bring weapons, skills, volunteers, and a commitment to the local fight. This symbiotic relationship provides the extremists a venue for proselytizing, recruiting, and training their membership. The global insurgents participate in these local conflicts to co-opt some or all members to their own, broader goals. As they succeed in persuading more Muslims of their vision, they attempt to drive them toward the extreme end of the spectrum of commitment and violence. Complete success is unnecessary; merely shifting people's goals and increasing their acceptance of violence are enough to expand the movement.

In areas they seek to exploit, global insurgents, in concert with local insurgents, seek to establish two competing dynamics: one between the people and the state, and one between themselves and the people. The insurgents profit most if they can establish and sustain these two dynamics simultaneously.

First, they seek to delegitimize the established government in a given country. Much of the extremists' action against the Pakistani government, for example, consists of pointing out that the government is an imperfect representation of Islam. They describe the regime as corrupt, irreligious, and lacking legitimacy because it seeks to copy the West. The insurgents want to show the national leadership to be ineffective or unwilling to meet the legitimate demands of the people and then use violence to emphasize this point. They hope ultimately to alienate most of the population from the Pakistani government, thereby making it seem less effective and legitimate, which in turn alienates still more of the population.

The insurgents also often use nonviolent efforts to reinforce a virtuous relationship between themselves and the people. They offer alternative organizations and solutions to problems afflicting the state. In particular, as we are seeing in the Federally Administered Tribal Areas of Pakistan right now, they are effectively exploiting the media, using them to spread disinformation and their own, unflattering depiction of Western society, and to increase dissatisfaction with governments they seek to undermine. Moreover, the combined efforts of al-Qaida and the Taliban in the FATA are providing alternative options for security, health care, and education to disenfranchised, dislocated people. They establish and use these organizations to create a sense of identity and common purpose. In short, they establish their loose alliance as the "party" of better governance.

The driving factor in both of these dynamics is the global insurgents and their supporting networks of clerics and nongovernmental organizations. They are able, by using violence, to set the pace of governmental delegitimization, to direct all other efforts of the local insurgents against apostate regimes and their supporters, especially the United States.

Eventually, our adversary will want to transform the insurgency into "victory." The enemy has no discrete theory of victory, such as unconditional surrender, that would identify when the insurgency is successful. Instead, the adversary will most likely benefit from a "cumulative" strategy. This is a nonlinear strategy that depends on gross accumulation of "victories," not sequential action. That makes fighting more important than winning, and it coincides nicely with the ideology of jihadism. It's an optimal strategy for a nonmonolithic movement and allows almost any incident or attack to be counted as a victory. Further, the strategy obviates the need for strict command and control. It also allows the insurgents to work three dimensions; inside Muslim regimes and regions, in lawless ungoverned spaces of weak or failing nation states, and inside liberally governed countries.

This third dimension, Western and Western-style democratic states, presents some difficult challenges for us. Not only are these states often targets themselves, but the key features of these states—the rule of law, freedom of movement, ethnic, racial, and religious tolerance, right to privacy, freedom of speech, freedom of press, due process—ironically make them havens for the insurgents. In the free nations of Europe, North and South America, and Asia, global insurgents can obtain expertise, funds, technology, documents, and transportation, all the raw materials of their warfare. It is not a coincidence that these countries become the staging grounds and locations of many attacks. Prominent French scholar of modern Islam Gilles Kepel has written in *The War for Muslim Minds* a penetrating analysis of how this is being accomplished through physical and virtual means every day in Western Europe.

The global insurgents will apply all their tools, as they are able, to achieve effects on any population they can, whenever they see or can create the opportunity. They will need to continue scoring such victories so that they can continue to prove their greater effectiveness and legitimacy in the Islamic world.

This cumulative victory strategy is mainly opportunistic, and will not play out in a linear manner; it will sometimes seem aimless or directionless, but that does not indicate anarchy.

Indeed, the global insurgency is distinctly non-Western because, one, it does not seek unity of command, though it has achieved broad unity of effort and strives toward a common vision; two, it has no defined endpoint and no distinctive "theory of victory," yet, by virtue of those very facts it is resilient abroad; and three, it considers victory to be the accumulation of local and social victories for its vision of Islam and of strikes against apostate regimes and their Western allies, whether they operate in Morocco, France, Pakistan, Indonesia, or Australia. In this way they achieve their aims: fighting is winning.

If our understanding of the adversary is correct, the next question is: What is the appropriate strategy for dealing with this new type of adversary? My view has been that since 9/11, we haven't developed a national strategy adequate for dealing with a global insurgency. For the most part, we look at the threat more narrowly, that is, we view operations tactically, and do not place them in the larger strategic context that would lead to an appropriate strategy.

There are some fundamental ideas that apply to any strategy that might be developed for dealing with this global insurgency. One is a realization that no nation, however powerful or rich, can deal alone with the major problems that we face in this world. This certainly is true for dealing with a global insurgency. A second is that to fulfill the strategy we will have to be able to harness all our instruments of national power—military, economic, informational, and diplomatic—and all instruments of international power if we are to succeed.

Today we are much too reliant on the military instrument, in part because we haven't properly described our adversary, and also because, in practical terms, it is easier to employ the DoD to deal with what we are calling a *war*. In determining our strategy, we first must look at the adversary's vulnerabilities and determine what opportunities they create for the United States and our friends and allies.

Most important, the insurgency itself faces a paradox. The adversary is an extremist element that lives in a symbiotic relationship with a sympathetic element in the Muslim world, on which it depends for moral, financial, and physical support, and for a population of eligible candidates to radicalize and adopt into their own ranks. However, for the extremists to attract the adherents they require, they need to conduct their offensive in a morally sustainable fashion.

As they fight across the three dimensions of the strategic landscape, they are compelled to fight in Muslim lands; in ungoverned spaces, because they require havens; and in Westernized "apostate" states. Therefore, the most extreme elements of the movement are separated from the bulk of the population by a fundamental contradiction: They are in a fight to win the souls of the Muslim people, but by waging war in unnecessary locations and against inappropriate foes, they risk killing Muslims and losing the very souls they seek. Further, because fighting is winning, they cannot stop. They recognize the corollary to this maxim is: Not fighting is losing. This particular point was most dramatically made in 2008 when the Sunni Awakening, tired of the violence destroying Iraq, successfully confronted and defeated al-Qaida in Iraq.

This strategic contradiction produces rifts between the various elements of the global insurgency, and between the global insurgency and the rest of Islam. It is these basic rifts that the extremists seek to bridge in order to build their insurgency, and therefore they are the fundamental rifts that the United States can take advantage of.

The terrorist-inspired global insurgency threatens to undermine the nation-state system from which the United States derives much of its strength. The enemy's will in the struggle of persuasion is clearly a center of gravity, but the loose organization, virtual operating space, and idea-based nature of the insurgency make the center of gravity immune to direct attack. That is why capturing Usama bin Laden or al-Zawahiri would have an impact on the al-Qaida movement. But it would not bring the conflict with violent extremism to an end.

Therefore, the U.S. grand strategy must attack the enemy's strategy; an American strategy must prevent the admixture of local grievances with global aims. This will require simultaneous efforts to defeat the global insurgents and to defeat, suppress, defuse, or prevent local insurgencies. A near-term effort will blunt the insurgency's galvanizing offensive; it will create the time needed for a long-term effort to split the global insurgents both from local insurgencies and from the Islamic resurgence.

This proposed counterinsurgency strategy must have three major goals. The first entails a number of concurrent efforts. First America must attack, disrupt, and defeat the terrorists themselves. Second, it must break the links of the regional and local struggles to the global insurgent movement (for example, separating al-Qaida Organization in the Islamic Maghreb from the global insurgents). And third, it must accommodate Islamic solutions, within limits.

With regard to the first goal, as I've emphasized, the United States alone cannot defeat the global insurgents. The intelligence, law enforcement, and military efforts needed to bring down these networks on all three strategic dimensions—weak, corrupt, and alien states; ungoverned space such as Somalia; and democratic Western states—will require the United States to work with local governments, regional alliances, and international institutions. Working through local governments and institutions could help counter the global insurgents' depiction of a United States–led crusade against Islam, and this would build the capability to find and attack terrorists routinely. Sometimes the imperative to prevent enemy victories will make it necessary to create working relationships with countries not normally considered to be American allies. This demands the greatest subtlety and most careful execution.

Those countries that sponsor terrorism must stop. Compelling states to stop supporting terrorists will often require military activity, which will be inherently controversial. This controversy can be mitigated by acting in concert with alliances and coalitions and under the imprimatur of international bodies. This will strengthen American rhetoric with visible action, and will help greatly to preserve international cooperation in a counterinsurgency; in essence, an international approach reduces the cost of unilateral American action, and this approach should be taken to the extent possible. However, we must move quickly, decisively, and alone if threats warrant it. Again, in these operations, efforts to emphasize the responsibilities of sovereignty will provide an important background of justification for unilateral military action.

Attacking the terrorists, while an imperative portion of the effort to defend the United States, is also critical to preventing terrorists from igniting wider conflict between Islam and the West. Repeated or catastrophic attacks against America would increase the chances of wider conflict by emboldening the terrorists, feeding the insurgency, and sparking calls for a massive response from the United States. Preventing attacks undermines the apocalyptic vision of the global insurgents.

The second major goal is breaking the link between local struggles and the global insurgency. Once one conceives the global insurgency as a symbiotic relationship between global insurgents and local populations, it becomes evident that breaking or preventing a link between the two is key to a successful strategy. As the global insurgents are denied a broad base of support, the problem of insurgency will be reduced to a problem of terrorism—a complicated and dangerous problem to be sure, but not the existential threat posed by the global insurgency.

"Defueling" this insurgency requires finding areas of potential local grievance and assisting local governments to ameliorate the problems to prevent their exploitation. It also suggests a need to increase the capabilities of local governments to combat local insurgents fomenting trouble in their countries. This will require training, military advice and advisers, and equipment. At the higher end of the spectrum of possible activities, it might also be necessary for the United States to support or wage full-scale counterinsurgency.

Under Adm. Tom Fargo's leadership in Pacific command we carried out such assistance on Basilan Island in the Philippines. The Abu Sayyaf group, affiliated with al-Qaida, had found a haven with the local population. We trained and equipped the Philippine Army to do the fighting (they weren't shooting straight—and the answer lay in issuing the troops glasses), advised them, put in all-season roads, and dug wells that provided safe drinking water for the residents (previously the death rate among children due to unsafe water was very high). Once the Abu Sayyaf group left, they weren't welcomed back.

Of all the aspects of the U.S. strategy, achieving goal two is the most ambitious and potentially the most costly undertaking. However, it is not an open-ended objective. The United States need not solve all the world's ills to stop terrorism, but our strategy must have the goal of preventing the global insurgents from exploiting economic, social, and political problems to further their aims. American efforts should directly challenge, or support alternatives to, the global insurgents, their proxies, and nongovernmental agencies, madrassas, and Islamic charities.

After the 9/11 attacks, the United States made its first concerted effort to dry up the dubious charitable private financial well that was funding violent extremist groups. We succeeded in convincing several of our closest allies to follow our lead. However, there remains a lot of work to be done in this area.

The need to undermine the false impression of American imperial designs merits emphasis. The purported desire of the United States to control Muslim lands and populations is a cornerstone of the global insurgents' rhetoric, and U.S. strategy should not reinforce that mischaracterization. Generally, the footprint of the United States' actions should remain as small as possible, and our efforts should be crafted to limit their scope and duration when practicable. Our principles must be to work, in descending order of preference, by proxy, covertly, or in a coalition, using unilateral activity, especially force, only as a last resort. These principles will focus and limit U.S. efforts in the counterinsurgency, and thus help decrease the cost to the United States, the unrealistic expectations of partners and intended beneficiaries, and the exploitable impression that American actions conceal imperial designs.

The third major goal involves accommodating Islamic resurgence. Neither the Muslim world nor the West is monolithic. The global insurgency will exploit deep cleavages in our culture and alliances. American strategy should endeavor to do the same to the global insurgents.

Furthermore, the global insurgents err in their conceptualization of the insurgency. It is not a struggle of Islam against the West; it is a struggle between the insurgents and the nation-states that enjoy the rights of, and exercise the responsibilities of, the international system that the insurgency seeks to undermine. The United States can undermine the insurgents' rhetoric by creating and maintaining a grand coalition that includes the active involvement of responsible non-Western states that understand and share America's point of view. Such a coalition will also quicken the resolve of the countries facing the insurgency. Recasting the issue as involving an insurgency against a modern world will reduce global toleration for the problem.

Ultimately, the only conclusive way to prevent the ignition of a wider, inter-civilization conflict is to bring Muslim society to an accommodation with the modern world. External voices lack authority in this struggle. The Islamic resurgence will likely produce voices and potential solutions that do not correspond precisely with Western ideas of governance and society. It may also produce some solutions or behavior we cannot accept. The United States can and must prevent this. American strategy must formulate "redlines" defining unsuitable behavior and broadcast them constantly and with consistency to ensure they are understood and acknowledged by Muslim leaders and opinion makers. These redlines should especially address the consequences for violations of sovereignty and the use of terrorism to achieve national and international goals. It needs to be clear that such behavior will not be tolerated.

In this sense, our communications strategy must be proscriptive, not prescriptive: We cannot decree beliefs for others to hold, but can decree how others may not behave. Rather than telling Muslims what they must be or become, America should simply tell them what behavior is not acceptable: The United States can never accept state or societal support of terrorism against our interests or those of our allies, and America cannot accept violence against other societies or countries as part of the internal struggle within Islam.

Transmitting redlines to the Muslim world will require the establishment of multiple channels of communication. Such channels currently exist almost exclusively with governments we support and a small circle of Western-centric Muslim academics. Establishing wider channels that include nontraditional voices that are spread across the political spectrum will require research, outreach, and a deeper understanding of Islam and its cultural expressions. Broader communication will produce a double benefit; it will allow the United States to broadcast our redlines, but will also demonstrate, without meddling, America's understanding of and interest in the Islamic resurgence.

Westerners will be tempted to inject their voices into the inter-Islamic conversation. They must not. Nor need Westerners fear the ultimate result. The global insurgents' visions are either quixotic or apocalyptic. The latter cannot stand the practical scrutiny of a debate over visions of future governance, and the former, as grand as visions of a global Caliphate have become, are so poorly conceptualized as to be impractical.

Muslims will create a range of acceptable visions for their future, a range that will isolate extremist views at the end of the spectrum. Some Muslim voices will urge solutions that might not be suitable to the Western way of life, but will not threaten it. If the United States can prevent the global insurgents from dominating the debate and proscribe unacceptable conclusions, the Islamic resurgence will produce an expression with which we can coexist.

America faces several paradoxes in this strategic approach. Actions that the United States government must take to defeat global insurgents may poison the dialogue within the Muslim world. Our government may need to cooperate with the security services of regimes whose legitimacy is the subject of local grievance, and we may need to kill or capture terrorists who are currently popular or protected. We may also need to continue affording committed terrorists fewer rights than we provide common criminals. Our involvement in local struggles may undermine our ability to ameliorate them and prevent their cooptation to global jihad. We may have to prop up or strengthen regimes whose legitimacy is questionable. And we may need to support regional leaders trying to arbitrate local struggles, creating the impression these leaders are U.S. government surrogates.

The mere presence of American government personnel in the country or region may provide a catalyst for the enemy's cause. The United States may need to operate in ways that both transcend sovereignty and reinforce it. For instance, our government may need to physically attack terrorists within the boundaries of sovereign states, even as it recognizes the concept of sovereignty or recognizes the concept of sovereignty is the subject of this struggle. We may also need to confront the enemy in the virtual realm in arenas in which international laws and protocols have yet to be developed. Finally, the United States may need to rely more on traditional bilateral and regional partnerships to defeat the enemy. Hopefully any actions taken through these partnerships would be consistent with those supported by the international community. However, if necessary, the U.S. and its partners must be prepared to undertake actions without the support of international organizations like the United Nations.

These paradoxes will require artful execution of strategy. It will be impossible to create cookbook solutions or a comprehensive roadmap for solving all these problems. But the paradoxes can be anticipated and they can be balanced and mitigated in the policy-making process.

In discussing what it will require to win, so far I've talked about appropriately characterizing the adversary and then coming up with a strategy to deal with that adversary. The final part of this discussion has to do with several intangibles and one tangible action.

On the intangible side, we hope we will be able to convince the rest of our friends and allies that what we are facing is a global insurgency and not just the tactical fights in Iraq or Afghanistan, or wherever the insurgency raises its head. And achieving success in this counterinsurgency will require great patience, great will, and the resolve of the American people. Our adversary has said many times that we are culturally weak and don't have the patience, will, or resolve for this long struggle. To ensure we do possess the resolve, all of us will need to engage in one very tangible pursuit: good, honest public discourse.

Unfortunately, in my view, as a nation we haven't been able to engage in this public discourse since the summer before the 2004 national elections when the efforts in Iraq and Afghanistan became much more politicized, much more partisan. The strident and often vitriolic language on both sides of the debate made such discourse difficult, if not impossible. The media were just an amplifier for this partisan discourse.

In my farewell speech in at Fort Myer, Virginia, on September 30, 2005, I made this point one last time. Our national security debate has to be elevated, especially given the enormous stakes. There is an opportunity now with a new administration to work toward a more unified national security debate.

I'd like to offer some concluding thoughts about the threat we face and how we might deal with it. The first is that the ultimate, final defeat of the insurgency can only come from within the Muslim world, when Muslims themselves conclude that the apocalyptic vision of the global insurgents offers neither the end they desire, nor the means they prefer. Second, America is in large measure fighting a war of persuasion. Ideas, not violence, will be decisive. But the challenge for America is to recognize its "voice" is unwelcome. America's voice will only be "heard" in the actions we take to protect the nation, communicate redlines, and undermine the exaggerated rhetoric and dishonest initiatives of the global insurgence. Carefully and thoughtfully executed, however, this strategic approach will cause the insurgency to collapse under its own weight.

With this in mind, it is important to remember that the final success of our global counterinsurgency efforts will be hard to discern. If waged successfully, ultimately, the War on Terror will not so much be won as dissipate.

13

THE MOST IMPORTANT NATIONAL SECURITY CHALLENGES AMERICA WILL FACE

Protecting the Future of Democracy

N ational security has to be any President's primary concern. The first year our new Commander in Chief is in the White House the nation will face profound security challenges. Inevitably, many of these challenges will be both critical and urgent. As the new administration outlines it key policy initiatives during its inaugural year, I want to address what I think will be the most important security challenges that our forty-fourth President will face.

ADMINISTRATION LEADERSHIP IN TIME OF WAR

In time of war, the executive branch of government, the United State military, American citizens, and the international community will all expect decisive leadership. President Obama is clearly mindful of this.

To provide this leadership, it's crucial that the President's key advisers be in place in the White House, in the Department of Defense, and throughout government. Yet historically, other than some key cabinet officials confirmed by the Senate before the inauguration, there will be hundreds and hundreds of important appointees who will not be sworn in for months. We must address this problem; without the second, third, and even fourth tier of political appointees in place, vital work will go undone.

One possible course of action is to carry over some political appointees. It took almost an entire year for Secretary Rumsfeld to fill all of the key deputy positions. Because of this delay, he held over the deputy secretary from the Clinton Administration, Rudy de Leon, until Paul Wolfowitz was sworn in on March 16, 2001, two months after the new administration came to office. De Leon did a terrific job of providing continuity in the Office of the Secretary of Defense while the nominations ground through the slow official process. If President Obama's transition plan works as currently articulated, this method may be a good prototype for future presidential transitions.

During both Bush administrations, a year often passed between nomination of key political appointees and their governmental positions' being filled. This includes not only the critical positions here in Washington, but our United States Ambassadors as well.

With this example in mind, there are certainly some things that a new President can do to get the people he wants and needs confirmed by the Senate and into their jobs as quickly as possible.

First, he can work with the Senate to ensure expeditious handling of the nominees who are presented to it for confirmation. This should be easy for a former senator.

Second, the President needs to pressure the bureaucrats who handle the cumbersome security clearance process to make the completion of security reviews a national priority. The paperwork regarding financial disclosure and potential conflicts of interest must be completed expeditiously. Appointees must be able to enter their positions fully prepared to support the President. President Obama's selection to continue Defense Secretary Robert Gates in his position goes a long way toward ensuring continuity in this wartime transition.

Third, the President and his key advisers must ensure that appointees have the requisite skills for the positions they're going into. He should not default to selecting nominees on a political basis. While we're at war and while men and women in the United States armed forces are putting their lives on the line every day, they are counting on the President to find the most capable and talented individuals for the various positions in our government regardless of their previous political contributions. It's a good sign that the Secretary of Defense is staying on through the transition.

Just as President Bush did with de Leon in Defense, he may similarly decide to hold over some of the Ambassadors from the previous administration to ensure continuity of effort in those important countries where we need a strong ambassador and a strong country team. My experience suggests that, if we're to be successful in our international security efforts, particularly in places like Afghanistan, Iraq, and Pakistan, we need our most able Ambassadors leading our country teams. Unfortunately, when there are months-long gaps in ambassadorial terms in key countries, or when Ambassadors are appointed who don't have the required skills, we make little progress and sometimes lose ground in meeting our security objectives. I've seen both of these situations in Iraq and Afghanistan. In wartime, country teams always must have well-qualified leaders in place.

REORGANIZING AMERICA'S NATIONAL SECURITY APPARATUS

As several recent studies have noted, the new President and his administration also have to realize that the United States' interagency and national security apparatus, as currently organized, can't deal effectively with the threats of the twenty-first century. This is particularly true when confronting the global insurgency threat. The last major reorganization of this apparatus was the National Security Act of 1947, just after World War II. And while it's been modified several times, the current system is incapable of reliably bringing all instruments of national power to focus on U.S. security priorities. In a sense, we remain perfectly organized for World War II. Yet today's security challenges require unprecedented interagency integration, execution, and accountability; sustained political will; and broad international cooperation.

The U.S. governmental security apparatus is designed for nation-to-nation state interaction and is biased toward a peacetime context of short-duration contingencies. Much as our military was before the Goldwater-Nichols Act, the United States government is stovepiped: All departments and agencies tend to stay in their own vertical hierarchy. At times there is very good integration, but it is the exception rather than the rule. Inherent differences in cultures, resources, bureaucracies, and leadership of the various federal departments and agencies mean the U.S. government is often focused on deconfliction among the organization rather than on sustained effort and integrated approaches.

However, neither the U.S. government nor the military can simply be dismantled and reorganized to address the challenges of national security. Too many functions predating 9/11 remain important today, and existing legal and legislative mechanisms and equities would make this difficult, if not impossible, to accomplish. Moreover, the dismantling of long-established structures and procedures could inadvertently undermine our government's ability to pursue other critical efforts. Therefore, a practical reorganization should follow some principles: First, it must establish procedures and bodies that supplement the current organs of government without usurping them. Second, the bodies must be quick-acting, enabling integration without unnecessarily adding bureaucracy. And third, the overall design must permit agility when addressing challenges as they arise from the dynamic security situation we face.

One way to meet this requirement for additional integrative function without reorganization is by "matrixed" organizations and the development of strong transorganizational links. This "reorganization within an organization" provides the ability to direct efforts centrally while preserving core functions of individual agencies. It fosters institutional agility by permitting rapid establishment and dissolution of functional organizations as requirements dictate, while leaving open the possibility of permanently institutionalizing valuable and viable mechanisms as their worth is proven.

The issue to date, and certainly through my tenure in the Joint Chiefs of Staff, is that below the President there is no one person, head of a department, or head of an agency who has been tasked with or is responsible for the strategic direction and integration of all elements of national power, so the United States can properly execute a strategy for Iraq, Afghanistan, or a global counterinsurgency. And while there are people who are tasked to do parts of this job, nobody brings it all together. In particular, nobody has the authority and influence needed across the whole U.S. government to be responsible, and held accountable, for strategic planning and execution. We need some new constructs and some new matrixed organizations.

Using the global counterinsurgency strategy as an example, these new organizations and constructs would need to perform three tasks to carry out an overarching strategy. First, a central entity must be established to integrate the interaction of the three elements of the U.S strategy as outlined in Chapter Twelve and to analyze the costs and benefits of policy decisions and mitigate their negative effects. Another must be dedicated to attack the global insurgency, and to optimize the complex interagency and transnational initiatives that task will require. Finally, one is also needed to conduct those myriad activities that will work within the nation-state system to prevent the global insurgents from infiltrating and radicalizing local conflicts; it should be optimized for the traditional state-based activity.

The central organization would be the U.S. government's highest integrative body empowered to develop, direct, and implement the strategy to counter the global insurgency. The body must then be led by a new cabinet-equivalent officer assigned to the executive office of the President and responsible directly to the President. This person would not be in the chain of command for field operational purposes, but would be responsible for the strategic planning government-wide and for overall execution of the integrated plan.

Of course, this director would require a dedicated staff to develop a strategic counterinsurgency campaign framework, and to integrate the efforts of the U.S. government agencies into it. It would be a matrixed organization consisting of any government department or agency involved in the counterinsurgency. The members would belong to their parent departments but take daily direction from the new director. The collective body would also be empowered to plan, align, and direct interagency counterinsurgency efforts. In this manner, major departments would participate in the planning of the strategy, commit themselves to executing it, but retain the ability to rationalize the strategy with the other goals and requirements of their departments. Properly led, the director's staff would be a powerful but self-limiting mechanism for the planning, integrating, and execution of the counterinsurgency strategy.

The new cabinet-level official would take options and decisions through a council, which could be the National Security Council, or a subset of that body. This group would have to be at the principals level and include the Secretaries of State, Defense, and Treasury; the Attorney General; the Director of National Intelligence; the Director of the CIA; and the Chairman of the Joint Chiefs of Staff. It would need to complement, but not supplant, the NSC process and should not rupture already established executive branch structures. This would allow the heads of agencies to balance tasking and priorities from the director of this counterinsurgency effort with their other statutory and strategic responsibilities.

Neither the director, nor his staff, nor the council would be permanent. Their functions could be eliminated or incorporated into the normal structure of the NSC when the insurgency sufficiently dissipates. By creating these as temporary organizations without adding additional governmental duties or entities, the President would be able to continue to meet all statutory responsibilities.

I saw a system very similar to this work when I was the Assistant to the Chairman. One was for Plan Colombia, a strategy that was designed by the U.S. government, in cooperation with the Colombian government, to help train and equip the Colombian military to deal with the FARC terrorists and the drug trade. The day-to-day execution of the plan was given to the Deputy Secretary of State, Tom Pickering. Pickering was empowered with the authority to gather those from various governmental departments and agencies who had the responsibility for executing Plan Colombia and ensuring that people were doing what they were supposed to be doing. From an organizational standpoint, this was an effective way to integrate the various departments and agencies to carry out our strategy.

I also saw it, again when I was Assistant to the Chairman, in how the U.S. government organized to deal with Russia in the mid-1990s. There were several Russia-U.S. and Russia-NATO issues that were coming to a head, which would result in a summit between President Yeltsin and President Clinton in Helsinki in spring 1997. Here again, the Deputy Secretary of State was empowered, and held accountable, by the President to lead the interagency effort to put together the various proposals, including a NATO-Russian charter, which would help ameliorate some of Russia's concerns with NATO expansion; an outline of the principles for a new round of nuclear arms limitations (START III); and an agreement on limitations they wanted on our ballistic missile defense capabilities, specifically our tactical ballistic missile defense capabilities. The details of these issues were contentious inside our government, but we worked through them during meetings with Deputy Secretary of State Strobe Talbott leading our group. We were all empowered to speak for our various departments and agencies and we always had a chance to go back to our departments and agencies to get the principals to weigh in if there was a position we didn't agree on. But we didn't waste a lot of time in the bureaucratic process. Secretary Talbott kept the process moving along and it resulted in a very successful summit on all of the subjects.

Some aspects of this reorganization of our national security apparatus may require congressional approval. At the same time, Congress may want to look at how they're organized to support our integrated national security efforts. Congress is stovepiped in its committee structure and rarely takes an integrated approach to national security matters. There were also several instances in which Congress and the law precluded doing things in the most effective manner, for example, training the police in Iraq or Afghanistan. Under normal circumstances, this is a State Department function, but in these unique cases the mission was best suited to the Defense Department. Once the bureaucratic hurdles were overcome in the executive branch, we had to overcome several in the legislative branch. The result was a delay in training the very forces that could get our troops home sooner.

Unless someone is given the responsibility across government, has the authority, and is held accountable, no strategy for dealing with current or emerging threats, however good, is likely to be fully successful.

DEVELOPING A GRAND STRATEGY

Once the key players are in place, the administration will need to craft a grand strategy to guide the actions of the United States as it deals with myriad challenges it will confront in protecting our vital national interests. This strategy must match our "ends," protecting and promoting our vital national interests, with our strategic "means," which include all instruments of power and persuasion—including nonmilitary instruments ("soft power"), such as public diplomacy, economic measures, and information programs.

The crucial grand strategy issue facing our President will be focusing our government's efforts on effectively crafting strategic tools to actually *defeat* the insurgency. Given that this new strategy will include contributions from across government, he must also realize that the entire U.S. government will not focus on such an important undertaking unless he is personally driving the process. This is one task that can't be delegated.

His first and most important task will be to persuade the country of the seriousness of this threat. As 9/11 recedes in our national memory, most Americans don't believe the United States is engaged in an existential struggle. The President can start a fresh dialogue, explaining to American citizens that we indeed are threatened, that there's a lot at stake, and that we can't just wish it away.

All instruments of national power need to be brought to bear on the problem. In this long fight against violent extremism, the military instrument will not be the primary implement. Instead, it will be the other tools of national and international power that, in the right strategy, will lead to a more permanent peace between the Muslim world, and those violent extremists who live in it, and the West and our friends and allies.

The United States needs to lead the development of this strategy, but it also has to work with the international community and international organizations. Our friends and allies need to acknowledge the nature of the threat we face. The threat will not disappear if they ignore it. However, there are large differences between the way that many European countries, for instance, look at the challenge from violent extremism, and the way the United States sees the problem. But a common definition of the adversary is absolutely necessary if we are to lead the international community in a strategy for making our world safer. Driving to consensus will require considerable energy. And the further away from 9/11 and other major attacks we get, the less either America or the rest of the world will remember just how determined and ruthless this adversary is.

IRAQ AND AFGHANISTAN

An element of the strategic campaign against global insurgency strategy is the integration of the Iraq and Afghanistan conflicts into this strategy. The new administration must continue to find ways to seek progress and help the Iraqi and Afghan governments to succeed, moving both countries toward greater stability. To do this, the new administration must seek progress in the political and economic realm as well as the security realm.

Success in these countries is more a question of political progress than a security issue, particularly in Iraq. For example, for the Iraqi government to succeed it must be seen as legitimate and fair by all the ethnic factions in the country. Great progress has been made, but as Ambassador Ryan Crocker and Gen. David Petraeus have noted, it is fragile and there is further to go. Government legitimacy and concurrent popular support are essential.

Political, military, and economic progress in these two conflicts have to move forward together. You can't ask for just one of those three items to move independently of the others—they have to be linked to advance simultaneously because they are synergistic and build upon and reinforce one another. One of the most important aspects of the surge strategy announced by President Bush in 2007 was that he called for progress along all three of these lines, the political, the military, and the economic.

In this regard, developing artificial timelines for withdrawing (or retaining) American troops is dangerous. Any troop movements need to be based on how best to help progress toward good governance and democratic principles. After all, both countries already have new liberal constitutions; they already have elected parliaments and governments. What they need is help from us and the international community in focusing on working through the multiple obstacles and challenges to good governance. The late-November 2008 Iraqi security agreement, which passed the National Parliament in Baghdad, established December 2011 as the final withdrawal for all Coalition forces.

The consequences of not doing this are profound. An Iraq in chaos would be very disconcerting for the Gulf States. Most people have forgotten that for the ten years leading up to the first Gulf War, the United States with our Saudi partners had an airborne warning and control aircraft flying twenty-four hours a day, seven days a week, 365 days a year. The sole reason was to prevent an Iranian air attack on Saudi Arabia. Now latent, these fears would quickly re-emerge if Iraq collapsed into chaos, and especially if it fell under Iran's sphere of influence.

Of course, instability in the Gulf would also have grave, far-reaching economic consequences, given the world's dependence on the region's oil. This volatility could also lead to serious, second-order security concerns. With Iran exerting more influence in the region through Iraq and apparently intent on developing a nuclear weapon, what would the regional reaction to the collapse of the Iraqi government be, particularly in Saudi Arabia? Would the Saudi government look at developing nuclear weapons itself? Would a regional arms race ensue? The possible scenarios are many and have profound implications for regional and global stability. So the consequences of an Iraq in chaos are among the most serious the next President will face.

The same holds true for Afghanistan. After all, Afghanistan was where al-Qaida trained volunteers for and developed the 9/11 plot. Continued chaos in Afghanistan would give violent extremists a haven in which to train and plan their next murderous deeds. Here the problem is a little different than that in Iraq, in that the biggest obstacles to stability are rebuilding Afghanistan's decrepit infrastructure and extending central governance throughout the country. Afghanistan does not have the natural resources that Iraq has, and it will take continued application of international resources, both monetary and intellectual, to help with the needed rural development.

Until there are decent roads, water, and power, many Afghans will lack viable alternatives to protect and provide for their families, and growing and selling opium poppies will remain their best economic option.

There is one problem that Afghanistan and Iraq share; outside influence from neighboring countries. In Iraq's case it's Iran, in Afghanistan's case it's Pakistan. There will not be long-term stability in Afghanistan as long as the Taliban and al-Qaida enjoy a sanctuary in the Afghanistan-Pakistan border region.

One thing is certain, an Iraq or Afghanistan in chaos would be a stark indicator that the global insurgency is strong and increase the likelihood of more terrorist attacks on the West.

IRAN AND NORTH KOREA

Another priority is developing effective regional and bilateral strategies for dealing with Iran and North Korea. I put them together because they present similar challenges to our security interests. Because of the weapons they either possess or are pursuing, the new administration must focus on these dangerous regimes.

Both of these nations have chemical and biological weapons of mass destruction. North Korea has six hundred to seven hundred missiles with the range to strike all our forces in the Pacific as well as parts of the continental United States. Iran is busy developing missiles of greater range and capability. Their missiles today already have a range of over two thousand kilometers and can reach Israel.

Both countries also actively spread weapons technology. In the case of Iran, they do it through some of the groups they support, such as Hezbollah and the Shia fighters inside Iraq, and likely in other ways we're not aware of. Of course, in North Korea's case, we recently saw that they were providing nuclear reactor technology, and potentially nuclear weapons technology, to Syria. And Iran is actively involved in aiding terrorism by its support of Hezbollah and Hamas.

Through this support for terrorism, Iran has kept the security situation in the Middle East, particularly in Lebanon, the West Bank, and Gaza, unstable to the point that any permanent peace in the Middle East is very difficult to achieve. Iran's government will also continue to attempt to influence events inside Iraq in every conceivable way. Indeed, Iran's regional position would be enhanced by weak, disorganized governments in neighboring Iraq and Afghanistan. Conversely, the last things Iran could tolerate is democratic Iraqi and Afghan governments on its borders.

The best way ahead with North Korea is to continue our reliance on the six-party (U.S., Russia, North and South Korea, Japan, and China) talks to convince Pyongyang to give up its nuclear weapons. China is key to the success of the six-party talks because of the tremendous influence it exercises over North Korea. These talks will likely have to be rejuvenated, because of the uncertainty surrounding Kim Jong-Il's health and Korea's obvious intent to wait out the Bush administration in its waning months. Much responsibility will fall on the new administration to re-energize the six-party talks and convince North Korea its interests are best served by giving up its nuclear weapons and, for that matter, its chemical and biological weapons, which also threaten the region and the United States. Currently there are no "attractive" military options for dealing with North Korea, which would lose in any conflict. But in the fight, the many North Korean artillery pieces just north of the DMZ could wreak devastation on Seoul and the surrounding areas. Thus it's in the interest of all involved parties to find a peaceful solution.

In the case of Iran, the last couple of years have seen some success. The United States used to be the lone voice calling for Iran to open up to nuclear inspections and stop production of fissile material suitable for nuclear weapons. Since 2006 the United Nations has joined in this chorus, issuing five Security Council resolutions since 2006, imposing sanctions and calling for Iran to stop all uranium enrichment activities. The current focus on dealing with Iran, through the United Nation, should continue. But I would also look for opportunities to forge a new cooperation with Russia on this issue.

Russia is deeply involved in the nuclear technology being provided to Iran. Russia is also very worried about Islamic extremism on its borders, and has been for a long time. Perhaps because it has such a long southern border on which Islamic extremism is present, Russia started to take this threat seriously long before we did. It's already affected their country, all the way to Moscow. In Beslan, North Ossetia–Alania, an autonomous republic in the North Caucasus region of Russia, armed rebels took more than one thousand people hostage at School Number One in 2004. On the third day of the standoff, Russian security forces stormed the building, killing 331 of the hostages, including 186 children. There were more than 700 wounded. Chechen separatist warlord Shamil Basayev took responsibility.

Add to this the recent strain in Russia and U.S. relations over Georgia and there is good reason to search for common ground on a major issue, such as a nuclear-armed Iran. Arguably, Russia might be able to play a role similar to that China is playing with North Korea.

However the issues of Iran and North Korea are handled, one thing for certain is that the new President will have to make this issue an early priority if we are to keep more weapons of mass destruction from falling into the wrong hands. The nexus between violent extremists and WMD is a grave danger to people everywhere. We should be worried that nations that help spread weapons of mass destruction could arm violent extremists, directly or indirectly, giving them the means to carry out horrible acts. The new President and his administration are going to have to find ways to deal with these two countries that are effective in thwarting the danger they pose.

CHINA

One of the most critical bilateral and regional decisions our forty-fourth President will have to take is how to engage China not just over the course of his term, but for the next decade. This is a subject of much debate. Clearly, China is an emerging economic power and is rapidly modernizing its outdated military. Its air force, missile force, and naval modernization have been particularly impressive.

In my view, China does not want a confrontational posture with the United States. What it does want is more influence in Asia and the Pacific and strategic relationships with key resource suppliers around the world. As it seeks to develop its influence in the Asia-Pacific region, it naturally would seek to diminish U.S. power and influence in that area. China has done a good job of developing capabilities useful in countering American force projection military capability. Its recent satellite shoot-down is one example; its aggressiveness in cyber warfare is another. We must always be alert to China's espionage efforts against the United States and our friends and allies, as Beijing attempts to close the gap in military capabilities more quickly. However, such activities, even if sometimes quite dramatic, are fairly natural between nation-states and do not mean conflict is inevitable.

In fact, our military-to-military efforts at increasing transparency and building relationships with China since the EP-3 incident of April 2001 have improved dramatically. President Bush made this a priority and there has been steady progress in our relationship. Although the transparency between China and the United States has been too one-sided, in that we have shared many more of our military capabilities with the Chinese than they have with us, this has continued to improve since I left office.

Beyond the military realm, there are many economic areas where China and the United States are profoundly intertwined. The only outcome of conflict would be economic catastrophe for both sides and for the world economy. Furthermore, China is wrestling with many fundamental internal issues. When I was in China, in 2006, our hosts wanted us to see one of the small villages where so many of China's 350 million people who live in poverty reside. Add the millions in poverty to China's environmental concerns, the inadequacies of its food production, and the fact that it is now a net importer of oil, and you have a China where external conflict would only exacerbate these problems. The Chinese leadership is too capable and too globally involved to see conflict as being in its national interest.

The Taiwan situation is the only real problem area here. For now, as long as the leadership in Taiwan doesn't seek independence, I don't think we're going to see any pressure from China to come to a violent solution for the China-Taiwan issue. Again, any conflict between China and Taiwan would be detrimental to both of their economies, to the U.S. economy, and to the overall world economy. But it is the one area where conflict could arise if the rhetoric from either side gets out of hand. I remember late in my tenure as Chairman, during a visit to China, sitting with then-President Jiang Zemin, discussing Taiwan (it's interesting that Taiwan wasn't the first thing we talked about, which it would have been just a year earlier).

Former President Jiang Zemin put his hand on my arm and said, "Well, you know, if Taiwan declares independence, we'll have to go to war."

And I looked right back at him and responded, "If you go to war with Taiwan, of course we'll be there, too, and that would not be good for either one of us, or Taiwan." The situation looks better since the 2008 election of Taiwan's new government.

So part of our Asia-Pacific strategy has to include working with the Taiwanese in a supportive manner, but not letting Taiwan's politicians lead us to war.

In short, a key element of our grand strategy should be to continue building our military to military relationships and promote economic cooperation, while at the same time encouraging China to be a responsible player in the international community.

PROLIFERATION OF WMD

Any successful American grand strategy has to include the sweeping transnational challenge of combating the proliferation of weapons of mass destruction, which goes beyond the threats posed by North Korea and Iran. The threat is particularly dangerous when considering nuclear or biological weapons' falling into the hands of violent extremists. This is a critical problem, because violent extremists would not hesitate to use a nuclear device or biological agents. This dangerous nexus makes having a robust grand strategy centered on the global insurgency even more important. Use of nuclear fissile material or biological weapons by violent extremists would make the tragedy of 9/11 pale by comparison.

To deal with this threat, one of the things the new administration must not only continue but reinvigorate is the proliferation security initiative that many nations have joined. It's been an important piece of the puzzle in preventing the movement of WMD, particularly by sea. But the issue of the proliferation of weapons of mass destruction needs attention beyond U.S. leadership. It needs leadership in the international community and the United Nations. The international community must come to realize that the threat of nuclear material or biological weapon material in the hands of people who would not hesitate to use it is one of the bigger threats our world needs to confront and neutralize.

The only way to stop these weapons from falling into the hands of extremists is for the international community to unite against their proliferation. Indeed, one of the great strategic victories the global insurgents could achieve is a WMD attack against the civilian population of a liberal democracy. We must always remember they are a patient, persistent, and ruthless adversary.

ENERGY SECURITY

Energy security is one of the important transnational concerns facing the United States in the twenty-first century. Without an appropriate energy policy we risk jeopardizing our national security in several different ways as we compete for scarce energy resources. Not only is oil demand skyrocketing even as supply levels off, but much of the world's oil comes from or through dangerous neighborhoods. Major production, transit seaports and routes, and pipelines lie in the Middle East, the Caucasus, Central Asia, and the Caspian regions. These areas are characterized by latent conflicts that flare up periodically, evolving legal regimes, and varying degrees of political stability. Russia's threat last year to curtail oil supply to Europe and some Central Asian countries in response to the Georgian issue is fairly typical. The supply of oil is tight and the potential vulnerability to supply disruptions is a serious consideration.

I'm amazed that such a basic issue is hostage to partisan politics. The Bush administration and Congress could not develop a comprehensive energy policy for our country. It's obviously past time for a sweeping energy policy that includes conservation, renewable sources, nuclear power, and alternative fuels. President Obama must champion a bipartisan policy that will serve this country well for decades to come.

STRATEGIC SURPRISE:
SAUDI ARABIA AND PAKISTAN,
"THOUGHT EXPERIMENT" SCENARIOS

Finally, as most strategists know, the administration must have a robust intellectual and resource "kit bag" to deal with the surprises it will inevitably face despite effective strategic planning. Perhaps the most vivid example of this is the shift in strategic focus that resulted from the 9/11 surprise attack. Disregarding the probability of a strategic surprise is irresponsible. For the sake of argument, I offer a couple of places in the world where potential instability could have a significant impact on our national interests. While not predicting this will happen, I'd argue that a strategic planning approach that allows for scenarios like these is essential. Two such scenarios are potential instability in either Saudi Arabia or Pakistan. These are good U.S. allies and I'm certainly not predicting instability, but if they were to destabilize the consequences would be dire.

From 2001 to 2004, many newspaper headlines and intelligence reports discussed the potential for instability in Saudi Arabia. It doesn't take much imagination to think about the impact such instability could have on the flow of oil from the Persian Gulf and the consequences for our worldwide economic system. Any disruption in the eastern Saudi Arabian oil fields would be disastrous.

If their eastern oil fields, for example, were to come under the influence of violent extremists, what would American and international reaction be? This scenario raises lots of questions: Would the Saudi government want the United States or some international group to intervene? If the Saudi government did not want external intervention or help, under what authorities could we intervene if required? What would the Muslim world say about outside (non-Muslim) forces in the country that hosts the two most holy Muslim sites? If intervention was called for, would anyone have the capability to act quickly enough to stop a severe shock to the global economy?

In Pakistan, the problem is different. With its nuclear arsenal and potential extremist haven, the worry is that this arsenal could fall into the hands of extremists. How would this affect the region? As a nation, how would we respond? Would we consider a preemptive move? Again, the questions and the possible courses of action associated with them are vast. Needless to say, how we might address them could have a dramatic impact on regional and global security.

Pakistan and Saudi Arabia are our friends and allies, and we need to continue to work with them to avoid scenarios in which they could destabilize. On the other hand, from a grand strategy perspective, the new administration should immediately begin thinking about how to deal with instability in either of these two important countries, especially since many violent extremists come from these parts of the world. That makes having a strategy to deal with violent extremism all the more important. In short, these scenarios portend some very difficult issues.

The administration that entered office in January 2009 should repeatedly conduct these strategic thought experiments and others that envisage profound threats to American's vital interests. They won't identify all the scenarios or address them perfectly, but this approach will increase the administration's intellectual arsenal for dealing with inevitable strategic surprises.

NATIONAL SECURITY
AND THE U.S. BUDGET

Once a viable grand strategy is crafted, our nation's budget priorities must reflect it. The new President and administration are going to have considerable problems with the federal budget. There are going to be profound pressures on the budget, especially due to the global financial crisis, as well as the issues of Social Security, Medicare, Medicaid, and the national debt. No doubt dealing with these pressures will consume much of the new President's time. And while the defense budget has grown substantially, it has not been able to make up for the lack of defense modernization funds in the 1990s.

In my view, if the military is to continue to be asked to play such a large security role, the percentage of our gross domestic product that's devoted to defense is going to have to stay about where it is now: approximately 4 percent of our gross domestic product (GDP).

This administration needs to pay particular attention to the procurement budget in the Defense Department and in the military services. The procurement portion of the budget shrank disproportionately during the draw-down in the 1990s, when all the services were cut by about a third, in terms of manpower, and all the budgets were slashed. This decrease reflected the twin pressures of the post–Cold War manpower and budget cuts, while the services were being asked to increase their deployments and operational missions. Consequently, budget priorities went to the Operations and Maintenance (O&M) accounts that funded these deployments, and the only place to find additional O&M funds was in the procurement part of the budget.

Indeed, procurement suffered to the point that there was bipartisan support for increasing DoD procurement budgets by the late 1990s. In President Clinton's last budget, the DoD budget increased for the first time in many years. And this increase provided a badly needed increase in procurement funding.

All the services suffered from the "procurement bathtub or holiday" of the nineties, but it particularly affected the capital-intensive Air Force and Navy. As a result the Air Force is now flying very old equipment, and the Navy is sailing very old ships, and there is not enough money in the budget to procure new items in a timely fashion. In the Air Force's case, this was highlighted by an incident in which F-15 essentially split in half in the skies above Missouri—the result of metal fatigue. In fact, Air Force F-15 and F-16 fighter aircraft are on average over twenty-five and eighteen years old, respectively. The B-52 bombers and our refueling tanker fleet are on average over forty-six years old.

The number of vessels in the Navy is decreasing because we can't build them fast enough to keep up with the rate of retirement of older ships. According to the American Shipbuilding Association, if current Navy shipbuilding budget trends continue, the naval fleet will drop from 288 ships today to fewer than 200 ships by 2015.

The Army and Marine Corps have sweeping problems as well. Not only do they have to modernize, they have to replace or refurbish equipment (tracked and wheeled vehicles, helicopters) that for the last seven years has been driven, flown, worn out (or shot up) as much as ten times the predicted peacetime rate.

Adequate resourcing is a huge issue not only for the Defense Department, but also for other parts of our government. I've been critical of the lack of people and resources coming forth from the State Department, and the other departments and agencies, as we tried to bring all instruments of national power to bear on the conflicts in Iraq, Afghanistan, and elsewhere. As part of Secretary Rice's Advisory Committee on Transformational Diplomacy, my eyes were opened to the scope of State's resource challenges. There is not a level playing field in the national security arena. Other than the Defense Department, most departments are not funded adequately for the new security challenges we face. For example, while the DoD has sufficient personnel to ensure positions are filled when someone is assigned to a year-long educational oppor-

tunity, there is no such capacity in the Department of State. When State de-
cides to send someone to a school for a year, a position goes vacant somewhere
in the department. It's also difficult for these departments to find qualified people to send overseas to help rebuild countries such as Iraq and Afghanistan
without affecting their domestic responsibilities. Therefore, there are departments and agencies that require additional resources to help confront the security challenges we face.

All of these issues will have to be dealt with in the first budget that our the
forty-fourth President submits to Congress. Decisions about federal budget priorities will have a significant impact on our ability to deal with the many security challenges facing our nation and on the shape of our armed forces for years
to come.

The development of a comprehensive, coherent grand strategy based on our
vital national interests will be essential to dealing with the myriad security
challenges facing this administration. Because of the global insurgency threat,
the security environment will require the administration to pursue some radically different solutions.

Time is of the essence. Our President and and our country need to work
on these security issues from a strategic as well as a tactical perspective. It
will take several years of focused leadership and hard work to identify and implement the courses of action critical to ensuring our liberty, prosperity, and
security.

Index

Photo Credits

Pg 1—all author

Pg 2—all author

Pg 3—both US Air Force Photo

Pg 4—top two photos—author; bottom photo—US Air Force Photo

Pg 5—both author

Pg 6—top, US Air Force Photo; bottom, Government of Japan Photo

Pg 7—top, US Air Force Photo; bottom, US Army Photo

Pg 8—top, US Air Force Photo/Ron Hall; middle, Japan Air Self Defense Force Photo; bottom, US Air Force Photo

Pg 9—top, author; middle, US Air Force Photo; bottom, Joint Staff Photo/Mamie Burke

Pg 10—top, Joint Staff Photo/Mamie Burke; bottom, White House Photo

Pg 11—top, White House Photo; middle and bottom, Joint Staff Photo/Mamie Burke

Pg 12—top, Kansas City Chiefs Photo; bottom, US Air Force Photo

Pg 13—top, US Army Photo; bottom, White House Photo

Pg 14—top, White House Photo; middle, Department of Defense Photo; bottom, White House Photo

Pg 15—top, Joint Staff Photo/Myles Cullen; middle, US Marine Corps Photo; bottom, White House Photo

Pg 16—top, Joint Staff Photo/Myles Cullen; middle, Kansas State University Photo; bottom, Joint Staff Photo/Mamie Burke